A glorious high throne

A glorious high throne

Hebrews simply explained

Edgar Andrews

EVANGELICAL PRESS

EVANGELICAL PRESS
Faverdale North Industrial Estate, Darlington, DL3 0PH, England

Evangelical Press USA
P. O. Box 825, Webster, New York 14580, USA

e-mail: sales@evangelicalpress.org

web: http://www.evangelicalpress.org

First published 2003
Reprinted 2009

British Library Cataloguing in Publication Data available

ISBN 978 0 85234 547 4

Other titles by Edgar Andrews:
Christ and the Cosmos
Free in Christ — The message of Galatians
From Nothing to Nature — A basic guide to evolution and creation
The Spirit has come — The Holy Spirit's work in the Christian's
heart and life

Printed and bound in Great Britain by Athenaeum Press Ltd.,
Gateshead, Tyne & Wear

To Samuel William Clark (1932-1998)
who loved to preach
the unsearchable riches of Christ

Contents

Part 3. The new covenant in Christ (7:1 – 10:39)

Part 4. Faith and its fruits (11:1 – 12:29)

Part 5. The law fulfilled by love (13:1-25)

Foreword
by Dr John Blanchard

Other than Revelation, Hebrews is the most difficult New Testament book to understand clearly. It has often been said that in order to do so the reader must have a pretty thorough knowledge of the Old Testament, and especially of Leviticus. This probably rules out a disheartening percentage of today's Christians — hence the need for books such as the one you are now holding.

Written by an anonymous author to Jews who had been converted to Christ and were suffering persecution as a result, Hebrews is at one time a tonic and a treatise, yet it is not difficult to grasp its overall theme. Many years ago I spoke at a West Country college whose motto was 'Beyond the best there is a better'. The phrase has stayed with me ever since, and forms a perfect summary of what Hebrews is all about. In its thirteen chapters the author points back to the best of Old Testament religious practices, then points to things that are better — a better testament, a better priest, a better sacrifice, a better promise, a better hope and a better country. In doing so, he relentlessly has in mind our glorious, unsurpassable Saviour, the Lord Jesus Christ. Professor Andrews makes the point perfectly: 'As a compass needle always seeks the north, so the epistle to the Hebrews always returns to Christ. He is never far from view, even when other matters intervene.'

Professor Andrews has tackled the task of unravelling the twists and turns of Hebrews with obvious enthusiasm and equally obvious integrity. None of the 'problem passages' is ignored, and none of the text is glossed over, while careful scholarship is made accessible by the use of apt illustrations such as the one just quoted. Best of all, every page is full of Christ and 'the grace of God that brings salvation' (Titus 2:11).

I predict that this volume will be of enormous help to the busy preacher, the enquiring student and the 'ordinary' Christian who wants to learn more about this wonderfully rich New Testament letter and to apply its teaching to the problems and pressures of living a godly life in a godless world. May the Lord graciously use these pages to his glory in pointing its readers to the one who is 'the radiance of God's glory and the exact representation of his being' (Heb. 1:3).

John Blanchard
Banstead, Surrey

Author's preface

Many books and commentaries on the epistle to the Hebrews already exist, but in writing this work I have tried to provide something rather different, namely, a full verse-by-verse commentary which at the same time can be read like an ordinary book. I hope, therefore, that it will be of value to preachers and Bible-teachers, while also providing a rich source of devotional material for the ordinary Christian. The riches, of course, reside in the pre-eminence that Hebrews accords to Christ, not in any efforts of the author. The chapters have been kept short enough for use as daily readings, if the reader so desires.

I am deeply grateful to those who have helped bring this book to completion, especially the late Bill Clark who urged and encouraged me to write it in the first place. John Blanchard, Roger Fay and Robert Strivens all read the draft manuscript with meticulous care and made many helpful suggestions for its improvement. John Blanchard has also kindly written the foreword.

I have used the New King James Version throughout, and the references are given in the 'author and short title' form, with the full bibliography in an appendix.

Edgar Andrews
Welwyn Garden City
September 2003

Introduction:
Understanding Hebrews

Whenever I read Hebrews, a verse from the prophecy of Jeremiah comes to mind: 'A glorious high throne from the beginning is the place of our sanctuary' (Jer. 17:12). Hebrews could be an exposition of that verse!

The epistle to the Hebrews begins by showing us the glory of Christ — the eternal Son of God who shares the everlasting throne of 'the Majesty on high'. It then demonstrates in entrancing detail how he descended from that throne to become a man, sharing our flesh and blood, that he might rescue his elect people from death, judgement and the power of sin.

The epistle shows us how he did so — by inaugurating a new covenant. It is a covenant with better promises, a better priesthood, a better sacrifice, and a better hope, than had hitherto prevailed under the law of Moses. In this new covenant, Christ, our great High Priest, offered himself as a sacrifice for sin, by which he appeased the wrath of God and so became his people's sanctuary from death and condemnation. By his one offering for sin for ever, he has perfected for all eternity those he has set apart ('sanctified') for his glory and who come to God through him. He is their advocate, their rest, their righteousness, their example and their 'exceeding great reward'.

In short, the subject of Hebrews is Christ and the new covenant. Notice that I say 'subject', not 'subjects'. For the Christ presented to us in this epistle *is* the Christ of the new covenant — the new covenant in his blood (1 Cor. 11:25) — determined from all eternity but now revealed in its fulness, to the praise of the glory of his grace.

Yet Hebrews is not simply a theological treatise. It is an eminently useful and practical epistle, written to people who were tempted to return to the shadows of the old (Mosaic) covenant in the mistaken belief, perhaps, that two covenants were better than one! But the epistle demonstrates, beyond all argument, the impossibility of sewing the new cloth of the gospel on to the old garment of 'the law'. Indeed, it shows in considerable detail how 'the law was our tutor to bring us to Christ' (Gal. 3:24).

In emphasising the continuity of redemption history, we must be careful not to *negate* the Bible's teaching on the new covenant. In his massive commentary on Hebrews, the Puritan John Owen puts it like this: 'The Scripture doth plainly and expressly make mention of *two testaments, or covenants*, and distinguishes between them in such a way, as what is spoken can hardly be accommodated unto a *twofold administration* of the same covenant.' He is careful to add: 'This old covenant is abrogated and taken away, as the apostle expressly proves, but the word of God in the books of the Old Testament abideth for ever.'[1]

This latter point needs underlining. Technically, the terms 'Old Testament' and 'old covenant' mean the same thing, but we use them today in completely different ways. The Old Testament means the books of the Bible from Genesis to Malachi. These Scriptures are as valid and relevant as they ever were. On the other hand, the old covenant means that specific covenant that God made with Israel at Mount Sinai, as is recorded in Exodus 19-40, elaborated in Leviticus and revisited in Deuteronomy. While the author of Hebrews teaches the demise of the old covenant, he uses the Old Testament — extensively and robustly — to prove his case!

In rejecting the idea of 'two administrations', of course, Owen deviates from mainstream Reformed teaching, but I believe he has the weight of Scripture on his side. However, even if we do not share Owen's specific viewpoint, it serves as a useful reminder that the Bible in general, and Hebrews in particular, majors on the failure of the old covenant and the glory of the new.

This being so, the writer of Hebrews argues that we should 'run with endurance the race that is set before us, looking to Jesus the author and finisher of our faith' (12:1-2). For we have not come to the fires and thunder of Mount Sinai, but 'to Mount Zion, and the city of the living God, the heavenly Jerusalem ... and to Jesus the Mediator of the new covenant, and to the blood of sprinkling that speaks better things than that of Abel' (12:18-24).

To understand this is to understand Hebrews, to walk by faith, and to please God (11:6; 13:16).

Authorship

Hebrews is the only anonymous document in the New Testament — its author is unknown. Because of this we shall refer to him throughout this commentary simply as 'the Writer' (using a capital 'W' to avoid confusion with other writers). In the Western church, uncertainty over the epistle's authorship delayed its acceptance into the New Testament 'canon', or list of authentic writings. It was finally accepted on the grounds of its self-evident quality and consistency with apostolic teaching.

From the earliest times, the Eastern church attributed Hebrews to Paul, and some still hold to that view. In favour of this tradition, the Writer obviously had a thorough understanding of the law of Moses; he knew Timothy; and may have been imprisoned (see 13:19 and 10:34 where, however, 'my chains' is a doubtful translation). Like Paul, he employed metaphors from the sporting arena, and there are other similarities.

However, there are also good reasons for discounting Pauline authorship:

1. The opening greeting and self-identification common to all Paul's epistles is absent from Hebrews. Furthermore, it is unthinkable that Paul would have placed himself among those who received the gospel from first-generation believers (2:3-4; cf. Gal. 1:11-12).

2. The Greek style is polished and the rhetoric elegant — quite unlike the down-to-earth language employed in Paul's writings (Luke and Acts come closest in Greek style to Hebrews).

3. The Writer consistently quotes from the Greek Septuagint translation of the Old Testament, never the original Hebrew text. This would seem strange in a letter addressed to Hebrews and coming from 'a Hebrew of the Hebrews' (as Paul described himself).

4. Equally, Hebrews employs concepts not found in any of Paul's writings, such as the priesthood of Christ. It can be argued that Paul's epistles were all written to Gentile churches, so that imagery borrowed from the Mosaic system would have been inappropriate. But Paul does not hesitate to appeal to the Mosaic economy when writing to Gentiles (for example, the tablets of the law and Moses' veil in 2 Corinthians 3).

5. The style of argumentation in Hebrews is quite different from Paul's straight-line approach. In Hebrews the argument constantly circles back to earlier passages

and builds upon them. This makes it particularly difficult to discern the structure of the epistle — unlike Paul's epistles where the structure is normally straightforward.

6. Hebrews is unusually strong on exhortation. For example, the expression 'let us' occurs on average twice as frequently in Hebrews as in Paul's epistles.

A Pauline authorship is unlikely, therefore, despite the early traditions to this effect. Other candidates have been suggested, including Luke, Apollos, Barnabas and Clement of Rome — even Priscilla. But there is no convincing case for any of them, and we must therefore accept the fact that the author is unknown. He is likely to remain so.

Date

The key factors in determining the date of the epistle are as follows:

1. From 2:3-4 the Writer appears to have been a second-generation Christian and certainly not a member of the apostolic 'circle'.

2. Hebrews 8:13 says that the old-covenant economy 'is becoming obsolete and growing old [and] ready to vanish away'. It is also implied in 10:1-2 that the temple sacrifices were still being offered at the time of writing. These verses would hardly have made sense if written *after* the destruction of the temple in A.D. 70, because the Mosaic system ended abruptly and absolutely with that event.

3. Timothy, who became a fellow-worker of Paul in about A.D. 49[2] was alive and well, having been set free from prison (13:23).

Although we cannot be entirely certain, it seems likely from these considerations that Hebrews was written between A.D. 50 and A.D. 70.

Destination

Again, we are largely in ignorance about those to whom the epistle was written, although they were clearly Jewish, as opposed to Gentile believers. 'The only explicit clue', say Carson, Moo and Morris, 'is found in 13:24; "Those from Italy send you greetings".'³ Clearly the Writer had with him some believers from that land, but this does not mean that he was in Italy when he wrote the epistle. Nor does it necessarily mean that he was sending their greetings home *to* Italy — although this option would make sense of the words he uses. Again, we must be content to remain in ignorance.

Nevertheless, the epistle was certainly written to a particular group of believers. The Writer refers to specific experiences through which they had passed (10:32-34). Some authorities believe that this group (perhaps a house-church) lived in Jerusalem, while others see Rome as their location. The persecutions referred to could have occurred in either place. The overall 'Greek flavour' of the epistle (in its style and its exclusive use of the Greek 'Septuagint' version of the Old Testament) tips the scales in favour of Gentile Rome rather than Jerusalem. Although the recipients were Jews, they would most likely have absorbed the culture of the society in which they lived.

In spite of our ignorance on these matters (and perhaps even because of it) the message of Hebrews is of enormous relevance to God's people in every age and every place. It transcends any purely local situation and illuminates for all of us the peerless gospel of God's grace in Jesus Christ.

For a more detailed discussion of authorship and related matters, see Carson *et al*, referenced in the notes, Bruce (introduction),[4] or any of the other technical commentaries on Hebrews cited in this book.

Part 1:
Christ is all (1:1 – 3:6)

1.
Christ the message of God

Please read Hebrews 1:1-2

Most writers unfold their dramas gradually, holding in reserve their highest themes. Not so the Writer to the Hebrews, as he pens his great epistle. The full brilliance of his subject bursts upon us at the outset. Spurning all introductions, and with a remarkable economy of words, he sets before us the surpassing glory of Christ.

The full impact of this portrayal is found in verses 2-4, which we shall consider presently. For the moment we dwell upon the Writer's opening words, which are no less important. For here he shows us Christ both as the messenger of the new covenant and the message of God.

Christ the messenger (1:1-2)

The epistle begins abruptly: **'God, who at various times and in various ways spoke in time past to the fathers by the prophets, has in these last days spoken to us by his Son'** (1:1-2). The word translated 'by' means, more literally, 'in'. God once spoke *in* the prophets as he now speaks *in* his Son. By using similar terminology of Christ and the Old Testament prophets, the Writer exalts the prophetic ministry and the continuity of divine revelation.

He does not put the prophets *themselves* on a par with Christ, of course. But he does liken the prophetic *word* to God's self-revelation in his Son. This is important, because it means that the Old Testament Scriptures are to be received and honoured as the word of the Lord — for God spoke through them just as truly as he now speaks through Christ. Jesus himself claimed that they testify of him (John 5:39).

As the epistle unfolds, we shall see just how significant this is. The Writer is going to rely heavily on Old Testament Scripture as he builds his case for the surpassing glory of Christ and the new covenant. His ringing endorsement of the Old Testament, as being the word of God to man, is neither accidental nor incidental to his message.

Nevertheless, the Writer does make a clear distinction between God's *manner* of speaking, through Christ and the prophets respectively. This is evident from the expression 'these last days' which, says John Owen, refers to 'the end of the Judaical church' and the 'days of the Messiah'.[1] In referring to 'these last days', therefore, the Writer deliberately divides God's written revelation into two phases, corresponding to two eras. During the first era, God spoke 'in' the prophets. That is, he raised up human servants, with all their frailty and foibles, to prepare the way for Christ. But in the new era, God reveals himself *directly* through his perfect and glorious Son. For 'No man has seen God at any time [but] the only begotten Son, who is in the bosom of the Father, he has [now] declared him' (John 1:18). By drawing this distinction between the prophetic era and the 'last days', the Writer anticipates the grand theme of his epistle, namely, the inauguration of a new order — the new covenant in Jesus' blood.

The distinction between Christ and the prophets is also brought out in the book of Malachi: 'Behold, I send my messenger, and he will prepare the way before me. And the Lord, whom you seek, will suddenly come to his temple, even the

Messenger of the covenant in whom you delight' (Mal. 3:1). In this passage, Malachi shows us two messengers. The first is John the Baptist, who prepared the way for Christ (John 1:23; Isa. 40:3). The second is Christ himself, the 'Messenger of the covenant'. John was the last of the prophetic messengers who, by their spoken and written words alike, pointed away from themselves to the ultimate Messenger — Jesus of Nazareth, the Son of God.

Messenger of the covenant (1:2)

Let us spend a few moments with Malachi. What does it mean that Christ was 'the Messenger of the covenant'? Several things.

Firstly, the Lord Jesus Christ came to *reveal* a new covenant. The power and glory of this mission are the central themes of Hebrews, for the new covenant is nothing other than the gospel of Christ. It had been foretold throughout the Old Testament, both directly and in types and symbols, but its full glory remained hidden. The prophets themselves were, to some extent, in the dark about it — they sought to know 'what … the Spirit of Christ who was in them was indicating' when he spoke through them (1 Peter 1:11). Indeed, Peter continues, even the angels desire to know more about these things! The full disclosure of the gospel only came through the teaching of Christ himself and later through that of the apostles and New Testament prophets — which is equally the teaching of Christ (Gal. 1:12; Eph. 3:2-5; Heb. 2:3). This new-covenant revelation is preserved for us explicitly in the New Testament Scriptures.

Secondly, Christ came to *inaugurate* the new covenant. Throughout Old Testament history the promised covenant was for the future (Jer. 31:31-32; 1 Peter 1:10-12). But Christ came 'in these last days' to fulfil the promises and to usher in a new era — one in which God's people would no longer have to say, 'Know the Lord', but would all know him, from the least to the greatest (Jer. 31:33-34). As Paul writes to the Galatians, 'When the fulness of the time had come, God sent forth his Son ... to redeem those who were under the law, that we might receive the adoption as sons' (Gal. 4:4-5).

Thirdly, Christ came to *enable* the new covenant. It was the new covenant made in his blood (1 Cor. 11:25), and until that blood had been shed it could not come into force. It was the fulfilment of the age-old covenant of promise — 'the promise of the Spirit' (Gal. 3:14) — but the Spirit could not be given until Christ had been glorified and had ascended on high (John 7:39; 17:1). It was the true covenant of grace, but the grace of Christ was only fully manifested in his death and resurrection (2 Cor. 8:9).

This does not mean that none who lived before Christ could benefit from the new covenant. Quite the reverse, for Old Testament believers were indeed justified by faith in the coming Messiah. Just as we look back to the finished work of Christ, so they looked forward to the Anointed One whom God would send to redeem his people. So, for example, not only was Abraham justified by faith (Rom. 4:9), but that faith embraced a clear view of Christ — Jesus said, 'Abraham rejoiced to see my day, and he saw it and was glad' (John 8:56). However, for them the enjoyment of the new covenant was posthumous. As Hebrews puts it later, 'These all died in faith, not having received the promises, but having seen them afar off... God provided something better for us, that they should not be made perfect *apart from us*' (11:13,40, emphasis added).

How does this affect us practically? If Christ is the ultimate messenger from God, we must listen to him, and him alone. Today we are confronted by many 'messengers', each claiming to show us the way to God. All religions lead to God, they tell us, and we must study and absorb their teachings. But Jesus warned us that many false (literally, pseudo-) 'Christs' would arise, drawing men after themselves, and his words have proven true (Matt. 24:24). A syncretic society affords many opportunities to create 'designer religions' for ourselves. A multiplicity of sects provide a religious supermarket, where we may pick and choose to our heart's content, if all we want is 'religion'. But only Christ brings the message of God. 'This is my beloved Son', declared the Father; 'Hear him' (Mark 9:7).

Christ the message of God (1:2)

But let us examine this matter of God's revelation more closely. Although both the prophets and Christ were involved in the *process* of revelation, we know from John 1:1-5 that Christ is, in a special way, the Word of God. He is not only the messenger of the covenant, therefore, but the *message itself.*

He is the 'Word of life' and 'that eternal life which was with the Father and was manifested to us' (1 John 1:1-2). God speaks to us in Jesus Christ in the special sense that Christ is, in himself, the utterance of God, the embodiment of his divine nature and eternal purpose. Lane comments, 'The eternal, essential quality of Jesus' sonship qualified him to be the one through whom God uttered his final word.'[2]

A mere messenger is a 'go-between'. He directs attention away from himself to (a) the sender of the message and (b) the content of the message. The Lord Jesus Christ certainly directs our attention to the Father, but only by pointing to himself. 'I am the way, the truth and the life', he declares. 'No one comes to the Father except through me' (John 14:6). It is *to* Christ that we must apply for salvation, therefore, and it is *in* Christ that we may find it. This is why the genuine gospel must always focus upon the Lord Jesus Christ. When the apostles preached, they preached 'Christ and him crucified', considering it unnecessary to 'know anything' other than his divine person and atoning work (1 Cor. 2:2).

It is very easy to be sidetracked from the purity of this apostolic message. The Athenians of old 'spent their time in nothing else but ... telling or hearing some new thing' (Acts 17:21). So people today demand novelty in religion. They want to know, 'What's new?' rather than 'What's true?'

Thus it is old-fashioned to believe that Scripture is the in-fallible Word of God; that man is dead in trespasses and sins; that he abides under the wrath of a holy God; that he faces eternal condemnation; that God chose by grace to redeem a great multitude from among mankind; that Christ shed his blood for these elect; that he rose physically from the dead to justify them; that he will come again in judgement and that the dead will return to face that awful day.

It is not sufficient (they say) simply to preach Christ. We must communicate the gospel by drama, music and art. We must provide for those who prefer discussion to doctrine, pop music to preaching, and spiritual 'highs' to spiritual hunger. But we must not be sidetracked from Christ. He alone is God's message to a fallen race, and only by seeking him can we dis-cover what God has to say to us.

In what other sense is Christ the message of God? The question is answered in the verses that follow. It is only by reference to him that we can understand God's purpose, God's nature and God's covenant — his gracious and glorious pro-vision for sinners like ourselves.

2.
Christ the image of God

Please read Hebrews 1:2-3

These verses contain an account of the glory of Christ that is unsurpassed anywhere in Scripture. God has spoken in his Son, we read, **'whom he has appointed heir of all things, through whom also he made the worlds; who being the brightness of his glory and the express image of his person, and upholding all things by the word of his power, when he had by himself purged our sins, sat down at the right hand of the Majesty on high'** (1:2-3). We see here Christ's limitless inheritance, creative power, divine glory, perfect representation of the Father, awesome providence, single-handed redemption, and exaltation to the throne of God. The statement is all the more breathtaking for its brevity, as the infinite excellencies of Christ are somehow compressed into human language, at once simple and profound.

Thus the Writer lays the 'chief cornerstone' of the new covenant — the person of Christ by whose blood that covenant is sealed. 'For there is no other name under heaven given among men by which we must be saved' (Acts 4:12).

Heir of all things (1:2)

God the Father has **'appointed [his Son] heir of all things'** (1:2). It is both the Father's purpose and his pleasure to bestow the highest honour conceivable on his beloved Son. Among men, ancient rulers were known to offer up to half their kingdom to those they wished to honour (e.g., Mark 6:23). But the honour which God has purposed for his Son, the Lord Jesus Christ, is not so finely calculated. It is total, for he will inherit *all* his Father's incomprehensible wealth and glory. What this implies is beyond our comprehension. We cannot even understand what God has planned for those who believe in Christ (1 John 3:2); so how shall we ever comprehend what he has prepared for his only begotten Son, in whom he is well pleased? (Mark 1:11).

Nevertheless, the immediate lesson is plain. If God so honours Christ, ought not men to do the same? Christ stands pre-eminent in the Father's esteem. Where does he stand in ours? Many claim to follow Christ who actually dishonour him. Some dishonour him by their behaviour. Others simply fail to give him pre-eminence in their religious schemes, for truly Christ-centred teaching is the exception rather than the rule. Yet we are told, 'He that does not honour the Son does not honour the Father who sent him' (John 5:23). To worship Christ is to worship the triune God, for 'in him dwells all the fulness of the Godhead bodily' (Col. 2:9). God has exalted his Son and we must do the same.

What will Christ inherit? Certainly, heaven, earth and cosmos, together with their inhabitants. It was for him that 'all things were created, that are in heaven and that are on earth, visible and invisible, whether thrones or dominions or principalities or powers' (Col. 1:16). 'The inheritance of the Son of God', says Bruce, 'is not limited to earth; it embraces the universe, and particularly the world to come.'[1]

Yet amazingly, amidst all this vast heritage, it is 'the riches of the glory of his inheritance in the saints' that means most to the Lord Jesus Christ (Eph. 1:18). That is, his chief joy will be to possess the redeemed and glorified church, which he will present to himself 'a glorious church, not having spot or wrinkle or any such thing, but ... holy and without blemish' (Eph. 5:27). Amid all the awesome universe, Christ treasures most the sinners he redeemed. 'He is the heir', says Calvin, 'so that he may make us wealthy by his riches.'[2]

Maker of the worlds (1:2 cont.)

Through Christ, continues the Writer, God **'made the worlds'** (1:2). The word 'worlds' means literally 'ages'. Hebrews uses this word several times, along with the more common term 'cosmos' which is also rendered 'world' in English. When the New Testament writers refer to 'ages' they present a view of the created order that emphasizes its temporal nature. Unlike its maker, the creation is neither eternal nor changeless. It is a creature of time, subject to change and transition. This does not diminish the glory of Christ as its maker, but only under-lines his transcendence over all created things.

What does it mean that the worlds were made **'through'** Christ? The word 'through' could equally well be translated 'by means of'. That is, God (either the triune God or the Father) appointed the Son creator as well as heir. As Paul explains to the Colossians, 'All things were created *through* him and *for* him' (Col. 1:16, emphasis added). There is, therefore, a close relationship between Christ's roles as creator and heir. He cre-ated in order to inherit. He inherits because he created. This serves to emphasise that creation was purposeful, that is, it had an end in view. That end was, and is, the creation, re-demption and glorification of the church to be the bride of Christ (see Col. 1:16-20).

The brightness of his glory (1:3)

The creator-heir is no mere agent, as if God had deputed the task of creation to some lesser being. Creation is a work of God himself, for 'In the beginning *God* created heavens and the earth' (Gen. 1:1, emphasis added). He did so by his word, and that Word was Christ, 'who was God' (John 1:1-5).

Thus the Writer continues to delineate the full deity of Christ in unforgettable terms. He is **'the brightness of [God's] glory and the express image of his person'** (1:3). It is 'highly probable', comments John Brown, that there is a comparison here between Christ and the visible 'Shekinah' glory that filled the inner sanctum of the tabernacle under the Mosaic covenant.[3] The Writer is emphasising that the new covenant is not lacking in visible glory, but that this glory is to be found in Jesus Christ rather than the tabernacle — 'we beheld his glory, the glory as of the only begotten of the Father, full of grace and truth' (John 1:14).

'Brightness' means 'outshining'. As a lighthouse reveals its presence by its beam, and the sun illuminates and warms the earth by its rays, so Christ reveals in his person the glory of God. The essential idea here is that of unveiling or revelation. 'No one has seen God at any time. The only-begotten Son, who is in the bosom of the Father, he has declared him' (John 1:18). Again, Paul writes, 'God … has shone in our hearts to give the light of the knowledge of the glory of God in the face of Jesus Christ' (2 Cor. 4:6). Very simply, to see God's glory we must look at Christ.

This looking is not done, of course, by physical sight. It requires spiritual sight, that is, God's gift of faith. If we look merely at the human Jesus we shall see no beauty in him (Isa. 53:2-3). But as we gaze upon him by means of faith, we shall behold his glory in essentially the same way as did John and the other apostles.

God himself is invisible. But Christ is 'the image of the invisible God' (Col. 1:15). In Christ, the invisible, unknowable God is manifested and made known. Philip's memorable plea, 'Lord, show us the Father', received the devastating answer: 'He who has seen me has seen the Father... I am in the Father and the Father is in me' (John 14:8-11).

What does this mean for us in practice? It means firstly that we seek God in vain if we seek him anywhere other than in Jesus Christ. This is true for those who follow other religions or none, but it is equally true for those who call themselves Christians. There is a great deal of 'Christless Christianity' around, that is, a Christianity that has at its core something other than the glorious person and saving work of Jesus Christ. That core may be ritualism, intellectualism, polity, morality, ethics, self-interest, social concern, entertainment — even religious zeal. But if Christ is not the focus and glory of our religion, it is not Christianity.

This has particular application in our day to those who claim that many who follow non-Christian religions are, in fact, 'anonymous Christians'. These people, they say, are saved by Christ without knowing it, since they exercise faith in God, however dimly they perceive him. But 'faith' as a human attitude can do nothing for the soul — only Christ (through faith *in him*) can save.

Upholding all things (1:3 cont.)

Christ is not only the creator, but also the sustainer of the cosmos, for he is even now **'upholding all things by the word of his power'** (1:3). This concept is even more challenging to our thinking than the creatorhood of Christ. Creation lies in the past, long before the incarnation. It is therefore possible in our minds to distance the 'cosmic Christ' from the man Christ

Jesus. But that is not an option when we confront the present-tense activity of Christ in providence. 'Upholding all things' means just what it says. It means that one who lived on earth, a man among men, is the sovereign ruler of the physical universe. Nature, history and the political affairs of men and nations, along with the personal experiences and destinies of people like ourselves, all lie in his omnipotent hands.

In Scripture, providence (God's purposeful control of events) is ultimately ascribed to the Father. Not a sparrow falls to the ground without his express intent (Matt. 10:29). He works all things according to the counsel of his will (Eph. 1:11). Who, then, is in control — the Father or the Son? The answer is the same for providence as it is for creation. God upholds all things *through* his Son, so that either can properly be called the 'upholder of all'. Colossians tells us that 'in him [Christ] all things consist' (Col. 1:17). That is, all things 'hold together'. The universe derives its integrity from Christ, and this is the way God the Father has ordained it. There is no conflict between the persons of the triune God. The Father always acts through the Son. As Owen puts it, '... as to operation he [the Father] works not but by the Son.'⁴

How does Christ uphold all things? 'By the word of his power', we are told. The term 'word' implies 'command'. It signifies that Christ's mind and purpose are continually being expressed in actuating power. Just as a general commands his army by a flow of orders and commands, so Christ 'does according to his will in the army of heaven and among the inhabitants of the earth. No one can restrain his hand or say to him, "What have you done?"' (Dan. 4:35).

As far as the physical universe is concerned, the 'word of power' can be equated with the laws of nature. In a physical sense, it is these laws that 'uphold' the natural universe. Where did these laws come from? Who devised them and who enforces them? The Bible's answer is Christ. He does so on a moment-by-moment basis, for providence, unlike creation, is ongoing and present-tense.

He purged our sins (1:3 cont.)

The heart of the gospel is the atonement: Christ **'purged our sins'** (1:3). Literally, he 'carried out a cleansing' in which the sins of the elect were removed from them as if by washing. Sometimes Jesus is presented as a victim, passively bearing the punishment for our sins. That is true, but it is not the whole truth. Christ's death was a positive work, not just a passive suffering. The purpose and effect of that work was the removal from his people of all stain of sin, so that they stand before God in utter purity — the sinless purity of Christ.

Zechariah illustrates this beautifully. He saw Joshua, the high priest, standing before the Lord, 'clothed with filthy garments'. Then the Lord said, 'Take away the filthy garments from him... See, I have removed your iniquity from you, and I will clothe you with rich robes' (Zech. 3:1-5). So Christ removes our sins by virtue of his death. But he does not leave us naked. He clothes us with the rich apparel of his own perfection — 'the garments of salvation' (Isa. 61:10). He was made 'to be sin for us, that we might become the righteousness of God in him' (2 Cor. 5:21).

Later in Hebrews, the Writer reminds us that 'according to the law almost all things are purged with blood, and without the shedding of blood there is no remission' (9:22). Christ could not cleanse his people without himself suffering as their substitute. The wages of sin is death, so sin cannot go unpunished. But he took our place and 'suffered once for sins, the just for the unjust, that he might bring us to God' (1 Peter 3:18).

Finally, notice the importance the Writer attaches to the words 'by himself'. These words are omitted in the NIV, but this does not alter the fact that salvation is the work of Christ alone. Neither angels, nor 'saints', nor other intercessors, nor rituals of whatever kind, can help Christ redeem a single soul. Redemption is not a co-operative effort between God and man. Nor can the sinner himself assist Christ in the work of purging sins. Augustus Toplady understood this when he wrote:

Not the labour of my hands
Can fulfil thy law's demands;
Could my tears for ever flow,
Could my zeal no respite know,
All for sin could not atone;
Thou must save, and thou alone.

The Majesty on high (1:3 cont.)

Having accomplished the redemption of his elect, Christ **'sat down at the right hand of the Majesty** [greatness] **on high'** (1:3). The one who 'humbled himself and became obedient to death' has been 'highly exalted and given … the name which is above every name' (Phil. 2:8-9). This statement presages the entire epistle. The overriding view that Hebrews gives of Christ is as one enthroned. Having triumphed over all his enemies, he has taken his rightful place as the Son and heir of the Most High God. It is concerning Christ that Jeremiah cries, 'A glorious high throne from the beginning is the place of our sanctuary' (Jer. 17:12).

Notice first that Christ has **'sat down'**. His work is done. His mission, planned from all eternity, has been accomplished. Nothing remains to be achieved. 'I have glorified you on the earth. I have finished the work which you have given me to do', he prayed, even before his crucifixion. 'And now, Father, glorify me together with yourself, with the glory which I had with you before the world was' (John 17:4-5). It was an answered prayer.

His work is a finished work in more senses than one. It was complete in time, yes, but it was also complete in its accomplishment. Later in Hebrews we read, '... this man, after he had offered one sacrifice for sins for ever, sat down at the right hand of God... For by one offering he has perfected for ever those who are being sanctified' (10:12-14). The finished work of Christ is a most precious doctrine. It bids men abandon their religious works and self-effort, and flee to him for justification. Christ has left nothing to be done in the matter of salvation, and to realise this is to embrace the gospel and find peace with God. But where is Christ seated? He is at the **'right hand'** of God. This is the place of privilege, authority and esteem. The Father is well pleased with his Son and declares his pleasure by setting him at his right hand. Nothing that the Son desires will be withheld. None for whom he intercedes will be rejected. 'He is able to save to the uttermost those who come to God through him, since he ever lives to make intercession for them' (7:25).

This has great practical implications. Firstly, it is from the Father's right hand that the glorified Christ sent the Holy Spirit to his people, the church (John 7:39; 16:7). We shall have much more to say about this in due course. Secondly, it is from this position of 'all authority in heaven and on earth' that he sends his servants 'into all the world [to] preach the gospel' (Matt. 28:18; Mark 16:15). Thirdly, Christ's presence at the right hand of the Majesty on high is the source of our confidence as we make this gospel known. Regardless of the opposition and the cost, the great commission of the exalted Christ will be carried to completion.

Finally, the Father is aptly described as **'the greatness on high'**. His majesty defies our imagination. He whom we know in Christ is nevertheless ineffable — beyond our knowledge.

The one we worship through his Son transcends our worship. That such a glorious Being as the Father holds the Lord Jesus in high esteem should give us a new understanding of the glory of Christ.

The things above (1:3 cont.)

The psalmist confesses, 'Such knowledge is too wonderful for me. It is high, I cannot attain it' (Ps. 139:6). And he was only talking about God's providence, not his person! What practical value can there be, therefore, in contemplating the glory of Christ? I would suggest three things.

Firstly, *it will assist our worship.* For many professing Christians, worship is a matter of outward form. This can be true for evangelicals as well as ceremonialists. For example, it must be wrong to distinguish between 'worship' services and other kinds of service, such as evangelistic meetings. Surely, we can never approach God, or meet together in his name, without worship. To focus on the transcendent nature of God and his beloved Son is the wisdom with which worship begins.

Secondly, *it will concentrate our minds on 'things above'.* Paul exhorts his readers, 'Seek those things which are above, where Christ is, sitting at the right hand of God. Set your mind on things above, not on things on the earth. For you died and your life is hidden with Christ in God' (Col. 3:1-3). It is the unbelieving who are preoccupied with the things of earth (Matt. 6:25-34). God knows we have need of these things, such as food and clothing, but *because* he knows and cares, we can safely leave the matter to him! Our responsibility is to 'seek first the kingdom of God and his righteousness'. Heaven should be in all our thinking.

Finally, the sovereign power of the enthroned Christ is *our joy and confidence in all that life can bring.* Because he is on the throne, '… all things work together for good to those who love God, to those who are the called according to his purpose.' It follows that nothing 'shall be able to separate us from the love of God which is in Christ Jesus our Lord' (Rom. 8:28,39). Here lies our peace and perseverance.

3.
Christ the Son

Please read Hebrews 1:4-6

The Writer now begins to work out in greater detail the majestic themes broached in his opening verses. This is characteristic of the epistle. Just as an orchestral symphony first introduces and then elaborates its melodic themes, so Hebrews returns again and again to the glorious attributes and saving ministry of Christ. The first theme to be developed is that Christ is the Son of God.

The Jews were much preoccupied with angels. They believed that these mighty and mysterious beings exercised an unseen influence in the affairs of men. What better subject could there be for speculation and spiritual intrigue? But their obsession with angels led to dangerous confusions. One such idea was that Christ himself had emerged from this world of shadows and was just a special kind of angel. If that were so, then he would be a created being, superior to other such beings, perhaps, but nevertheless inferior to God. Such opinions live on today among Jehovah's Witnesses and other Unitarians. Hebrews sets out to demolish such thinking. The angels are servants, but Christ is the 'only begotten Son' (John 1:18).

An excellent name (1:4)

In the preceding verses, the excellence of Christ has been declared in absolute terms and by reference to his own divine attributes. But now it is set forth in comparative terms, by reference to the inferiority of angels. Jesus Christ, we read, has sat down at the throne of God, **'being made so much better than the angels, as he has by inheritance obtained a more excellent name than they'** (1:4). '*Made* so much better' does not mean that Christ's superiority is of recent origin. It is not some kind of promotion earned through his obedience to God. Christ has been God's Son and heir from all eternity, for he was 'in the beginning with God' (John 1:2). Lane translates this verse: 'having been exalted as far above the angels as the name which he has inherited is superior to theirs'.¹ That is, Christ occupies the place of pre-eminence, and always has done, because he alone is the Father's Son.

Verse 2 declares that Christ is the sole heir of his Father's wealth and glory. But more than that, verse 4 tells us that he has inherited a **'name'** or title which *proclaims* his unique status. What is that name? It is the **'more excellent'** name of Son. Traditionally, a man's heir was his oldest son. All his wealth passed to this one special person, no matter how many other children he might have. Even today, in monarchies, it is the oldest child of a king or queen who inherits the crown, the throne and the title 'Majesty'. Thus the Writer draws an analogy. Christ inherits the throne and majesty of God because he is the Son. He does so in the sense that he *shares* that throne and title with his Father. He does so *uniquely* because, unlike the most glorious of created beings, he alone has been begotten by the Father.

It is a grave offence against the majesty of God to diminish the status of his Son. Yet this is what the Hebrews were in danger of doing. It is the same today. Those who deny the deity of Christ are the chief offenders, of course. But even as trinitarians we can neglect to honour the Son. We do so if we deny that he has 'authority over all flesh', acting in absolute sovereignty when he bestows the gift of eternal life (John 17:2). We do so if we embrace materialistic theories of origins and ignore his creative power and providential care. We do so again if we forget that he will be the Judge of all the earth (John 5:27). He is the compassionate Saviour of sinners. But he is also the sovereign Lord.

The only begotten Son (1:5)

The Writer is not content to make assertions about Christ. He is anxious to justify his claims by appeal to Scripture. He first cites Psalm 2:7: **'You are my Son, today I have begotten you'** (1:5; cited also at 5:5 and Acts 13:33). To which of the angels did God ever say *that*, he asks? Clearly, to none of them. It was to Christ that these words were addressed. Looking back at the psalm, we find that the citation is a decree of the Most Migh God. This serves to emphasise how important and unchangeable is the pronouncement he makes concerning Christ.

The importance lies, of course, in the word **'begotten'**. The term 'sons of God' is used variously in Scripture to describe both men and angels (Heb. 2:10; Job 1:6). What is utterly different about Christ is that he is the 'only begotten Son' (John 1:14). When the word 'begotten' is applied to Christ in the New Testament it has three distinct connotations. A failure to recognise this can cause confusion. The three meanings are:

1. Christ *the eternal Son*, being of the same essence or substance as the Father (John 1:14,18; 3:16,18; Col. 1:15).

2. Christ *the incarnate Son*, the 'first-born' brought into the world (1:6; Rom. 8:29). Kistemaker says, 'His appointment to the office of Son — specifically his appearance in the flesh — is reflected in the clause "today I have become your Father".'[2]

3. Christ *the first-born from the dead*, referring to his resurrection (Acts 13:33; Col. 1:18; Rev. 1:5).

Our quotation from Psalm 2 is applied in various senses at different places in the New Testament (1:5; 5:5; Acts 13:33). Here in Hebrews 1:5 I believe the Writer intends the first meaning. The context and purpose of his argument require this. What is he saying? Christ is God because 'like generates like'. A human being cannot beget an ape or a bird, nor an animal a human being. The whole point of 'begetting' is that the offspring, though a separate individual, shares the essence (or essential nature) of the parent. Thus God can beget nothing but God. He can *create* angels and men, but he cannot *beget* or generate them. Of course, the word 'begotten' is a metaphor. It has no sexual connotation here and implies nothing about the mechanism of generation. It simply teaches the single truth set out above, namely that Christ the Son is of the same essence as God the Father. As the Nicene Creed puts it, he is 'begotten, not made, being of one substance with the Father'.

On the other hand, when Psalm 2:7 is quoted in Acts 13:33, the context and argument concern the resurrection of Christ. Paul is preaching in the synagogue at Antioch in Pisidia. God has fulfilled his ancient promise, he declares, 'in that he has raised up Jesus. As it is also written in the second psalm, "You are my Son, today I have begotten you"' (Acts 13:33). Again, writing to the Colossians, Paul calls Christ 'the head of ... the church, the first-begotten from the dead' (Col. 1:18). That is, Christ was the forerunner for every believer, since all believers will be raised from death to glory when Christ returns. Similarly, in Revelation 1:5 he is 'the first-born from the dead'.

The double meaning of the psalmist's statement helps to explain why he says, '*Today* I have begotten you' (Ps. 2:7, emphasis added). Some interpret this to mean that the Father pre-existed the Son, as human parents must exist before their children. Thus, they say, Christ cannot be the eternal Son. Yet we read in John's prologue that before creation Christ, the Word, was 'in the beginning with God' (John 1:2). Others acknowledge that Christ is eternal, but suggest that the title 'Son' was bestowed on him *only* after his incarnation or his resurrection. But then how could John write that 'God so loved the world that he sent his only begotten Son ...'? (John 3:16). Clearly, the Son was begotten before he was sent. These mistaken ideas arise from a confusion of the two meanings of the verse.

When the passage is interpreted as a prophecy of Christ's resurrection, the word 'today' signifies the historical reality of the event. But when it is used by the New Testament writer to describe the basic relationship between Christ and the Father, the word 'today' has no temporal significance at all. Just as 'begotten' is a metaphor, taken from the temporal human experience of fatherhood, so is 'today'. There can be no time with God, for time itself is a created thing. There were no 'days' before God created time, and we know that Christ was already *there* when that occurred (see John 1:1-3). The whole decree, therefore, is a metaphor, couched in the language of human generation so that we may better understand it. A human baby shares its essence with its parents, but marks its separate existence from its date of birth. So Christ is of one essence with the Father and yet is a distinct and separate person. Far from undermining the doctrine of the Trinity, the decree underlines it.

That Christ is begotten of the Father has further implications. John tells us, 'No one has seen God at any time. The only begotten Son, who is in the bosom of the Father, he has declared him' (John 1:18). Because Christ is of the essence of God, he is able to 'declare', or reveal, the Father. He who has seen Christ has, of necessity, seen the Father, for they are one (John 14:9). Scriptural revelation concerning God has been given through the prophets. But only in Christ can a man *know* God, since only Christ is his express image

Christ, the son of David (1:5)

The Writer presses his case with the aid of two further Scriptures. The first, from 2 Samuel 7:14 states, **'I will be to him a Father and he shall be to me a Son'** (1:5). Historically these words were spoken by God through the prophet Nathan concerning King Solomon. His father David had desired to build a house for the ark of the covenant but God would not allow him to do so. The privilege of erecting the temple was granted instead to Solomon. The Writer to the Hebrews takes up this story and applies it to Christ, 'great David's greater son'. Solomon built a temple of stone, but Christ is building one of 'living stones', that is, his church. Peter writes, '… you also, as living stones, are being built up as a spiritual house, a holy priesthood, to offer up spiritual sacrifices acceptable to God through Jesus Christ' (1 Peter 2:5).

Quite apart from the way Solomon pictures Christ, the text makes a plain statement concerning the relationship of Jesus to God. Under the guidance of the Holy Spirit, the Writer applies the Scripture to show that Jesus is uniquely the Son of God. Again he asks whether God ever addressed an angel thus. Again the implied response is, 'Never'. As before, the suggestion of time ('he *will* be') arises only from the historical context and is not descriptive of the Father-Son relationship, except in so far as that relationship was fully *revealed* at the incarnation.

Worthy of worship (1:6)

The Writer makes his third appeal to Scripture: '**… when he again brings the first-born into the world, he says: "Let all the angels of God worship him"**'(1:6). Although some have suggested that 'again' refers to the Second Coming of Christ,[3] the verse can and should be read: 'Again, when he brings …'

The quotation, 'Let all the angels of God worship him', is taken from the Septuagint rendering of Deuteronomy 32:43. The words are not found in the Hebrew Old Testament text, but only in the early Greek translation, the Septuagint, and in a fragment from the Dead Sea Scrolls.[4] The statement may have been lost from the Hebrew version through some accident of transcription, or may be an insertion into the Mosaic text. Regardless of how the discrepancy came about, we see here an example of the way New Testament authors often quoted from the Greek translation of the Old Testament rather than directly from the Hebrew. In doing so, of course, they wrote under the Spirit's guidance, so that their words are no less inspired than if they had used the original text.

The reference is clearly to the incarnation of Christ, for it was only then that he came into the world (cf. John 1:9-11). His description here as the 'first-born' may thus refer to the unique event in which God's Son became man. Guthrie comments, 'The primary reference must be to the incarnation to draw attention to the fact that when Jesus was born the function of the angels was to worship him.'[5]

But this may not be the case. We have already seen that the term 'first-born' as it is applied to Christ is also an honorific title, signifying pre-eminence. Thus Colossians 1:15 tells us that 'He is the image of the invisible God, the first-born of [over] every creature: for by him all things were created …' Again, Psalm 89:27 says of Christ, 'I will make him my first-born, the highest of the kings of the earth.' It is possible that the word is used in this honorific sense in our present verse.

This 'first-born one' is of higher rank than any in the world to which he came. Did he not create that world and its inhabitants? But he also ranks higher than the exalted 'angels of God'. Clearly so, for they are called upon to worship him. And this they did, as Luke records in Luke 2:1-14. Barely had the astonished shepherds taken in the message that '... there is born to you ... a Saviour, who is Christ the Lord', than a multitude of angels appeared, 'praising God and saying, "Glory to God in the highest, and on earth peace, good will towards men!"'

Plainly, the only one to whom the angels render worship is God himself. On no account could angels worship their fellow angels, nor could they accept the worship of others. When the apostle John fell down to worship his angelic guide, he was sharply rebuked: 'See that you do not do that! I am your fellow servant... Worship God!' (Rev. 19:10). It follows that 'Christ the Lord', whom they were *commanded* to worship, must be God in human form. As Charles Wesley sings:

Veiled in flesh the Godhead see,
Hail the incarnate Deity!

Or, as Mary was told, '... that holy one who is to be born will be called the Son of God' (Luke 1:35).

Let us be clear, therefore, that Christ is to be worshipped. If the angels must revere him as God, so should we. He is the friend of sinners, but we should never presume upon his friendship. He received sinners and ate with them, but our familiarity must be tempered with awe. We may call him 'Jesus', for he saves his people from their sins, but we must never forget that he is 'Jesus, the Lord'. John leaned on Jesus at that final Passover (John 13:23), but he 'fell at his feet as dead' when he saw Christ in his ascended glory (Rev. 1:17).

4.
Christ the King

Please read Hebrews 1:7-9

Christ is God the Son, but he is also God the King. He is enthroned, the ruler of men and angels, the Lord of lords and the King of kings. He shares not only the substance of his Father, but his Father's glory and sovereign power. By contrast the angels, though they are 'a flame of fire', are but 'ministers' or servants for the heirs of salvation. Thus the Writer continues to delineate his portrait of Christ by introducing the *kingdom* — not the earthly throne of David but the new-covenant kingdom which men and women enter by the regenerating power of the Holy Spirit (John 3:5-6).

Flames of fire (1:7)

Psalm 104 praises God for his creative works: 'O Lord my God, you are very great: you are clothed with honour and majesty'. It is from this sublime hymn to the Creator that the Writer takes his next quotation. 'You are the one', continues the Psalm, 'who walks on the wings of the wind, **who makes** [creates] **his angels spirits,** [and] **his ministers a flame of fire** ... who laid the foundations of the earth' (1:7, quoting Ps. 104:1-4). This statement concerning angels is embedded in an extended description of the physical creation, and this is

significant. It emphasises that angels are just as much part of
the created order as are mountains or men.

What are angels? The word means 'messengers' or 'agents'.
Angels, therefore, are those who do God's bidding and thus
can properly be called 'ministers', or servants, as here. If we
turn to Hebrews 1:14 we see the point reiterated. 'Are they
[angels] not all ministering spirits?', asks the Writer. In his
sovereign rule over all things, it pleases God to appoint means
to accomplish his ends. So it is that he employs angelic agents
to carry out his purposes.

Psalm 103 expresses this fact in words of great clarity and
beauty: 'Bless the Lord, you his angels, who excel in strength,
who do his word, heeding the voice of his word. Bless the
LORD ... you ministers of his, who do his pleasure' (Ps.
103:20-21). Yet the angels' service is seldom evident to the
eyes of men. Their ministry is normally a hidden one, lest they
become the object of our praise instead of God (see Col. 2:18).

The angels, we are told, are 'spirits'. They are part of the
created order, but not of the physical world. They remain unseen, part of an invisible world that we glimpse in passages
such as Colossians 1:16. There, Christ is named as the creator
of 'all things ... that are in heaven and that are on earth, visible
and invisible, whether thrones or dominions or principalities
or powers'.

The angels are described as **'a flame of fire'**. What does
this mean? Hebrew poetry makes statements which are then
repeated or mirrored in different words. The psalms give eloquent testimony to the power and beauty of this structure.
Bearing this in mind, we would expect the phrase '[he makes]
his ministers a flame of fire' to echo its antecedent, 'he makes
his angels spirits'. The 'flame of fire' is therefore a poetic statement of the spiritual, as opposed to physical, nature of the
angels. Some see the reference to wind and fire as signifying
that angels are insubstantial. Bruce comments, 'If this is the

way in which our author understands Psalm 104:4, then he is
contrasting the evanescence of angels with the eternity of the
Son.'[1]

Nevertheless, as fire purifies, the angels that serve God are
pure, unfallen creatures. They may be physically insubstantial
but, like fire, they are mighty in their influence and effect —
they 'excel in strength' (Ps. 103:20). As we shall see later, it is
a matter of great comfort to believers that God's agents operate with such divine authority and power.

The throne of Christ (1:8)

While the angels are servants, Christ is King. The Writer continues: '**... to the Son he says: "Your throne, O God, is for
ever and ever; a sceptre of righteousness is the sceptre of
your Kingdom"**' (1:8). The quotation is from Psalm 45:6-7,
which declares itself 'a composition concerning the King' (Ps.
45:1). The striking thing about this verse is that in a single
breath it provides a threefold identification of Christ as Son,
God and King. Nowhere in Scripture can there be a more comprehensive statement of the full nature and glory of the Lord
Jesus Christ. 'This king', says Hywel Jones, 'sits on a throne,
is addressed by God (by Jehovah), is a perfect king for God (a
man after God's own heart in all respects) and is rewarded
with the gift of the Spirit for his people whom he takes into
union with himself.'[2]

According to our verse, God speaks to God and calls him
'**Son**'! Such is the mystery of the triune God. Pink remarks,
'This [verse] supplies us with one of the most emphatic and
unequivocal proofs of the Deity of Christ to be found in the
Scriptures.'[3] The teaching that God is one yet three, Father,
Son and Holy Spirit, is difficult to grasp and impossible to
comprehend. Many, applying human reason to this matter, have

rejected the deity of Christ as a logical contradiction. Yet this is the testimony of Scripture, and we cannot have the gospel of Christ without the deity of Christ. In fact, our inability to fathom the doctrine of the Trinity is a clear pointer to its truth! For if God is the transcendent Being we believe him to be, it would be strange if our finite minds could comprehend his nature.

Our text embraces another seeming contradiction. As we saw earlier, God is on the throne and Christ is seated at his right hand. But now we are told that Christ himself is the King enthroned. Who, then, is really on the throne? The answer is *both* the Father and the Son. In Revelation 22:1-3, John depicts 'the throne [singular] of God and of the Lamb' as the centrepiece of heaven. We have to recognise that the term 'throne' is a metaphor for the sovereign power and universal authority of the triune God. There is thus no contradiction that first one and then another of the divine persons is pictured as enthroned.

One awesome example of this is Isaiah's vision. He saw 'the Lord sitting on a throne, high and lifted up, and the train of his robe filled the temple. Above it stood seraphim ... and one cried to another and said, "Holy, holy, holy is the LORD of hosts; the earth is full of his glory."' Isaiah had no doubt whom he had seen: 'My eyes have seen the King, the LORD of hosts,' he cried in great distress (Isa. 6:1-5). Normally we rightly identify 'the LORD of hosts' with God the Father. Yet John tells us in his Gospel that Isaiah wrote these things of Christ, 'when he saw his glory and spoke of him' (John 12:39-41; cf. Isa. 6:10). It can be argued that all visions of God and 'theophanies' (appearances of God) recorded in Scripture are of the Son, the Second Person of the Godhead, since 'he is the image of the invisible God' whom 'no one has seen ... at any time (Col. 1:15; John 1:18).

An everlasting throne (1:8 cont.)

Christ's throne is **'for ever and ever'** (1:8). Unlike earthly dynasties, Christ's rule is eternal. This is true both in the past and future senses of 'eternity'. Concerning 'eternity past' Jeremiah declares, 'A glorious high throne from the beginning is the place of our sanctuary' (Jer. 17:12). Christ is our sanctuary from the guilt and power of sin and from the judgement of a holy God. But that sanctuary is a throne, glorious, high and established 'from the beginning'.

Similarly, concerning the eternal future, there will be no end to his dominion. 'You ... shall call his name Jesus', announced the angel Gabriel. 'He will be great and will be called the Son of the highest; and the Lord God will give him the throne of his father David. And he will reign over the house of Jacob for ever, and of his kingdom there will be no end' (Luke 1:32-33; see also Isa. 9:6-7; 2 Sam. 7:16).

Although Christ rules over all, there are in fact two distinct but interrelated kingdoms in view. The first is often referred to in Scripture as the 'kingdom of God', or the 'kingdom of heaven'. It is identified here as the 'house of Jacob'. This is the church of Christ, the spiritual Israel. The use of the name 'Jacob' is a poignant reminder that this kingdom is composed of sinners saved by grace. Like Jacob, the liar and schemer, they have been rescued from their sinful ways and transformed into 'Israel', the people of God.

The second kingdom is that cosmic realm which encompasses the church but also embraces 'all things', including both the material universe and the spiritual world of angels, principalities and powers. Concerning this more comprehensive kingdom Paul writes, '... it pleased the Father that in him all the fullness should dwell, and by him to reconcile all things to himself — by him, whether things on earth or things in heaven, having made peace through the blood of his cross' (Col.

1:19-20). This is the realm that will be involved when Christ 'delivers the kingdom to God the Father, when he puts an end to all rule and all authority and power' (1 Cor. 15:24).

Which of these kingdoms is of greater importance in the sight of God? Surprisingly, it is the first. For the Father has 'put all things under [Christ's] feet, and gave him to be the head over all things to [for the benefit of] the church, which is his body, the fulness of him who fills all in all' (Eph. 1:22-23).

The rod of righteousness (1:8 cont.)

One who occupies a throne also wields a sceptre — 'one of the badges of royalty ... an emblem of the integrity of the monarch in administering justice'.[4]

Historically, the sceptre was a rod or wand which symbolised authority and power. The rod of Moses is a good example of this symbolism. Whenever God commanded some mighty work or miracle, Moses and Aaron used their rods (Exod. 4:17). By Aaron's rod, the rivers of Egypt were turned to blood. The waters of the Red Sea parted as Moses stretched out *his* rod. With the rod he struck the rock, and water gushed out (Exod. 7:19; 14:16; 17:6). Probably, a rod or staff was originally used by those in authority as a 'domestic weapon' to chastise tardy servants or courtiers. It thus became a symbol of power — the man with the rod was the man in charge!

The **'sceptre of righteousness'** that characterises Christ's kingdom, therefore, signifies that his sovereign power is exercised in a righteous manner. Unlike mere men, he does not rule arbitrarily or unfairly. His motives are always pure, his intentions always gracious, his actions always self-consistent. Everything he does is done righteously, in a way that reflects and displays his righteous nature. This is true, whether we understand it or not.

This is a most important principle, and it is something that Scripture appeals to again and again. 'Shall not the Judge of all the earth do right?', asks Abraham, appealing to this very principle as he pleads that any who are righteous should be spared in the destruction of Sodom (Gen. 18:25). In the New Testament, Paul throws light on the mystery of predestination by reference to this same concept, namely that God cannot act unrighteously (Rom. 9:19-20). 'Let God be true and every man a liar', he declares elsewhere, and quotes Psalm 51:4 to the effect that God is always justified in his words and overcomes when he is criticised (Rom. 3:4). Otherwise he would not be the God of Scripture.

We often make the mistake of 'defending' God by denying his sovereignty. Has some natural disaster taken the lives of innocent people? Has some human action brought horror in its wake? 'Don't blame God', we cry. 'Leave him out of it! It's nothing to do with him. He does not control the elements. He cannot help what man does in his sinfulness.' But, of course, he can and does exercise such control, since he 'works all things according to the counsel of his will' (Eph. 1:11). We may not understand *why* he brings about certain events, nor why he allows the innocent to suffer. But because the sceptre of his kingdom is a righteous sceptre, we may be assured that he acts in perfect righteousness in everything he does.

Love and hate (1:9)

Christ both loves and hates: **'You have loved righteousness and hated lawlessness; Therefore God, your God, has anointed you with the oil of gladness more than your companions'** (1:9). Continuing his quotation from Psalm 45, the Writer demonstrates that Christ is passionate concerning righteousness and 'lawlessness'. The word 'righteousness' often comes across as something cold, clinical and theological. Admittedly, it is a technical term which has a precise and important meaning in Scripture. But with God it evokes strong emotion. Righteousness he loves; wrongdoing he hates. Guthrie writes, '[Righteousness] forms the centre of his affection. It is part of his nature — "Thou hast loved righteousness." '⁵ Furthermore, as darkness cannot exist in the presence of light, Christ's love of righteousness necessarily implies a hatred for iniquity and wickedness.

If we have the mind of Christ, we also will love what is right and hate what is wrong. We will not be indifferent to these things, shrugging our shoulders and mumbling, 'That's life.' There will be passion in our souls and in our lives concerning good and evil, righteousness and sin. The former we will practise and applaud. The latter we will shun and condemn. In doing so, however, we will remember that we too are sinners. Our attitude will be to condemn the sin, but point the sinner to Christ.

But this is not all. When we love something, we derive great pleasure from it. So to love righteousness is not simply to admire it, but actively to rejoice in it. Thus the psalm continues, **'Therefore God, your God, has anointed you with the oil of gladness more than your companions'** (1:9). Christ rejoices in righteousness with a gladness that is total. His joy is likened to an anointing oil, pure and fragrant, poured out upon his head and running down his garments. Why can he exult in righteousness 'more than his companions'? Because, among men, he alone was righteous. His followers (or companions) share his perfect righteousness by imputation and by union with him, but have no righteousness of their own. Paul's desire was to be 'found in him, not having my own righteousness which is from the law, but that which is through faith in Christ, the righteousness which is from God by faith' (Phil. 3:9). Thus believers, looking to Christ, can indeed rejoice in his perfection. But Christ, uniquely, rejoices in his own righteousness.

Commonly, righteousness is represented as something stern and unsmiling. It is good, many will admit, but it is not fun! Such a view may be Victorian, but it is not biblical. It is ungodly people who turn truth upside down and represent sin as enjoyable and righteousness as dull. No one on earth should be more joyful than one who has the righteousness of Christ laid to his account and the indwelling Holy Spirit implementing Christ's victory over sin in his daily life. 'Rejoice in the Lord always', writes the apostle. 'Again I will say, rejoice!' (Phil. 4:4; see also Phil. 3:1, 3).

5.
Christ the Creator

Please read Hebrews 1:10-14

Although it is often disregarded, the creatorhood of Christ is a recurrent theme of the New Testament. The fact that Christ is the Creator features prominently in John's Gospel, in Colossians and here in Hebrews. It is no accident that each of these books addresses the question: 'Who is Christ?' That is, they major on the person of Christ and his transcendence over all created beings, whether angels or men. The subject has already been raised in verses 1-3 of chapter 1 but the Writer is drawn back to the theme, irresistibly, in verses 10-12.

Nor is the creatorial role of Christ a 'stand-alone' subject. We have to bear in mind that creation was a means to an end, namely, to provide the sphere of redemption history and prepare the way for the new creation — which is the culmination of the new covenant. John speaks of this new creation and links it with Christ's kingly reign: 'Then he who sat on the throne said, "Behold, I make all things new"' (see Rev. 21:1-7; the one enthroned is the Judge of Rev. 20:11).

In the beginning (1:10)

The opening words of the Bible are both memorable and evocative. 'In the beginning God created the heavens and the earth'

(Gen. 1:1). They tell us who God is, namely, the maker of heaven and earth. They show us that biblical revelation is set in the context of eternity. They demonstrate that God, the Creator, transcends the creation. He is before, beyond, above, and altogether outside, the created order — yet he sustains and permeates it (Acts 17:24-28). And, comments Eveson in this context, 'What is true of God the Father is also true of the Son, Jesus Christ.'[1]

The New Testament takes up the evocative words of Genesis 1:1 and, with great deliberation and not the slightest hint of apology, applies them to Jesus Christ (John 1:1). Our passage further exemplifies this teaching: **'But to the Son he says ... "You, LORD, in the beginning laid the foundation of the earth, and the heavens are the work of your hands"'** (1:8,10).

The quotation is from Psalm 102:25. The Writer has inserted the word 'LORD', perhaps to remind us that the whole psalm is addressed to Jahweh (the name of God rendered 'LORD' in our English translation). But, crucially, the addressee of the psalm is identified not only as Jahweh but also as 'the Son', that is, Christ. 'The meaning is', says Barnes, 'that at the very beginning he existed, and that he would continue to exist to the very close, unchangeably the same.'[2]

The Writer is pointing out that Christ Jesus is a timeless, transcendent Being. If he is the Creator, he cannot be created. If he made all things, then he must be identified with Jahweh, the covenant God of Abraham, Isaac and Jacob. Christ and the Father are one (John 10:30).

Many are confused by the idea that the Lord Jesus Christ, who lived and suffered as a man among men, can at the same time be the creator and sustainer of the universe. It is, admittedly, a mind-boggling concept. Some rationalise the problem by making a distinction between the 'cosmic Christ' and the man Christ Jesus. But the New Testament will not allow this.

As we have seen, the one who 'uphold[s] all things by the word of his power', is also the one who 'purged our sins' (1:3). The Christ of creation *is* the Christ of the cross. Difficult as the idea may be for our finite minds to grasp, we have to accept that Christ is both Creator and the Saviour of sinners like ourselves.

One further point: it is as 'the Son' that Christ created. That is, he did not act independently of his Father when he created all things. Rather, he was carrying out the will and purpose of the Father in performing his creative work. Thus creation can be ascribed to both the Father and the Son, since the Father created all things *through* the Son. Equally, the Father created all things *for* the Son (Col. 1:16).

'You are the same' (1:11-12)

Continuing his quotation from Psalm 102, the Writer accentuates the timelessness of Christ: **'The heavens ... will perish, but you remain; and they will all grow old like a garment; like a cloak you will fold them up, and they will be changed. But you are the same, and your years will not fail'** (1:11-12).

Not only did Christ create the worlds 'in the beginning', but he will outlive and outlast the created order. Brown observes, 'The Son is represented not only as the creator of all things but as the Author of all the changes through which they are to pass.'[3] As we continue in Hebrews, we shall see that Jesus Christ, the ever-living Son and High Priest, is brought constantly before our view. The idea that Christ is eternal in his nature is central to the whole epistle, for it is this that guarantees the timelessness of the new covenant.

The created order is not itself eternal. It will 'grow old' and 'perish', like a worn-out coat. When it has served its purpose, it will be 'folded up' and 'changed' — that is, *exchanged* for something new. Peter elaborates. The first created universe will be 'burned up' or destroyed, he tells us, but not to leave mere chaos or void. Rather, the discarded order will be exchanged for a new creation. 'We, according to his promise', writes the apostle, 'look for new heavens and a new earth in which righteousness dwells' (2 Peter 3:10,13). Some apply these words to heaven, but since 2 Peter 3:10 refers to the destruction of the physical world, it seems better to understand the 'new' heavens and earth as a new created order (which may not, however, be a *physical* universe as we understand that term).

But whatever created orders there may be, now or in the future, the fact remains that Christ transcends them all: 'You are the same and your years will not fail.' He remains 'the same yesterday, today and for ever' (13:8). The timelessness of Christ is more than a philosophical concept. It is a strong ground of assurance for the believer. Not only can we depend on Christ for time and eternity, but we can depend upon his unchanging love. Because with him there is no 'yesterday' or 'tomorrow', his grace cannot fail or be rescinded: 'I am the LORD, I do not change; therefore you are not consumed, O sons of Jacob' (Mal. 3:6).

Christ the conqueror (1:13)

So far we have seen that Christ is the creator and sustainer of all things, who will also bring this present world to an end, folding it away like a worn-out garment. It comes as something of a shock, then, to be told that this almighty person has 'enemies'. Who would dare oppose omnipotence? What created being would be so foolish as to quarrel with the Almighty?

Yet the Writer to the Hebrews proceeds to quote from the Psalms: **'To which of the angels has he ever said: "Sit at**

my right hand, till I make your enemies your footstool"?'
(1:13). 'The usefulness of this testimony for the confirmation
of the dignity and authority of the Messiah', writes Owen, 'is
evidenced by the frequent quotation of it in the New Testament'[4] (see Matt. 22:44; Acts 2:34-35; 1 Cor. 15:25).

The word 'till' does not indicate that Christ's reign will
cease once his enemies are overcome, since his kingdom 'shall
stand for ever' (Dan. 2:44). Rather, it emphasises the fact that
he rules *now*, during the period when his foes appear to retain
some strength.[5] It is true that a time will come when Christ
'delivers the kingdom to God the Father' (1 Cor. 15:24). But
this means that he will dedicate or devote it to the Father,
rather than relinquish it.

The full quotation from Psalm 110:1-2 is as follows: 'The
LORD said to my Lord, "Sit at my right hand, till I make your
enemies your footstool." The LORD shall send the rod of your
strength out of Zion. Rule in the midst of your enemies.' Only
a portion of this passage is cited in 1:13, but the recipients of
the epistle would have known the context, and this context is
highly germane to the argument.

The psalm has three parties in view. They are, firstly, 'the
LORD' (Jahweh); secondly, the one whom the psalmist David
acknowledges as 'my Lord', and who is identified as the Christ
in Luke 20:41-44; and thirdly, the enemies of Christ. To these
categories the Writer adds a fourth, namely, the angels
(1:13-14). We will consider them in turn, beginning with 'the
LORD' and the 'Lord'.

1. 'The LORD' and the 'Lord'

Again and again in the Old Testament we are told that there is
only one God. On the threshold of the promised land, for
example, Moses exhorts the people in these terms: 'Hear O
Israel; the LORD our God, the LORD is one! You shall love the

LORD your God with all your heart, with all your soul, and with all your might' (Deut. 6:4-5). Again, we read in Isaiah, 'For I am God and there is no other. I have sworn by myself ... that to me every knee shall bow, every tongue shall take an oath' (Isa. 45:23). Yet this very verse is applied to Jesus Christ by the apostle Paul! (Phil. 2:10-11).

The only conclusion we can draw is that Jesus Christ is God and that he shares this divine nature with his Father. There is one God, but there are two persons, the Father and the Son. (Other Scriptures, of course, reveal that there is a third person in the Godhead, namely the Holy Spirit, a fact that gives rise to the name 'Holy Trinity' applied to God.)

It follows, then, that when the psalmist writes, 'the LORD said to my Lord', he is referring to the Father as 'the LORD' and to the Son as 'my Lord'. Clearly, such words could never be addressed to created beings such as angels. An even more explicit statement of the same truth is found in Psalm 2:7, which the Writer cited earlier in 1:5: 'The LORD has said to me, "You are my Son, today I have begotten you."'

But such is the union between the Father and the Son that even this tidy division of the divine titles is sometimes over-turned. In the prophecy of Zechariah, for example, we are told that 'the LORD of hosts' has sent 'the LORD of hosts' to dwell among his people! No, that is not a misprint; you can read it for yourself in Zechariah 2:8-10. Very simply, the Old Testament applies the titles 'LORD' and 'LORD of hosts' equally (even randomly) to both the Father and the Son. A prime example is Isaiah's vision in the temple, when he saw 'the Lord sitting on a throne, high and lifted up'. Whom did he see? None other than 'the King, LORD of hosts' (Isa. 6:1,3,5). But John tells us it was Christ, in all his glory, that Isaiah saw in his vision of the Majesty on high (John 12:41).

It is God the Father, therefore, who invites his Son to sit at his right hand, 'the position of honour and rank',[6] the place of privilege and power. It is the Father who promises to make his foes his footstool, that is, to subdue his enemies and make them serve him. Here we are privileged to view the awesome concourse of the Father with the Son. Hebrews 1:3 describes how Jesus, having purged our sins, was enthroned at the right hand of the Father, and the Writer returns again and again to this great theme (2:9; 10:12-13). The latter reference tells us specifically that Christ's session (being seated) began 'after he had offered one sacrifice for sins for ever'. Christ's enthronement in glory is a magnet for the Writer's thoughts as he pens the epistle.

2. The enemies

The Father tells the Son, 'Sit at my right hand, till I make your enemies your footstool. The LORD shall send the rod of your strength out of Zion. Rule in the midst of your enemies' (Ps. 110:1-2). It is the Father's work and undertaking to crush the enemies of Christ. Who are his enemies? They are firstly those men in all ages who oppose and reject his rule. During his time on earth, Jesus 'endured such hostility from sinners against himself' (12:3), and this rejection will continue till the end of time. However, we have the example of Saul of Tarsus to encourage us. His bitter enmity against Christ was subdued and he became the illustrious apostle Paul. So God in grace deals with many of his enemies from among mankind.

Secondly, Christ's enemies are 'the devil and his angels' (Matt. 25:41), the spiritual foes against which believers also wrestle in this life — 'principalities ... powers ... the rulers of the darkness of this age ... spiritual hosts of wickedness in the heavenly places' (Eph. 6:12-13). These are also the forces that underlie the activities of the 'antichrists' of this world (1 John 2:18; 4:3). In one sense, Christ has already defeated these enemies. When he redeemed his people on the cross, asserts Paul, he 'disarmed principalities and powers, he made a public spectacle of them, triumphing over them in it' (Col. 2:15). Not only has he triumphed over them, but he enables us to do so also. In the face of their attacks, says Paul again, 'we are more than conquerors through him who loved us' (Rom. 8:37). However, in the unfolding purpose of God, the 'rulers of darkness' are not *yet* utterly crushed beneath his feet. They persist in their harmful yet fruitless resistance, so that the warfare still rages. Nevertheless, Christ's victory is real and has practical consequences. Satan is a powerful enemy but, because Christ rules, we in our weakness are able to 'resist the devil and he will flee from [us]' (James 4:7; 1 Peter 5:9), knowing that 'he who is in [us] is greater than he who is in the world' (1 John 4:4).

Thirdly, Christ's enemies include the impersonal entities of sin, death and their consequences. We read, 'For he [Christ] must reign till he [the Father] has put all things under his feet. The last enemy that will be destroyed is death' (1 Cor. 15:24-26; Ps. 8:6). Jesus conquered sin when he died on the cross, and overcame death when he rose on the third day. But sin and death still hold mankind in their thrall, including, in some measure, those who are in Christ. Under the new covenant, believers are freed from sin (Rom. 6:6-14) — but they still struggle against it as it indwells the flesh (Gal. 5:17). Under that covenant also they have eternal life — but they must still suffer physical death until the day of resurrection. That is why death will be the last enemy to be defeated. Its abolition awaits the return of Christ in glory.

Nevertheless, Jesus reigns. He rules, notice, not in the absence but 'in the midst' of his enemies, and will do so until they are made his footstool. They still surround his church on earth; they still persecute his saints; they still rebel against his sovereign rule. But when they do their worst, his enemies (and ours) are 'gathered together to do whatever [God's] hand and [God's] purpose determined before to be done' (Acts 4:28).

3. The angels

The final entities referred to in 1:13 are the angels. The esteem with which the Father regards the Son sets him for ever apart from the angels, however mighty they may be. 'To which of the angels has he [the Father] ever said; "Sit at my right hand ..."'? asks the Writer. He is confident that no one will attempt an answer, for such an invitation is unthinkable. As Bruce points out, 'The most exalted angels ... "stand in the presence of God" like Gabriel (Luke 1:19), but none of them has ever been invited to sit before him.'[7] Angels are servants, not sons.

We must admit, of course, that both men and angels are designated 'sons of God' in Scripture. See, for example, Galatians 4:6 and Job 1:6. However, the distinction here is between the unique 'only begotten Son' (John 3:16) and a plurality of men or angels accorded the courtesy title 'sons' by virtue of their creation as sentient and moral beings.

Specifically, argues the Writer, angels are servants not only of God but also, amazingly, of Christian believers. **'Are they not all ministering spirits'**, he asks, **'sent forth to minister for those who will inherit salvation?'** (1:14). Although, in context, this is almost a 'throwaway' line, it is a statement of great comfort and importance to every true Christian.

Scripture is largely silent about this angelic ministry. There are specific cases where angels assisted God's people, such as Lot (Gen. 19:1-10) and Peter (Acts 12:7-10), but such accounts are rare. This implies that the ministrations of angels towards the 'heirs of salvation' are largely hidden from us, and deliberately so. The Lord employs their services for the

welfare of his people, but in a manner usually unseen and unknown, lest angels should become objects of devotion and
worship (cf. Col. 2:18). It is nevertheless comforting that the
often derided idea of 'guardian angels' has a basis both in Scripture and in every believer's experience of God's providential
care.

6.
Christ the Saviour

Please read Hebrews 2:1-4

The Writer now makes a powerful application of his arguments in chapter 1. 'If the word spoken through angels proved steadfast', he asks, 'how shall we escape if we neglect ... a salvation ... spoken by the Lord?' (2:2-3). Under the Mosaic covenant it could mean death to despise or 'neglect' the law. Yet that was a covenant 'spoken' (mediated) through mere angels. The gospel, however, is a covenant mediated to us by Christ himself, as the Writer tells us at the very beginning of the epistle (1:2). Since Christ is infinitely superior to the angels, so must his message (the gospel) transcend theirs (the law). Thus any who neglect the gospel are vastly more guilty than those who despised Moses' law. How can such people escape the fierceness of God's anger?

The need to listen (2:1)

'**Therefore**', exhorts the Writer, '**we must give the more earnest heed to the things which we have heard, lest we drift away**' (2:1). The 'things which we have heard' are the truths of the gospel, and this exhortation is the first of many like it. Throughout the epistle we find strong, even vehement, exhortations and directions addressed to the readers. The

Writer pulls no punches but, equally, he always builds his case on sound argument. Indeed, it is the very logic of the exhortation that lends it power. These are not arbitrary commands, but ones which gather strength from the force of truth.

How important it is that we should follow this pattern in our own day! Too often believers are taught the 'rules' of Christian behaviour as if they were arbitrary and ritualistic. They do things simply because their leaders say so. But only Scripture-based persuasion can guarantee Scripture-based obedience.

The word **'therefore'** in 2:1 refers us back to the detailed case already developed in chapter 1, namely, that Christ is the divine Son endued with all authority and power in heaven and in earth. What the Writer is about to say rests entirely on what he has already explained. As we proceed through the epistle, we shall see, again and again, that the Writer's whole message is based firmly on the foundation laid in Hebrews 1.

The Writer's first point is a positive one: **'we must give the more earnest heed'** to the gospel of Christ. In other words, we must listen carefully to what it has to say. Not only must we listen, but we must listen *earnestly*. Indeed, we must listen 'the *more* earnestly'. Owen comments, 'To attend ... unto the word preached is to consider the *author* of it, the *matter* of it, the *weight* ... of it, the *ends* of it, [and do so] with faith, subjection of spirit and constancy.'[1] Why must we so listen? Because God himself is speaking to us through his Son, and we insult the Almighty if we turn a deaf ear to what he has to say.

Sadly, many do just that. Remember that the Writer is not addressing unbelievers, but rather those who at least consider themselves Christians. This alerts us to the fact that professing believers can and do 'neglect' the gospel. That is, they pursue both their religion and their lives without due attention to the facts and implications of the gospel of Christ.

They may be taken up with good works and noble causes. They may be sincere in religious observances. But they do not hold the person and work of Christ central to their scheme of things or to their practical activities. It is vital, therefore, that we keep Christ central to all our teaching, ministry and worship. Otherwise we shall fall into the same trap. And we shall only listen 'more earnestly' if we make it our habitual practice to preach and to hear 'the unsearchable riches of Christ' (Eph. 3:8).

The positive exhortation to listen is reinforced, negatively, by the warning, **'lest we drift away'** (2:1). There is a danger, suggests the Writer, of departing from the true gospel by imperceptible steps, that is, by drifting.

The word 'drift' has a nautical overtone.[2] As any sailor knows, it is easier to drift with the current than to make headway against it. In order to drift, all we have to do is nothing! To remain true to the gospel takes effort. It requires us to 'earnestly contend for the faith' — to labour in it, fight for it, and defend it (Jude 3; Phil. 1:7). This will often mean being misunderstood and criticised, assaulted by Satan and by men.

The spiritual drifter faces no such problems. What he does face, however, is the danger of being denied by Christ in the Day of Judgement (Matt. 10:33). 'Therefore, we must give ... heed.'

The need to escape (2:2-3)

The Writer's basic argument is expressed in verses 2-3: **'If the word spoken through angels proved steadfast, and every transgression and disobedience received a just reward, how shall we escape if we neglect so great a salvation, which at the first began to be spoken by the Lord?'** The 'word spoken through angels' is, of course, the law of

Moses which 'was appointed through angels by the hand of a mediator' (Acts 7:38; Gal. 3:19).

Angels are not mentioned in Exodus where the giving of the law is described, though Moses features prominently as mediator. This is a case where the details of an event recorded in the Old Testament are filled out by New Testament Scriptures (other examples are found in Acts 7:38,53; Gal. 3:19; 2 Tim. 3:8 and Jude 9). Brown suggests that 'The audible voice in which the revelation from Mount Sinai was made, was produced by angelic agency.'[3]

This 'word' of the law, asserts the Writer, condemned all who transgressed it. A **'just reward'** (a fitting punishment) was meted out to those who ignored or disobeyed it: 'Anyone who has rejected Moses' law dies without mercy', he avers later (10:28).

Without question, then, the law given at Sinai through angels was **'steadfast'**. It was rock-solid in its condemnation of sin. It could not be circumvented or avoided, nor could its punishments be softened or ameliorated. There are many examples in the Old Testament of the severity of that law (see, e.g., Achan's punishment in Joshua 7).

If this is so, argues the Writer, how much *greater* punishment is to be expected for those who despise the message of grace — a message delivered not by angels but by Christ himself? The answer is self-evident. If a breach of Moses' law brought physical punishment or death, then nothing short of eternal and spiritual condemnation will result if we 'neglect so great a salvation' revealed by the eternal Son.

The use of words like 'escape' and 'salvation' indicate clearly that man stands in danger of condemnation. To ask, **'How shall we escape?'**, is to assert that we *need* to escape. From what, then, do we need to be saved?

The answer is implied rather than stated in our passage, but it is clear enough from other parts of Hebrews and from

Scripture as a whole. We need to be saved both from the power of our sin and from God's wrath against it. We need to escape the just punishment of our transgression against a holy God, for 'all have sinned and fall short of the glory of God' (Rom. 3:23).

The greatness of salvation (2:3 cont.)

The essence of the gospel is that God has provided a way of escape. He has provided **'so great a salvation'** (2:3) through his Son, Jesus Christ. The *greatness* of this salvation resides in several things.

Firstly, it is no bare escape that God provides. We do not escape, as it were, by the skin of our teeth. In Christ we escape from condemnation into a glorious acceptance. Not only is Christ the Son of God, but through him God brings 'many sons to glory' (2:10). That is, those who trust in Christ are saved according to God's purpose, namely, to be adopted as his own children in Christ and share his eternal glory.

Secondly, this salvation is great because it reveals the greatness of God's love and mercy. How does God demonstrate these characteristics? By sending his Son to purge our sins. Later in the epistle we shall read much concerning Christ's death, in which he offered himself as a sacrifice to atone for the sins of his people. God gave his utmost to redeem us to himself, and the salvation thereby provided is great beyond comparison.

Thirdly, this salvation is great on account of its perfection or completeness. This is another major theme of Hebrews, namely that Christ 'has perfected for ever' those he has 'set apart' (10:14). This means that, for God's elect, salvation is a complete and perfect work — one that befits and reflects the perfections of God himself.

To neglect, or treat lightly, such a salvation is the height of folly. It defies comprehension. Yet such neglect is all too possible — otherwise we would not be warned against it. Neglect occurs if we take our eyes off Christ and his redeeming work; if we turn to 'other gospels' which are, in fact, perverted gospels, in which human works take precedence over the grace of God in Christ (Gal. 1:6-9). Let us give greater heed, then, to these things.

Spoken by the Lord (2:3 cont.)

The fourth reason why the Writer insists on the greatness of the gospel is, of course, that it is brought to us by Christ himself — not by angels, not by prophets, but by the incarnate God. It was he who **'began'** to speak the gospel. This does not mean, of course, that the Old Testament contains no gospel revelation, or that John the Baptist's message was irrelevant. Both the Old Testament and John pointed to Christ. But until Christ came in the flesh, these anticipations went unrealised and, to a great extent, unrecognised. Witness the difficulty that even the disciples of Christ had in understanding his mission and message (see, e.g., Mark 8:14-21; Luke 24:25). It is only by the coming of Christ to earth that the secret, or 'mystery', that had previously been hidden from the majority of mankind was revealed in its fulness (1:2; Eph. 3:5-9).

However, in God's gracious purposes, his servants had a part to play. This gospel, continues the Writer, **'was confirmed to us by those who heard him'** (2:3). That is, Christ entrusted the gospel message to his apostles and prophets (as Ephesians 3:5-9 testifies) and it was *their* work to pass on this gospel to succeeding generations without loss or adulteration. This they did both by preaching and by writing the New

Testament Scriptures. This entrustment explains the sometimes fiery language employed by the New Testament writers when dealing with deviations from the gospel. These men were not only the *recipients* of the gospel but also its jealous *guardians*.

Notice that the Writer seems to suggest that he had learned the gospel from other, first-generation, believers. Kistemaker is adamant that 'The author ... and the readers of his epistle belong to the second generation of followers; they had not heard the gospel from Jesus himself.'[4] This bears upon the identity of the Writer, since it is hardly a statement that Paul, for example, would have made (cf. Gal. 1:12: 'I neither received [the gospel] from man, nor was I taught it'). Kistemaker's interpretation is probably correct, but the possibility remains that the Writer may have been putting himself in his readers' place rather than speaking of his own experience.

God bears witness (2:4)

Just as Christ himself had authenticated his words by signs and wonders (John 11:3-6; 14:11), so those to whom he first entrusted the gospel also enjoyed God's authentication. The word had been **'confirmed'** to the Writer's generation by those who learned it directly from Christ, **'God also bearing witness both with signs and wonders, with various miracles, and gifts of the Holy Spirit, according to his own will'** (2:4). It is quite clear *who* were thus authenticated, and *why* they were so favoured. There is no suggestion here that miracles were to be performed by believers in general, or were to remain a feature of the post-apostolic church.

Those to whom God bore witness in this dramatic manner are here identified as the men to whom Jesus first entrusted the gospel. As we have already seen, it was their privilege and responsibility to convey that message to future generations, and this they did, either by writing the New Testament Scriptures, or by their preaching and teaching (preserved by others in those same Scriptures). In short, this miraculous verification of their message was reserved for those whose teaching or writing gave us the New Testament.

It was fitting that these men — apostles, prophets and evangelists — should be marked out as the true messengers of God by 'signs and wonders' accompanying their teaching. Every New Testament miracle is an authentication of Christ himself. For example, when Peter healed the lame man at the temple gate, the healing was performed 'in the name of Jesus Christ of Nazareth' and to demonstrate that he was indeed the Christ of God (Acts 3:11-16). 'The purpose of this evidence', says Lane, 'is the validation that God has spoken definitively in Christ.'[5]

Finally, the Writer employs various terms to describe these acts of authentication — 'signs', 'wonders', 'miracles' and 'gifts' (2:4). These words are probably not intended to describe different categories of miraculous works, but rather to flesh out their significance. Thus a 'sign' is a pointer to the person of Christ. A 'wonder' is something that emphasises that the power of God is at work. A 'miracle' tells us that God is not limited by natural law and may manifest his activity by suspending such laws. Finally, 'gifts of the Holy Spirit' mean that the Spirit of God was working to reveal Christ's power and glory.

Notice that these gifts are given sovereignly by the Holy Spirit, 'according to his own will' (2:4). This alerts us the fact that such gifts, even in New Testament times, were not available at man's insistence or desire. As Paul tells the Corinthians, such gifts were distributed 'to each one individually as he [the Spirit] wills' (1 Cor. 12:11). For a fuller discussion of spiritual gifts, the reader is referred elsewhere.[6]

7.
Christ the Man

Please read Hebrews 2:5-9

The 'great salvation' made available in Christ is a privilege beyond description — that much is made clear in 2:3. But now the Writer unveils a further aspect of God's eternal and cosmic purpose. The redeemed, we are told, will inherit **'the world to come'** (2:5).

In order to make this new assertion, the Writer returns to an earlier subject, namely, the lowly role of angels in God's economy. He does so both to link his new thoughts to the earlier exposition and to introduce his next great theme, namely the humanity of Christ. This theme begins here in 2:5-9 but continues to the end of Hebrews 2, as we shall see. Jesus is the Son of God, the sovereign Lord and creator of all things — but, asserts the Writer, he is also true man. Even more, he is the *representative* man, in whom humanity achieves its zenith and fulfilment.

In him, therefore, we see what new-covenant humanity (in the form of the glorified church) will one day be.

The world to come (2:5)

Not only does Christ transcend the angels; the humblest believer also enjoys a status higher than theirs: **'For he [God]**

**has not put the world to come, of which we speak, in sub-
jection to angels'** (2:5). It is man who is destined to fulfil *that*
role.

A special feature of Hebrews is the Writer's command of
evocative phrases and powerful imagery. The poetry of his
writing survives even the 'insult' of translation. We have already
seen this in phrases such as 'the brightness of his glory' and
'the Majesty on high'. Here he introduces another such phrase,
'the world to come'. It is this world, he declares, 'of which we
speak'. This is not an aside. It reveals the heart of the epistle.

Notice that the Writer's concern is for a future world, not
the world in which we now live. It is, says Matthew Poole, 'a
world that must consist of heaven and earth ... distinct from
this present world'.[1] Some commentators disagree, suggesting that 'the world [economy] to come' is, in fact, the gospel
era, the age of the Messiah,[2] but this seems difficult to sustain
in the light of 2:8-9. John Brown may be closest to a true
interpretation when he writes, 'Some, by "the world to come",
understand the new heavens and new earth ... others understand by it the celestial state. I apprehend it includes both, but
is not confined to either; it is, generally, the order of things
introduced by the Messiah.'[3] In interpreting this verse we should
not forget that Abraham looked (and still looks) for a better,
heavenly country, an eternal city whose builder and maker is
God (11:10,16). The heirs of faith will follow his example, for
the world to come is, in the main, still a future prospect.

We are too often taken up with this present world and its
fashions. This is evident even in some forms of theology, such
as liberation theology and theonomy, both of which (in very
different ways) seek to establish the kingdom of God on earth.
The former seeks to improve the lot of the poor of this world
(a commendable purpose) but completely ignores their eternal welfare. The latter desires to bring human society and institutions into obedience to God's Word, but in doing so

confuses the earthly kingdoms of men with the spiritual kingdom of God.

But this earth-bound perspective is also found in much 'evangelical' activity, where happiness and fulfilment in this life are the declared objectives. The Bible's emphasis is placed unashamedly on 'the world to come', for there lies the believer's true reward and glorious inheritance.

The angels will receive no such inheritance. Lane remarks, 'Although God has entrusted the administration of the terrestrial world to the angels, their prerogatives did not extend to the heavenly world to come.'[4] In *that* world they will only be servants, ministering to the heirs of salvation. Indeed, the redeemed will 'judge angels' (1 Cor. 6:3). How foolish, therefore, are those who worship angels rather than Christ alone!

The Writer, then, is profoundly concerned with the future of mankind. Yet not with its future in this present world, but rather in 'the world to come', a world that will be in subjection first to Christ and then to man in Christ. Positively, he is writing of such things as the eternal salvation, security and blessedness of the redeemed. Negatively, he warns of the eternal loss of those who spurn the gospel of God's grace in Christ. He wants his readers to consider not only the world that now exists, created through Christ and for him, but also the fact that Christ is the future heir of all things. Those who 'run with patience ... looking to Jesus' will find he is not only the author of their faith but also the one who brings it to perfection and fulfilment (12:2). How important, then, that we keep in view the end and object of our lives; that we live in the light of 'the world to come', the fulfilment of God's eternal purposes.

Dominion of this coming world, he tells us, has not been entrusted to angels, but to man in Christ. Not to man alone, as was the case with Adam and the physical creation. That arrangement did not work *then* and would fail again. It is to man *in Christ* — to the church and bride of Christ — that this entrustment has been made. To his disciples Jesus could promise: 'In the regeneration, when the Son of Man sits on the throne of his glory, you ... will also sit on twelve thrones judging the twelve tribes of Israel' (Matt. 19:28). Again, Isaiah tells us that when Christ the 'king shall reign in righteousness', then also 'princes will rule with justice' (Isa. 32:1). Scripture gives us only glimpses of this 'new heaven and new earth', so we cannot speculate about its detailed structure. But most certainly, 'the world to come' is of vital interest to the believer, for it is more enduring than the world that now exists.

What is man? (2:6)

The Writer develops his theme by citing Psalm 8: **'One testified in a certain place, saying: "What is man that you are mindful of him, or the son of man that you take care of him?"'** (2:6).

Well might the psalmist cry out in wonder, 'What is man that you are mindful of him?' The question he poses has been debated by philosophers down the ages. The answer we give will determine the direction of our lives and the nature of our society. The Scriptures have no doubt. Man is God's special creation, designed to serve him and enjoy an eternal destiny of glory. This destiny is fulfilled in Christ.

Christians are sometimes intimidated by the world's philosophies which claim the intellectual high ground and despise the simplicity of biblical truth. But we should not be intimidated by the arrogance of human wisdom. The New Testament authors certainly were not, for they saw that wisdom for what it is. 'Where is the wise?', asks Paul. 'Where is the scribe? Where is the disputer of this age? Has not God made foolish the wisdom of this world?' (1 Cor. 1:20). The wisdom of God, he tells us, is wiser than men.

Today all questions regarding the nature of man are usually answered in terms of the theory of evolution. Man, they say, is just a superior animal. He has risen from among the apes by a process of evolution over many millions of years. There was no divine purpose in his origin; it was merely a quirk of fate. Thus man is the offspring of that blind goddess, chance, and must endue his own existence with meaning.

How different is the Bible's account of human origin! Mankind is a special work of God, created by God in his own image and thereby differentiated from the animals. Although he shares much in common with the animal world, yet he is utterly different, possessing as he does a spiritual nature and an eternal soul. Furthermore, unlike the animals, he is accountable to God. Since he bears the image of God, he also bears responsibilities towards God. He alone among the inhabitants of the physical world is capable of sin and rebellion against his Creator.

It is obvious, even to a child, that what we believe about human origins must affect our behaviour in the world. If we are the products of evolution, then let our rule of life be the survival of the fittest. But if we are the offspring of a holy and righteous God, then let us serve him with reverence and fear!

Lower than the angels (2:7-8)

The psalmist expresses amazement that God should be **'mindful'** of man and **'take care'** of him — that he should be concerned in any way with human beings. God is so great and man so insignificant. God is so holy and man so sinful. God is eternal but man is mortal. Why, then, should God care about man at all? The psalm answers its own question — and does so by reference to God's plan and purpose: **'You made [man] a little lower than the angels, you crowned him with glory**

and honour and set him over the works of your hands. You have put all things in subjection under his feet' (2:7-8). For added impact the Writer continues: **'For in that he put all things in subjection under him, he left nothing that is not put under him'** (2:8).

Man's 'glory and honour' refer, initially, to his creation, when God gave man dominion over 'the works of his hands' (Gen. 1:28). This command to rule the natural world is sometimes called 'the cultural mandate' because it justifies man's development of civilisation, science, technology and industry, together with his exploitation of earth's resources. As created, man was indeed crowned with glory and honour, for he was the pinnacle of God's creation. Even though man is now a fallen creature, these truths retain significance, since they provide a divine context for man's dominance of (and responsibility for!) the world in which he lives.

But this creation mandate is clearly not the Writer's main concern for, remember, he is not speaking of this world but of 'the world to come'. Mankind's true glory, and God's great purpose for him, will only finally be revealed in the context of that future world. Only then will all things be 'put under his feet', with the emphasis on 'all'. 'There is', says Lane, 'a profound note of anticipation in the OT teaching about humanity. The words of the psalmist look forward into the future, and that future is inextricably bound up with the person and work of Jesus.'[5]

So man is higher than the angels because of the glorious destiny God has purposed for him, in the form of the church of Christ. But at the same time, he has been made **'a little lower than the angels'** (2:7). How are we to resolve this paradox?

Firstly, the words 'a little' are better translated 'for a little while'. They refer not so much to the *degree* of man's present subjection as to its *duration* (it will last until Christ returns in triumph — Rom. 8:21). In God's sovereign purpose, man did not step immediately from Eden's garden to eternal glory. Why not? Because then God's purpose for mankind would have usurped his purpose for his Son, namely, that he might have the pre-eminence, be glorified as the Redeemer of the lost, and become heir of all things (1:2).

As a result, man's potential is hidden in this present age, obscured by the ravages of sin and the curse of death. Thus **'now we do not yet see all things put under him'** (2:8). But all is not darkness. The man Christ Jesus, having died for his elect and risen from the dead, has entered into glory as their forerunner. He thus demonstrates what ultimately awaits the whole church in glory.

The coronation of the Crucified (2:9)

The Writer puts it thus: **'But we see Jesus, who was made a little lower than the angels for the suffering of death, crowned with glory and honour, that he, by the grace of God, might taste death for everyone'** (2:9).

When the eternal Son of God became man, he identified himself with man's humiliation, sin excepted. Just as man was 'made for a little while lower than the angels', so Christ also embraced this lowly estate for a time. During his 'little while' upon earth, he shared man's suffering, mortality and physical frailty. 'He was tempted in all points as we are' (4:15).

Why was this necessary? 'For the suffering of death', replies the Writer. This does not mean that Christ accomplished nothing by his *life* on earth. The opposite is true. The righteousness that is imputed to the believer is the righteousness Jesus earned during his life as a man on earth. Christ came to live as well as die.

However, his death was the culmination of his life, the fulfilment of his earthly ministry (John 12:27). It was the effectual means by which his people would be made righteous in the sight of God: 'For [God] made him who knew no sin to be sin for us, that we might become the righteousness of God in him' (2 Cor. 5:21). It is appropriate, therefore, that the death of Christ should be the focus of the Writer's thoughts as he summarises the earthly mission of the Man, Christ Jesus.

This emphasis upon the death of Christ is most important. Many today sanitise the gospel by playing down the suffering of Christ and the atonement. They find the idea of substitutionary death obnoxious. They reject the biblical teaching that Christ suffered the wrath and judgement of his Father upon human sin and died, 'the just for the unjust, that he might bring us to God' (1 Peter 3:18).

But, declares the Writer, Christ did not come merely to teach and sympathise and heal, nor simply to show us how we ought to live. He came to die; to offer his life as an atonement for sin — 'a ransom for many' (Mark 10:45). When the apostle Paul preached the gospel he preached 'Christ and him crucified' (1 Cor. 2:2; Gal. 3:1). This is one of the dominant themes of Hebrews and it is worked out in great detail in the remainder of the epistle.

Accordingly, **'by the grace of God, [he tasted] death for everyone'** (2:9). We should notice several things here. Firstly, the whole work of salvation is driven and motivated by the grace of God. Christ's atoning death for sinners was an act of pure grace; that is, it was unforced and utterly unmerited by man. No man deserves what God has done for us in Christ, and it follows that no human 'work' or activity can make us eligible for the benefits accruing from his death.

Grace and works are two opposing principles. If salvation is attributed to *anything* that a person does in the strength of human nature, then grace is negated. It is true that we are 'saved by grace *through faith*'. But the faith in Christ that we must exercise is itself the gift of grace — for Paul continues:

'... and that [salvation is] not of yourselves; it is the gift of God, not of works lest anyone should boast. For we are his workmanship ...' (Eph. 2:8-10).

The second thing to notice is that Christ **'tasted'** death. That is, he genuinely experienced all the bitterness that death involves for human beings. His status as the Son of God did not spare him any of death's terrors. He was our forerunner in every last detail, that he might be a perfect and complete substitute for God's elect. He identified completely with our condition, that he might 'save to the uttermost those who come to God through him' (7:25).

Thirdly, he died **'for everyone'**. Taken out of context, this statement might seem to support a universalistic view of Christ's atonement. If he died for everyone, then surely everyone may benefit from his saving work if they so desire? But we get a different picture if we consider the context of this statement. A few verses later we read, 'Here am I and the children whom God has given me' (2:13). The 'children' are those who are sanctified, or set apart, by his death, the 'many sons' whom he will bring to glory (2:10-11). Thus it is clear that 'everyone' in 2:9 must be understood to mean every one of these 'children', given to Christ by the Father before time began (John 17:2,9; 2 Tim. 1:8-9). Christ died for the elect, to save them from their sins.

Finally, the Writer reaches the climax of his argument. This same Christ who partook of our humanity and died for our sins, has now been **'crowned with glory and honour'** (2:9). This passage omits the steps leading to his coronation, subsuming the resurrection, ascension and session of Christ in a single reference to his 'crowning'. And, wondrously, **'we *see* Jesus'** thus crowned and glorified. Faith gazes upon Christ enthroned and derives both joy and comfort from the sight.

Moreover, we must not overlook the point that Christ has been 'crowned with glory' *as the representative man*. His crowning anticipates and represents the collective glorification of all his people, and thus the fulfilment of both God's purpose for mankind and the psalmist's prophecy: 'You have crowned him [man] with glory and honour.'

Of course, Christ is more than man. He alone shares 'the glory of the incorruptible God', a glory he had with the Father before the world was (Rom. 1:23; John 17:5). His uncreated glory must always exceed that of the redeemed. Nevertheless, the Writer's emphasis in this passage is upon the eventual glorification of mankind in the shape of the church. Christ's present honour as the exalted Saviour and representative man anticipates the glory of his people, his eternal bride.

8.
Christ the Deliverer

Please read Hebrews 2:10-18

This passage expands further the theme of Christ the man. In doing so, however, it begins to elaborate a subject briefly touched upon in 1:3 and 2:3 and which preoccupies the Writer increasingly throughout the epistle — the Saviour's work of deliverance. By coming as a man to lost mankind, the Lord of glory has delivered his people from Satan, death, fear, bondage, sin and temptation. In doing so, he brings God's chosen 'sons' to glory.

The Lord of glory (2:10)

The Writer continues: **'It was fitting for him, for whom are all things and by whom are all things, in bringing many sons to glory, to make the captain** [champion] **of their salvation perfect through sufferings'** (2:10). The ascription, 'for whom are all things and by whom are all things', refers here to God the Father. However, the Writer has applied almost identical terms to the Son in the opening verses of the epistle (see 1:2-3). As Paul writes in Colossians 1:16-17, 'All things were created through him [Christ] and for him. And he is before all things, and in him all things consist.'

We see, then, that the description of God as the one who made all things for his own glory attaches equally to the Father

and the Son. This strengthens even further the Writer's contention that Jesus is fully God. Hebrews never lets us forget
that Jesus is the Lord of glory, even when it has in view his
lowly estate as 'the man of sorrows'.

It was **'fitting'** (or appropriate) that in bringing **'many
sons to glory'** the Father should do so through the work and
sufferings of his eternal Son. The *fitness* of God's scheme of
salvation lies in the self-giving that was involved, which is
consonant with God's gracious nature. The **'sons'** are the elect,
whom he chose in Christ 'before the foundation of the world
… having predestined us to adoption as sons by Jesus Christ
to himself' (Eph. 1:4-6). Christ came from glory — a lonely
figure in a world of sin. However, he does not return alone,
but as the leader of a numberless multitude of redeemed sinners!

Christ is thus **'the champion' of their salvation'** (2:10).
A military leader, wounded in the battle, might nevertheless
lead his troops home, triumphant in victory. So, suggests the
Writer, Christ leads the sons of God to glory. More than that,
his sufferings were the *necessary* and *sufficient* means of victory and deliverance. It is in this sense that the Father made
him 'perfect (i.e., complete) through sufferings'.

It is central to the message of Hebrews that Christ's work
of deliverance is complete. Christ is the perfect Saviour because he saves perfectly. There is nothing partial, conditional,
or temporary about the salvation that is in Christ. Nothing is
left to chance. Nothing is left to man's fallible 'decision' or
'commitment'. Jesus' work of atonement is a finished work of
grace that has completely and eternally saved his elect. Their
entrance into 'glory' is assured.

Sanctified (2:11)

The sons who are being brought to glory are said to be 'sanctified' by Christ: **'For both he who sanctifies** [or 'the

sanctifier'] **and those who are being sanctified** [or 'the sanctified'] **are all of one, for which reason he is not ashamed
to call them brethren'** (2:11). This is the first mention of
sanctification in Hebrews. To sanctify has the basic meaning
'to set apart' or 'consecrate', with the further implication that the
thing sanctified is set apart for the special use and glory of God.

The present continuous tense, 'those who are being sanctified', although a legitimate translation, is not favoured by the
majority of translators and commentators, who prefer 'the
sanctified' or 'those who are sanctified [made holy; conse-
crated]' (see, for example, AV, NIV, NASB). Clearly, the statement can be understood in one of several ways.

Firstly, it could mean that sanctification is a *process* for
each individual (progressive sanctification). Secondly, it could
mean that the 'sons' are being set apart (sanctified) one by
one, as they are regenerated by the Spirit (positional sanctification). Thirdly, it can be understood simply to refer to those
who *are now* in an ongoing state of sanctification, without
reference to process or degree. This interpretation also implies positional sanctification and is probably the correct one.
Embracing this view, Doddridge interprets 'they who are being sanctified' as those who are 'consecrated and introduced
to God with such acceptance'.[2] 'No person can doubt', adds
John Brown, 'that by "the Sanctifier" we are to understand
Jesus Christ, and by "the sanctified" his saved people.'[3]

We shall have to take up this matter again when we consider Hebrews 10:14. For the present we leave the question
open and concentrate on something that is both unambiguous
and more important, namely, that it is *Christ* who sanctifies
and the believer who receives sanctification (2:11). 'It is by
his sacrifice of himself', says Bruce, 'in obedience to God's
will that they are sanctified.'[4] As Paul declares, Christ '*became* for us ... righteousness and *sanctification* and redemption' (1 Cor. 1:30, emphasis added). Here lies the essence of
the new covenant.

This is important for us to understand. Too often 'sanctification' is represented as a condition that the justified sinner
must attain by his own efforts and obedience to God. But
Hebrews teaches that the elect are sanctified (set apart for
God's special use) *by Christ*, through his redeeming and justifying work. Then, as a consequence (not a cause) of this sanctification, believers perform those good works that 'God prepared beforehand that we should walk in them' (Eph. 2:10).

Union with Christ (2:11-13)

The Writer's main point in verse 11 is that Christ and those he
sanctifies are 'all of one'. There is a fraternal union between
the Redeemer and the redeemed, so that **'he is not ashamed
to call them brethren, saying: "I will declare your name to
my brethren; in the midst of the congregation I will sing
praise to you"'** (2:11-12). While Christ is God's eternal Son,
believers are God's sons and daughters by adoption. They are
thus made 'brethren' of Christ. There is, of course, a vast difference between these two kinds of 'sonship'. Nevertheless,
the believer's 'sonship' is both real and glorious, deriving as it
does from his or her relationship with Christ. 'The reason of
the Son's incarnation', observes Poole, '[is] the necessity of
union in nature between the sanctifying Mediator and the sanctified sinner.'[5]
    The Writer's citation in 2:11 is from Psalm 22:22. This psalm
describes, prophetically and in some detail, the death of Christ
upon the cross. It is in the context of his passion, then, that
Jesus calls the elect his 'brethren'. And rightly so, for our adoption as sons and daughters of God rests on the atonement
wrought at Calvary: 'God sent forth his Son ... to redeem
those who were under the law *that we might receive the adoption as sons*' (Gal. 4:4-5, emphasis added). Furthermore, he
declares his relationship with them publicly ('in the midst of

the congregation'). Far from being ashamed of them, he rejoices over them. In words that presage the new covenant, the Lord says, 'I will make an everlasting covenant with them... I will put my fear in their hearts so that they will not depart from me. Yes I will rejoice over them to do them good...' (Jer. 32:38-41; cf. 8:7-13).

The two further citations are from Isaiah 8:17-18: **'"I will put my trust in him", and again, "Here am I and the children whom God has given me"'** (2:13). These references speak of the Messiah, who will be revealed in due time along with those he has redeemed. They serve, says Lane, 'to stress that Jesus identifies himself with the community of faith in his absolute trust and dependence upon God', a thought calculated to assure afflicted believers that they too could 'trust God in difficult circumstances'.[6] This passage also re-emphasises that the 'children' referred to are the elect, *given* to the Son by the Father before time began (John 10:29; 17:2; Eph. 1:4-5).

The terminology is familiar, but the truth expressed is precious beyond words. The objects of God's saving grace have not simply been forgiven their sins and delivered from his wrath. They have been incorporated into the family of God. The Father is *their* Father. Christ is their brother. They themselves are 'members one of another' (Rom. 12:5) and of the body of Christ (1 Cor. 12:13). A changeless intimacy has been established between the elect and the eternal God — an intimacy that is manifested in the true church on earth but will only be worked out in its fulness in glory.

Deliverance (2:14)

This being the case, continues the Writer, it must surely be clear why Christ had to clothe himself with humanity. **'Inasmuch as the children have partaken of flesh and blood, he**

**himself likewise shared in the same, that through death
he might destroy him who had the power of death, that is,
the devil'** (2:14).

It was only by becoming man that Christ could die. And
only by dying could he engage the devil in mortal conflict,
invade the citadel of darkness, and lead 'captivity captive' (Eph.
4:8).

Satan, we are told, 'had the power of death'. This does not
mean that he had usurped God's sovereignty over life and death
(Ps. 90:3; Job 2:6). Rather, it was through Satan's agency that
'sin entered the world and death through sin, and thus death
spread to all men, because all sinned' (Rom. 5:12; see Owen[7]).
By luring men into rebellion and unbelief, the devil controlled
their destinies — and still does so.

Under the over-arching sovereignty of God, Satan has been
given authority over those who die in their sins — they abide
under 'the power [authority] of darkness' (Col. 1:13; compare the parable of Dives and Lazarus — Luke 16:20-25).
Scripture offers no support for the belief that the unsaved dead
can, in some way, receive a second chance of salvation. The
Mormon idea that we can deliver our dead ancestors from hell
by being baptised on their behalf and the Roman Catholic teaching about purgatory and prayers for the dead are both equally
wrong.

However, through his death and resurrection, Christ has
robbed the devil of his power to control the destinies of the
elect. 'He has delivered us from the power of darkness and
translated us into the kingdom of the Son of his love' (Col.
1:13). In doing so, Christ has in one sense 'destroyed' the
devil, 'having disarmed principalities and powers [and] made
a public spectacle of them, triumphing over them in it' (Col.
2:15).

At his second coming, Jesus will complete the destruction
of Satan (Matt. 25:41; Rev. 20:10) — but he has already destroyed the devil's power over death! Those who die believing

in Christ are ushered instantly into the presence of their Lord (Phil. 1:23). These 'spirits of just men made perfect' await the consummation, namely the resurrection of their bodies at Christ's return (12:23; Phil. 3:20-21).

Not only have the chains of death been loosed for the elect, but the *fear* of death has thereby been removed. For Christ has **'released those who through fear of death were all their lifetime subject to bondage'** (2:15). The fear of death is an ever-present reality. Witness the grief and pain of those bereaved. People fear both their own death and that of their loved ones, and much of this fear lies in a dread of the unknown. Is death the end? Does some shadowy purgatorial existence lie beyond the grave? Is there a heaven and a hell? Uncertainty breeds fear, and fear brings mental bondage, casting an inescapable shadow over life and robbing man of lasting peace or joy. But for those who are in Christ, all uncertainty has been removed, for he has passed through death and become the first-born from the dead (Col. 1:18). We follow in his train.

Christ the High Priest (2:16-18)

Skilfully, the Writer now introduces another of his major themes — Christ is our great High Priest. There are no fewer than sixteen references in Hebrews to the high priest, so we shall deal briefly with the subject here and develop it at greater length later.

This is also the point in the epistle at which the Mosaic law is first invoked, and it sets the tone for all that follows. Jesus Christ is God; he is King; he is man; and he is Redeemer. All this we have seen in the first two chapters of Hebrews. But now he is declared to be the intercessor and mediator between God and man. As such, our verse implies, he has both fulfilled and replaced the high-priesthood of the old covenant.

Christ **'does not give aid to angels, but he does give aid to the seed of Abraham. Therefore, in all things he had to be made like his brethren, that he might be a merciful and faithful High Priest in things pertaining to God, to make propitiation for the sins of the people'** (2:16-17). The passing reference to angels is significant. The Writer is still concerned to divert his readers from their preoccupation with angels — so that they might fix their eyes instead on Christ. How important this is even today! People are too often distracted from the worship of Christ by religious icons, whether they be angels, Mary, spirits, rituals, or even theological hobbyhorses. Had Christ come to redeem angels, he would have had to become an angel. But his mission was to redeem man.

Therefore, he assists (literally, 'lays hold of'[8]), not angels, but 'the seed of Abraham'. Not men in general, notice, nor Jews alone, but those who are 'of faith', for these are the true offspring of Abraham and heirs of the promise (Gal. 3:7,29). They are 'his brethren', and he was 'made like' them in order to perform the functions of high priest on their behalf.

What are these functions? We are told briefly but succinctly. Firstly, as a *merciful* High Priest, he exercises mercy towards them. As rebels and sinners, they no more deserve God's favour than the generality of men. But God has been gracious to them, showing them the mercy they need rather than the justice they deserve: 'But God, who is *rich in mercy*, because of his great love with which he loved us, even when we were dead in trespasses, made us alive together with Christ' (Eph. 2:4-5, emphasis added). Notice how Paul identifies God's mercy as a concomitant of his love in fulfilling his purposes of grace.

Secondly, our High Priest is *faithful* to his calling. This concept is worked out in detail in the passage that follows (3:1-6) and we shall defer discussion till then. Thirdly, and fundamentally, he makes '*propitiation* for the sins of the people'. Under the Mosaic covenant, it was the high priest's special responsibility to enter the inner sanctuary once each year on the Day of Atonement. He carried with him the blood of the sacrifices, a bull and a goat, to atone for his own sins and the sins of the people respectively (9:7; Lev. 16). So Christ makes 'propitiation' (reconciliation, appeasement, atonement) for the sins of *his* people. The difference is that Christ offers, not the blood of bulls or goats, but his own blood — a sacrifice of infinite value, as we shall see.

Fourthly and finally, the high priest offers *succour* to those who look to him in their trouble. **'In that he himself has suffered, being tempted, he is able to aid those who are tempted'** (2:18). 'Temptation' here is to be understood as 'testing' and includes not only temptation to sin but also any kind of trial experienced by mankind. Because he was truly man, Jesus is able to empathise with us in our trials, whatever their nature. Divine comfort is always available to those who come to him in faith, bringing their needs and burdens. 'Come to me', he said, 'all you who labour and are heavy laden, and I will give you rest' (Matt. 11:28).

9.
Christ the faithful Son

Please read Hebrews 3:1-6

The Writer now calls on his readers to **'consider the Apostle and High Priest of our confession'** (3:1). Both 'apostle' and 'priest' refer to human offices, so the use of these terms underlines the humanity of Christ as set out in the foregoing verses. But these offices are also metaphors which speak of his divine nature, especially as that nature is expressed in his mediatorial role. 'If ... we want to look up at him properly', says Calvin, 'we must consider his nature: he must be endued with his own power, in case we catch hold of an empty shadow instead of him.'[1]

Christ is the 'Apostle' in that he is both the message and the messenger of God, as we have seen. He is also the High Priest, in that he represents men before the presence of a holy God. In both capacities, asserts the Writer, his ability to act effectively stems from his unique relationship with the Father. This passage, therefore, links Christ's humanity and mediatorial work to his eternal sonship.

We must not underestimate the profundity, and even difficulty, of the task the Writer sets himself at this point. Familiar as we are with the idea that Jesus Christ is the God-man, this concept continues to defy the comprehension of the human mind. How, then, does the Writer go about the matter? He does so by using Scripture to show that Christ transcends even the greatest of God's purely human servants, namely Moses, the 'man of God'. Indeed, he tells us, Moses, with all that he accomplished in the service of God, was primarily a picture of Christ.

Our heavenly calling (3:1)

The Writer addresses his readers as **'holy brethren, partakers of the heavenly calling'** (3:1). How graciously he regards them! They are precious in his sight, as they are in God's. The word 'holy' means 'set apart', or 'separated'. Believers are holy because, from eternity, they were set apart for salvation, as the elect of God. They are holy, secondly, because they have been set apart ('sanctified') by the regenerating work of the Holy Spirit (see 2:11; 1 Peter 1:2; 2 Thess. 2:13).

The believer's holiness is not of his own making, for Christ has become to him 'righteousness and sanctification and redemption' (1 Cor. 1:30). Very simply, Christians have been set apart by God himself for his own glory and service. That is why the New Testament frequently calls them 'saints'. Even the highly imperfect (even 'carnal') Corinthians, Paul tells us, 'were washed ... were sanctified ... were justified in the name of the Lord Jesus and by the Spirit of our God' (1 Cor. 3:1; 6:11). Accordingly, they ought to live in a manner consistent with their high calling.

Not only are believers holy — they are also 'partakers [sharers] of the heavenly calling'. That is, they participate in God's eternal purpose to redeem a great multitude that no man can number (Rev. 7:9). They are the objects of saving grace — adopted by the Father, redeemed by the Son, and made heirs of God's heavenly kingdom (Gal. 4:4-7). They are called to repentance and faith in Christ, that they might share his glorious inheritance (Luke 24:47; Acts 11:18).

These high privileges bring responsibilities. Because we have been made partakers of the heavenly calling, we must live as those whose citizenship is in heaven and who serve a holy and righteous God. We no longer serve sin, but Christ (Rom. 6:17-18). We are no longer sons of Adam, but children of the living God. Our treasure is not laid up on earth but in heaven. All this should be evident in the life of the believer. As Paul says, 'The life which I now live in the flesh, I live by faith in the Son of God who loved me and gave himself for me' (Gal. 2:20).

The Apostle of our confession (3:1 cont.)

We are to **'consider'** Christ (3:1). This is not the only place where the reader is urged to do this. In Hebrews 12:3, for example, we read, '... consider him who endured such hostility from sinners against himself, lest you become weary and discouraged in your souls.' The Writer's purpose in that place is to strengthen weary believers lest they stumble and faint in the spiritual race. When he urges us to 'consider' Jesus, therefore, he has a serious pastoral purpose in mind. He intends us to dwell upon the matter — to obtain enlightenment, comfort and strength from meditating on Christ. What spiritual benefit, then, can we derive by focusing on Christ as **'the Apostle ... of our confession'**? (3:1).

'Our confession' is the gospel we profess. 'It connotes the essential core of Christian conviction that the Writer shared with his audience,' explains Lane.[2] Jesus Christ is 'the Apostle' of that gospel because he was the one the Father *sent* (Greek *apostello*) to bring it to us. Indeed, in the deepest sense, he *is* the gospel, for 'No one knows ... the Father except the Son, and the one to whom the Son wills to reveal him' (Matt. 11:27).

It is only because Christ has visited us in the flesh that we have received the good news of God's saving purpose. Without the apostleship of Jesus we would remain in darkness, having only the unfulfilled shadows of the old covenant to enlighten the gloom.

But Christ has brought us the revelation of God in his person, and the knowledge of salvation through his work. Once he had come, of course, the Messianic message came into focus, so that we can read the gospel in almost every line of Old Testament prophecy. But this is only because we have the New Testament to interpret the Old! Until the divine Apostle came, there could be no full understanding (2 Tim. 1:10).

But Christ was sent not just to *inform*, but to *redeem*. He was a man with a mission, and that mission was to save his elect people. He 'finished the work' that God had given him to do (John 17: 4). And having, by himself, purged our sins, he ascended to the right hand of the Majesty on high (1:3). Christ did not return to his Father apologetically, regretting that he was unable to accomplish the task he had been set. He did not discharge his mission partially, as if it were too difficult to complete in full. No! He perfectly and fully accomplished the Father's eternal purpose and returned triumphant to his place in glory.

This has great implications for our understanding of the cross of Christ. That he was God's own Apostle, or emissary, means that his success was guaranteed. A perfect God cannot perform an imperfect work. An absolute God cannot implement a conditional atonement. A God who sees the end from the beginning cannot leave himself at the mercy of human choice. Christ's atoning work is finished, full and final. We may depend upon it, for he was God's Apostle, sent to accomplish that very purpose.

Christ the High Priest (3:1 cont.)

We are also to 'consider' Christ as **'the ... High Priest of our confession'** (3:1). We began to see what this means at the end of the previous chapter, and the subject of high-priesthood of Christ is developed at great length in the fourth to the tenth chapters of Hebrews.

Among the Jews, the high priest was a most important person. In one sense he ruled the nation. He was the prime mediator between God and man, offering as he did the annual sacrifice on the Day of Atonement. This symbolised the forgiveness that God extends to those who repent of their sins and trust in God's provision for them. It was therefore a highly significant title to attach to Christ, especially for the Jewish readers of the letter. It implies, firstly, that Christ is the ruler and leader of his confessing people, namely, those who obey the gospel ('our confession'), whether Jews or Gentiles. Secondly, it reminds us that 'there is ... one mediator between man and God, the man Christ Jesus' (1 Tim. 2:5).

There are some today who seek to promote Mary as the mediatrix. Others, such as cult leaders and those who claim to be channels of special revelation, also effectively interpose themselves between their followers and the exalted Christ. All such pretensions are false. Every believer has direct access to the Lord who died for him or her — God does not respect persons (8:11). Before the throne of God, all believers are equal, and all are equally 'in' Christ.

The faithfulness of Christ (3:2-4)

Christ, we are next informed, **'was faithful to him that appointed him, as also Moses was faithful in all his house'** (3:2). The reference to Moses comes from Numbers 12:1-9.

His brother Aaron and his sister Miriam had criticised him for marrying an Ethiopian woman. Perhaps this was an early example of racial prejudice! God's anger was aroused against them, for Moses was his chosen servant and mouthpiece, and should have been respected, not despised. There are lessons here for us, and they are emphasised in such New Testament passages as Matthew 7:1-6 and James 4:11-12, where criticism of fellow believers is forbidden.

In the process of defending Moses, God says that his servant 'is faithful in all my house' (Num. 12:7). God's 'house' or 'household' refers here, of course, to Israel under the law — which Moses led faithfully, that is, in full obedience to God's commands. Thus the Writer draws a parallel with Christ, who was faithful to his Father who appointed him head of a greater household, namely his church.

Palmer Robertson points out that Paul's expression, 'the Israel of God', in Galatians 6:16 draws a clear line of distinction between national Israel and those who are justified by faith in Christ, that is, the new-covenant church.[3] Although the church of Christ is inclusive of the believing remnant among Old Testament Israel, it clearly cannot embrace the *unbelieving* majority of that nation. Israel can be called 'the Old Testament church', and was a *type* of the true church — but it cannot be *equated* with that church in any spiritual sense.

Thus the 'house' analogy is remarkable for its contrasts as much as its comparisons. The Writer goes on to point out further distinctions between Moses and Christ.

Firstly, this man was **'counted worthy of more glory than Moses inasmuch as he who built the house has more honour than the house'** (3:3). As a man, Christ (like Moses) was fully qualified to lead the people of God. But how different is this leader! The prophet led God's people Israel, and did so faithfully, but he did not choose or create them. By contrast, Christ not only leads the redeemed, but he *is* their Redeemer.

He is not only their Master, but their Maker. Moses led Israel, and God honoured him notably. But Moses was himself *part* of that household, whereas Christ is the builder and maker of the church (11:10).

How has Christ built the church? By atoning for her sins and making her members his children (2:14). He 'gave himself for us', explains Paul, 'that he might redeem us from all iniquity and purify unto himself a special people, zealous for good works' (Titus 2:14). Peter adds, 'You are a chosen generation, a royal priesthood, a holy nation, a special people; that you should show forth the praises of him who has called you out of darkness into his marvellous light. Which in times past were not a people, but are now the people of God' (1 Peter. 2:9-10). Since Peter's readers were formerly 'not a people', the term 'the people of God' must refer to the new-covenant church as distinct from Israel.

More honour attaches to Christ, therefore, than to Moses — the most revered of the Old Testament prophets and mediator of the old covenant. But that is not all. The Writer cannot resist the conclusion that, to be the builder of God's household, Christ himself must be God! **'For every house is built by some man'**, he continues, **'but he that built all things is God'** (3:4).

The reasoning is straightforward. Every earthly dynasty owes its existence to some human patriarch or founder. The heavenly household, by analogy, derives from a heavenly founder. Not only did this person build the church — he was responsible for the creation of all other things as well. Who is this person? Christ, by whom 'all things [were] created, that are in heaven, and that are in earth, visible and invisible, whether thrones or dominions or principalities or powers; all things were created by him and for him' (Col. 1:16; cf. 1:2). Only God can have done this, so Christ must be God.

Thus we may legitimately read this statement as follows: '… he that built all things [that is, Christ] is God.' Unless we *do* read it in this way, it makes no sense, for it would reduce to a statement that 'God created all things'. This would be true, of course, but wholly irrelevant to the argument.

Christ the Son (3:5-6)

Finally in this section, the Writer draws a different contrast between Moses and Christ. In the earlier analogy, Moses belonged to a household, whereas Christ built a household. Now the metaphor changes, and Moses is a servant in his household while Christ is the Son and heir over his. Indeed, he has already entered into his inheritance and has become the Lord, or owner, of the household. **'Moses indeed was faithful in all his house as a servant, for a testimony of those things which were to be spoken after, but Christ as a Son over his own house'** (3:5-6).

The service Moses rendered was not just to lead Israel, but also to provide 'a testimony to those things which were spoken after'. What were these later revelations? Clearly, the gospel of Christ. The Writer continually draws contrasts between the former things, taught by the law and the prophets, and the later things revealed in and through the incarnate Christ. Indeed, this is exactly the note he strikes in the opening words of the epistle.

But it is important to recognise the *nature* of the contrast. It is not that the former things have no relevance to the gospel. Far from it. Rather, Moses, and the Old Testament generally, was 'a testimony' which pointed forward to the gospel era and to Christ himself. That is, the Old Testament and its provisions, such as the law, bore witness to the coming Messiah

— to both his person and his redemptive work. Palmer Robertson writes, 'Even as Moses was the representative head who
led old covenant Israel through the desert, so Jesus stands at
the head of a new covenant people, leading them into the realisation of their heavenly calling.'[4]

But what specific 'testimony' is borne to Christ by Moses'
leadership of the nation of Israel? As a nation, Israel *pictured*
the church, so that God's dealings with them become a rich
source of enlightenment regarding his dealings with his people
today. Israel was a chosen nation, a redeemed nation, a nation
which enjoyed the presence and blessing of God, and one which
was subject to the law of God. Likewise, the church is also
elect, redeemed, inhabited by God through the Spirit, and subject to the law of Christ (not the old covenant but the new; see
8:13). Other examples include the manna in the desert and the
blessings of the promised land. God's many warnings to Israel
also have parallels for us in our modern situation. In short, the
Old Testament, as Paul reminds us, was written 'for our learning, that we through the patience and comfort of the Scriptures might have hope' (Rom. 15:4; see also 1 Cor. 10:11).

Secondly, Moses is a type of Christ, a human analogy of
the incarnate Son. It is this aspect that the Writer chooses to
emphasise. Moses cared for Israel as a servant *in* the house of
God. But Christ cares for (and rules *over*) the church as the
Son and heir. The picture is that of a great household, created
by the Father through the Son, and inherited by the Son. God
has 'appointed' him 'heir of all things' (1:2) and made him
'head over all things to the church' (Eph. 1:22). Moses served,
but Jesus reigns.

Holding fast our confidence (3:6 cont.)

If the Israelites were privileged, how much more those who
belong to the 'spiritual Israel', the church of Jesus Christ? God

gave the Jews a physical land to inherit, but he has given us an 'inheritance incorruptible and undefiled ... reserved in heaven' (1 Peter 1:4). They were led by Moses, but we are wed to Christ. Could anyone in his right mind turn his back upon this? Yet again and again, the Writer finds it necessary to warn his readers against defecting from the true gospel. The warning here is indirect, but no less real. He speaks of **'Christ ... whose house are we if we hold fast the confidence and the rejoicing of the hope firm unto the end'** (3:6). To participate in the promised land of salvation, leading to glory, we must 'hold fast' to certain things.

This statement has sometimes been taken to signify that a believer may lose his salvation through failing to 'hold fast' his faith — whether through sin or carelessness. But all such reasoning is back-to-front. The Bible teaches that perseverance is the *result* of genuine faith, and that the believer's good works stem from (and demonstrate the reality of) his security in Christ. The saving work of Christ is the *cause* of our salvation, and nothing we do (or fail to do) can negate that work. Our continuation in Christ, and the service we render, are alike the *consequences* of a saving relationship to Christ. If we confuse cause with consequence we shall fall into bondage and condemnation.

Why, then, does the Writer bother to warn his readers? He wants them to give attention to the danger of apostasy, in which men believe themselves to be truly saved when they are not. The consequence is that eventually they fall away, in spite of once having made a fair profession of faith in Christ. Such people need to be warned of their condition while they are still receptive towards spiritual things, so that they might turn to Christ in true repentance and faith before it is too late. There have always been professing Christians who have no true experience of salvation. They are relaxed about their spiritual condition, but not regenerate; devoted but dead; sincere but asleep. To such endangered souls the gospel thunders, 'Awake, you who sleep, arise from the dead, and Christ will give you light' (Eph. 5:14).

What, then, must we 'hold fast' if we are to demonstrate the reality of our faith? The answer is, 'the confidence [or courage] and rejoicing of the hope'. By 'hope' the Writer means an expectation of all that is promised to us in the gospel of Christ — the settled assurance that what God has promised us in Christ he will surely fulfil. Hope is the certain knowledge that in life we have his presence, grace and power; that in death we have the promise of resurrection; and that in heaven we have a place reserved, where we shall behold the glory of Christ and inherit the riches of his kingdom.

This, then, is our hope. We have to hold it fast, embracing it with courage, confidence and joy. By referring to 'courage' the Writer admits that this quality is needed by those who would remain faithful to Christ in the face of persecution.[5] We must rest our full weight upon the promise of God, committing ourselves to him alone and having no other expectation. We have to reject all spiritual 'insurance policies', enticing as they may be, and put our irrevocable trust in Christ.

Part 2:
Unbelief and the throne of grace

10.
The deceitfulness of sin

Please read Hebrews 3:7-19

As a compass needle always seeks the north, so the epistle to the Hebrews always returns to Christ. He is never far from view, even when other matters intervene. Nevertheless, the Writer does here turn from his contemplation of the excellencies of Christ to an altogether more sombre matter, namely, the sin of the human heart. That is why we begin a new 'part' to the commentary at this point in the epistle.

Clearly, an understanding of the human condition is essential if we are to appreciate the gospel. The disease must be properly diagnosed before the correct remedy can be applied. Yet even in this section of the epistle, extending from 3:7 to 6:20, the Writer finds it impossible to dwell *exclusively* on man's sinfulness. Instead, he alternates between his analysis of sin and the gracious provision for the sinner that God has made in Christ. In this part, therefore, we shall learn not only about transgression but also about grace — and that dispensed from an exalted throne.

But first, in 3:7-19, comes a solemn warning! The Writer quotes at length from Psalm 95:7-11 and then applies the lesson with this dire yet tender caution: **'Beware, brethren, lest there be in any of you an evil heart of unbelief, in departing from the living God'** (3:12-13).

It is unusual in our easygoing days for Christians to be warned. Indeed, there is such a spirit of toleration abroad that language of the kind used here would be considered inflammatory. Yet the Writer's words flow from a deep pastoral concern for his readers, and where such care exists, even today, it will always find expression in biblical terms. Warning is still appropriate in our modern times, and even more so because there are few preachers who are willing to risk opprobrium by proclaiming, without fear or favour, the whole counsel of God. The dangers facing the church and individual believers are just as great — and just the same — as those that threatened believers in the first century. Let us read, then, and learn, to our own spiritual benefit.

The inspired Scriptures (3:7)

The Writer introduces his extract from Psalm 95 with significant words: **'Wherefore, as the Holy Spirit says...'** He then proceeds to quote from the psalm at some length. There could be no clearer statement of the stature accorded to the Old Testament Scriptures.

Their ultimate author was the Spirit of God, for 'holy men of God spoke as they were moved by the Holy Spirit' (2 Peter 1:21). The psalm, of course, had a human author, as did all the other Scriptures. Furthermore, these authors employed their personal styles and expressed their own character in what they wrote. Nevertheless, here as elsewhere, the Bible teaches that ultimately all Scripture is 'God-breathed' or inspired (2 Tim. 3:16). This means that even the individual words in Scripture are present (in the original writings, of course) by the direct intention of God himself. He has accomplished this result without violating the minds of the human authors or using any kind of 'automatic writing' process. This is the doctrine of the verbal, or 'plenary', inspiration of Scripture, and any departure from it is a slippery slope from which few recover.

However, the claim that the Old Testament Scriptures are God's own words is not *just* doctrine! The Writer's purpose in emphasising the divine origin of Scripture is to bring its full authority to bear on a *present* issue. If the ancient Scriptures were merely the words of man, they would have lost all force with the passage of the years. But if they are God's Word, their significance is timeless. The Writer wants his readers to feel the full force of God's Word, and so should we. The doctrine of verbal inspiration is as important today as it was then.

Lessons from the wilderness (3:7-8)

What, then, does the Holy Spirit say to us through the psalm? **'Today, if you will hear his voice, do not harden your hearts as in the rebellion, in the day of trial in the wilderness'** (3:7-8; Ps. 95:7-8). Although the reference is to ancient Israel, Bruce reminds us that 'The record of Israel's rebellion and punishment in the wilderness has been preserved "for our admonition", lest we should imitate their disobedience and be overtaken by comparable judgement' (1 Cor. 10:6 ff; Jude 5).[1] Looking at the passage from a new-covenant standpoint, therefore, the first note sounded is one of urgency. Action is required 'today' — not tomorrow or at our future convenience. To hear the voice of God is a privilege, not a right.

Of course, in times of gospel freedom we may hear the Word preached at any time we choose. But will we 'hear his voice'? We cannot presume that God will speak to our hearts at any time. We may hear the preaching, or read the Bible, but we may do so without hearing his voice in a direct and personal way. When the Spirit of God moves our souls concerning some matter, then is the time to respond. The time is of God's sovereign choosing, not our own.

There should, therefore, be urgency in both our preaching and our hearing. Perhaps we have become over-cautious about *urging* folk to respond to God's Word. Some caution is valid, in the light of the abuse by certain evangelists who major on emotional pressure and human persuasion. But we must not forget that apostolic preaching was often urgent and forceful. The New Testament exhorts men to repent and believe immediately or, if they already profess to be Christians, to return with haste to the paths of faithfulness while they have opportunity. The Writer was clearly burdened with a sense of responsibility for his readers. They must heed his warning *now*, not later.

What was his warning? That they should not harden their hearts against the truth. It is clear from what follows that a 'hardened' heart is the same as 'an evil heart of unbelief' (3:12). That is, the Writer discerns that the root of the problem is unbelief — a failure to trust God's Word and act upon it.

This was the essence of Israel's sin in the wilderness. It began, of course, with their refusal to enter the promised land. They simply did not believe that God could deliver what he had promised. They looked at the walled cities and the giants who would oppose them, and forgot that God had defeated the might of Egypt without their help. They turned their backs on God's declared purpose and repeated promise.

In doing so, declares the Writer, they were 'departing from the living God' (3:12). This is important. To dismiss God's Word is to depart from God. We cannot disbelieve the living God and still maintain a relationship with him. He demands our trust, our utter confidence — for otherwise we are not treating him as God at all.

That professing believers may succumb to unbelief is apparent, since otherwise no warning would be needed. We harden our hearts against the truth if we reject the clear teaching of Scripture. There is evidence enough of such attitudes today. Not only do theological liberals pick and choose what they will accept or reject from Holy Writ, but some who claim to be 'evangelical' do the same. They often do so covertly, claiming to be 'reinterpreting' Scripture, or understanding the Bible 'in the light of modern scholarship' or 'scientific progress'. But the final result is the same. The Scriptures cease to be the Word of God, reliable in every part, and become a playground for human speculation and philosophy. This is unbelief, and we should learn to recognise it.

Unbelief is not necessarily intellectual, however. It is a basic characteristic of the unregenerate human heart, and can be defined as the absence of spiritual wisdom (1 Cor. 2:8,14). Ordinary people betray their unbelief when they give no place to God in their lives, or follow those who compromise the veracity of Scripture. They substitute human preferences and prejudices for the authority of the Word of God. They display their unbelief whenever they prefer the opinions of false teachers to God's own Word — and so we could continue. But all unbelief takes leave of God.

Unbelief among those who profess to know God is a special offence to him. As the Writer tells us later in the epistle, '... without faith it is impossible to please God, for he who comes to God must believe that he is, and that he is a rewarder of those who diligently seek him' (11:6).

Unbelief provokes God's anger (3:9-11)

The quotation from Psalm 95 continues: **'Your fathers tested me, proved me and saw my works forty years. Therefore I was angry with that generation and said, "They always go astray in their heart, and they have not known my ways"'** (3:9-10). What a devastating analysis! They saw God's works but did not know his ways.

Yet this is the case with all unbelief. God has not left himself without witness (Acts 14:17). All who are born into this world 'see' the evidence of God's existence and goodness around them, and are 'without excuse' in rejecting him (Rom. 1:20). This 'unbelief' does not necessarily take the form of atheism. The Jews in the wilderness believed in both the existence and the presence of God (they saw his works and proved his faithfulness). Their problem was a lack of submission, thankfulness and trust. Their view of God was utilitarian; he existed to meet their needs. They had no concept of his majesty, compassion and love.

Many are like them today. God exists, but he is there to satisfy their needs. Man is the focus of their thinking, the pivot around which their religion revolves. Such unbelief still evokes God's anger. Hebrews was written to abase such man-centred thinking and replace it by a Christ-centred apprehension of the glory and grace of God.

The Writer implies that his readers stood in danger of the same divine displeasure as the Jews of old. God's anger against unbelief is no futile raging — it has serious consequences. **'So I swore in my wrath'**, he continues, **'"They shall not enter my rest"'** (3:11). Unbelief kept Israel from the promised land. Since that land epitomises salvation, the warning is topical and severe. Those who fail to submit to God — who do not trust his Son as their only Saviour from sin — have not attained God's rest. They have not been saved from their sins, whatever profession they may make.

Departing from the living God (3:12-13)

The application follows: **'Beware, brethren, lest there be in any of you an evil heart of unbelief in departing from the living God; but exhort one another daily, while it is called**

"Today" lest any of you be hardened through the deceitfulness of sin' (3:12-13).

One of the most consistent features of Hebrews is the way the Writer warns those he calls 'brethren' of the danger of apostasy. These warnings are Scripture-based, trenchant and sustained. The present 'warning passage' persists through to 4:13, and similar exhortations are to be found in 6:1-12; 10:26-39 and 12:12-29.

Scripture teaches uniformly that those who are redeemed by Christ cannot fall away and be lost. But among those who profess to follow Christ (and even make a fair show of doing so) are some who remain unregenerate. They have 'evil' hearts, that is, says Newell, 'hearts wilfully inclined to a state of unbelief and rejection of the living God'.[2]

They lull themselves into a false sense of security, often aided and abetted by their teachers, who tolerate the absence of spiritual fruit in people's lives and fail to apply Scripture vigorously to their hearers. It is vital that believers should be 'diligent to make [their] calling and election sure' (that is, 'to make sure of their calling and election' — 2 Peter 1:10).

The Writer gives specific advice. Firstly, professing Christians should **'beware'** of departing from the living God. How might they depart? Clearly, by turning away from the everliving Christ, the express image of God's person, to worship lifeless idols. The consistent message of Hebrews is that any religious system, doctrine or devotion is idolatrous if it does not focus upon Jesus. We must be Christ-centred in everything we believe and do.

Secondly, we must **'exhort one another daily'** while there is time (**'while it is called "Today"'**). Notice that exhortation is a *communal* duty, not that of the preacher alone. We must 'consider one another in order to stir up [AV, 'provoke'] love and good works, not forsaking the assembling of ourselves together ...' (10:24). This mutual provocation involves far more than warning people about apostasy. Rather, it entails stirring up others continually by our own example and the practice of love and good works; by our own faithful attendance on the means of grace; by our own display of fellowship in the gospel, encouragement of others, and spiritually edifying conversation.

This spiritual consideration of others will provide an antidote to the 'deceitfulness of sin' and the hardening of heart that sin produces. Without the godly example of others, and the exhortation to live a life worthy of Christ, sin can gain the upper hand in our lives. It does so 'deceitfully', that is, by stealth. Slackness creeps into our spiritual walk; carelessness invades our devotional life. Indiscipline erodes our attendance at church, and our gathering for Bible study and prayer. The heart is progressively drawn away from spiritual delights towards sensual and material pleasures. It becomes hardened towards God. How vital that we should heed the warnings and directions given here!

Partakers of Christ (3:14)

The Writer continues his exhortation, but now turns for ammunition to the historical events themselves, rather than the psalmist's record of them. He briefly re-quotes Psalm 95:7-8 (3:15) to remind us that we *are* looking at an actual historical precedent, and then emphasises its relevance to New Testament believers by an 'up-front' statement. **'We have become partakers of Christ'**, he declares, **'if we hold the beginning of our confidence steadfast to the end'** (3:14).

This statement introduces two important strands of New Testament teaching. Firstly, believers are 'partakers' (sharers) of Christ. This signifies two things. They are (1) beneficiaries of all that Christ has done and (2) united with Christ in such a manner as (in some sense) to share 'the divine nature' (2 Peter 1:4). They are Christ's body and bride — heirs of the new covenant and of glory.

Secondly, those who are truly converted to Christ do, indeed, endure in the faith to the end. The final proof of our salvation is that we do not fall away during our lifetime here on earth. On the contrary, we 'hold fast the beginning of our confidence'. That is, we maintain our initial profession of trust in the saving work of Christ for the remainder of our lives. This is the grand doctrine of 'the perseverance of the saints'.

This truth is taught at several points in the New Testament. In Matthew 10:22 the Lord says, 'You will be hated by all for my name's sake, but he who endures to the end will be saved.' Each of the letters to the seven churches in Revelation promises eternal blessedness and safety to the one 'who overcomes' (Rev. 2:7,11,17,26; 3:5,12,21).

It is easy to misunderstand this teaching as meaning that endurance *qualifies* us for heaven. But that would contradict the fact that Christ's sheep, given to him by the Father, are eternally secure. 'I give them eternal life', says the Saviour, 'and they shall never perish; neither shall anyone snatch them out of my hand' (John 10:28-29). Our verse does not say we *become* partakers of Christ by remaining steadfast. It says we *have* become partakers of Christ *if* we do so. That is, endurance confirms the believer's claim to have a secure and personal interest (share) in the saving work of Christ. As Calvin remarks, 'We shall be stable and free from the danger of wavering provided we are on the foundation of faith.'[3]

By the same token, however, those who fail to endure as Christians demonstrate that they were never truly saved. Writing of some who had defected from the faith, John observes: 'They went out from us, but they were not of us; for if they

had been of us they would have continued with us' (1 John
2:19). It is this same lesson that the epistle drives home. It
does so by reverting to the story of Israel in the wilderness.

Rebellion in the wilderness (3:15-19)

The Writer repeats part of his earlier quotation from Psalm
95: **'Today, if you will hear his voice, do not harden your
hearts as in the rebellion'** (3:15). The Israelites, implies the
Writer, had 'heard' the voice of God. What did they hear? The
promise of God to give them a homeland: 'See, I have set the
land before you; go in and possess the land which the LORD
swore to your fathers' (Deut. 1:8). The analogy is clear. The
recipients of Hebrews had heard and welcomed a greater promise — the promise of the gospel. They had heard a greater call
— to possess salvation and eternal glory through faith in Christ
alone. Would they now turn their backs on that gospel, as the
Israelites forsook the promised land and perished in the wilderness when their hearts became discouraged? (Deut.
1:27-28).

The Writer brings home the enormity of Israel's rebellion.
'Who, having heard, rebelled?', he asks; **'Was it not all
who came out of Egypt, led by Moses? Now with whom
was he angry forty years? Was it not with those who sinned,
whose corpses fell in the wilderness? And to whom did he
swear that they would not enter his rest, but to those who
did not obey?'** (3:16-18). With their own eyes they had
watched God defeat their enemies by supernatural power. They
had witnessed the dividing of the Red Sea. They had followed
the pillar of cloud and fire, and trembled before God's glory at
Mount Sinai. The Writer's tone is one of incredulity. How
could these, of all people, reject God's way out of craven fear?

The application is self-evident. The recipients of the epistle had been delivered by the supernatural power of the gospel from their own 'Egyptian' captivity — bondage to sin and Satan. Christ had nailed their sins to his cross and had brought them out of darkness into the marvellous light of his kingdom. They had been emancipated, not by Moses but by the incomparable and eternal Son of God. How could they now turn their backs on all this, reverting to the spiritual desert of . Judaism? If they did so, would they not suffer the same fate as the Israelites of old? Would they not be shrivelled by God's wrath and perish in their chosen wilderness?

But the greatest tragedy of all was that these who 'did not obey' God's command to possess the land never saw that land, nor did they enter into the 'rest' it symbolised (see 4:10 and discussion thereon). So also, those who dabble in the gospel, but never really obey its command to repent and believe on Christ, can never know eternal rest.

Of ancient Israel, the Writer concludes sombrely: **'So we see that they could not enter in** [to the promised land] **because of unbelief'** (3:19). In the same way, those who turn away from Christ display their unbelief and bring upon themselves similar retribution — exclusion from salvation and heaven.

11.
The promise of rest

Please read Hebrews 4:1-10

The Writer elaborates his warning with more quotations from Psalm 95. In doing so he develops a dimension briefly introduced at the end of our previous chapter — the promise of rest and the danger of losing it.

In a world of turmoil, rest is highly sought after. Enormous effort is expended by modern-day counsellors and therapists, as they attempt to bring rest to unhappy and restless souls. The escapism so widely practised by Western society is another symptom of the insecurity suffered by many in our day. How precious, then, is true rest of soul!

The Hebrews were no different from ourselves, though unlike most people today they *were* seeking rest in religion. In this, the Writer both encourages and warns them. There is indeed rest to be found in religion. But it will only be obtained if the object of our faith is the person and work of Christ. Any other kind of religion, even if it calls itself 'Christianity', will lead us to destruction, not peace. Furthermore, the rest of which the Bible speaks entails far more than mere tranquillity of mind. It is a rest that characterises God himself and which — though knowable in this life — will find its fulfilment in the eternal glory of his presence.

It will help us understand this passage if we realise that it features three distinct 'rests'. In chronological order they are, first, the rest of a finished creation: 'God blessed the seventh day and sanctified it, because in it he rested from all his work which God had created and made' (4:4; Gen. 2:2). Second is the rest of the promised land, denied to unbelieving Israel (4:3; Deut. 12:9; Ps. 95:11). And, third, there is the rest enjoyed by those who abandon their own works as a means of salvation — who believe the gospel and trust in Christ alone (4:10).

Concerning the first two 'rests', Pink comments, 'The Hebrews might well say, "We have always enjoyed the Lord's Sabbath, and our fathers have long occupied Canaan; why then do you speak so much about entering into God's rest?" The verses which follow meet this objection, showing that neither of those "rests" was meant by David in Psalm 95, nor by [the Writer] himself here in Hebrews 4. '[1]

In contrast to the former 'rests', the Writer explains that this third rest **'remains'** (4:1,9). That is, both the promise of this rest and the rest itself are fruits of the new covenant, which will never pass away. It is available only to those who truly trust in Christ. Professing Christians must be careful not to forfeit this rest through unbelief.

The necessity of faith (4:1-2)

The Writer begins by stating his conclusion, anticipating the argument he will shortly develop. What is this conclusion? That **'a promise remains of entering into [God's] rest'** (4:1). This promise is fulfilled in everyone who **'has ceased from his works'**, trusting Christ alone for salvation (4:10). But waverers must be warned — **'let us fear lest any of you seem to have come short of [the promise]'** (4:1).

The Writer senses that among his readers are some who are not fully persuaded that Christ is the only way to God. They hanker after the rituals and ceremonies of the Mosaic law, thinking that observance of that law will commend them to God. They believe in Christ intellectually, but their trust lies elsewhere, in their own religious experience and works.

Many are like them today. They are found not only in cults and the ranks of ritualistic churches but also among evangelicals who substitute the 'three Es' (excitement, experience and entertainment) for faith in the person and work of Christ.

Today the watchword in religion is, 'Anything goes'. The validity of religious experience is judged in terms of 'feel-good factors', rather than in relation to objective truth or scriptural warrant. We are no longer bidden to 'seek first the kingdom of God and his righteousness', but instead to strive for self-fulfilment, inner healing and 'spiritual highs'. In our age of inclusiveness, there is neither fear nor concern that religious profession, sincerity and practice might not, after all, be enough to save us.

The Writer has a solemn warning for us all — **'let us fear'**. Calvin comments, 'This fear is commended to us, not as something that drives away the assurance of faith, but as something that inspires us with concern that we do not grow slack with carelessness.'[2] Just as the Israelites stopped short of the promised land, so professing Christians may 'come short' of God's promised rest and be shut out from salvation and heaven.

Jesus himself warned, 'Not everyone who says to me "Lord, Lord" shall enter the kingdom of heaven, but he who does the will of my Father in heaven' (Matt. 7:21). And what is that will? 'This is the will of him who sent me', replies Christ, 'that everyone who sees the Son and believes in him may have everlasting life' (John 6:40). To do God's will, then, is to 'believe in him whom [God] has sent' (John 6:29). Thus the Writer labours to fix both our sight and our hope on Christ. Only through faith in him can we enter the kingdom of heaven. Nothing else avails.

To drive home the lesson, the Writer reverts to the example of Israel in the wilderness. **'For indeed'**, he says, **'the gospel was preached to us as well as to them; but the word which they heard did not profit them, not being mixed with faith in those who heard it'** (4:2).

How was the gospel 'preached' to the Jews in the wilderness? Some commentators point out that **'gospel'** here can simply mean the 'good news' about the promised land They do not, therefore, apply it to the gospel of Christ. Brown, for example says, 'It is not the design of the Apostle in these words that "the gospel" in the ordinary sense of that word was preached to ... their ancestors.'[3]

However, this may not be the case. There is a real sense in which the gospel of Christ *was* proclaimed to the nation that came out of Egypt, namely, through symbols: the Passover, the crossing of the Red Sea, the water from the rock — together with the prolific symbolism of the tabernacle, priesthood and sacrifices. For those who had eyes to see it, all these events were replete with the message of salvation through faith in Christ. Likewise, the commandments should have served as their 'tutor to bring [them] to Christ', revealing their sin and need of salvation (Gal. 3:24).

Tragically, they were unable to understand the meaning of these symbols, namely, that they pointed to a coming Messiah who would 'save his people from their sins'. They saw the symbols as ends in themselves, external experiences and rituals without spiritual content. And this, of course, was the problem with the readers of Hebrews — they were putting their trust in the external symbols of the old covenant rather than in the Christ they symbolised.

Their inability to understand the symbolic gospel of the Mosaic system is neither excused nor indulged by the Writer. He calls it by its name of unbelief (or absence of faith). For the preached gospel to take effect it must be met by ('mixed with') faith in the hearer, and such faith can only be obtained as God's gift of grace through the righteousness of Christ (2 Peter 1:1).

Had the readers of this epistle received the gospel by 'the hearing of faith'? Or did their understanding go no further than the symbols of the old covenant? (Gal. 3:2). If the latter, then the gospel of Christ, however clearly set forth, would no more profit them than the Mosaic order profited the Jews in the wilderness.

Entering rest (4:3-4)

The 'rest' of an accomplished creation, and that of entry to the promised land, both symbolise the true rest obtained by those who believe: **'For we who have believed do enter that rest'** (4:3). This rest, he implies, was prepared from the dawn of creation and was part and parcel of the created order. Having referred to the Jews' failure to achieve rest he adds, **'although the works were finished from the foundation of the world. For ... God rested on the seventh day from all his works'** (4:3-4).

The conjunction 'although' introduces the 'Sabbath rest' of creation into an already complicated argument.

The reason for this is probably that the Writer sees God's plan of redemption as an intrinsic part of his creation purpose. Thus 'the works' of creation embrace not only the material world-order but also those spiritual designs that God prepared before time began but unfolds within the physical world of time and space.

If this is so, the verse can be paraphrased as follows: 'Even though God had ordained a rest for his people as an intrinsic part of his preordained creation purpose, the Jews of old were not the intended beneficiaries of the promise, even though they did eventually enter the promised land. It follows that the eternal purpose — signalled by the "creation ordinance" of the Sabbath — must be fulfilled in some other way and enjoyed by some other constituency (4:6).'

This interpretation not only makes sense of an otherwise confusing passage, but also points to an essential link between creation and redemption. The link, of course is Christ, for he is the author and beneficial heir of both.

Although seldom noticed, this interlinking of Christ's roles in creation and salvation is common in Scripture. We saw it in Hebrews 1:3. It appears in such passages as Isaiah 42:5-7, and again in Colossians 1:16-18 and Romans 8:22-24. The Bible presents the 'cosmic Christ' as the Christ of the cross, and vice versa. God did not create the universe as one isolated act, and redeem the church as another. These various 'works' of God are joined seamlessly in the overarching and eternal purpose of God in Christ. One day we shall understand these glorious mysteries more fully.

Many who profess to be Christians are loath to admit the eternal character of God's plan of redemption, preferring to see the gospel as God's response to the misfortune of human sin. Yet this eternal character is written so plainly in Scripture that it cannot be missed. The Father 'chose us in [Christ] before the foundation of the world, that we should be holy and without blame before him in love', declares the apostle Paul (Eph. 1:4). God has 'saved us and called us ... not according to our works, but according to his own purpose and grace which was given to us in Christ Jesus before time began' (2 Tim. 1:9). Jesus spoke of 'the elect' (the chosen ones; Matt. 24:31), while Luke records that 'as many as had been appointed to eternal life believed' (Acts 13:48).

Furthermore, the rest that God prepared for those who love him was not only ordained before the physical creation, but is pictured by it. For just as God rested on the seventh day, so his elect now enter by faith into that same peaceful and perfected state ('we who have believed do enter that rest').

Ceasing from works (4:5-10)

The Writer repeatedly states that the enjoyment of this rest was forfeited by the Jews of Moses' day because of their unbelief. **'And again ...'**, he writes, ' **"They shall not enter my rest." Since, therefore it remains that some must enter it, and those to whom it was first preached did not enter because of disobedience ...'** (4:5-7). But that is not all. He next asserts that even Joshua, who *was* a man of faith, failed to secure the promised rest for Israel when he conquered Canaan: **'If Joshua had given them rest, then [David] would not afterward have spoken of another day'** (4:8). The argument is clear. David, writing Psalm 95 centuries after the conquest of Canaan, was *still* talking about a rest available **'today'** (4:7-8). This is implied rather than stated in Psalm 95, but the Writer argues that (1) God's rest was prepared from the creation and must therefore be possessed by someone; (2) the Jews of Moses' day did not obtain it; (3) neither did Joshua's nation, because if they had done so Psalm 95 would have told us; therefore (4) the promised rest remains to be possessed by those for whom it always was intended.

Who, then, *do* possess this divine rest? **'The people of God'**, replies the Writer (4:9). And who are they? Those who have **'ceased from ... works, as God did from his'** (4:10). Although heaven is the ultimate rest for believers, this is not the Writer's primary concern here. Rather, the rest is that obtained by faith in Christ during this life — the rest of ceasing from self-justifying works and trusting in Christ alone for pardon and acceptance. Owen concurs: 'It is here ... plainly affirmed that believers do here, in this world, enter into rest in their gospel state.'[4]

Clearly, when the Writer speaks of ceasing from works, he does not mean that God's people are *without* good works. Indeed, he later exhorts his readers, 'Do not forget to do good, and to share, for with such sacrifices God is well pleased' (13:16). The works that must cease before we can enter God's rest are our attempts to earn salvation by our actions. These actions may take the form of religious rituals or observances, deeds of moral and practical goodness, acts of self-denial, or other things. In themselves they may be commendable. But as means calculated to obtain salvation they are futile.

We can only be saved, and enter God's rest, by faith in Christ: 'To him who does not work but believes on him who justifies the ungodly, his faith is accounted for righteousness' (Rom. 4:5). Just *how* Christ justifies the ungodly is the unfolding story of the epistle to the Hebrews.

12.
The accountability of man

Please read Hebrews 4:11-13

In the previous chapter we saw that those who 'come short' of God's promised salvation may seem to be genuine Christians. The epistle addresses its warnings to professing believers, not to pagans. The Writer is careful to alert us all to the dangers of spurious Christianity.

He is in good company. The Lord Jesus Christ often returned to this same theme. Many of the parables reflect his concern, including those of the sower, the dragnet, the unforgiving servant, the wedding garment, the wise and foolish virgins, the talents, and the sheep and the goats (to cite just Matthew's Gospel). In every case the warning is clear. Many claim to be followers of Christ who are nothing of the kind, because they neither know Christ nor obey his word. Such people will be shut out of God's eternal rest.

The Writer wants to impress on his readers just how serious it is to make false claims of discipleship. They will not be judged by man, but by one to whom they must 'give account' (4:13) and who is 'a consuming fire' (12:29). Furthermore, they may hide their hypocrisy from men, but they cannot conceal it from either God or from themselves. Let everyone, therefore, who claims the name 'Christian' be diligent to seek and secure the 'rest' of true salvation. The alternative is too dreadful to contemplate.

Diligence (4:11)

'Let us therefore be diligent to enter into that rest', urges the Writer, **'lest anyone should fall after the same example of disobedience'** (4:11). The 'example' referred to is that of Israel in the wilderness who, as we have seen, spurned the promise through unbelief.

It is easier to reject God's promises than we may think. Firstly, we do so if we neglect them. Scripture is replete with the promises of God, but do we *know* our Bibles sufficiently to realise this? We should, for it is only by these 'exceedingly great and precious' promises, says Peter, that we are made 'partakers of the divine nature' and escape 'the corruption that is in the world through lust' (2 Peter 1:4).

Again, merely *knowing* the promises is not sufficient of itself. The Jews knew all about the promised land, yet did not believe that God would give it to them. Do we trust the Lord to *deliver* his promises? Or do we hedge them around with 'ifs and buts', not really trusting God's ability or willingness to do what he says? Of course, we have to understand what it is he promises. We often 'ask and do not receive because [we] ask amiss' (James 4:3). Nevertheless, we are frequently guilty of unbelief in our approach to the living God — we do not 'let God be God'.

However, the Writer's main concern here is not the weak faith of God's true people, but the unbelief that keeps professing Christians from true salvation. There are times when the leader in a marathon, having outstripped his rivals, collapses from exhaustion within sight of the finishing line. He never completes the course, and the crown goes to another. So it is with any whose profession is not grounded on genuine faith — they 'fall after the same example of disobedience'.

How can we avoid such a fate? We must **'be diligent'**, replies the Writer. In urging diligence he echoes Peter: '…

giving all diligence, add to your faith virtue, to virtue knowledge, to knowledge self-control, to self-control perseverance,
to perseverance godliness, to godliness brotherly kindness, and
to brotherly kindness love ... be even more diligent to make
your calling and election sure, for if you do these things you
will never stumble' (2 Peter 1:5-11).

There is nothing 'quietistic' about the Christian life. We
rest from our own works, trusting in Christ alone for salvation.
But true salvation issues in a life of fruitfulness to God. 'By
this my Father is glorified', declared Jesus, 'that you bear much
fruit; so shall you be my disciples' (John 15:8). This fruit-
bearing requires effort, hence the need for diligence. Of course,
'the branch cannot bear fruit of itself ... without me you can
do nothing' (John 15:4-5). The fruit we bear to God is the
fruit of the indwelling Holy Spirit (Gal. 5:22-25). But we only
bear that fruit as we 'walk in the Spirit', and that requires
understanding, determination and diligence.

Those who are diligent, says Peter, make their 'calling and
election sure'. This does not mean that they *obtain* their calling and election by diligent obedience. That is impossible, since
both election and calling must necessarily *precede* conversion
to Christ (Eph. 1:4; Gal. 1:15). It means, rather, that diligence
and its fruits provide evidence (to ourselves and others) that
we are indeed God's children — the subjects of his saving
grace.

The two-edged sword (4:12)

The Writer now presents a dramatic picture: **'For the word
of God is living and powerful, and sharper than any two-
edged sword, piercing even to the division of soul and spirit,
and of joints and marrow, and is a discerner of the thoughts
and intents of the heart'** (4:12). The 'two-edged sword' is a

metaphor, of course, as are the references to separating soul from spirit and marrow from joints. The *reality* they picture lies in the way Scripture 'pierces' our defences to reveal 'the thoughts and intents of the heart'.

The opening word, **'for'**, indicates that the statement made here is linked with what precedes it. But what exactly is the connection between being 'diligent' to avoid disobedience, and the Scriptures ('the Word of God')?

There are two possible answers. Firstly, by way of encouragement and help, the Word of God provides an antidote to error, and is thus the basis of all gospel diligence. We are therefore exhorted to use it on ourselves, lest we also err. Alternatively, these words can be taken as a warning — God's Word will seek out and expose any hypocrisy or false profession. According to this interpretation, the readers are told plainly that they cannot hide their unbelief from themselves, even though they may hide it from others. They are in for a rough ride, therefore, as long as they continue to sit under the ministry of the Word. As they listen to that Word, they will be seized by an inward sense of sinfulness and by the terror that attends it.

It is not unreasonable to take the passage both ways, as a warning and as an encouragement. Indeed, this reflects the balance of the whole epistle, where warnings, encouragements and exhortations alternate in quick succession. Admittedly the tone in verse 12 is sombre, so that the warning element is uppermost. But the help extended to the storm-tossed believer by Scripture's penetrating work is also real.

First, then, the warning. The false professor can have no peace of soul. As one who still professes Christ, he will continue to hear the Word of God expounded (or at least remember it). But it will give him no rest, since it will continually challenge and condemn his hypocrisy. It will discern **'the thought and intents of [his] heart'**, discovering his perfidy and condemning him to abject misery until he cries out for mercy and for true salvation. As indicated above, the references to 'soul and spirit' and 'joints and marrow' are figurative; the Word of God (the sword of the Spirit — Eph. 6:17) is ruthless in its separation of truth from error, sin from righteousness, falsity from reality. It pierces through our best-constructed defences and searches out the innermost thoughts of our hearts.

The question arises, of course, whether the Word of God is ministered today in a manner that actually achieves this end. To be effective, a sword must be wielded skilfully. Those who preach and teach the Word have a solemn responsibility to do so in a way that can be used, by the Spirit of God, to bring conviction and discomfort to any whose profession is insincere. Here lies the rub. We do not like to discomfort our hearers. We are constantly in danger of crying, '"Peace, peace!" where there is no peace' — producing a superficial 'healing', perhaps, but not dealing with the true disease (Jer. 6:14). Clearly, the Writer has no such inhibitions.

Nevertheless, these stern words also embody solid comforts. **'The word of God is living and powerful'** (4:12). Firstly, it is 'living'. As with the 'living water' in John 4:10, the adjective denotes something 'having vital power in itself and exerting the same upon the soul'.[1] Thus 'the Scriptures ... are able to make [us] wise for salvation through faith which is in Christ Jesus' (2 Tim. 3:15). Christians are 'born again, not of corruptible seed but incorruptible, through the word of God which lives and abides for ever' (1 Peter 1:23). Scripture 'lives' because it is the Word of the living God and is the vehicle by which the Holy Spirit brings life to the human soul, both in regenerating and sustaining the believer.

Secondly, this sword is **'powerful'** or active. 'The Bible', says Kistemaker, 'is not a dead letter, comparable to a law that is no longer enforced.'[2] In Scripture, God has provided us with a powerful and effective weapon, whether we use it against our spiritual foes or our own sinful tendencies. This is why we must learn to use this 'sword' with skill, whether in our own private devotions or in public ministry. The present writer must confess that if you placed a rapier in his hand he would be hard put to use it, lacking the necessary training. Although the Holy Spirit is not limited by our lack of expertise, each of us nevertheless has a responsibility to 'be diligent to present [himself] approved to God, a worker who does not need to be ashamed, rightly dividing the word of truth' (2 Tim. 2:15). Let us be diligent, then, learning to use the Scriptures effectively, both in our own lives and in our service to God.

God sees all (4:13)

Having delineated the central role of Scripture in discerning falsehood, sin and error, the Writer issues his ultimate warning to those who make false professions of faith. They may conceal their duplicity from their Christian friends, but they cannot hide it from God. **'There is'**, he declares, **'no creature hidden from his sight, but all things are naked and open to the eyes of him to whom we must give account'** (4:13). The words 'naked' and 'open' in the Greek both imply exposure with an element of violence, as in 'stripped bare' or 'forced open'.[34] Those who make false claims to faith are in for a rough time!

God's knowledge is total, whether of outward circumstances or inward thoughts. No created being can conceal even their most secret thoughts from God. As the psalmist declares, 'O Lord you have searched me and known me ... you understand my thoughts afar off, you comprehend my path ...' (Ps. 139:1-6). Our transparency to the gaze of God can be a source of comfort for the believer, for even 'if our heart condemns us, God is greater than our heart and knows all things' (1 John 3:20). John's statement here is addressed to the doubting Christian, who is 'of the truth' but lacks heart-assurance of this fact. At such times, advises John, we should trust God, who justifies the ungodly, rather than trust our hearts.

But what is comfort to the true believer is a terror to any whose profession is false. God sees through our camouflage and reads our hearts and minds. Is prayer a pretence? God knows it. Is worship an outward sham? God sees the reality behind the mask, and is angry. Our motives are laid bare; our thoughts and intentions stand naked before his holy gaze.

But, even worse for any who do not abide in Christ, we also **'must give account'** (4:13). 'We must all appear before the judgement seat of Christ', says Paul, 'that each one may receive [reward or punishment for] the things done in the body ... whether good or bad' (2 Cor. 5:10). We shall not be judged according to our *profession* of faith, for not everyone who calls Christ 'Lord' will enter the kingdom of heaven (Matt. 7:21). Only those who *do* God's will, and bring forth the fruits of repentance and of the Spirit, will be received. No wonder Paul continues: 'Knowing, therefore, the terror of the Lord, we persuade men ...' (2 Cor. 5:11).

Giving account to God is a constant theme of Scripture. Several of the parables are built around this idea. A king calls his servants to account and discovers that one owes him enormous debts (Matt. 18:23-27). A landowner calls for his tenants to render up the fruits of a vineyard (Matt. 21:33-43). A master returns from afar and his servants must account for their actions during his absence (Matt. 25:14-30; Luke 19:11-27). God requires the soul of the rich fool (Luke 12:16-21) and demands fruit from a barren fig tree (Luke 13:6-9).

In Hebrews, those who are elders among God's people are said to 'watch out for your souls as those who must give account' (13:17), and we are all called to 'render ... to God the things that are God's' (Matt. 22:21). Accountability to God is not a popular concept today. Many, even Christians, conduct their lives as if they were answerable to no one but themselves. That is the spirit of the age, no doubt. But it does not alter the fact that each of us is accountable to God. If we are not convinced of that now, we shall be persuaded in the day of reckoning — but then it will be too late. Paul strove to please God, knowing that he must appear before Christ's judgement seat to give an account of his stewardship. We should be moved by the same godly fear that motivated the apostle. For, one day, we too must give account.

13.
The throne of grace

Please read Hebrews 4:14-16

Against the sombre backcloth of the preceding verses, heavy with the displeasure of an all-seeing God, the Writer now sets his recurrent theme of Christ the Saviour. The reversion is brilliant, as he sweeps our gaze from the trembling sinner to the source of all help: **'Seeing then that we have a great High Priest ... let us hold fast our confession'** (4:14). The dark foreboding of the preceding passage is scattered by the light of grace. It is not that the dangers have vanished, or the warnings lost their force, but rather that the way of escape from apostasy and unbelief is so gloriously revealed. What is that way? A person, Jesus Christ the righteous. As Isaac Watts rejoices:

> Jesus my great High Priest
> Offered his blood and died;
> My guilty conscience seeks
> No sacrifice beside:
> His powerful blood did once atone,
> And now it pleads before the throne.

The Writer's theme in this passage, therefore, is **'mercy and ... grace'** (4:16). All who are tempted to dally with unbelief; all whose consciences are dull or fearful; all who tremble at the wrath of God — let them behold Christ as their Intercessor-King, a 'priest on his throne'. According to the prophecy of Zechariah, this exalted Saviour 'shall bear the glory', shall 'rule on his throne', and shall establish 'the counsel of peace' between a needy people and their holy God (Zech. 6:13). To that **'throne of grace'** we are bidden to come.

A great High Priest (4:14)

'Seeing then that we have a great High Priest ...' (4:14). The words signify possession — having a close relationship, being closely joined, or even clinging, to this great High Priest. Access to Christ is not just some resource, to be used or neglected at our whim. The identity that Christ has established with his people, so fluently set forth in 2:10-18, is both real and practical. Christ's oneness with believers avails them mightily in their hour of need.

This is the third time in the epistle that Christ is designated **'High Priest'**. In 2:17 he is described as 'a merciful and faithful High Priest ... to make propitiation for the sins of the people'. Again, in 3:1 he is called 'the Apostle and High Priest of our confession'. But here there is a major development. Not only is he a faithful High Priest, but one also who is **'Jesus the Son of God'**, who is **'great'**, and has **'passed through the heavens'** (4:14). The implied superlatives are pregnant with meaning. In this name, says Calvin, 'there inheres that majesty which drives us to awe and to obedience'.[1]

Christ's greatness as High Priest resides chiefly in two things. Firstly, he is great because of his unique person — he is no mere man like Aaron, but the eternal Son of God. Secondly, he is great because of his unique work — he has not passed into an earthly tabernacle, but through the heavens. So far does the new covenant excel the old.

The Writer here begins to weave together the several offices of Christ. Previously, his glorious sonship and atoning work have been described, as has his leadership as the 'Apostle ... of our confession' (3:1). But these roles have hitherto been viewed separately. Now, however, the attributes and offices of Christ are skilfully assembled to provide an awesome portrait of omnipotent grace.

As we have just seen in Zechariah, Christ uniquely combines the offices of high priest and king. The Mosaic priests stood to minister, but this High Priest, his work complete, sits upon a throne. Nor is his kingship of any ordinary kind, for he is 'Jesus the Son of God'. This re-emphasises that Christ is both God and man. Guthrie comments, 'The Writer does not appear to use the different names [of Christ] indiscriminately. It is highly important for him to establish without question that our high priest is none other than the historical Jesus.'[2] But even more important, Jesus is 'a name given him from the work he had to do. He was to "save his people".'[3] 'Jesus', therefore, is a most fitting name for our great High Priest to bear.

Human as he is, this Jesus has **'passed through the heavens'**. This last phrase is a metaphor, denoting passage *from* mortal sight, *through* a curtain or veil and *into* a heavenly place. It therefore signifies three things.

Firstly, Christ has ascended to take his rightful place of 'all authority' upon the throne of God and of the Lamb (Acts 1:9; Matt. 28:18; Rev. 22:1). His divine priesthood is of an entirely different (and greater) order than that of Aaron and his sons. For what does a priest do, but intercede between man and God? Yet this priest *is* both man and God! He perfectly joins the supplicant to the one supplicated. Christ's enthronement, therefore, while it hides him from our sight, does not distance him from us. Rather, it creates an unbreakable chain between the believing sinner and the holy God in heaven.

Secondly, passing 'through the heavens' refers not only to Christ's ascension and enthronement, but also to his having entered the true 'holy of holies', the 'more perfect tabernacle not made with hands' (9:11-12). Under the old covenant, on the Day of Atonement, the high priest would pass through the veil and enter the holiest-of-all to make atonement for the people with the blood of animal sacrifices. This annual ritual, argues Hebrews, was symbolic of the work of Christ. To inaugurate the new and everlasting covenant (13:20), he has entered the heavenly sanctuary once for all, bearing a perfect and permanent offering — his own shed blood. Enthronement and atonement! Separately, each speaks of Christ's surpassing power to save. Together, they show why 'he is also able to save *to the uttermost* those who come to God through him' (7:25, emphasis added).

Thirdly, he has 'passed through the heavens' as our forerunner. He has entered 'the inner part [of the true tabernacle] behind the veil' as our representative (6:19-20). We who believe shall surely follow him into the glory prepared for his people — the immediate presence of the triune God.

Holding fast (4:14-15)

This being the case, urges the Writer, **'let us hold fast our confession'** (4:14). Kistemaker translates 'confession' as 'the faith we profess'[4] and cites Hughes' definition of this faith as 'the belief that is both inwardly entertained by the heart and outwardly professed before men'.[5]

As professing believers, his readers had both put their faith in Christ and confessed him before others. His atoning death and imputed righteousness were the whole ground of their hope and confidence — for time and eternity. To abandon this confession, therefore, would be to abandon hope. Whatever threats or inducements might tempt them to turn back, they dare not do so.

Today, as then, believers are continually assailed and tempted to 'let go' rather than 'hold fast'. Persecution, false teaching, love of the world, and many other distractions, can cause Christians to lose heart and relax their grip on Christ. Were it possible, even the elect would be deceived (Matt. 24:24). But, of course, it is not possible for the elect to abandon Christ, because Christ cannot abandon his elect! The Writer's exhortation is addressed primarily to those whose faith is suspect and whose response to his exhortation will settle the matter one way or the other. Are they true believers? Then they will 'hold fast' their profession.

But this exhortation applies also to those who *are* holding fast their confession of Christ — and thereby demonstrating the reality of their faith. Tenacity in the face of trials or persecution is never easy, and encouragement is always welcome. The call to hold fast can, of itself, rouse the soul to greater reliance on our great High Priest. The more clearly we see him enthroned on high, and interceding for us, the more firmly will we be able to hold fast. But the encouragement does not stop there! The exhortation is backed by a further, and tender, assurance.

'**For**', continues the Writer, '**we do not have a High Priest who cannot sympathise with our weaknesses, but was in all points tempted** [tested] **as we are, yet without sin**' (4:15). Owen points out that 'a double negation ["we do not ... who cannot"] doth strongly and vehemently affirm'.[6] Christ has passed through the heavens, but he is still most surely 'touched with the feeling of our infirmities', as the Authorised Version puts it.

Before we apply the text we need to consider an objection. If Christ, as God, was incapable of sin, how could he experience genuine temptation? Can he truly empathise with fallen sinners, seeing that he himself could not yield to temptation?

The answer is twofold. Firstly, and basically, we cannot know what Jesus endured by way of temptation. We do know that he suffered superhuman deprivations in the wilderness, and that 'his sweat became like great drops of blood' in an agony of trial before his crucifixion (Mark 1:12-13; Luke 22:41-44). Clearly, temptation was no easy thing for the incarnate God. Secondly, we have to trust the Word of God when it declares that he did, indeed, suffer in such a way as to experience the selfsame trials as we ourselves. We may also note that Christ's very immunity to sin guaranteed that he would experience the full force of temptation. We ourselves often give way while the pressure is light.

Reverting to the earlier part of the verse, we can now consider its strong message of encouragement. Enthroned as he is on high, and engaged in the business of the heavenly sanctuary, Christ nevertheless still draws near to help (sympathise with) his children in their weakness here on earth. This is important to grasp. It is not simply that Christ, having experienced testing and temptation during his earthly life, knows how we feel. That is itself a gracious truth, but our verse implies more. It tells us that Jesus *actively* succours his people in the midst of their trials, graciously upholding them and strengthening them in their time of need. There is more than sympathy available; there is support, for 'The eternal God is [our] refuge and underneath are the everlasting arms' (Deut. 33:27).

He renders this support and comfort, of course, in the person and power of his Holy Spirit (John 14:16-18). The Spirit has been given to Christ's people expressly as their 'Helper' and 'Comforter' (John 14:15-18). He 'also helps in our weaknesses. For we do not know what we should pray for as we ought, but the Spirit himself makes intercession for us with groanings which cannot be uttered' (Rom. 8:26).

Many today have lost sight of this great truth, living their Christian lives in almost total ignorance of the Holy Spirit's ministry in them and to them. Perhaps the excesses and

unbiblical teachings of the charismatic movement have fright-
ened believers into ignoring the present work of the Spirit in
the heart and in the church. But a neglect of experimental theology is not new. It always characterises periods of church
history when lifeless orthodoxy prevails.

The New Testament provides the corrective. It is by the
Spirit that we are 'born again' and translated from death to
life (John 3:6-7). God's gift of faith is imparted by the Spirit,
and by that same faith the believer receives the Spirit in conscious awareness (Eph. 2:5-9; Gal. 3:2). The Holy Spirit reveals the glory of Christ to the believer, and teaches him all
things (John 16:14; 14:26). The Spirit 'bears witness with our
spirit that we are the children of God', crying 'Abba, Father'
in our hearts, confirming the reality of our adoption (Rom.
8:16-17; Gal. 4:6-7). God strengthens us 'with might through
his Spirit in the inner man, that Christ may dwell in our hearts
through faith', that we might 'know the love of Christ which
passes knowledge [and] be filled with all the fulness of God'
(Eph. 3:16-19). The indwelling Spirit bears fruit in our lives
to the glory of God (Gal. 5:22-25; John 15:8).

To summarise, then, Christ's throne-gift of help and sympathy is actualised in our experience by his Spirit. It is the
believer's right and privilege to live in the conscious experience of this reality.

Grace to help (4:16)

The Writer draws his conclusion: **'Let us therefore come
boldly to the throne of grace, that we may obtain mercy
and grace to help in time of need'** (4:16). Our great High
Priest, the Son of God, has ascended to his throne. Yet this
throne, declares Calvin, 'is not marked by a naked majesty
which overpowers us, but is adorned with a new name, that of

grace'.[7] He has offered his own blood to atone for our sins. He knows our needs and provides for them abundantly through the ministry of his Holy Spirit. What further reassurance do we need? We should not linger uncertainly but draw near in faith, nothing doubting (James 1:6).

The Writer bids us come **'boldly'**, or 'with boldness'. The words mean 'confidently', 'frankly' and 'without concealment'. We should not seek to hide our sins and our weakness, however much we are ashamed of them. Our very frailty in these matters constitutes a claim upon the great High Priest. Is this really so? Yes, because we come first of all to **'obtain mercy'**, and only sinners need that.

The starting point, then, is confession of sin and repentance towards God. Yet, amazingly, we are bidden to seek this mercy 'boldly' — not hesitantly or fearfully, but eagerly and with full assurance. How can this be? Because Christ has died for our sins and made full and final atonement for them. To apply boldly for mercy, therefore, is to express confidence in the finished work of Christ on our behalf — whereas to come fearfully would cast doubt on its efficacy. Our boldness does not reside in ourselves; we are bold in Christ.

But the Saviour's throne affords more than mercy. We may also **'find grace to help in time of need'** (4:16). After all, it is a throne *of grace*! The concept of 'grace' is a major building block of biblical theology, and perhaps this is why it is so often misunderstood. The nature of grace is succinctly explained by Berkhof. 'Grace is not an abstract quality', he writes, 'but is an active working principle, manifesting itself in beneficent acts... In the first place grace is an attribute of God, one of the divine perfections. It is God's free, sovereign, undeserved favour or love to man in his state of sin and guilt... In the second place the term "grace" is used as a designation of the objective provision which God made in Christ for the salvation of man.'[8]

In Scripture, grace is never a commodity that passes from God to man, so as to be infused into the human soul. It is a very ancient error that grace is somehow transferred to men through the sacraments, but many still subscribe to it. This erroneous view of grace focuses on man — 'How much grace have I received by my religious observance?' Seen in this way, grace is subtly transformed into human merit, which is the very opposite of what it really is.

Let us be clear. Grace (or more strictly, graciousness) is first and foremost an attribute of God, namely, his propensity to give. It describes the divine generosity which lies at the heart of all God's dealings with his creatures. It manifests itself in 'common grace', concerning which the psalmist exclaims, 'You open your hand and satisfy the desire of every living thing' (Ps. 145:16). It reaches its culmination in the gospel of grace, in which God provides for the sure salvation of a multitude of undeserving sinners in Christ. Paul expresses it perfectly. Believers, he writes, are 'predestined ... to adoption ... according to the good pleasure of [God's] will, to the praise of the glory of his grace, by which he has made us accepted in the Beloved. In him we have redemption through his blood, the forgiveness of sins, according to the riches of his grace' (Eph. 1:6-7).

The recipients of saving grace are rich! They dwell continually in the warm and wondrous climate of God's grace. As a once-frequent visitor to the Gulf Coast of America, the author often travelled from a cold British winter to the welcome warmth of Texas. How good it was to shed one's scarf and overcoat for a few days and drink in the scented balm of a semi-tropical climate! In the same way, the believer has passed from the desolate winter of sin into the glorious climate of grace, with its gentle rain of mercy and the sunshine of God's constant favour. Nor is the Christian a mere visitor to this kingdom of grace, but rather a permanent resident.

The expression **'find grace'** (4:16) is borrowed from the Old Testament Scriptures, and the epistle's first recipients would have fully understood its meaning. In almost every instance of the use of 'grace' in the Old Testament, the word is coupled with the verb 'to find'. 'Noah found grace in the eyes of the LORD' (Gen. 6:8; see also Moses in Exod. 33:12). Ruth asks Boaz, 'Why have I found favour [grace] in your eyes, that you should take notice of me, since I am a foreigner?' (Ruth 2:10). It is clear that to 'find grace' is a Hebrew idiom — 'to be looked upon with favour by one who owes nothing to the person favoured'. We cannot earn grace; we can only 'find' it at the footstool of the God of grace.

And because it is dispensed from a throne, it is by definition *sovereign* grace that we receive from our great High Priest. That is, this grace is given according to the counsel of God's own will and in accordance with his sovereign purposes in Christ (Eph. 1:5,11). Moreover, as regards its quality, this grace is powerful (as befits the intentions of a king) and compassionate (as befits the intercession of a priest). As regards its quantity, it is abounding grace, sufficient for all our need, in time and in eternity (Rom. 5:20).

As regards its effect, it succours us **'in time of need'** (4:16). Believers are in constant possession of the riches of 'the grace of our Lord Jesus Christ' (2 Cor. 8:9). But there are certain times of special need, when afflictions abound or temptations press us sorely. At such times, the Writer assures us, we may find superabundant comfort, special strength, at the grace-throne of our priestly King. Let us therefore come boldly to the throne of grace!

14.
The author of salvation

Please read Hebrews 5:1-11

Having launched the theme of Christ's high-priestly office, the
Writer pursues it with vigour. This subject will, in fact, occupy most of the next six chapters of the epistle. The Writer's
presentation of the unique priesthood of Christ, which began
in 4:14, contributes vitally to our understanding of salvation.
But it also serves as an introduction to the covenants, old and
new, which emerge explicitly (albeit gradually) throughout
Hebrews chapters 5-8 .

The approach is slow but sure. The Writer's strategy is
first to establish the incomparability of Christ, both in his divine person and the great salvation he has wrought for sinners. This he has done in chapters 1-3. But now, as he enlarges
upon the offices of Christ, the necessity of a new covenant
begins to emerge as an unavoidable consequence of these offices — especially that of High Priest.

A sacrificing High Priest (5:1-3)

In this passage, Jesus' credentials as a high priest are further
established. It is typical of the Writer's methodology that a
proposition is first advanced and then justified. In the foregoing verses (4:14-16), the high-priesthood of Jesus was

asserted in the most positive terms. But now the assertion is vindicated by a variety of arguments — drawn in turn from analogy, Scripture and the life of Christ himself.

Scripture invariably uses logical argument to establish its doctrines. Of course, it starts with certain assumptions, such as the existence of God and the validity of his self-revelation in Scripture and in Christ. For 'he who comes to God must believe that he is, and that he is a rewarder of those who diligently seek him' (11:6). All reasoning, of whatever kind, must have a starting point.

That being said, however, we cannot read the Bible without our minds being engaged and our reason led step by step to logical conclusions. We misuse the Bible if we pick out statements at random to justify human fancies. Rather, we must pay attention to the context and follow the argument; only then will we arrive at a true understanding of Scripture. This is why expository preaching is so valuable, since it seeks to explain a passage, set it in context, draw out the spiritual truth it contains, and then apply it to our lives. But such preaching, if it is truly faithful to the message of Scripture, will always be full of Christ — otherwise it is of little value. That is never a problem with Hebrews, for Christ fills our view wherever we turn in this remarkable epistle!

The first argument advanced here to support the high-priesthood of Christ relates to a high priest's role. What is that role? To **'offer gifts and sacrifices for sin ... [and] have compassion on those who are ignorant and going astray'** (5:1-2). Since these are the very things that Christ performs (or has performed), contends the Writer, he perfectly fits the high-priestly profile. He offers to God the 'gift' of a perfect life (he was 'without sin', 4:15). Like the incense offered by the priests of old, he is in himself 'the fragrance of Christ' to the Father (2 Cor. 2:15). He offered himself as a sacrifice for sins — an offering more complete, more perfect and more effectual than anything performed by man. Yet, since he lived among us as a man, he can supremely 'sympathise with our weaknesses' (4:15).

While Christ's ministry parallels that of human high priests, the Writer is careful to make distinctions where necessary. Thus the compassion shown by a human high priest is based upon his own human frailty, **'since he himself is also beset by weakness. Because of this he is required as for the people, so also for himself, to offer sacrifices for sins'** (5:2-3). This is not true of Christ, whose compassion stems from strength, not weakness (he was tempted in all points yet without sin). Nor is it necessary for Christ to offer sacrifices for his own sin, for he had none. In these regards he stands apart from all human priests. Nevertheless, his high-priesthood is discerned by analogy with the office of Aaron and his sons.

An appointed High Priest (5:4-6)

A second thing that qualifies Christ as a high priest is that he **'is called by God, just as Aaron was'** (5:4). The Writer argues that no legitimate high priest attains office by his own choice, for **'no man takes this honour to himself'** (5:4). Neither did Christ **'glorify himself to become High Priest'** (5:5). On the contrary, he was appointed by God, who said to him, **'You are my Son, today I have begotten you,'** and further declared, **'You are a priest for ever after the order of Melchizedek'** (5:5-6). These were the all-important words of divine commission and ordination.

The argument that Christ's high-priesthood is valid and genuine on account of divine appointment would have been important for the readers of the epistle, steeped as they were in Old Testament law. Under the old covenant there were severe penalties for any who usurped priestly authority — witness the dreadful fate of Nadab and Abihu, sons of Aaron though they were, who offered 'strange fire' before the Lord (Lev. 10:1-7). The law was both strict and severe, allowing no deviation from the divine pattern in man's approach to God. But Christ is no usurper. He has been appointed by the Father to a unique and *legal* high-priesthood — of Melchizedek's order — of which the Writer still has 'much to say' (5:11).

For us also, it is important that Christ has been appointed to his high-priesthood by the Father. This fact provides further assurance, if any were needed, that Christ has a *right* of access to Almighty God on our behalf. And if Christ has such rights of audience and acceptance, then those who are 'in Christ' also partake of those rights. That is why Paul can say, '... having been justified by faith, we have peace with God through our Lord Jesus Christ, through whom also we have *access by faith* into this grace in which we stand' (Rom. 5:1-2, emphasis added).

This is the first mention of Melchizedek in Hebrews, but by no means the last. In the whole Bible he is mentioned just eleven times. He appears in his original historical context in Genesis 14:18 and in a prophetic setting in Psalm 110:4. The other nine references are in Hebrews (5:6,10; 6:20; 7:1,10,11,15,17,21). Like the Writer, we shall have much more to say about him.

A diligent High Priest (5:7-8)

The Writer's third argument in support of the legitimacy of Christ's priesthood relates to the diligence with which the Lord fulfilled this office. In the affairs of men, people appointed to high office often fail to discharge their responsibilities. Although apparently qualified, they are found wanting in practice. A true high priest is one who not only holds the office, but who *fulfils* the appointed role. Does Christ qualify by this criterion? Undoubtedly, declares the Writer. For **'in the days of his flesh, when he had offered up prayers and supplications, with vehement cries and tears to him who was able to save him from death, [he] was heard because of his godly fear'** (5:7).

This verse needs a little explanation. The reference is clearly to Christ's agony in the Garden of Gethsemane, recorded in Matthew 26:36-46, when Jesus prayed, 'O my Father, if it is possible, let this cup pass from me; nevertheless, not as I will, but as you will.' A cursory reading of Hebrews 5:7 might suggest that Christ was praying to be spared from crucifixion, but this is clearly not so. We are told that he 'was heard', that is, his prayer was answered. But since he *did* die on the cross, his answered prayer could not have been for deliverance from that death!

It is true that Jesus shrank from the prospect of the cross. He knew that he would there carry the sins of his people and suffer the wrath of his Father in their place. Equally, the Father could have spared his Son and abandoned his purpose of redemption. But, surely, the chief object of Christ's agonised prayer was that his suffering might be effective in the salvation of the lost. 'Jesus' prayers were a sacrificial offering,' says Lane.[1] Only this interpretation is consistent with his intercessory function as our great High Priest. The Writer has not suddenly changed the subject, but wishes to demonstrate the diligence and pain with which Christ carried through the priestly work of mediation.

His prayer was heard **'because of his godly fear'**. What does this signify? It can be translated 'dutiful love'.[2] On this reading, it refers (according to Lane) to 'the recognition of God's sovereignty and submission to the divine will'.[3] Jesus said, 'Nevertheless, not my will but yours be done' (Luke 22:42). As Anne Cousin wrote:

Death and the curse were in our cup,
O Christ, 'twas full for thee!
But thou hast drained the last dark drop,
'Tis empty now for me.
That bitter cup, love drank it up,
Now blessing's draught for me.

However, Calvin interprets the verse differently. 'I have no doubt', he declares, 'that the apostle means that Christ was heard [and thus delivered] out of that which he feared, so that he was not overwhelmed by and did not give way to these evils, nor was he overcome by death ... at no time was he deprived of God's mercy and help.' He adds, 'From this we can take it that God often answers our prayers even when it is least apparent.'[4]

Either way, Christ fulfilled to the uttermost his role of High Priest, working through the implications of his office as no priest has ever done before or since. With prayers, supplications, cries and tears he carried his own blood into the sanctuary to make atonement for his elect. What agony of soul was his, we shall never know. But we do know that 'It was for us he hung and suffered there.'

'Though he was a Son', continues the Writer, **'he learned obedience through the things which he suffered'** (5:8). This may seem confusing. Did not Christ obey his Father's will *before* he suffered on the cross? How, then, could the later suffering teach him the former obedience? Probably the reference here is not to the sufferings of the cross, but rather to the things Jesus endured during his earthly life prior to the climactic act of redemption. By serving an apprenticeship in the school of suffering, he was *prepared* (he learned what was needful) for his supreme act of submission to the Father's will.

Many commentators interpret this differently. Feeling that Christ could have nothing to 'learn' in the moral realm, they take 'learned obedience' to mean that Christ entered into an experimental knowledge of obedience and its consequences. Thus Brown states, 'To "learn obedience" is, I apprehend, to become experimentally acquainted with obedience.'[5] This is undeniably true, but perhaps does not go far enough. Everything that Christ experienced 'in the days of his flesh' (5:7) was preparation for his supreme act of obedience and atonement — and preparation is a process of 'learning'.

That Christ needed such preparation underlines the truth that he was truly human as well as truly God. Although he was the exalted Son of God (5:8), 'he made himself of no reputation, taking the form of a servant ... and being found in appearance as a man, he humbled himself and became obedient to death, even the death of the cross' (Phil. 2:7-8). He fulfilled his high-priesthood, not just in his supreme work of atonement, but throughout his life on earth.

A perfect High Priest (5:9-11)

The fourth and final argument for the authenticity of Christ's high-priesthood is that his intercession has achieved its defined purpose, namely, the **'eternal salvation [of] all who obey him'** (5:9). This was something never accomplished by the Aaronic priesthood and marks Christ out, not only as a true High Priest, but as one unparalleled in excellence. To quote the text in full, **'And having been perfected, he became the author of eternal salvation to all who obey him, called by God as High Priest "according to the order of Melchizedek"'** (5:9-10).

We have already encountered the idea that Christ was 'made perfect', back in 2:10. There, as here, Christ was designated the 'author', or originator, of salvation and we were told that 'it was fitting' that the Father should make him 'perfect through sufferings'. Commenting on that verse, we noticed that Christ's sufferings were the *necessary* and *sufficient* means of victory and deliverance, and that it was in this sense that the Father made him 'perfect through sufferings'.

The word 'perfect' means 'complete'. Until he died on the cross, Christ was not a perfect Saviour for the simple reason that his work was not complete. He was already a perfect man, the sinless incarnate God. But his saviourhood only became complete when he was able to cry, 'It is finished!' (John 19:30). The same Greek verb translated 'finished' in John 19 is rendered 'made perfect' in 5:9. In John the reference is to a finished work of atonement, and in Hebrews to a 'finished' or perfected Saviour, but the ideas are inseparable.

It is one of the key concepts of Hebrews (and indeed of Scripture generally) that Christ's work of atonement is a *finished* work. Whereas human priests must make continual sacrifices, Christ died 'once for all' and made an end of sacrifice for sin for all time and for all who obey him (10:1-3,10-14). This is one of the major differences between the old and new covenants. We shall enlarge on this idea when we come to Hebrews 10, but for the moment we note only the consequence — that by virtue of his effectual sufferings on behalf of his people, Christ is a *perfect* High Priest. We need no other.

Moreover, the salvation he has procured for his elect is 'eternal salvation' (5:9). 'Christian salvation is eternal', comments Bruce, 'like the "eternal redemption" of 9:12, the "eternal inheritance" of 9:15 and the "eternal covenant" of 13:20, because it is based on the sacrifice of Christ, once for all accomplished, never to be repeated, and permanently valid.'[6] Such a salvation cannot be lost or forfeited, nor is it 'conditional' on our faithfulness, as the Wesleyan Methodists taught (and still teach). The reality of a person's faith will certainly be demonstrated by 'patient continuance in doing good' (Rom. 2:7), but this will be the *consequence* of Christ's saving work, not the *cause* of our final salvation.

Furthermore, 'eternal salvation' implies 'eternal life' which, said Jesus, he gives to his sheep so that 'they shall never perish; neither shall anyone snatch them out of [his] hand' (John 10:28). Christ is a 'perfected' Saviour because he saves perfectly, finally, fully and eternally. The source of all our assurance and peace is the finished work of Christ.

Although, by these various tests, Christ is demonstrated to be a true High Priest, even in the old-covenant sense, the Writer is careful to show that his high-priesthood does not derive from that covenant. Christ is not a high priest after the order of Aaron, but is of an entirely different order — the appropriately mysterious order of Melchizedek. Paul describes the gospel as 'the mystery of Christ which in other ages was not made known to the sons of men' (Eph. 3:4-5), and there are few greater mysteries (or secrets) in the historical unfolding of redemption than the role and significance of Melchizedek.

The Writer is clearly excited and anxious to reveal this mystery to his readers: 'Of [Melchizedek] we have much to say', he declares, 'and hard to explain' (5:11). But he is forced to interrupt his exposition of the mystery of Christ. Why? Because his readers **'have become dull of hearing'** (5:11). How often this is true, even today! The gospel of the glory of Christ is obscured; our appetites for its wonders are dulled; and our Christian lives become drudgery, our devotions perfunctory. Why should this be? The Writer explores the problem in the verses that follow.

15.
The need to progress

Please read Hebrews 5:12 – 6:2

The Writer is finding it 'hard to explain' the high-priesthood of Christ. This is not because it is inexplicable, but because his readers are not sufficiently mature, spiritually speaking, to take it in. They need to move on from **'the elementary principles of Christ'** (6:1) — not in the sense of leaving them behind, but in the sense of building upon them.

This is a timely reminder that we cannot stand still in the Christian life. One of the classic evidences of life (of any kind) is growth. When something ceases to grow it is usually dead, and this is the Writer's great concern. The full extent of his concern is revealed in the verses that follow our present passage, where the danger of apostasy is frankly addressed. But in the verses now before us, the emphasis is on the need to grow up, or mature, in the knowledge of Christ.

This is important for two reasons. Firstly, as we have already noted, growth is the best evidence of life. But secondly, growth is also an indication of good health. This is just as true in the spiritual realm as in the physical. Some may be satisfied to be merely alive, but no one would deny that without good health we cannot fully enjoy life. The New Testament wants us not just to live, but to live to the full. Jesus said, 'I have come that they may have life, and that they may have it more abundantly' (John 10:10).

The veil reimposed (5:12)

'Backsliding' is a word that is easily misapplied. People often use it to describe a loss of faith that should be termed apostasy. But there *is* such a thing as true backsliding. The Writer breaks off his discourse on the high-priesthood of Christ to describe it: **'For though by this time you ought to be teachers, you need someone to teach you again the first principles of the oracles** [revelation] **of God'** (5:12). The rebuke throws considerable light on the condition of the Hebrews and thus on the reason why the epistle was written.

These people had been converted to Christ some years before, perhaps even early in the post-Pentecostal era. Some commentators believe that the letter was written to the churches of Judaea.[1] Whether or not this is the case, the recipients were clearly Jews, well-instructed in the 'oracles of God' (that is, God's revelation in the Old Testament Scriptures). They had received Christ as the fulfilment of those oracles. They ought, therefore, to have understood clearly that the life and atoning work of Christ had rendered the Mosaic system redundant (see 8:13). They, more than any, were in a position to be teachers of these things and instructors of the Gentiles, who lacked their grounding in the Old Testament Scriptures.

Tragically, however, the reverse was the case. Knowing the 'oracles of God', they now failed to discern their most elementary teachings (their 'first principles'). What are these teachings? We are told in Hebrews 6:1 — they are the 'elementary principles *of [i.e. concerning] Christ*' (emphasis added). This is profoundly important and the key to the whole passage.

They had not forgotten the Scriptures as such, but had neglected to search and understand them in a Christ-centred way. In their reading of the Old Testament they saw ritual, not redemption; legalism, not liberation ('If the Son shall make you free, you shall be free indeed'). The veil that had once kept the

Jews from understanding the books of Moses had been taken away in Christ (2 Cor. 3:14). But somehow, for these Christians, it had been reimposed. In reading the Old Testament they were turning away from the truth of the gospel and back to the shadows of the old covenant (10:1). Bruce remarks: 'To such people, the exposition of the high-priestly service of Christ, with the corollary that the old order of priesthood and sacrifice had been abolished once for all, might well have been unacceptable.'[2]

The Writer is anxious to move on with his exposition of the high-priesthood of Christ. But how could his readers follow such exalted teaching if they had forgotten even the first principles of Old Testament Scripture? No doubt we share the Writer's surprise and indignation at their folly. But let us pause for a moment. Is it possible that we could fall into the same trap? The epistle to the Hebrews is evidence enough that the correct way to interpret Old Testament Scripture is in a Christocentric manner. Quite apart from its specific teachings, the letter viewed overall makes this abundantly clear. Jesus himself showed 'in all the Scriptures the things concerning himself' (Luke 24:25-27) and told the Pharisees that the Old Testament testified of him (John 5:39). Hebrews provides an exemplary demonstration of this fact.

Yet today, even evangelical Christians often forget this 'first principle' of Old Testament interpretation. They find many things of value in the Old Testament, such as history, ecclesiology, the holiness and sovereignty of God, incomparable moral teaching, the nature of man, and much more. But, fatally, they often fail to discern Christ in all the Scriptures.

As a result, they teach many things from the Old Testament that are actually inconsistent with the gospel of God's free grace in Christ. They teach salvation by works, bondage to law, false notions of theocratic government, priestly orders, and the like. And all because they do not see that these things had no value in themselves but prefigured a *new* covenant and a *new* order which is established in Christ.

Milk or meat? (5:12-14)

The Writer presses home his point with an illustration. **'You have come to need milk and not solid food'**, he chides. **'For every one who partakes only of milk is unskilled in the word of righteousness, for he is a babe'** (5:12-13). 'Milk', says Calvin, 'is the elementary teaching with which the ignorant begin.'³ In spiritual things they had reverted to babyhood. They needed to be taught from scratch, as if they were spiritual infants, newly born of the Spirit.

They had become unskilled in 'the word of righteousness'. Although there are alternative interpretations of this phrase,⁴ this is probably a reference to the Hebrews' failure to view the Scriptures through new-covenant eyes. Thus Hughes believes that the 'word of righteousness' is 'the teaching about righteousness ... the insistence on Christ as our righteousness'.⁵ The Hebrews lacked skill in reading the Old Testament and could not discern therein 'the righteousness which is from God by faith' (Phil. 3:9).

It does indeed require skill to unearth the full Christology of the Old Testament. Some Messianic passages are obvious to all, but to apply a consistent and uniform Christological interpretation to the Old Testament is a significant challenge to the best of us. But that, the Writer intimates, is where the skill comes in: **'Solid food belongs to those who are of full age, those who by reason of use have their senses exercised to discern both good and evil'** (5:14). Using the methodology of the New Testament, and instructed by the Spirit of God (who takes the things of Christ and reveals them to us — John 16:14), believers today can exercise such skill. They are enabled to discern 'good and evil', that is, truth and error concerning the doctrine of Christ.[6]

Now, as then, we need to rediscover the gospel of God's grace in Christ alone — to understand anew what it means to 'live by faith in the Son of God who loved [us] and gave himself for [us]' (Gal. 2:20). The Writer says, 'You need someone to teach you again' (5:12) and is prepared to be that teacher! That is why Hebrews has such value for us today. It will teach us these basic principles of Christ-centred thinking.

Foundations (6:1-2)

Although the Writer is prepared to teach these erring Christians, he does not propose to do so by entering into a **'discussion of the elementary principles of Christ'** or (what amounts to the same thing) by **'laying again the foundations'** of the gospel as found in these Old Testament Scriptures (6:1). As we shall see presently, his method is to remind them of what they already know. Building on *that* knowledge, he exhorts them to **'go on to perfection'** ('completeness' or 'maturity' — 6:1). They are to grow and mature, to become 'full grown' in understanding (1 Cor. 14:20). Here is encouragement to us all. Even the apostle Paul had 'not ... already attained' and needed to 'press on [to] lay hold of that for which Christ Jesus ... laid hold of [him]' (Phil. 3:12-13). So also must we persevere and grow. But the Writer sternly reinforces the lesson by holding before them the dreadful prospect of apostasy for those who have no interest in spiritual growth.

But before we consider this, it is instructive to see what the Writer considers to be **'foundations'**, or foundational doctrines relating to Christ. **'Not laying again'**, he says, **'the foundations of repentance from dead works, and of faith towards God, of the doctrine of baptisms, of**

laying on of hands, of resurrection of the dead, and of eternal judgement' (6:2).

Notice that these foundations are all associated with the basic truths of the gospel of Christ. Repentance and faith are the response of the sinner to the gospel, as the Spirit of God gives him ability to exercise them. Both repentance and faith lie beyond the power of the natural man, but are imparted as gifts by the Spirit in the great work of regeneration. Nevertheless, they are things the sinner must *do*; he must 'repent and believe the gospel' if he is to be saved.

Baptism follows, being the outward profession of repentance and faith in Christ. **'The doctrine of baptisms'** simply means the teaching concerning the significance of baptism. Those who submit to baptism need to understand what it means, for there are many false teachings on this matter (such as baptismal regeneration, which supposes that baptism is necessary for salvation and actually brings about the regeneration of the individual — notions that are entirely false and contrary to Scripture).

Commentators find difficulty here because 'baptisms' is plural, suggesting that there are more than one kind of baptism. Indeed, there are several! Scripture tells us of John's baptism of repentance; of water baptism into Christ; and of baptism in the Spirit. John's baptism had already become redundant (see Acts 19:3-5), but both water baptism and Spirit baptism are basic to the believer's experience and witness (Acts 2:38-39; 1 Cor. 12:13).

An alternative explanation is that baptism was normally administered to a group of people at the same time. Plural baptisms often marked the establishment of a new local church in New Testament times, which adds special significance to the fact that several were baptised at the same time.

The next foundation — the **'laying on of hands'** — at first seems out of place. Today we tend to think that the laying on of hands relates to such things as ordination to the gospel ministry and hardly falls into the category of 'foundations'. But the practice was employed more generally in New Testament times. Jesus laid his hands on little children (Matt. 19:15). Hands were laid on the sick that they might recover (Mark 16:18); the first deacons were set aside for their social function in this manner (Acts 6:6); on rare occasions the Spirit was given by the laying on of the apostles' hands (Acts 8:17-18; 19:6); and Timothy received some unspecified spiritual gift by this means (1 Tim. 4:14). 'The laying on of hands', says Jones, '[refers to] the gift of the Holy Spirit and his ministry.'[7]

It is helpful to view the laying on of hands as an act of identification and transmission. This is the Old Testament usage, where the priests laid hands on the sacrificial animals before they were slaughtered (Lev. 8:14-22, etc.). The animals were thereby identified with the people, whose sins were transferred (typologically) to the sacrifice.

We have no biblical evidence, but it is quite possible that the laying on of hands was practised when individuals were admitted to church membership. This would have been very natural if regarded as an act of identification. Whether or not this was the case, the laying on of hands emphasised the corporate nature of New Testament Christianity; believers are 'members one of another' (Rom. 12:5; Eph. 4:25). The practice is foundational in this sense, if none other.

The last two foundations require little explanation. The **'resurrection of the dead, and ... eternal judgement'** are clearly basic doctrines. Paul explains the importance of the doctrine of resurrection in 1 Corinthians 15:12-19: 'If there is no resurrection of the dead, then Christ is not risen... And if Christ is not risen, your faith is futile, you are still in your sins!' Similarly, a belief in eternal judgement is important because this is the fate from which Christ has saved us.

It is perhaps significant that these two doctrines are often glossed over in our day. The general resurrection of the dead, with its implications of judgement to come (Rev. 20:11-15) is not currently a popular subject among evangelicals — who are more often preoccupied with spiritual problems, benefits and experiences 'here and now'. Yet if we lay aside such foundational truths, we make nonsense of the gospel and diminish the work of Christ.

16.
The danger of apostasy

Please read Hebrews 6:3-8

The Writer to the Hebrews has one great desire — to see his readers 'go on to perfection' (6:1). In the previous section we saw how he rebukes them for their lack of progress and, indeed, their backsliding. 'Let us go on,' he cries, adding, '**... this we will do if God permits**' (6:3).

There is always a balance in Scripture, even a tension, between the responsibility of man and the sovereignty of God. Hebrews recognises here that progress in the Christian life, while it remains the believer's responsibility, can only be made with the help of God. We are utterly dependent on the grace of God for all, or any, attainment in the pursuit of holiness.

It is important to remember this and to maintain the balance of Scripture. Some shrug off their responsibilities, claiming that only God can make things happen. Others overemphasise human effort and obedience as the source of blessing and security. But the reality is that we only 'grow in the grace and knowledge of our Lord and Saviour' (2 Peter 3:18) as we take up, and use with diligence, the means of grace that he has given us, depending wholly on Christ for strength to do so. There is no contradiction between 'going on' with Christ and 'leaning on' God's enabling grace. The new-covenant believer will do both.

In the passage now before us, the Writer chooses to emphasise the believer's responsibility. He does so by issuing a dire warning. Those who fail to move beyond the basic principles are in danger of forsaking even these. Whatever spiritual experiences they may have, their erstwhile profession of faith will be revealed as false. They will fall away (become apostate) from Christ and cannot be restored.

Tasting, tasting (6:4-6)

The Writer explains the problem of apostasy in sombre terms: **'For it is impossible for those who were once enlightened, and have tasted the heavenly gift, and have become partakers of the Holy Spirit, and have tasted the good word of God and the powers of the age to come, if they fall away, to renew them again to repentance, since they crucify again for themselves the Son of God, and put him to an open shame'** (6:4-6).

These verses have been a source of much debate and perplexity. The experiences outlined here correspond so closely to those of believing Christians that many have concluded that the people described *were* true believers. And if that is so, it follows that true believers can fall away and be lost. But that, of course, is contrary to the uniform teaching of the New Testament, namely that no one can snatch from Christ's hand the sheep that his Father gave him (John 10:28-30).

Many commentators believe that the passage is dealing with a hypothetical situation. Guthrie says, 'It must be borne in mind that no indication is given ... that any of the readers had committed the kind of apostasy mentioned. The Writer appears to be reflecting on a hypothetical case, although in the nature of the whole argument it must be supposed that it was a real possibility.'[1] But if it is 'a real possibility' it can hardly be just 'hypothetical'.

What we have to understand is that the experiences described in these verses attach, not to the elect, but to some who mimic true believers, being manipulated by the deceiver of souls. Of course, such terms as 'enlightened' and 'partakers of the Holy Spirit' can be (and are) applied to genuine followers of Christ. But that is where the mimicry comes in. Calvin puts it thus: 'God certainly bestows his Spirit of regeneration only on the elect... But I do not see that there is any reason why he should not touch the reprobate with a taste of his grace, or illumine their minds with some glimmerings of his light, or affect them with some sense of his goodness.'[2]

The idea that false discipleship can imitate the real thing is found throughout the New Testament. The parable of the sower is so familiar that we perhaps overlook the fact that it teaches this very truth. The stony ground and the weed-infested soil both yield initial evidence of germination. The seed settles and grows, but not for long. Yet until the seedlings become shrivelled or choked, they look genuine enough. 'We have ... here', remarks Trench, 'a state of mind not stubbornly repelling the truth, but woefully lacking in all deeper earnestness ... whatever was fair and beautiful in Christianity ... had attracted [the hearer] ... but not its answer to the deepest needs of the human heart.'[3]

Similarly, John tells us that the counterfeit disciples of his own day were only *recognised* as such when they eventually defected: 'They went out [from us] that they might be made manifest, that none of them were of us' (1 John 2:18-19). The whole epistle of Jude is devoted to the condemnation of 'certain men [who] have crept in *unnoticed* ... ungodly men who turn the grace of our God into licentiousness and deny the only Lord God and our Lord Jesus Christ' (Jude 4, emphasis added). Judas Iscariot is, of course, the prime example (Luke 22:3). Thus it is wholly consistent with the rest of the New Testament to ascribe to false disciples certain experiences that mimic those of the elect.

These apostates, firstly, were **'once enlightened'**. Notice the past tense. Some see this as a reference to baptism.[4] Whether this is so or not, they had apparently understood the gospel of Christ, at least intellectually. They had approved it mentally. They were no longer ignorant concerning the way of salvation. But somewhere along the line, all this had been lost. They did not *remain* enlightened, but relapsed into the darkness of works-religion and ritualism. This is never true of one born of the Spirit, for the Holy Spirit never ceases to enlighten the child of God concerning Christ (John 16:14-15). The Spirit gives 'wisdom and revelation in the knowledge of [Christ]... the eyes of [our] understanding being enlightened ...' (Eph. 1:17-18).

Secondly, apostates **'have tasted the heavenly gift'**, and become **'partakers of the Holy Spirit'**, having **'tasted the good word of God and the powers of the age to come'**. The word 'tasted', which is repeated, can mean to 'perceive the flavour of, partake of, enjoy, feel, make trial of, experience'.[5] Although the word can be used of genuine spiritual experience (e.g. Ps. 34:8; 1 Peter 2:3) it can equally signify something temporary or superficial. Everything depends on the context. Since the context here is that of 'falling away', the Writer obviously means a temporary enjoyment of heavenly impressions and powerful emotions. Owen points out that the Holy Spirit 'may be received either as unto personal inhabitation or as unto spiritual operations' and 'is present with many as unto powerful operations, with whom he is not present as to gracious inhabitation'.[6] Put simply, this means that the Spirit 'inhabits' the true believer, but may merely 'operate' upon the unregenerate.

The word 'tasted' may be a reference to participation at the Lord's Table.[7] However, it probably has a wider significance. Perhaps these people had been caught up in seasons of outpouring of the Spirit on the early church. They had been there when it was all happening. They had felt the force of heaven, and been deeply impressed by the 'good word' preached in power. Like the stony-ground hearers, they had tasted the joy of the gospel (Matt. 13:20-21). But it was all superficial; there was no root. These various experiences and impressions were not accompanied by regeneration, and no fruit was borne to life eternal. They had 'insulted the Spirit of grace' (10:29).

Falling away (6:4-6 cont.)

'It is impossible', declares the Writer concerning such people, **'if they fall away, to renew them again to repentance, seeing they crucify again for themselves the Son of God and put him to an open shame'** (6:4-6). The word 'fall away' means to deviate from the right path, turn aside, or wander.

Although their overpowering impressions and feelings fall short of genuine spiritual experience, these people are not ignorant of the gospel and its power. When they 'turn aside' from the truth, therefore, they do so knowingly and deliberately. They thus despise the blood of Christ and reject his atoning work. In so doing they effectively 'nail him back upon the cross', counting his sacrifice of no significance as they turn again to their own righteousness.

When those who once professed to know Christ fall away, the name of the Lord Jesus is defamed. He is put to 'open shame' before a scornful world. 'So much for Christianity!' they jeer. 'So much for your precious gospel!' There is nothing theoretical about this, for it happens all the time. The pastor who taught the Scriptures leaves his wife and family to live with another woman; the high-profile preacher and author resigns to cohabit with another man and promote 'Christian homosexuality'; the 'Christian' international cricketer is banned from his sport for life for taking bribes to 'fix' matches. These are all real-life cases that happened within a twelve-month period. What is the effect? Whether high-profile or low-profile, all such events bring sore reproach upon the name of Christ.

Of course, we should never rule out the possibility that such people may truly repent of their sin and return to Christ. But if they are indeed apostate, declares the Writer, it is impossible to renew them to repentance. Not just because they have no desire to repent, but because God's hand is implacably against those who deliberately dishonour his Son. This emerges more clearly in the following verses.

Back to the soil (6:7-8)

Earlier, we referred to the parable of the sower. It is interesting, therefore, that the Writer concludes his condemnation of apostates with a simile closely resembling that parable: **'For the earth which drinks in the rain that often comes upon it, and bears herbs useful for those by whom it is cultivated, receives blessing from God; but if it bears thorns and briars, it is rejected and near to being cursed, whose end is to be burned'** (6:7-8).

These verses tell us two things. Firstly, we see that the fault does not lie in the gospel 'rain', but in the nature of the 'soil' on which it falls. This, of course, is essentially the message of 'the sower' (though there it is seed that falls, not rain). Gospel truth is always health-giving and capable of bearing fruit. But what happens depends on the hearts of those who hear it. In some cases, the heart is good ground, prepared by grace to receive the message of salvation. The result is blessing from God.

In other cases the same rain falls upon soil that harbours seeds of thorns and briars, though this is not at first apparent. Only as the rain germinates the residual seed, do we see the unhappy result. This is a picture of apostasy, which is thus revealed as an *inherent* condition. The apostate was never going to bear fruit to eternal life, whatever initial profession he may have made. Rather, 'They stumble, being disobedient to the word, to which they also were appointed' (1 Peter 2:8). To summarise, therefore, the apostate is not a true believer who has found the way too hard, but a person who was always destined to fall away.

The second lesson to be learned is that apostates will be severely judged. The ground that yields only thorns and briars, says the Writer, is rejected, being fit only for burning. It is, in effect, cursed by God. So also is the apostate. This, ultimately, is why repentance is impossible for such people. The apostate can know no repentance because God has simply closed the door. Repentance is God's gift, but he will not give it to such people (Acts 11:18).

17.
The need for diligence

Please read Hebrews 6:9-12

Having warned his readers in such severe terms in 6:1-8, the Writer now calms them with assurances, while continuing to exhort to diligence. This 'carrot and stick' approach is found throughout Hebrews, where stern warnings and fulsome re-assurance follow in quick succession. Paul employs the same approach in Galatians and, to some extent, in 2 Corinthians and Colossians. It is legitimate, therefore, to use it today. We are prone to the same wanderings and errors as first-century believers. Like them, we need to be alerted to the dangers of spiritual shipwreck — of deviating from the path of righteousness and truth. But we also need encouragement, comfort and reassurance. Both have their place under the new covenant in keeping us diligent in our spiritual work and warfare.

Owen writes, 'The special design of the apostle in [this passage] is to declare his good will towards the Hebrews [and] his judgement of their state and condition.'[1] Their spiritual 'state and condition', of course, is judged according to the new-covenant criteria of faith, fruitfulness and gospel obedience.

Things that accompany salvation (6:9)

Had the Hebrews actually become apostate? Not in the Writer's opinion, for he continues: **'But, beloved, we are confident** [we remain sure] **of better things concerning you, yes, things that accompany salvation, though we speak in this manner'** (6:9). This verse answers two questions. Firstly, it makes even more clear that the various spiritual experiences rehearsed in 6:4-5 do not necessarily 'accompany salvation'. Although these experiences *sound* like the genuine article, they do not necessarily imply the presence of saving faith. Secondly, it emphasises the Writer's conviction that his readers are true Christians, born of the Spirit and the subjects of saving grace. Otherwise, why should he take the trouble to write his epistle? '"Better things"', says Hewitt, 'suggests a fruitful spiritual life in contrast to a life bringing forth thorns and briars, and a destiny of eternal blessedness in contrast to the curse of perdition.'[2]

None of this means that the warnings are unnecessary. The Writer maintains his right to **'speak in this manner'**, and actually returns to the subject in Hebrews 10. Why? For one thing, in the final analysis, apostasy happens to *individuals*, not groups. We often speak of 'apostate churches', but they are only so because their leaders and members apostatise individually. Among any group of professing Christians, therefore, some individuals will be tempted to stray, and the only sure way to warn such people is to warn everyone. Secondly, even true believers sometimes need to be spurred into action. We easily become 'sluggish' in our Christian walk (6:12), and shock tactics, like these warnings of apostasy, are not without their value.

Nevertheless, the Writer's words are tender: **'Beloved ... we are confident of ... you.'** The Writer does not wish to be seen as a taskmaster, whip in hand. Rather, he adopts the role of a concerned parent, worried about his spiritual children and anxious for their welfare. Although the New Testament writers often rebuke us forcefully, they are careful always to be 'speaking the truth in love' (Eph. 4:15). We need to follow their example in applying spiritual or church discipline. Too often we err, either by withholding the truth for fear of offending people, or by dealing harshly with them. All discipline must have as its objective the restoration of the offender (Gal. 6:1-2) and be applied with this in mind. The New Testament knows nothing of the unfeeling harshness and unforgiving spirit that often passes for church discipline today.

God is just (6:10)

What persuaded the Writer that his readers had really been saved? He gives two reasons, which are two sides of a single coin. Firstly, they had borne fruit in their spiritual walk. Secondly, God would be unjust to forget this and will not do so. He writes, **'For God is not unjust to forget your work and labour of love which you have shown toward his name, in that you have ministered to the saints, and do minister'** (6:10).

The church to which this epistle was written had performed 'a labour of love' towards their fellow believers ('the saints'). Moreover, this was not just an enthusiastic phase through which they had passed, but an ongoing feature of their corporate life. They had ministered (served) in the past, and continued to do so in the present. Such ministrations are, says the New Testament, evidence of spiritual life. We see this clearly in John's first epistle. 'We know that we have passed from death to life, because we love the brethren', asserts the apostle (1 John 3:14). It was Christ's 'new commandment' that his followers should 'love one another' as he had loved them (John 13:34).

It is important that their ministrations were a 'labour of love', for without love all our efforts and activities are worthless in the sight of God. 'Though I bestow all my goods to feed the poor ... but have not love, it profits me nothing', declares Paul (1 Cor. 13:3). Furthermore, works of compassion and kindness do not make a person righteous in the eyes of God. We cannot be saved by works. But when the works flow from a heart of love, they reveal their source as that 'love of God [which] has been poured out in our hearts by the Holy Spirit who was given to us' (Rom. 5:5). Needless to say, the Holy Spirit is given only to those who are truly God's elect children and heirs (Gal. 4:6-7).

This is why the Writer, discerning not only the outward acts of kindness and mercy, but also the source and nature of those acts, can write with such confidence about his readers. Furthermore, since their works are the genuine product of grace, he can assert that 'God is not unjust to forget your work and labour of love.' Calvin cautions against finding here any doctrine of salvation by works: 'God is not paying us a debt that he owes us [on account of our works]', he explains, 'but he is keeping the promise he has already made ... he looks not so much on our works as on his grace in our works... He is not oblivious of our works, because he recognises in them himself and the work of his Spirit.'[3]

God never forgets what his children do. That is a sobering thought, but also an encouragement. Even human parents remember fondly the trivial actions of their offspring. Many of us, as adults, have listened while our parents recounted things we did as children — sometimes to our acute embarrassment. How much more will God remember! And in so far as those actions have glorified his name, even if they amounted to very little in our own sight, God remembers graciously. Jesus declared: 'Whoever gives one of these little ones only a cup of cold water in the name of a disciple, assuredly, I say to you, he shall by no means lose his reward' (Matt. 10:42). Were it otherwise, God would be unjust. But he is not unjust, and must therefore deal kindly with his people. It has been well said that 'God is no man's debtor.'

Desire and diligence (6:11-12)

This being so, the Writer expresses his wish: **'We desire that each one of you show the same diligence to the full assurance of hope until the end, that you do not become sluggish, but imitate those who through faith and patience inherit the promises'** (6:11-12). The word 'desire' is a strong word indicating longing or yearning. The Writer reveals the true heart of a pastor as he exhorts and encourages his readers. As Lane remarks, 'Pastoral concern for his friends is evident in every line of this extended section.'[4]

He desires that 'each one' should give attention to their spiritual health. There is here, perhaps, a hint of what we suggested earlier — that the Writer's concern was not so much for the whole company but for certain persons within the church. Whether or not this is the case, it does remind us that, in the last analysis, we are individually responsible for our standing before God. It is not enough that the church leaders should 'watch out for [our] souls' (13:17) — 'each one' must accept his or her spiritual responsibilities.

What are those responsibilities? The Writer lists five things: to show diligence; to seek assurance; to persevere to the end; to watch against 'sluggishness'; and to imitate those who have gone patiently and triumphantly before us. Who said the Christian life was undemanding?

'Diligence,' firstly, is the key to fruitfulness. As Peter explains, '... giving all diligence, add to your faith virtue, to virtue knowledge, to knowledge self-control, to self-control perseverance, to perseverance godliness, to godliness brotherly kindness, and to brotherly kindness love. For if these things are yours and abound, you will be *neither barren nor unfruitful* in the knowledge of our Lord Jesus Christ' (2 Peter 1:5-8, emphasis added).

Secondly, diligence is also essential if we are to find **'full assurance'**. Peter continues: 'For he who lacks these things is short-sighted, even to blindness, and has forgotten that he was cleansed from his old sins. Therefore, brethren, be even *more diligent to make your call and election sure*, for if you do these things you will never stumble; for so an entrance will be supplied to you abundantly into the everlasting kingdom of our Lord and Saviour Jesus Christ' (2 Peter 1:5-11, emphasis added). This does not mean, of course, that 'doing these things' *secures* our call or our election. It is God's prerogative both to choose us in Christ and call us to Christ (Eph. 1:4; Rom. 8:30). What it does mean, however, is that our personal assurance that God has chosen and called us is confirmed and made abundant as we bear fruit to God. The fruit is the produce of the indwelling Spirit, but the diligence must be our own.

Perseverance is the third responsibility. We are to show diligence **'until the end'**, says the Writer. Again, Hebrews accords with other Scriptures. God grants eternal life, declares Paul, 'to those who by patient continuance in doing good seek for glory, honour and immortality' (Rom. 2:7). Jesus says, 'He who endures to the end shall be saved' (Matt. 24:13), and promises the blessings of his kingdom to the one 'who overcomes and keeps my works until the end' (Rev. 2:26). Some have found this difficult to reconcile with the believer's security in Christ ('Once saved, always saved'). If endurance is needed for final salvation, how can we be sure that we are saved *now*?

The question is based on a misunderstanding. The elect, once born again, are indeed right to feel secure. So much so, that God gives them his Holy Spirit as an 'earnest', or guarantee, that they have been purchased by his death and will most certainly enter glory (see Eph. 1:13). These must and will 'endure to the end'. But, as we have already seen, there will be

'stony-ground' hearers who endure only for a while. Endurance to the end (of life) and faithfulness 'unto death' are characteristics of the true believer. His endurance is the *proof* that
he does indeed possess eternal life and will never perish (John
10:28).

Perseverance, therefore, is a characteristic of the truly saved
person, but is not accomplished without effort on that person's part. Christians are not automatons, moved to continuance by some external force. Rather, by the grace and power
of the indwelling Spirit, our hearts and wills are motivated to
willing obedience, despite the opposition of the flesh (that is,
the sin that dwells within our mortal minds and bodies — Rom.
7:17-18; Gal. 5:17).

Imitation (6:12 cont.)

Our fourth responsibility is to avoid becoming **'sluggish'**
(6:12). The word means slow, indolent, dull or languid. These
are the symptoms of spiritual ill-health, a disease of the soul
that, if neglected, could prove fatal. The exhortation is given
us so that we may be alert to such symptoms whenever they
arise and be quick to deal with them. The Song of Solomon
provides us with an example.

'I sleep', says the Shulamite, 'but my heart is awake; It is
the voice of my beloved! He knocks, saying, "Open for me,
my sister, my love..."' But the sleepy woman replies: 'I have
taken off my robe; how can I put it on again? I have washed
my feet; how can I defile them?' She continues: 'My beloved
put his hand by the latch of the door, and my heart yearned for
him.' But it was too late: 'I arose to open for my beloved...
But my beloved had turned away and was gone... I sought
him, but I could not find him; I called him, but he gave me no

answer' (S. of S. 5:2-6). If we are spiritually lazy and sleepy, we too shall forfeit fellowship with Christ and the comforts of his presence.

What can we do to correct our tendency to slothfulness in the Christian life? We should fulfil the fifth responsibility, namely, to 'imitate those who through faith and patience inherit the promises' (6:12). Earlier, we considered the wrong kind of imitation, in which the apostate mimics the true believer. But here is a *commendable* imitation, in which believers both study and follow the example of those who have gone trium- phantly before. The full value and power of this exhortation will be seen when we come to the eleventh chapter of He- brews, where the Writer displays the 'gallery of faith'. There he sets out the struggles and victories of past generations, people who teach us how to 'run with endurance the race that is set before us, looking unto Jesus, the author and finisher of our faith' (12:2). Those Old Testament believers never saw the coming Christ, but still believed in him and embraced his lordship and his kingdom. How much more privileged are we, who live in the full light of the new covenant!

'By faith and patience', we are told, believers **'inherit** [are inheriting] **the promises'** (6:12). Wilson comments: 'The Greek present tense can have a durative force, "are inherit- ing", which would lend colour to ... [the] suggestion that our author has the example of contemporaries in mind.'[5] Thus the Writer seems to embrace here not only the Old Testament saints but also the Hebrews' contemporaries, who were making bet- ter progress than they.

This is almost the first reference in the epistle to the prom- ises of God, the only preceding mention being in 4:1. The present reference relates to the promises made to Abraham, as the verses that follow make clear. Why is this important? Because this quiet introduction of the concept of 'promise' actually launches the epistle into its remaining major themes. These are (1) the new covenant in Christ and (2) the necessity of faith as the means by which we participate in that covenant.

Although Hebrews never uses the term 'covenant of promise', the concept is always present. We are told, for example, that Christ 'is the Mediator of the *new covenant* ... that those who are called may receive *the promise of the eternal inheritance*' (9:15, emphasis added). We may compare this with Paul's assertion in Galatians that '... the law [of Moses], which was four hundred and thirty years later, cannot annul the covenant that was confirmed before [to Abraham] by God in Christ. For if the inheritance is of the law, it is no longer of promise; but God gave it to Abraham by promise' (Gal. 3:17-18). As we proceed in Hebrews, we shall see how the covenant of promise blossoms into the new covenant in Christ, displacing and replacing the old covenant made at Sinai.

18.
The unchanging purpose

Please read Hebrews 6:13-20

At the close of the previous chapter we saw how the Writer introduces the promise-covenant that God made with Abraham. He now proceeds to enlarge upon the glorious distinctives of this covenant.

In discussing the old covenant and the new covenant, we often forget that there ever was a 'covenant of promise'. Yet this was the first covenant between God and man that pointed unmistakably to Christ. God made this covenant with Abraham, and confirmed it to Isaac and Jacob (Gen. 12:1-3; 15; 17:1-8; 26:3-4; 28:13-14). There had been earlier covenants, such as the promise that the woman's Seed (that is, Christ) would bruise the serpent's head, and the promise to Noah that the earth would never again be overwhelmed by water (Gen. 3:15; 9:9-11). But Scripture gives a special place to the covenant with Abraham because it so completely foreshadows the coming Christ. He himself declared: 'Your father Abraham rejoiced to see my day, and he saw it and was glad' (John 8:56). The covenant of promise was, in effect, the new covenant 'in waiting'.

The magnificent promise (6:13-17)

The Writer, therefore, is anxious to underline the profound significance of the covenant with Abraham: **'When God made** a promise to Abraham, because he could swear by no one greater, he swore by himself, saying, "Surely blessing I will bless you, and multiplying I will multiply you." And so, after he had patiently endured, he obtained the promise' (6:13-15). This verse invites us to consider two things: firstly the greatness of the promise, and secondly the manner of its appropriation.

With regard to the latter, the Writer is simply illustrating the principle already stated in verse 12. Abraham, the revered father of the Jewish nation, 'obtained the promise' when he saw his descendants multiply following the deliverance of Isaac (the context requires that, in this instance, the promise cannot refer to the birth of Isaac[1]). But Abraham obtained the promise only after years of patient trust in the promise of God. The Hebrews ought to follow his example of perseverance.

But the Writer's chief point, which he proceeds to develop, is that the promise itself is infallible and magnificent beyond comparison. During his lifetime, Abraham received only a partial and earthly fulfilment of that promise. But God's covenant also set before him a glorious and eternal hope, a hope into which all true believers now enter (as we shall see in 6:18-19). In short, the promise to Abraham was not merely that his seed would become a great nation, but that his Seed (namely Christ; Gal. 3:16) would bring blessing to *all* the nations of the earth (Gen. 12:1-3). Moreover, that blessing would be found not in the temporal land of promise but in the everlasting joy of salvation and glory.

A judge today is often called upon to 'construe' a contract or legal document — that is, to interpret its true meaning. In the same way, the Writer places an important 'construction' on the terms of the covenant of promise. He identifies not only a promise but also an oath — 'God ... swore by himself.' The promise is clear enough: 'I will bless you.' But where is the oath?

It is found in Genesis 22:16: 'Then the Angel of the LORD called to Abraham a second time out of heaven, and said: "*By myself I have sworn*, says the LORD, because you have done this thing, and have not withheld your son, your only son; blessing I will bless you, and multiplying I will multiply your descendants as the stars of the heaven and as the sand which is on the seashore ... and in your seed all the nations of the earth shall be blessed' (emphasis added).

The repetition, 'blessing I will bless you', signifies emphasis, and a particularly strong one at that. By placing the word 'blessing' first in the sentence, the Lord puts his full weight and credibility behind the promise.

The Writer presses home his point: **'For men indeed swear by the greater, and an oath for confirmation is for them an end of all dispute. Thus God, determining to show more abundantly to the heirs of promise the immutability of his counsel, confirmed it by an oath'** (6:16-17). In swearing an oath *at all*, God provided strong confirmation that his promise was true and irrevocable. In swearing *by himself*, he puts the issue beyond challenge or dispute, for there is none greater than God.

John Brown points out that God's promise *alone* was sufficient ground for confidence and that 'The declaration was not in reality made more certain by the addition of an oath, but [the oath] ... was calculated to give a deeper impression of its certainty.'[2] Why should the sovereign Lord go to such extremes? Why, indeed! The answer is as remarkable as it is reassuring. He was determined 'to show more abundantly' that his purpose to redeem believing sinners to himself is immutable. Such massive condescension ought to leave us speechless, in wonder and in worship.

The final beneficiaries of this condescension are called here 'the heirs of promise'. God's covenant of promise, therefore, has all the characteristics of a testament or will, in which the donor makes a disposition in favour of his heirs. The disposition is the Father's 'immutable counsel', a purposive intent of pure grace, by which he guarantees his Son a bride for all eternity. The heirs are the elect, chosen in Christ from before the foundation of the world (Eph. 1:4). They will constitute the bride, the redeemed and glorified church.

Strong consolation (6:18)

By confirming his promise in this way, the Lord gives his children deep and abiding comfort ('strong consolation'). By making both a promise and an oath, God reassures our hearts **'by two immutable things, in which it is impossible for God to lie [that] we might have strong consolation'** (6:18). The Hebrews were not alone in their need for such comfort. Doubts and questions often afflict the people of God, engaged as they are in lifelong spiritual warfare. Am I truly saved? Do things always 'work together for good to those who love God'? (Rom. 8:28). Does my labour for the Lord make any difference? Will I endure to the end? Is death really the gate of heaven for the follower of Christ? It is to such questions that these verses are addressed. God cannot lie! He has promised an inheritance to the heirs of salvation. He has confirmed the promise with an oath. What more can he say or do to convince us?

> How firm a foundation, ye saints of the Lord,
> Is laid for your faith in his excellent Word!
> What more can he say than to you he has said,
> You who unto Jesus for refuge have fled?

The anonymous hymn reminds us that the fortunate recipients of this comfort are those **'who have fled for refuge to lay**

hold of the hope set before us' (6:18). Since the ancient promise is finally fulfilled in Christ, only those can benefit who have fled to him for salvation. 'There is no other name under heaven given among men by which we must be saved' (Acts 4:12). We flee to Christ from God's wrath upon our sin; we abandon our trust in human effort and outward religion; we drop everything in which we once trusted and run to Christ. In the words of Augustus Toplady:

> Nothing in my hand I bring,
> Simply to thy cross I cling.
> Naked, come to thee for dress,
> Helpless, look to thee for grace;
> Foul, I to the fountain fly;
> Wash me, Saviour, or I die.

In fleeing to Christ, however, we do more than find refuge from judgement — we lay hold of a hope. By 'hope', of course, Scripture never implies uncertainty, as in our modern usage of the word. Biblical 'hope' means 'future certainty', a certainty that derives, not from any human source or confidence, but from the immutability of God's promise, certified by oath.

What, then, is this hope? It is the expectation of glory and eternal life 'through the redemption that is in Christ Jesus' (Rom. 3:24).

An anchor for the soul (6:19-20)

And what benefit such hope provides! **'This hope we have as an anchor of the soul, both sure and steadfast, and which enters the inner part behind the veil, where the forerunner has entered for us, even Jesus'** (6:19-20). As Paul emphasises in Romans 5:5, 'Hope does not disappoint [deceive, or put to shame]'. The hope God sets before us is no mirage that will fade from our sight even as we grasp at it. All too often, hopes based on human promises and prospects prove illusory. As the old proverb (Palladas, *fl.* A.D. 400) says, 'There is many a slip twixt the cup and the lip.' Such is the human condition that things seldom work out the way we expect or wish.

But the hope that is built on God's promise in Christ is altogether different. It is a veritable anchor for the soul! The metaphor conjures up pictures of a small ship on a stormy sea. Mountainous waves crash over the tiny craft as it is tossed around like a cork. Yet, miraculously, the ship survives. A strong hidden force restrains it from destruction, from being dashed to pieces on the jagged rocks. It has an anchor, resilient and firm. And so do we, declares the Writer, if we have fled to Christ for refuge. Our anchor is our hope in the unchangeable promises of God. This is more than poetic imagery; it is the reality experienced daily by every true child of God. It is important, therefore, that we should not let go of this all-sufficient hope.

But an anchor is only as safe as its lodgement. A ship will drag its anchor unless that anchor has grappled on to a rock or other solid foundation. How secure is our anchor of hope? Highly so, for it 'enters the inner part behind the veil, where the forerunner has entered for us, even Jesus'. The 'inner part' is the holy place of the tabernacle, which contained the ark of the covenant and lay beyond the second veil. It is sometimes called the 'holiest-of-all'. Hagner points out that 'this is the first occurrence [in the epistle] of imagery that will be vitally important in chapters 9 and 10',[3] where the tabernacle and its old-covenant ministration are used extensively to illustrate the high-priestly ministry of Christ.

The Writer is telling us that the security of our hope in Christ flows from his presence and work within the holiest place, that is, in the presence of God. It is based, therefore, on

Jesus' 'enthronement and atonement' which we considered at length when commenting on 4:14-16. Christ 'has embedded [the anchor] in the immovable ground of the presence and throne and character of God', comments Gooding.[4] The divine kingship and efficacious work of our great High Priest is the basis of our security. There can be no greater safety.

The order of Melchizedek (6:20 cont.)

Back in Hebrews 5:5-11 the Writer cited Psalm 110:4 and applied it to Christ: 'You are a priest for ever according to the order of Melchizedek.' Having introduced the holy place, with its overtones of high-priestly ministry, he now returns to this theme using almost identical terms — he refers to Jesus **'having become High Priest for ever according to the order of Melchizedek'** (6:20). There is a sense in which Melchizedek is the Writer's 'secret weapon' against the Judaisers' 'back to Moses' teaching. He attaches enormous importance to this obscure and mysterious person. By doing so he underlines the fact that Jesus Christ did not come from the family of Aaron, and thus could not be a priest of the old covenant. He belongs to an altogether different priestly order, as befits his new-covenant ministry.

But what order is that? Is there any legitimate priesthood apart from Aaron and his sons? Has the Writer forgotten how jealously God guarded that priesthood against usurpers and interlopers? Does Scripture provide evidence of any other priestly order? Yes, indeed, declares the psalmist: 'The LORD said to my Lord, "Sit at my right hand till I make your enemies your footstool" [and] "You are a priest for ever after the order of Melchizedek"' (Ps. 110:1, 4). Here again we see the 'priest upon his throne', the King-Priest seated at the right hand of God the Father.

Even before the Writer begins to elaborate his teaching on Melchizedek (as he does at length in Hebrew 7) he sketches the outlines of this radical priesthood. Firstly, unlike Aaron and his sons, the members of this order are kings as well as priests! Remember Jeremiah's words that 'A glorious high throne from the beginning is the place of our sanctuary' (Jer. 17:12), and Zechariah's prophecy that 'the Branch' would be 'a priest upon his throne' (Zech. 6:12-13).

Secondly, their priesthood is not the temporal office of the old covenant, but one that endures 'for ever'. Only such a priesthood befits the Son of God who 'ever lives to make intercession' for 'those who come to God through him' (7:25). These key features, then, mark out the order of Melchizedek and set it for ever apart from the priesthood of Sinai and the law. In Part 3 of this commentary we shall see the full outworking of this dramatic teaching.

Part 3:
The new covenant in Christ

19.
An eternal priesthood

Please read Hebrews 7:1-10

The subject of Part 3 of this commentary is the new covenant, mediated by a new High Priest, 'Jesus Christ the Son of God'. The Writer has already introduced the subject by implication earlier in the epistle, but it is only now that he launches into a full exposition of this, its central theme. He argues powerfully that a new priesthood signals a new covenant. You cannot graft Christ's high-priesthood on to that of the Mosaic order. Nor can the Mosaic priesthood survive under the 'better covenant' established in Christ's atoning blood. There *is* a new covenant and a new priesthood, and former things have passed away.

In the passage before us, the Writer emphasises the 'otherness' and transcendence of Christ's priesthood by tracing it back to the priestly order of Melchizedek. This Old Testament character is thus established as a 'type' of Christ — especially in respect of his priestly and kingly offices, and his eternal existence. The typology is rich with significance, for it establishes more firmly than ever that Christ *alone* provides the sinner with righteousness and peace.

Righteousness and peace (7:1-2)

The psalmist declares that 'Mercy and truth have met together; righteousness and peace have kissed' (Ps. 85:10). This happy confluence of righteousness and peace is characteristic of the gospel of Christ, for he is both our righteousness and our peace (1 Cor. 1:30; Eph. 2:14).

These new-covenant blessings are prefigured in Melchizedek and especially by the titles given to him. **'For this Melchizedek, king of Salem, priest of the Most High God, who met Abraham returning from the slaughter of the kings and blessed him, to whom also Abraham gave a tenth part of all, [is] first being translated "king of righteousness" and then also king of Salem, meaning "king of peace"'** (7:1-2). The reference is, of course, to the events recorded in Genesis 14:18-20, which occurred after Abraham rescued Lot from the marauding armies of certain local kings.

The Writer could have treated 'Melchizedek' as just a name, and Salem (later Jerusalem[1]) as simply the region over which he ruled. Instead, he sees foreshadowed in these titles the primary benefits enjoyed by believers under the new covenant — righteousness through faith in Christ, and peace with God. That Melchizedek was 'king' in respect of these blessings implies that Christ is both rich and sovereign in bestowing them on his people.

He was not only a king, however — he was also 'priest of the Most High God'. Guthrie comments that 'the title here given to God ... draws attention to the exalted character of God', and points out that 'any priesthood is evaluated according to the status of the Deity who is served'.[2] A transcendent God implies an exalted priesthood. Aaron and his sons served the same high God, of course. But the Writer is concerned, firstly, to establish that Melchizedek did not serve some lesser deity and, secondly, that his priesthood reflected the highest attributes of the true and living God.

Who was Melchizedek? (7:3)

Continuing his description, the Writer tells us that Melchizedek was **'without father, without mother, without genealogy, having neither beginning of days nor end of life, but [being] made like the Son of God, remains a priest continually'** (7:3). These statements raise an intriguing question.

Who was this mysterious person? Some have suggested that Melchizedek was none other than the pre-incarnate Christ. McCaul writes, 'Cunaeus ... believes, as Ewald does, and I do, that Melchizedek was the second person in the Ever Blessed Trinity, the divine Angel of the Lord, who continually appeared to the Fathers under the Old Testament dispensation ... if Melchizedek was "without beginning of days or end of life", but "abideth a priest continually", how can it be believed of him that he was a mere mortal? ... Melchizedek, as the Divine *Logos*, existed from eternity.'[3]

In support of this position, the Old Testament records a number of 'theophanies' (appearances of God) in which God manifested himself in human form. When three 'men' visited Abraham before the destruction of Sodom and Gomorrah, we are told that 'The LORD appeared to him by the terebinth trees of Mamre' (Gen. 18:1). Two of the men eventually departed for Sodom and were, in fact, the angels to whom Lot gave refuge.

But the third 'man' was 'the LORD' himself, who disclosed to Abraham his intention to destroy the wicked cities (Gen. 18:16-22). Another theophany occurred when Joshua met 'the Commander of the army of the LORD' prior to the assault on Jericho (Josh. 5:13-15). In yet another example, 'the Angel of the LORD' appeared to Gideon, and we read that 'The LORD turned to him and said, "Go in this might of yours and you shall save Israel... Have I not sent you?"' (Judg. 6:11-24). In all these cases, it was the Second Person of the Godhead who appeared, for 'No one has seen God [the Father] at any time. The only begotten Son, who is in the bosom of the Father, he has declared him' (John 1:18).

If Melchizedek's brief appearance on the stage of biblical history was a theophany, then the language used here in Hebrews is fully appropriate. He would, indeed, have been 'without father, without mother, without genealogy, having neither beginning of days nor end of life, but made like the Son of God'. Some commentators adopt this interpretation, but the greater number reject it. Melchizedek, say the majority, was a real historical person (some go as far as to identify him with Shem) who simply typifies Christ. Calvin asserts: 'It is certain that [Melchizedek] was begotten by parents, but the apostle is not discussing him here as an individual man, but rather setting him forth as the type of Christ.'[4]

According to this interpretation, the Writer uses the absence of any *record* of parentage, genealogy or death as symbolic of the eternal nature of Christ. Lineage was all-important to a priest under the Mosaic covenant, and was the seal of authenticity (see, e.g., Neh. 7:63-65). The absence of any such authentication for Melchizedek implies that his priestly authority, like Christ's, lay within himself. As Guthrie says, 'He stands mysteriously apart from all need to establish his genealogy.'[5] In support of this view of Melchizedek, as a type of Christ rather than Christ himself, it can be further argued that he was a local king and belonged to a priestly 'order', neither of which fits with a fleeting theophany.

On the other hand, the statement that Melchizedek was 'made like the Son of God' resembles the description applied to another undoubted theophany, when Nebuchadnezzar saw one whose 'form ... is like the Son of God' walking in the midst of the fiery furnace with Shadrach, Meshach and Abed-Nego (Dan. 3:25). The point here is that the use of a simile ('*like* the Son of God') does not necessarily rule out a theophany. The present writer is sympathetic towards the theophanic view, but would not wish to be dogmatic on the question.

Either way, the Writer seeks to establish that, unlike the priests of the Mosaic covenant, Melchizedek (and thus the Christ he represents) 'remains a priest continually' (7:3). Christ's priesthood is eternal and unchanging, and therein lies the believer's security.

Homage to Christ (7:4-10)

Melchizedek's priesthood was not only different from that of the Mosaic order — it was altogether superior. The Writer sets out his argument in a long passage which we cannot easily divide: **'Now consider how great this man was, to whom even the patriarch Abraham gave a tenth of the spoils. And indeed those who are of the sons of Levi, who receive the priesthood, have a commandment to receive tithes from the people according to the law, that is, from their brethren, though they have come from the loins of Abraham; but he whose genealogy is not derived from them received tithes from Abraham and blessed him who had the promises. Now beyond all contradiction the lesser is blessed by the better. Here mortal men receive tithes, but there he receives them, of whom it is witnessed that he lives. Even Levi, who receives tithes, paid tithes through Abraham, so to speak, for he was still in the loins of his father when Melchizedek met him'** (7:4-10).

This passage is almost self-explanatory. The transcendence of the order of Melchizedek is here witnessed by three things. Firstly, the great patriarch Abraham rendered homage to him by giving tithes and receiving a blessing. Melchizedek, therefore, is greater than Abraham. Secondly, since Levi was 'still in the loins' of Abraham when all this happened, the Aaronic priesthood, figuratively, also rendered homage to Melchizedek (and by implication submitted to his priestly order). Melchizedek, therefore, is greater than Aaron. Thirdly, unlike the priests of the Mosaic covenant, Melchizedek was not a mortal man but one who lives for ever (this can be taken either literally, according to the theophanic view, or typologically). Either way, Melchizedek pictures Christ.

The upshot of all this is that Christ, having been appointed a priest for ever after the order of Melchizedek, is necessarily superior to the priests of the old covenant. Indeed, his priesthood transcends the Mosaic order in every way. The Hebrews, therefore, must look to Jesus, not to the law, for access to God, because only Christ has an eternal priesthood. They must learn that 'A glorious high throne from the beginning is the place of our sanctuary' — the throne of God and of the Lamb (Jer. 17:12).

Many so-called Christian churches today hanker after the rituals of the old covenant. They create 'priests' who seek to mimic Aaron and his order — by their dress, by their priestly 'offerings' and by interposing themselves between God and the people. They even seek to perpetuate their priesthood, not by physical descent but by something remarkably similar — an 'apostolic succession' in which priestly authority is passed from generation to generation. Tragically, they seem never to have heard of Melchizedek. Or if they have heard, they do not understand.

20.
An endless life

Please read Hebrews 7:11-19

The Writer begins to tighten his argument. In this important passage he shows that there is an indissoluble link between a priestly order and the law (or covenant) over which it presides. His main propositions are, firstly, that Jesus Christ has inaugurated a new priesthood; secondly, that a new priesthood necessitates a new law; and thirdly, that Christ's high-priesthood can have nothing to do with the law of Moses (the old covenant) but must presage a new and better hope.

The Hebrews were living in a twilight world in which they were seeking to graft the new covenant in Christ on to the Mosaic covenant. They believed in Christ, but clung to the law, fearful of abandoning what was familiar and comforting. But, insists the Writer, we cannot live under two covenants or follow two laws. We cannot mingle the old and the new. The very fact that Christ has been appointed a priest according to the order of Melchizedek, and not that of Aaron, demonstrates that there has been a change of priesthood and therefore a change of law or covenant. 'So closely was [the Levitical priesthood] connected with the law', says Hywel Jones, 'that there could not be any change in it without the law being affected.'[1]

A further need (7:11-12)

'Therefore', asks the Writer, **'if perfection were through the Levitical priesthood (for under it the people received the law), what further need was there that another priest should rise according to the order of Melchizedek, and not be called according to the order of Aaron?'** (7:11).

Christ's designation as a priest according to the order of Melchizedek occurs, of course, in Psalm 110:4. It thus post-dates the giving of the law on Sinai by hundreds of years. The Mosaic system was well established, its priesthood ongoing, its governance of the Jewish nation unchallenged. But suddenly the psalmist unveils a new priesthood, established by a solemn oath from God himself.

Why? Such an innovation would be totally unnecessary if the Levitical priesthood were able to make men perfect in the sight of God by its offerings and intercessions. Therefore, concludes the Writer, the old-covenant priesthood was obviously *not* adequate to meet the needs of sinners. A new priesthood, established on different foundations, was required.

But it is not only the Levitical priesthood that was found wanting; it was the Mosaic law in its totality: **'For the priesthood being changed, of necessity there is also a change of the law'** (7:12). The people had 'received' that law under the imperfect Levitical priesthood and the law was subject to the same imperfection as the priesthood itself. Bruce comments: 'Paul and our author are agreed that the law was a temporary dispensation of God, valid only until Christ came to inaugurate the age of perfection.'[2]

Some commentators see 'the law' here as referring only to the 'ceremonial law', that is, the priestly ordinances and sacrifices, rather than the whole law of Moses. However, it is difficult to justify any such distinction on *biblical* grounds. Brown is clear on the point, citing Ebrard with approval: 'The law in every respect opened up and imposed a number of problems without solving any of them. It set up in the decalogue the ideal of a holy life, but it gave no power to realise that ideal. By the law of sacrifice it awakened the consciousness of the necessity of an atonement; but it provided no true, valid offering for sin. In the institution of the priesthood it held forth the necessity of a representation of the sinner before God, but it gave no priest able to save men [to the uttermost]. In short, it left everything unfinished.'[3]

The statement that the people received the law 'under' the priesthood of Aaron and his sons cannot refer to the giving of the law at Sinai, since the Levitical priesthood was set up *by* that law, not the other way around. The Writer's point is, rather, that the people received the *administration* of the Mosaic law at the hands of the priests.

But in what sense was the Mosaic law imperfect? Surely it had been given by God and should therefore be without fault? Paul answers the point clearly. 'The law is holy', he declares, 'and the commandment holy and just and good' (Rom. 7:12). However, he goes on to say that there was something 'the law could not do in that it was weak through [on account of] the flesh' (Rom. 8:3). That is, the law *cannot save*. Salvation can only come through the atoning work of Christ, applied in regenerating power by the Spirit (Rom. 8:3-4). The problem with the law was not any intrinsic imperfection, but the fact that it required human obedience.

Such obedience is never forthcoming, since all men are 'in the flesh', that is, they are sinners incapable of meeting the demands of God's law. Thus the law is inadequate, not in itself, but because of the weakness of fallen human nature ('the flesh'). If men are to be made perfect in God's sight, something *entirely different* is required, based on new principles that do not depend on the weak link of human obedience. This requirement is met by the new covenant (or law, see 7:12) in Christ.

The power of an endless life (7:13-17)

The Writer feels it appropriate to provide further evidence that a new priesthood has, indeed, been inaugurated. He advances two arguments. Firstly, Christ was born of the tribe of Judah, not Levi, and could not, therefore, belong to the Levitical priesthood. Secondly, being appointed according to the order of Melchizedek, Christ's priesthood derives its authority, not from an external law, but from his own glorious person.

On the first issue, the Writer asserts: **'For he of whom these things are spoken belongs to another tribe, from which no man has officiated at the altar. For it is evident that our Lord arose from Judah, of which tribe Moses spoke nothing concerning priesthood'** (7:13-14). The 'things spoken' refer both to Psalm 110:4 and to the original story of Melchizedek in Genesis. The Writer is clear that these Old Testament passages speak explicitly of Christ. It is not that the ancient scriptures just *happen* to illustrate the person and work of Jesus Christ. Rather, they were written expressly to testify to the coming Christ and 'the new covenant in [his] blood' (1 Cor. 11:25).

Once again, we see that the whole burden of the Old Testament is to reveal Christ, albeit in shadow and type. We need to apply this principle today as we seek to read and expound the Old Testament Scriptures, for unless we find Christ in those Scriptures we shall err both in our understanding and use of them.

Jesus' membership of the royal tribe of Judah reminds us again of his kingship: 'He will be great, and will be called the Son of the Highest; and the Lord God will give him the throne of his father David', promised the angel Gabriel. 'And he will reign over the house of Jacob for ever, and of his kingdom there will be no end' (Luke 1:32-33). Although the Writer is still preoccupied with Christ's priesthood, he never loses sight of the throne. As a compass needle returns unerringly to its pole, so the Writer's thoughts return continually to the priest *upon his throne*.

And, indeed, this is exactly what happens as the Writer turns to his second point, for he continues: **'And it is yet far more evident if, in the likeness of Melchizedek, there arises another priest who has come, not according to the law of a fleshly commandment, but according to the power of an endless life. For he testifies: "You are a priest for ever according to the order of Melchizedek"'** (7:15-17). Melchizedek was not only the king-priest, but also (either literally or typologically) enjoyed 'an endless life'. He thus typifies the Son of God, whose throne is eternal in the heavens and whose reign brings righteousness and peace to needy sinners like ourselves. The 'endless [indestructible] life' of Christ is intrinsic to his priesthood, being the 'power' that underwrites the gift of eternal life bestowed upon his people.

The Mosaic priesthood operated under 'the law of a fleshly commandment'. That is, the old covenant depended on the obedience of men. It was an outward rule of life that addressed itself to the natural man (man in the flesh). That is why it displayed **'weakness and unprofitableness'** (7:18), for we know that 'The natural man does not receive the things of the Spirit of God, for they are foolishness to him; neither can he know them, because they are spiritually discerned' (1 Cor. 2:14). The law itself 'is spiritual', explains Paul, 'but [we are] carnal, sold under sin' (Rom. 7:14). Being an external (or 'fleshly') commandment, the law is not capable of inducing a spiritual response in those who are 'dead in trespasses and sins' (Eph. 2:1). That is why it is weak and can make **'nothing perfect'** (7:19).

Once again we are reminded here of a vital principle, namely, that true Christianity is essentially *spiritual* in character. It can never consist in the outward observance of religion, or good works empowered by human nature (the flesh). Millions of professing 'Christians' worldwide fail to grasp this, and their leaders encourage them in their delusions. Genuine Christianity only exists where people have been brought to life spiritually by the gracious work of the Spirit of God. Only such people possess the spiritual sight to understand the things of God, and the spiritual power to respond to them appropriately. In a derivative sense, they share with Christ 'the power of an endless life', being indwelt and empowered by his Spirit (Rom. 8:11).

A better hope (7:18-19)

The Writer draws his conclusions: **'For on the one hand there is an annulling of the former commandment because of its weakness and unprofitableness, for the law made nothing perfect; on the other hand, there is the bringing in of a better hope, through which we draw near to God'** (7:18-19).

Thus the new priesthood creates an entirely new situation. As the Levitical priesthood has been made redundant by the coming of the Priest-King Christ Jesus, so also 'the former commandment' — the law of Moses — has served its purpose and has been annulled. According to Lane, 'the term "annulment" is a stronger term than "alteration" (v. 12). Its force is brought out in the papyri, where it assumes a technical legal sense for the annulment of a decree or the cancellation of a debt... The Writer views the whole OT law under the aspect of the priesthood and sacrifice.'[4]

The law, then, has been replaced by a new arrangement (covenant) which, unlike the Mosaic system, is both strong to save and eternally profitable to its beneficiaries. Paul declares, 'I am not ashamed of the gospel of Christ, for it is the power of God to salvation for everyone who believes' (Rom. 1:16). The gospel of the new covenant is able to save sinners from judgement and the thrall of sin, and bestow upon them the everlasting riches of salvation through Christ.

Not only has the old covenant been annulled, but it has been replaced by 'the bringing in of a better hope, through which we draw near to God' (7:19). Lane remarks, 'The new covenant ... can be described as 'better' because it is effective: the approach to God is guaranteed by Jesus in his office as eternal high priest.'[5]

'Hope' is an important word in the New Testament. As we saw earlier with reference to Hebrews 6:18-19, 'hope' signifies 'future expectation'. In apostolic thinking, hope is the keen anticipation that the promises of God will be fulfilled. The 'better hope' of which the Writer speaks is the final outcome of the new covenant, which brings not only righteousness and peace to those who believe, but the prospect of an eternity of glory, peace and joy in the presence of Christ.

In our present pragmatic world, Christian hope has been devalued, even among believers. We major on the present benefits of the gospel and are so engaged with the affairs of this life that we are ashamed to look for 'a better, that is, a heavenly country'. Yet, in reality, believers are 'strangers and pilgrims on the earth' who 'seek a homeland' in heaven (11:13-16). The hope of heaven and of glory, the anticipation of marriage to the Lamb and the everlasting enjoyment of his presence ought never to be far from our thoughts. As Paul declares, 'We ... rejoice in hope of the glory of God' (Rom. 5:2).

Furthermore, if properly cultivated, this hope enables us 'to draw near to God'. Nothing facilitates our fellowship with God, and the enjoyment of his felt presence, more than the contemplation of his eternal glory and the things that 'God has prepared for those who love him' (1 Cor. 2:9). We ought to exult with the apostle John: 'Beloved, now we are children of God; and it has not yet been revealed what we shall be, but we know that when [Christ] is revealed, we shall be like him, for we shall see him as he is.' John underlines the lesson as he continues: 'And everyone who has this hope in him purifies himself, just as he is pure' (1 John 3:2-3). Hope is not only a source of peace and joy, but also a powerful motivation to holiness.

21.
A perfect Saviour

Please read Hebrews 7:20-28

The Writer seems to be going round in circles, for he now quotes Psalm 110:4 for the fourth time (previously in 5:6,10 and 7:17). Perhaps so, but the circles in question are not the aimless wanderings of a tethered goat, but the rotations of a penetrating drill! That is, at each repetition of his great 'proof text', the Writer uncovers new layers of truth and provides us with new insights into the high-priesthood of Christ. In this passage we discover that Christ is the surety of a better covenant; that he has an unchanging priesthood; that he ever lives to make intercession for his people; that he is able to save them to the uttermost; that he has become higher than the heavens; and has been perfected for ever.

These verses provide a launching pad for the theological climax of the epistle, which is reached in Hebrews 8-10, as the epistle presents a devastating comparison between the old and new orders and unveils the full glory of the new covenant.

A better covenant (7:20-22)

Returning to Psalm 110:4, the Writer describes the manner of Christ's appointment as our great High Priest: **'And inasmuch as he was not made priest without an oath (for they have**

**become priests without an oath, but he with an oath by
him who said to him: "The LORD has sworn and will not
relent, you are a priest for ever according to the order of
Melchizedek"), by so much more Jesus has become a surety
of a better covenant'** (7:20-22). Under the Mosaic law, Aaron
and his sons were appointed priests with all due ritual and
solemnity. But they 'have become priests without an oath',
that is, their ordination was not accompanied by any oath or
commendation from God. By contrast, God the Father appointed Jesus Christ to the priestly order of Melchizedek under
his own immutable oath: 'The LORD has sworn and will not
relent.'

The Writer to the Hebrews is almost unique in appealing to
the oaths of God. Luke refers to such oaths, once in his Gospel and once in Acts, but otherwise they are not mentioned
apart from the five references in Hebrews (eight if we include
the word 'swore' applied to God). In Old Testament thinking,
oaths were important. They represented solemn and binding
undertakings, and were treated with great respect. Specifically addressing Hebrew Christians, then, it is not surprising
that the Writer appeals so strongly to the oaths of God. They
were nothing less than God's seal upon the promise of the
new covenant.

The fact that Christ's priesthood was established by an oath,
claims the Writer, has *covenant* implications. It is by virtue of
the oath that 'Jesus has become a surety of a better covenant'.
The Greek word translated 'surety' is found only here in the
New Testament. It could be rendered 'guarantor', 'sponsor',
or 'mediator'. It signifies that by appointing Jesus Christ as
his great High Priest, God the Father has *guaranteed* the im-
plementation of the new covenant. It also indicates that Christ
himself *sponsors and promotes* this covenant, that is, he puts
it into effect by his priestly work of atonement. Brown explains: 'To be the "surety" or mediator of a divine covenant or

economy in reference to fallen men, is the same thing as to be a priest, who does for man what man cannot do for himself.'[1]

The new covenant is, says the Writer, 'a better covenant'. We shall see in what way it is 'better' when we come to Hebrews 8:7-13. The word 'better' signifies 'more useful, more serviceable, more advantageous [and] more excellent'.[2] Although 'better' is a gentle word, lacking any superlative or triumphal overtone, it carries with it the strength of understatement. The new covenant is so *evidently* superior to the old that the Writer sees no need for 'hype'. Some things speak for themselves.

This covenant, says Jesus, is 'the new covenant in my blood' (1 Cor. 11:25). From all eternity it existed as the covenant of grace, established between the Father and the Son (2 Tim. 1:9). Throughout Old Testament times it existed as the covenant of promise which the law could not annul (Gal. 3:15-18). But it was only by the advent and high-priestly work of Christ that the Father actualised what he had both purposed and promised: '[God's grace] has now been revealed by the appearing of our Saviour Jesus Christ, who has abolished death and brought life and immortality to light through the gospel' (2 Tim. 1:10). Once again we see that the priesthood and the covenant are inseparable.

Perhaps surprisingly, our verse features the first use of the word 'covenant' in the epistle. Does this mean that the old and new covenants are secondary to the Writer's main purpose? Not at all. As Bruce points out, 'This is the first occurrence of the term "covenant" in this epistle, but the term is about to play such a central part in the argument to follow that the whole epistle has been described as "the Epistle of the *Diatheke* [covenant]".'[3]

If this is so, why has the Writer delayed so long in introducing the covenants of God? One possible answer is that he did not want to urge upon his readers a mere change of covenants, as if he was advocating a switch from one set of rules to another. Such an approach would, no doubt, have appealed to the flesh, as it does even in our own day. Various cults flourish on the basis of new and supposedly superior rules to live by. They take the gospel and add to it the commandments of men. Being wary of this danger, the Writer begins his epistle by proclaiming the transcendent glory of the person of Christ, and follows this with an exposition of his wondrous saving work as our great High Priest. Put simply, he preaches 'Jesus Christ and him crucified' (1 Cor. 2:2). Once he has established Christ as the heart of the gospel, he then introduces the new covenant as (1) the inevitable *implication* of the work of Christ and (2) the foreordained *scheme* under which God imparts the benefits of salvation.

This must always be the right order. Our remit is to preach Christ first and foremost, and afterwards, to proclaim the benefits of the new covenant in Christ. If we reverse this order we are in danger of promoting a man-centred gospel, in which the benefits to man are exalted above the one through whom they come. This has happened to a great extent in our own day. It is a trend that needs to be reversed, and Hebrews helps us mightily to regain the priority of a Christ-glorifying gospel.

An unchangeable priesthood (7:23-25)

Not only is there a better covenant — there is an unchangeable priesthood. The two are connected, of course, for the superiority of the covenant resides largely in the quality of its priesthood. Under the old covenant, '**... there were many priests, because they were prevented by death from continuing. But [Christ], because he continues for ever, has an unchangeable priesthood**' (7:23-24). The Writer draws a trenchant conclusion from the fact that Christ, in the manner of Melchizedek, ministers in the power of an endless life.

There is a profound difference between the death of the Mosaic priests and that of Christ: 'He dies *as* a priest', comments Pink, whereas 'they died *from* being priests'.[4] In their case, death terminated their office. In his case death and resurrection fulfilled his office.

Later in the epistle we read that 'Jesus Christ is the same yesterday, today, and for ever' (13:8). It is this timeless continuity that guarantees the eternal efficacy of the gospel and the eternal security of the elect. In the realm of salvation by grace, nothing changes, nothing fails, nothing decays. How unlike the material world and the affairs of men and nations! Here, nothing is certain, nothing is for ever. 'Change and decay' are all around us and, indeed, within us. Even religion, in so far as it is mediated by human priests, lacks this essential ingredient of continuity. One imperfect instrument is replaced by another, as death terminates even the most influential of human ministries. Although human religious systems outlive their practitioners, they still change to accommodate a changing society. But the gospel and ministry of Christ do not change, for they derive from one who ever lives in changeless glory. 'Christ, having been raised from the dead, dies no more. Death no longer has dominion over him' (Rom. 6:9).

We should derive much comfort from this fact. In times of failure we can remember God's words in Malachi 3:6: 'I am the LORD, I do not change; therefore you are not consumed, O sons of Jacob.' In times of doubt and discouragement we may assure ourselves that Christ remains our refuge and his love does not change. 'For I know the thoughts that I think toward you, says the LORD, thoughts of peace and not of evil, to give you a future and a hope' (Jer. 29:11). Our spiritual experience ebbs and flows, but our unchanging High Priest remains constant in his care, compassion and mercy towards us. Let us then take heart!

Specifically, asserts the Writer, '**... he is also able to save to the uttermost those who come to God through him, since he always lives to make intercession for them**' (7:25).

Christ's everlasting intercession is not to be seen as his pleading with a reluctant Father, nor an endless repetition of his offering on Calvary — for '... this man, after he had offered one sacrifice for sins for ever, sat down at the right hand of God' (10:12). The intercession of which the Writer speaks consists in Christ's *presence* at the right hand of God. His eternal priesthood, in and of itself, constitutes an effectual plea for the forgiveness of those who are 'in Christ'. To intercede for us, the priest upon his throne needs to say nothing and do nothing; the fact that he is *there*, 'in the midst of the throne ... a Lamb as though it had been slain', is sufficient intercession of itself (Rev. 5:6).

This eternal intercession means that 'he is ... able to save to the uttermost [or for all time] those who come to God through him'. This, says Lane, 'asserts emphatically that Jesus' capacity for effectively acting on behalf of his people is unlimited. He is able to meet every need of the Christian.'[5] Christ saves finally, completely, perfectly and utterly. Here is no partial salvation, as many teach, leaving man to complete a work that Christ began. Here is no temporary salvation that can be lost through neglect or inadvertence. There would be no point in Christ's everlasting intercession if it did not secure an equally complete and durable salvation. A perfect Saviour must provide a perfect salvation for all 'who come to God through him'. But let us be sure that we do come through Christ, for he alone is 'the way, the truth and the life, [and] no one comes to the Father except through [him]' (John 14:6).

A perfect Saviour (7:26-28)

The Writer reserves till last the all-important issue of Christ's perfection. Not only does he have an unchangeable priesthood, but he is the perfect, altogether fitting, or *suitable*, High Priest — and that in several ways. Firstly, he lived a sinless life on earth: **'For such a High Priest was fitting** [precisely appropriate] **for us, who is holy, harmless, undefiled, separate from sinners'** (7:26). That is, Christ entirely meets our needs because he was entirely righteous as a man. It is this human righteousness that sinners lack and that Christ has earned on their behalf. This is the righteousness that God imputes to those who trust in Christ. If we are to be made righteous in God's sight (and we have no greater need than this), it is essential that, during his life on earth, our Saviour should have been 'holy, harmless, undefiled and separate from sinners'. It was this that constituted Jesus' obedience to the law, an obedience that (imputed to us by grace) redeems us from its curse and fits us for adoption as children of God (Gal. 4:4-5).

Secondly, Jesus is a suitable High Priest because he **'has become higher than the heavens'** (7:26). This is, says Lane, 'a spatial metaphor [used] to denote the highest possible exaltation'.[6] Christ's obedience on earth led to his exaltation: 'Being found in appearance as a man, he humbled himself and became obedient [unto] death, even the death of the cross. Therefore God also has highly exalted him and given him the name which is above every name' (Phil. 2:8-11). Being thus exalted, Christ has been given 'authority over all flesh that he should give eternal life to as many as [the Father] has given him' (John 17:2). Not only has Jesus earned for us the righteousness we lacked, but he has the sovereign authority to bestow it on needy sinners like ourselves.

Thirdly, he is a suitable High Priest because he has offered a perfect sacrifice: **'[He] does not need daily, as those high**

priests, to offer up sacrifices, first for his own sins and then for the people's, for this he did once for all when he offered up himself. For the law appoints as high priests men who have weakness, but the word of the oath, which came after the law, appoints the Son who has been perfected for ever' (7:27-28). The once-for-all sacrifice that Christ offered was himself. Unlike the Mosaic priests, he had no sins of his own for which to atone. His death was therefore truly substitutionary: 'For Christ also suffered once for sins, *the just for the unjust*, that he might bring us to God' (1 Peter 3:18, emphasis added). The human priests of the old covenant were 'men who have weaknesses' and who must continually sacrifice for their own sins as well as those of the people. Such imperfect priests could never offer themselves as substitutes, for the lamb must be without blemish. That is, only a perfect sacrifice is acceptable to God. Unlike the Levitical priests, Christ has uniquely 'been perfected for ever', through his obedience to the law and to his Father's will (see comment on 2:10). It is *such* a high priest that God appointed by the word of his oath. He alone is suitable for our salvation, the only ground and cause of our acceptance with God.

22.
A revealed pattern

Please read Hebrews 8:1-6

At this point in the epistle the Writer stops to draw breath. 'He wants to crystallise his message', says Jones; he 'is not content just to state truth correctly. He wants to inform minds so as to affect lives.'[1] Thus the Writer summarises the arguments developed, and conclusions drawn, in Hebrews 4-7. In doing so, of course, he adds new material that serves to illuminate and underscore his earlier teaching. Nevertheless, this passage provides pause for thought and reflection. This is valuable for both the Writer and his readers. For the reader it brings into clearer focus the closely reasoned thesis that has been built up in the preceding chapters. For the Writer it gathers ammunition for the final campaign, namely, the presentation in chapters 8-10 of the glorious new covenant in Christ.

Such a High Priest (8:1-2, 6)

The Writer begins: **'Now this is the main point of the things we are saying: We have such a High Priest, who is seated at the right hand of the throne of the Majesty in the heavens, a Minister of the sanctuary and of the true tabernacle which the Lord erected, and not man'** (8:1-2). The Greek word rendered 'main point' can be translated 'principal thing' or 'sum'. When used in the latter sense, it normally refers to a sum of money. Perhaps the Writer is using it as a metaphor to signify that what he is 'summarising' are truths of surpassing value. Whether or not this is so, no one can deny that to possess *such* a great High Priest, seated at the right hand of the Majesty in the heavens, makes the believer rich beyond all reckoning.

Oddly, some commentators fail to find any summary in these verses, treating the material as essentially new.[2,3] However, as Owen remarks, 'The apostle in this and the ensuing verses doth both briefly recapitulate and also declare what is the principal thing that he had contended for and proved.'[4] The Writer's summary is clear enough and consists of three points here in verses 1-2, and a further two points in verse 6. These are as follows.

Firstly, we have a great High Priest, Jesus the Son of God. His greatness resides both in his divine person and his perfect and finished work of atonement for sinners. This has been spelled out and elaborated in the preceding chapters.

Secondly, this High Priest is enthroned at the right hand of **'the Majesty in the heavens'**. That Christ is a priest upon his throne is evident from his membership of Melchizedek's order, as discussed earlier. The picture is of two thrones, one for the Father and another for the Son and High Priest. The Son is set on the right hand of the Father, the place of privilege, favour and authority. In other scriptures, the two thrones are viewed as one, as in Revelation 22:1,3. There is no contradiction here, since it is common for a king and his consort, for example, to occupy two thrones which can be viewed as a single emblem of monarchy. The great High Priest is *seated* because his work is finished; he is enthroned as the sovereign Lord, having authority to bestow eternal life on those that the Father has given him (John 17:2). He is exalted, having received the name that is above every name (Phil. 2:9-11).

Thirdly, Christ is **'a Minister of the sanctuary and of the true tabernacle which the Lord erected, and not man'**. This statement amplifies a theme only lightly touched upon previously (4:14; 6:19-20; 7:26) — the exalted Saviour ministers in heaven, not on earth. Unlike the priests of the Mosaic covenant, Christ inhabits the true (that is, heavenly) sanctuary, where the ineffable God is present in person and where sovereign authority resides. He does not serve in an earthly shrine but in that heavenly sphere of which the tabernacle was merely a picture.

Although Christ's redeeming work is complete, it is still being *implemented* in human experience, both in the calling and regeneration of the elect and in their preservation and blessing in life. Christ, therefore, is still ministering to his people and, in that sense, continues to fulfil his high-priestly office in the most practical manner possible. Our access to the throne of grace is but one example of this present-tense ministry (4:16).

Verses 3-5 of Hebrews 8 amplify the concept of the heavenly tabernacle, and we shall consider them in a moment. But they are parenthetical in the sense that the Writer returns in verse 6 to his summary of things already proven. His fourth conclusion, therefore, is that Christ **'has obtained a more excellent ministry, inasmuch as he is also Mediator of a better covenant'** (8:6). The new covenant, inaugurated and mediated by Christ's high priesthood, was shown to be 'better' in 7:12-28. It is better because it rests on the 'power of [Christ's] endless life' (7:16), because it is the consequence of the Father's solemn oath, and because it is able to 'save to the uttermost those who come to God through [Christ]' (7:25). Moses was the mediator of the covenant of Sinai (Gal. 3:19). But one greater than Moses is here, of whom Moses was only a type.

Fifthly and finally in his summary of things already established, the Writer points out that this 'better covenant' is '**established on better promises**' (8:6). The promises in question are, firstly, those implied and revealed by the priesthood of Melchizedek — the certainty of God's oath, the eternal validity of Christ's priesthood and the merging of the priestly and kingly offices. All these 'promise' better things than Sinai, weak as it was through human failing. The old covenant promised earthly blessing in return for obedience. The new covenant guarantees heavenly riches as a consequence of the obedience of Christ (2 Cor. 8:9).

But the Writer also has in mind the promise made to Abraham (see comment on 6:13-15). Paul makes much of the promises to Abraham in Galatians 3:6-29, showing how they were ultimately fulfilled in and through Christ — by his saving work and the bestowal of 'the promise of the Spirit' (i.e. the gift to his people of the indwelling Holy Spirit — Gal. 3:14).

The centrality of Christ (8:1-2, 6 cont.)

Before we turn to verses 3-5, we should notice one more thing about the Writer's fivefold summary, namely, the centrality he accords to Christ. He, *Jesus,* is our great High Priest; it is *he* who reigns at the right hand of the Majesty on high; it is *he* who ministers for us in the heavenly sanctuary; it is *he* who mediates to us the better covenant; and it is in *Christ* that the better promises are fulfilled. Although the Writer is about to launch on his definitive comparison of the two covenants, his summary is first and foremost concerned with the person and work of Jesus Christ, the Son of God.

This is both logical and consistent with his emphasis throughout the epistle. Christ is the foundation on which all else rests. Are believers heirs of the promises and beneficiaries of the new covenant? Then it is only in and through Christ that they possess these inestimable gifts. Are they absolved from the strength and penalty of sin? Then it is through Christ's high-priestly sacrifice that this freedom is obtained. Do they have free access to a throne of grace, where they obtain mercy and find grace to help in time of need? Then it is to Christ's throne that they come, to avail themselves of Christ's mercy and Christ's help.

We should be quick to take note of these things and to imitate the Writer. The gospel is 'the gospel of the glory of Christ' — the New Testament knows no other (2 Cor. 4:4). Yet today it is fashionable for churches and preachers to major on the needs of men rather than the glory of Christ. The gospel is offered as a palliative for the human condition, a medicine for troubled hearts and minds. What people find comforting, encouraging, helpful, attractive and entertaining is considered to define the gospel. User-friendliness is the criterion of success. But this man-centred gospel is not what the apostles proclaimed. They preached nothing else, and nothing less, than 'the unsearchable riches of Christ' (Eph. 3:8).

We also fall into error if we construct foundations from our theologies, our intellectualism, our historical confessions, our ecclesiastical structures, our eschatologies, our rules of life, our Christian sociology, or our ministries of compassion. Many of these things have their place and function, but it must not be that of the foundation. Only Christ can perform that function, 'for no other foundation can anyone lay than that which is laid, which is Jesus Christ' (1 Cor. 3:11). Let us follow the example and exhortation of Hebrews and lay Christ at the heart of all we believe, proclaim and do.

Shadows of the true (8:3-5 cont.)

We now turn to the 'parenthesis' of 8:3-5. This interrupts the Writer's summary of his conclusions to date and represents an elaboration of verse 2, where Christ is portrayed as a 'Minister of the sanctuary and of the true tabernacle which the Lord erected, and not man'. Although parenthetical, these verses are significant because they represent the first use by the Writer of an important principle, namely the *positive* use of the rituals of the old covenant to represent the spiritual realities of the new covenant. The Writer has, of course, already contrasted the old and new covenants, especially with regard to their respective priesthoods. But he now begins to show how the provisions of the old covenant are 'the copy and shadow of the heavenly things' (8:5). Paul confirms the concept. Old-covenant rituals, he tells the Colossians, 'are a shadow of things to come, but the substance is of Christ' (Col. 2:17).

Every consistent Bible expositor knows this, of course. The typology of the Old Testament, correctly interpreted, enriches our understanding and appreciation of the person and work of Jesus Christ. He is our Passover lamb, our manna from heaven, our great High Priest, great David's greater son. He is our rock and hiding place, our high tower, our Prophet and our King. But the Writer to the Hebrews, uniquely, works out the details of the Mosaic law in terms of their prophetic and typological representation of Christ. They are the shadows, while he is the substance. But the shadows are rich with meaning as long as we see them for what they are.

Something to offer (8:3-5 cont.)

The first shadow-truth is presented in 8:3: **'For every high priest is appointed to offer both gifts and sacrifices. Therefore it is necessary that this one also have something to offer.'** Here is an important analogy. What are the functions of any priest? To offer gifts and sacrifices, replies the Writer. Gifts betoken praise and worship — things offered to God in recognition of his great and glorious being. Sacrifices, on the other hand, represent atonement for sin — the essential prerequisite for admission to the presence of God. What is true of earthly priests (and clearly understood by the readers of this epistle) is also true of Christ.

His atoning sacrifice of himself, together with its effects in time and eternity, is the burgeoning theme of Hebrews 8-10, as we shall see. Concerning this offering Bruce says, 'It is not implied that Jesus is continually or repeatedly presenting his offering; this is excluded by Ch. 7:27 ... the tense and mood of the Greek verb "to offer" also exclude the idea of a continual offering.' A better translation, he adds, would be: 'this one too must have *had* something to offer'.⁵

Although Christ's offering is paramount, his priestly 'gifts' are also meaningful, relating as they do to the worship of the Father. They signify that the ineffable God can only be truly worshipped through Christ, for 'no one comes to the Father except through [him]' (John 14:6). This well-known verse is normally applied to Christ's work of reconciling sinners to the Father, and rightly so. But it also has a continuing application. *Whenever* we come to the Father we must come through (and in) Christ, and this is particularly true of our worship. We approach God in the name of Jesus Christ, for we are 'accepted in the Beloved' and 'through him we ... have access by one Spirit to the Father' (Eph. 1:6; 2:18). Elsewhere, Paul asserts: 'We are the circumcision, who worship God in the Spirit, rejoice in Christ Jesus, and have no confidence in the flesh' (Phil. 3:3). We can only worship 'in Spirit and in truth' if we are trusting and rejoicing in Christ, who alone is 'the truth' (John 4:23-24; 14:6).

Our worship, therefore, must be Christ-centred if it is to please the Father. How tragic it is when churches lose sight of this basic requirement — when 'worship' becomes an indulgence of the flesh and people seek entertainment, excitement and emotional experience instead of desiring only Christ and his honour! Let us worship in such a way that our great High Priest will gladly bear that gift of worship before the Majesty of God.

Heavenly things (8:3-5 cont.)

The second shadow-truth found in our passage explores both the contrast and similarities between the Mosaic system and the ministry of Christ. Our great High Priest must serve in a *heavenly* sanctuary, argues the Writer. **'For if he were on earth, he would not be a priest, since there are** [already] **priests who offer the gifts according to the law'** (8:4). There is simply no place for Christ in the earthly sanctuary! Of necessity, therefore, he cannot be absorbed into the old-covenant order, as some of the Hebrews apparently desired. His ministry transcends that of the law as heaven transcends the earth.

Nevertheless, the Mosaic system still serves a valuable purpose in being **'the copy and shadow of the heavenly things'** (8:5). 'The two words ... copy ... and shadow ... both imply a deeper reality behind what is seen', explains Guthrie. 'The Writer's purpose is not to reduce the glory of the shadow, but to enhance the glory of its substance.'[6] It is precisely *because* the tabernacle and all that went with it was designed to provide a representation of Christ and his ministry that **'Moses was divinely instructed when he was about to make the tabernacle'** to **'make all things according to the pattern shown ... on the mountain'** (8:5).

Why wasn't Moses allowed to use his own imagination and initiative when he constructed the tabernacle and ordained the priesthood and sacrificial system of the law? Because the 'pattern' provided by God prefigured the glorious person and saving work of Christ. It must therefore be both perfect in itself and authored by God alone without the aid of man. Otherwise the law could not have been 'our tutor to bring us to Christ', because it would not have typified him correctly (Gal. 3:24). This has practical implications. First of all, the provisions of the old covenant still testify to the person and work of Christ. They do so to such an extent that they point men to Christ, 'that we might be justified by faith' (Gal. 3:24). How? We shall see many examples as we continue in Hebrews 8-10, but let us give one here.

The elaborate system of animal sacrifices under the old covenant helps us to understand the *concept* of substitutionary atonement. That is, it teaches us that an innocent sacrifice is acceptable to God as a substitute for the human sinner, who deserves to die for his sins. This concept of substitution is basic to a right understanding of the death of Christ. No other religion teaches that a God-man had to die in place of those he would redeem from death. The concept is foreign to the reasoning of the natural man. The Old Testament 'shadows', paradoxically, cast light upon this matter. They help us understand that Christ 'suffered once for sins, the just for the unjust, that he might bring us to God' (1 Peter 3:18).

There is a tendency today for preachers and theologians of the 'neo-evangelical' school to play down the idea of substitution in the death of Christ. They seek to eliminate the element of God's judicial wrath against sin and, therefore, against Christ as he bore that sin upon the cross. Jesus' death is represented as an act of self-sacrifice and compassion, but not as a satisfaction of divine judgement. This is bound up with a reinterpretation of sin itself, which is presented as human imperfection deserving divine sympathy, rather than rebellion against God requiring retribution. A proper understanding of the way the old covenant foreshadows Christ and the atonement is a powerful corrective in such matters. Let us be clear — God's 'pattern shown on the mountain' accurately prefigures the true nature of the work of Christ. The pattern cannot save us, but it testifies faithfully to the one who can.

Commentary on 8:6 appears earlier in this chapter.

23.
A new covenant (I)

Please read Hebrews 8:7-10

The Writer reaches the climax of his argument as he unveils the fulness of the new covenant. His timing is perfect and his method masterful. He has now made various references, direct or implied, to the new covenant, and his readers are ready to be told what this 'better covenant' actually entails. As to his method, the Writer risks no contradiction from his Hebrew audience, for he presents the new covenant in terms of solid Old Testament Scripture!

Hebrews 8:6, which immediately precedes our passage, speaks of 'a better covenant' built on 'better promises'. As we saw, this verse is part of the Writer's summary of the previous chapters. But the verse is more than a summary, for it provides the Writer with his opportunity to open up the radical nature of the new covenant in Christ. He does so by citing at length — and with very little comment of his own — a passage from Jeremiah (31:31-34). Evidently, he feels that this scripture is so clear and explicit that it requires little or no elaboration from him.

Altogether different (8:7-9)

The Writer presses a now familiar line of argument. **'If that first covenant had been faultless'**, he reasons, **'then no place**

would have been sought for a second' (8:7). Yet God himself, speaking through the prophet Jeremiah, declares: '**"Behold the days are coming", says the** LORD, **"when I will
make a new covenant with the house of Israel and the house
of Judah"'** (8:8, cited from Jer. 31:31). The inclusion of both
Israel and Judah implies a reunification of the separated kingdoms of Jeremiah's day. But in applying the prophecy to the
new covenant in Christ, Hebrews sees here an even greater
reunification — one in which 'there is neither Jew nor Greek
... for you are all one in Christ Jesus' (Gal. 3:26-29).

The making of a new covenant, argues the Writer, demonstrates that the covenant of Sinai was defective and in need of
replacement. He has already used this argument effectively in
relation to the high-priesthood of Christ, contending that the
new priesthood, based on the order of Melchizedek, signalled
the inadequacy of the Levitical order. Now he hammers home
the same lesson — God himself, **'finding fault'** (8:8) with the
old order, deems it necessary to announce a new covenant.
'The covenant of the Law', says Calvin, 'was neither stable
nor lasting.'[1]

The new covenant is to be radically different from the old.
It is **'not according to the covenant that I made with their
fathers in the day when I took them by the hand to lead
them out of the land of Egypt; because they did not continue in my covenant, and I disregarded them, says the**
LORD**'** (8:9). The negative 'not according to' is immensely
important to our understanding of the new covenant in Christ.
If I buy a defective dishwasher, I expect it to be replaced by a
perfect specimen of the same model. But if the defect lies in
the basic design of the model, the only remedy is to have it
replaced by an entirely different machine designed on different
principles.

In the same way, the new covenant is not just another arrangement of the same general character as the old but having

a different set of rules. The Writer is telling us that an *entirely different type* of arrangement was required if people were to be saved. 'This new covenant', declares John Brown, 'was ... to be entirely of a different kind.'[2] The old *kind* of covenant was unable to deliver what was needed for the fulfilment of God's plan of redemption. Why was this so?

The covenant of Sinai was God's own covenant ('my covenant'). Its failure, therefore, lay not in itself. As Paul declares, 'The law is holy, and the commandment holy and just and good' (Rom. 7:12). The fault of the old covenant lay in its external character which required the obedience of fallen man. That is, it was a covenant of works, for only such a covenant can be broken by disobedience. Guthrie comments, 'A covenant normally involves the full co-operation of both parties. If one party defaults, the covenant becomes invalid. This is virtually what happened to the old covenant.'[3]

Notice that Hebrews 8:8 says that God found fault with, and disregarded, **'them'** (the Israelites to whom the law was given), not the law itself. In God's wisdom, the law was impotent to save, but only because it was 'weak through the flesh' (Rom. 8:2). It could demonstrate God's holy requirements for human conduct, and provide the outlines of his saving provision in Christ. But because it was an *external* rule, addressed to fallen human nature ('the flesh'), it could do nothing to make a man righteous in the sight of God. It could only reveal his sin and condemn his every attempt to mollify an offended God. An external rule could do nothing to redeem a man from sin — it could only make him more aware of it, for '... by the deeds of the law no flesh will be justified in his sight, for by the law is the knowledge of sin' (Rom. 3:20).

The new covenant would, therefore, have to be a radically different kind of covenant. Just *how* different is made clear in the quotation from Jeremiah. The new covenant would involve the transformation of the individual and a new kind of

relationship with God. Hebrews 8:10-12 sets out four characteristics of the new covenant that distinguish it dramatically
from the law of Sinai. These are (1) its internal nature; (2) a
new relationship between God and his people; (3) a direct
personal knowledge of God; and (4) the experience of God's
mercy and forgiveness in Christ. We shall consider these in
turn.

God's laws in the mind (8:10)

Firstly, under the new covenant, God's laws would be internalised: **'For this is the covenant that I will make with the
house of Israel after those days, says the LORD: I will put
my laws in their mind and write them on their hearts'**
(8:10). God's holy requirements would no longer stand as
external rules, as in the Mosaic covenant, or as an all-pervading
consciousness of right and wrong (see Rom. 2:14-16). Instead
they would be inscribed upon the minds and hearts of his
people. Many commentators point out that 'mind' and 'heart'
are interchangeable words, signifying the inner person, and
conclude that they have no separate significance in this passage. However, John Owen makes a distinction, pointing out
that 'The first real effect of the internal promised grace of the
[new] covenant is on the mind ... this in the New Testament is
expressed by the renovation of the mind (Rom. 12:2, Eph.
4:23) and the opening of the eyes of our understandings (Eph.
1:17-18).'[4] In fact, it makes little difference whether or not
'heart' and 'mind' are the same since, either way, all would
agree that the new covenant involves both a *knowledge* of
God's will ('mind'?) and a *love* for it ('heart'?).

Consider first the internalised *knowledge* of God's laws.
Under the new covenant, God's people would be so wrought
upon that they would have an instinctive spiritual knowledge
of God's will. How does this come about? It results from the

work of the Holy Spirit in regeneration. The beneficiaries of the new covenant are, says Jesus, 'born of the Spirit' (John 3:1-8). Endued with new life, such people are no longer 'in the flesh', unable to 'please God', but 'the Spirit of God dwells in [them]' and they are 'led by the Spirit of God' (Rom. 8:8-14). As a consequence, they 'set their minds on ... the things of the Spirit' (Rom. 8:5).

These verses from Romans 8 demonstrate an important truth — the mind of the regenerate person is profoundly engaged with the things of God, not least with his holy requirements as set out plainly in Scripture. As a result, 'The righteous requirement of the law [is] fulfilled in [those] who do not walk according to the flesh but according to the Spirit' (Rom. 8:4). The laws of God, revealed in the written Word of God, and internalised in the mind, have the power to rule our thoughts and actions in a way that an external rule could never do. Paul prays for the Colossians that they might 'be filled with the knowledge of [God's] will in all wisdom and spiritual understanding; that you may walk worthy of the Lord, fully pleasing him, being fruitful in every good work and increasing in the knowledge of God' (Col. 1:9-10). We see here, once again, the essential link between the *knowledge* of God's will and a life pleasing to him.

But how exactly do we obtain this knowledge of God's will? We acquire it, says Colossians, as we are 'filled' with it by the work of the Holy Spirit. In other words, it is a revealed knowledge, as is taught consistently throughout the New Testament (e.g. Matt. 16:17; 1 Cor. 2:15-16; 1 John 2:20-21). But the New Testament writers are not talking about mere spiritual impressions, as taught by the Quakers, 'Moral Rearmament' and other heterodox movements, including the modern advocates of direct (or continuing) revelation. On the contrary, the Holy Spirit reveals this knowledge to us *through the Scriptures of truth* (John 6:68; 17:17; 2 Tim. 3:15; 4:2-4).

A consequence of this is that we ourselves must be active in acquiring a knowledge of God's will. In Romans 12, Paul urges his readers: 'Do not be conformed to this world, but be transformed by the renewing of your mind, that you may prove what is that good and acceptable and perfect will of God' (Rom. 12:1-2). If we are to know the will of God, our minds must be transformed by the work of God's Spirit. But, at the same time, 'be transformed' is a command, which implies some measure of responsibility and activity on our part.

That is, believers are not passive in this work of mental transformation, but are consciously active in *learning* what the Spirit teaches. It is not the Spirit's work to decant the pre-digested knowledge of God's will into our dormant minds. Rather, our minds are enlivened by the Spirit to explore and discover the 'acceptable and perfect will of God'. This we do through the Holy Scriptures as we read and meditate upon them and as they are preached and taught in the authority of the Spirit. It is from these Scriptures that the Holy Spirit takes the things that pertain to Christ and reveals them to us, glorifying Christ in the process (John 16:14-15).

Which laws? (8:10 cont.)

What, then, are these laws that God puts in his people's minds under the new covenant? They cannot simply be the covenant of Sinai, for the Writer's whole purpose is to show how *that* covenant has been made obsolete. Equally, the laws concerning the priesthood and the sacrifices no longer apply under the new covenant, so *they* cannot be the laws that God puts into the mind. On the other hand, these internalised laws will surely include the enduring moral precepts of that law, summed up in Jesus' words: 'You shall love the LORD your God with all your heart, with all your soul, with all your strength, and with all your mind, and your neighbour as yourself' (Luke 10:27).

However, the laws placed within the mind under the new covenant cannot be limited to Old Testament principles, but must surely include all that is revealed in Scripture, both Old and New Testaments, concerning God's will for mankind. Owen declares, 'The "laws of God", therefore, are here taken largely, for the whole revelation of the mind and will of God.'[5]

Consider, for example, Jesus' Sermon on the Mount. It is sometimes claimed that this is no more than an exposition of the Ten Commandments, but this is clearly not the case. The sermon certainly mentions three of the Ten Commandments, but it does so in a way that transforms them from external rules to internal motives. Furthermore, the sermon teaches moral principles that are hard to discern in the Mosaic law, such as loving our enemies and 'going the second mile'.

As it draws to a close, the Sermon on the Mount leaves us in no doubt as to where the Christian must look for moral instruction: 'Whoever hears *these sayings of mine*, and does them', says Christ, 'I will liken him to a wise man who built his house on the rock' (Matt. 7:24, emphasis added). We conclude, therefore, that the laws that God puts in the mind are the laws of Christ, and include every moral precept made known to us in all the Scriptures. We shall find these precepts in the Decalogue and elsewhere in the Old Testament, but we shall also find them in the Gospels and the epistles of the New Testament, where they are revealed in the clearer light of the new covenant.

But will not such a weight of moral teaching overburden us? Not at all. The whole point of God's laws being put within our minds is that we shall respond *instinctively* to his requirements, gladly approving their wisdom and hastening to follow their direction. Although there will always be a conflict between the flesh and the Spirit, we are promised help from the Spirit and power over the flesh (Gal. 5:16-18), so that obedience will be a joy and not a burden.

Written on the heart (8:10 cont.)

The new covenant provides not only a *knowledge* of God's laws but also a *love* for them as the revealed will of God. Paul illuminates the basis of all true Christian discipleship when he tells servants to perform their duties 'not with eye-service, as men-pleasers, but as bondservants of Christ, *doing the will of God from the heart*' (Eph. 6:6, emphasis added). This verse suggests not only a heartfelt desire to do God's will, but also the spiritual ability to perform it through the indwelling Christ (Phil. 4:13). When Jeremiah returns to the subject of the 'everlasting covenant' in Jeremiah 32:38-40, God declares, 'I will give them one heart and one way, that they may fear me for ever... I will put my fear in their hearts so that they will not depart from me. Yes, I will rejoice over them to do them good.'

Paul writes to the Romans: 'But God be thanked that though you were slaves of sin, yet you obeyed *from the heart* that form of doctrine to which you were delivered' (Rom. 6:17, emphasis added). This refers specifically to obeying the gospel, that is, to conversion, but it underlines the general principle that all Christian obedience is 'from the heart'. The believer's obedience is willing and happy obedience, because the laws he obeys are written on his heart. He 'delight[s] in the law of God according to the inward man' (Rom. 7:22; we consider later the struggle described by the apostle in Romans 7).

Perhaps the most memorable statement of this truth is found in 2 Corinthians 3:2-7, where Paul declares, 'You are our epistle written in our hearts, known and read by all men; clearly you are an epistle of Christ, ministered by us, *written not with ink but by the Spirit of the living God, not on tablets of stone but on tablets of flesh, that is, of the heart* ... for the letter kills, but the Spirit gives life' (emphasis added). Although this passage makes no explicit mention of God's laws, they are clearly implied. Christ-honouring lives result, not from the external commandments of the Decalogue written on stone, but from that which the Spirit of God writes upon the heart.

The believer's love of God's laws is nowhere expressed more fervently than in the Psalms. The longest of them all begins: 'Blessed are the undefiled in the way, who walk in the law of the LORD! Blessed are those who keep his testimonies, who seek him with the whole heart!' The psalmist continues, 'Oh how I love your law! It is my meditation all the day', and again, 'How sweet are your words to my taste, sweeter than honey to my mouth!' (Ps. 119:1-2,97,103). The same intensity of love for God's law is evident throughout this long psalm, as its author extols the precepts of God both for their intrinsic worth and the benefits they confer.

But was it not the law given at Sinai that the psalmist loved? It is true that the five books of Moses would have constituted most if not all of the psalmist's 'Bible' and that the law of Moses would therefore have featured prominently in his thinking. But the Hebrew word translated 'law' is *torah* (instruction) and is commonly applied to the entire Pentateuch, not just to the covenant of Sinai. Furthermore, the psalmist employs many different words to describe the object of his delight, including 'law', 'precepts', 'word', 'testimonies', 'commandments', 'statutes' and 'judgements'. These terms are so comprehensive that they must delineate, not just the law of Moses, but all the Scriptures then available. By extension, therefore, it is the whole of Scripture that should engage our hearts. We should love every commandment, injunction and exhortation of God's Word.

The conflict (8:10 cont.)

Before we leave the subject of God's laws written on the heart, we need to comment on the conflict to which Paul refers in

Romans 7: 'I delight in the law of God according to the inward man, but I see another law in my members, warring against the law of my mind and bringing me into captivity to the law of sin which is in my members' (Rom. 7:22-23).

Put briefly, the laws of God written in the heart and mind of the believer are opposed by a contrary principle, the law of sin. The same conflict is referred to in Galatians 5:17: 'The flesh lusts against the Spirit, and the Spirit against the flesh; and these are contrary to one another, so that you do not do the things that you wish.' The term 'the flesh' here refers to the old nature that lingers on in the body and mind of the regenerate person, and will only be finally destroyed by death.

Thus, throughout his lifetime, the believer has two contrary natures — 'the new man ... created according to God, in righteousness and true holiness' (Eph. 4:24), and the old nature, variously called 'the flesh', indwelling sin and 'this body of death' (Rom. 7:17,24,25; Gal: 5:17). Although these two natures co-exist throughout the believer's lifetime, the New Testament teaches that it is normative for the new man and the indwelling Holy Spirit to have victory over the 'flesh' (Rom. 8:4, 9; Gal. 5:24-25). Only by 'walking in the Spirit' can believers live lives that, while not sinless, are yet pleasing to God and bear the Spirit's fruit of practical righteousness — 'love, joy, peace, long-suffering, kindness, goodness, faithfulness, gentleness, self-control' (Gal. 5:22-23).

This is enormously important, for such practical righteousness is the only real evidence that an individual *does* have God's laws written on his heart and mind. Only those who have this testimony of a holy life are 'the people of God', as we shall see as we continue to consider the content of the new covenant in Christ.

24.
A new covenant (II)

Please read Hebrews 8:10-13

In the previous chapter we began to explore the nature and implications of the new covenant, as set out by Jeremiah and cited by the Writer. We saw that the first distinguishing feature of the new covenant was the internalisation of God's laws. In contrast to the old Mosaic economy, the new order puts God's holy requirements within the believing heart and mind so that his laws are obeyed instinctively and 'from the heart'. In this chapter we continue to examine the radical nature of the new covenant in Christ.

God and his people (8:10 cont.)

Because God's laws are implanted in the hearts and minds of his new-covenant children he can declare, **'I will be their God, and they shall be my people'** (8:10). Jeremiah uses the future tense, denoting that under the new covenant a new and different relationship would be established between God and his own.

It may be objected that exactly the same terminology is employed under the old covenant to describe the relationship between God and Israel: 'I will take you as my people, and I will be your God. Then you shall know that I am the LORD your God who brings you out from under the burdens of the Egyptians' (Exod. 6:7; see also Lev. 26:12). However, this relationship was conditional on obedience, as Jeremiah makes clear: 'This is what I commanded them, saying, "Obey my voice and I will be your God and you shall be my people..." Yet they did not obey' (Jer. 7:23-24).

Thus it could be argued that the 'God / people' relationship was never fully implemented under the old covenant but only foreshadowed. Palmer Robertson observes that 'The new community within humanity brought into existence by the cross of Christ in its uniting of Jews and Gentiles into one new people of God — is the community that may be designated as "the Israel of God".'[1]

However, it is probably correct to say that a 'God / people' relationship exists wherever a covenant is in force, but that the nature of that relationship *depends on the nature of the covenant*. Thus the Lord *was* the God of Israel under the old covenant, and they *were* his people, but the relationship was, for the most part, external, meritorious and judicial. By contrast, under the new covenant, the 'God / people' relationship is internal ('Christ lives in me' — Gal. 2:20), gracious ('by grace you have been saved ... not of works' — Eph. 2:8-9) and redemptive ('Christ has redeemed us from the curse of the law' — Gal. 3:13). But was God not gracious under the old covenant? Yes, for he is always gracious in his dealings with his people. But there is nevertheless a clear distinction in this relationship between the old and new covenants, and one that is brought out clearly in 8:11-12 (see below). Peter testifies of those who have believed on Christ that they are 'a chosen generation, a royal priesthood, a holy nation, his own special people' (1 Peter 2:8-10). John also makes the distinction plain as he writes of the believer's riches in Christ: 'Of his fulness we have all received, and grace for grace. For the law was given through Moses, but grace and truth came through Jesus Christ' (John 1:16-17). What this all means in terms of the practical experience of the new-covenant believer, we shall see in the following sections.

Knowing God (8:11)

The new 'God / people' relationship becomes clearer when we consider the next aspect of the new covenant, namely, the believer's knowledge of God. **'None of them shall teach his neighbour, and none his brother, saying, "Know the Lord", for all shall know me, from the least of them to the greatest of them'** (8:11). Every member of the new-covenant family will possess a direct and personal knowledge of God, regardless of status and maturity. Jesus makes the matter plain in his 'high-priestly prayer', saying, 'This is eternal life, that they may know you, the only true God, and Jesus Christ whom you have sent' (John 17:3).

Under the old covenant, Israelites had a responsibility to teach others, especially children, about the living God. We read many injunctions like Deuteronomy 4:9: 'Only take heed to yourself, and diligently keep yourself, lest you forget the things your eyes have seen, and lest they depart from your heart all the days of your life. And teach them to your children and your grandchildren.'

Similarly, Deuteronomy 6:7 says, 'These words which I command you today shall be in your heart; you shall teach them diligently to your children, and shall talk of them when you sit in your house, when you walk by the way, when you lie down, and when you rise up.' Joshua was told, 'This book of the law shall not depart from your mouth,' indicating that Moses' successor should not only apply God's law to himself but teach it to others also (Josh. 1:8).

Does Hebrews 8:11 mean that such teaching is no longer required? Not at all, for Paul exhorts Timothy: 'The things that you have heard from me among many witnesses, commit

these to faithful men who will be able to teach others also'
(2 Tim. 2:2). Teaching is an essential function of church elders,
who must be 'able to teach' (1 Tim. 3:2). What, then, does the
Writer mean when he says, **'None of them shall teach his
neighbour'**?

The teaching declared redundant here is the specific exhortation to 'know the LORD'. Sadly, under the old covenant, very
few Israelites had a personal, saving knowledge of God, because very few shared Abraham's faith in the coming Christ.
They witnessed the sacrifices and the Levitical priests at work,
but few of them saw beyond the types to the 'great High Priest'
and the 'Lamb of God'. There were some who did, of course,
and their exploits are recorded in Hebrews 11, to which we
shall come in due course. But Israel as a people were in spiritual darkness, having no true faith in the living God. It was
appropriate, then, that those who *did* know God (often called
'the remnant') should exhort their brethren to 'know the LORD'.

But the national Israel was a 'type' of the church of Christ.
And whereas very few in Israel truly knew the Lord, the reverse is true of the new-covenant church, for its membership
is *defined* by the very fact that they all know 'the only true
God, and Jesus Christ whom [he has] sent'. By 'church', of
course, I do not mean any human organisation or denomin-
ation, but the company of all who have been born of the Spirit
and have believed savingly in Christ. 'The right knowledge of
God', writes Calvin, 'is a wisdom that far exceeds what can be
comprehended by human understanding, and therefore no one
can attain it except by the secret revelation of the Spirit.'[2] Owen
adds: 'The knowledge of the Lord may be here taken, not
objectively and doctrinally, but subjectively, [to mean] the renovation of the mind in the saving knowledge of God.'[3]

When a person is born again, he is immediately aware that
he knows God on a personal level. The Lord has 'shone in our
hearts to give the light of the knowledge of the glory of God

in the face of Jesus Christ' (2 Cor. 4:6). 'The Spirit himself bears witness with our spirit that we are children of God' (Rom. 8:16). This direct (or 'immediate') knowledge of God through Christ is, by definition, universal among believers: **'All shall know me, from the least of them to the greatest of them'** (8:11).

Such knowledge is essential, because those who lack it are 'without Christ, being aliens from the commonwealth of Israel and strangers from the covenants of promise, having no hope and without God in the world' (Eph. 2:12). On the other hand, says Boston, the one who possesses this knowledge of Christ has 'communion with him; in which he launches forth into an ocean of happiness, is led into a paradise of pleasures, and has a saving interest in the treasure hid in the field of the gospel, the unsearchable riches of Christ'.[4]

Yet many who profess to be Christians are strangers to this intimate and experimental knowledge of God. This may be true even in evangelical circles, where a desire for spiritual 'experiences', excitement and entertainment often drives out all hunger and thirst for the living God himself. Many today need to ask whether or not they truly know God as a matter of personal experience. Paul exhorts: 'Examine yourselves as to whether you are in the faith. Test yourselves. Do you not know yourselves, that Jesus Christ is in you? — unless indeed you are disqualified' (2 Cor. 13:5).

For those who *do* know God, there is still much to do. Peter urges us to 'grow in the grace and *knowledge* of our Lord and Saviour Jesus Christ' (2 Peter 3:18, emphasis added). From the moment of regeneration, we have the knowledge of God, but we do not have it to the full. Just as in human relationships, there is room for this knowledge to grow, develop and mature. To this end, says Peter again, we must give all diligence, adding to our faith virtue, knowledge, self control, perseverance, godliness, brotherly kindness and love. 'For if

these things are yours and abound, you will be neither barren
nor unfruitful in the *knowledge* of our Lord Jesus Christ'
(2 Peter 1:5-8, emphasis added). But none of this is possible
until we first 'know' God personally through the regenerating
work of the Holy Spirit.

Forgiveness (8:12)

The final characteristic of the new covenant is that its subjects
are forgiven, permanently and absolutely, for Christ's sake:
**'For I will be merciful to their unrighteousness, and their
sins and their lawless deeds I will remember no more'**
(8:12). In electing grace, God has determined 'to make known
the riches of his glory on the *vessels of mercy*, which he has
prepared beforehand for glory' (Rom. 9:23, emphasis added).
Mercy is an essential element, both of God's glory and the
believer's glorification.

In themselves, the children of the new covenant are no more
righteous than those of the old. By nature they are 'dead in
trespasses and sins', being 'children of wrath, just as the others'
(Eph. 2:1-3). But whereas the old covenant could offer no
relief for innate human sinfulness, the new covenant extends
mercy to the unrighteous. (The same is true, of course, of the
'covenant of promise' — which looked forward to the coming of Christ during Old Testament times and should not be
confused with the old covenant made at Sinai — see Gal.
3:17-18.)

Paul extols this new-covenant mercy as he continues in
Ephesians: 'But God, who is rich in mercy, because of his
great love with which he loved us, even when we were dead in
trespasses, made us alive together with Christ (by grace you
have been saved)' (Eph. 2:4-5). The new-covenant believer is
the subject of God's rich mercy and free grace, and will be

abundantly *conscious* of this fact. This consciousness should be cultivated, for it is a powerful antidote to the sins of pride, ingratitude and lovelessness. The believer has come to Christ's throne of grace and has there obtained mercy as the first and abiding gift of grace (4:16). It is important that we never lose sight of the mercy God has shown us in Christ, for otherwise we shall grow cold and careless. John Stocker's hymn, if not always on our lips, should be constantly in our hearts and minds:

Thy mercy, my God,
Is the theme of my song,
The joy of my heart,
And the boast of my tongue;
Thy free grace alone,
From the first to the last,
Hath won my affections,
And bound my soul fast.

Exactly what it means to 'have mercy on their unrighteous- ness' is further explained by the words that follow: **'… their sins and their lawless deeds I will remember no more'** (8:12). The implications of this statement are weighty. Under the old covenant, declares the Writer in 10:1-3, 'there is a reminder of sins every year'. This reminder occurred on the annual Day of Atonement, of which we shall have more to say. But under the new covenant there is, instead, a divine forgetfulness — 'I will remember no more'.

This does not mean that God has amnesia, but that he no longer requires satisfaction for his people's sins at their own hands. They are no longer 'treasuring up for [themselves] wrath in the day of wrath and revelation of the righteous judgement of God' (Rom. 2:5). Why not? Because Christ, by his death, has suffered that wrath and judgement on their behalf, thus satisfying the justice of God. Therefore, God has no need to 'remember' their sins, since he will not ask them to account again for a debt that Christ has paid.

The words 'no more' add a note of finality to the grand and awesome transaction of Calvary. While Christians, despite all their efforts, sin daily, yet 'the blood of Jesus Christ cleanses [or keeps on cleansing] us from all sin' (1 John 1:7). There is simply no end, in time or eternity, to the efficacy of Christ's redeeming work; his blood atones for his people's sins yesterday, today and for ever!

While God 'forgets' the sin and transgressions of his people, he will not allow us to forget the cause of his forgetfulness, namely, the death of his Son. We are instructed to remember and proclaim Christ's redeeming work by gathering regularly to partake of bread and wine at the Lord's Table (1 Cor. 11:23-26). Forgetfulness of sin is God's prerogative, not ours. Yet we may, and must, put our sins behind us, forgiven as they are, for that is the essence of our trust and rejoicing in Christ.

A fading covenant (8:13)

Having set forth, albeit briefly, the glories of the new covenant, the Writer returns to his theme of the redundancy of the old. He continues, **'In that [God] says, "A new covenant", he has made the first obsolete. Now what is becoming obsolete and growing old is ready to vanish away'** (8:13). He does not say that the old covenant has already passed away, but that it is 'ready' to do so. Some commentators seem to suggest that God intended the two covenants to run in parallel for a time, but this would be contrary to the whole burden of Hebrews. It would also invalidate Paul's strictures on the Galatians and the Colossians (see, for example, Gal. 3:10,26-29; Col. 2:20-23). It is more in harmony with the rest of the epistle to understand verse 13 as a simple statement of fact — unconverted Jews were still observing and trusting in the Levitical rites. For Christians, God *himself* had already made the old covenant 'obsolete' — he had abolished it in spiritual terms, if not yet in a historical sense. Furthermore, although it was still being extensively practised by others, its end was in sight. Assuming that Hebrews was written before A.D. 70, this verse is prophetic of the destruction of Jerusalem in that year, with the consequent cessation of temple worship and the whole sacrificial system.

Let us conclude this chapter with the words of John Brown: 'The new covenant has been introduced. The former is now old and, as *old*, is about to vanish away. It had done two things: it had served its purpose as a figure, and as a schoolmaster; and it had also clearly showed that it could not serve the grand purpose of a saving economy; and therefore it was removed out of the way — an honourable end was put to it, in all its requisitions having been fulfilled in Christ.'[5]

25.
A symbol of Christ (I)

Please read Hebrews 9:1-5

Having pronounced the demise of the old covenant in the closing verse of Hebrews 8, the Writer immediately returns to it! He does so by citing the **'divine service'** (Greek *latreia* meaning 'ministration') that took place under that covenant.

At first sight this reversion is surprising, but it is fully consistent with the Writer's method. We have noticed before that he introduces a theme, lays it by for a while, and then returns to it in greater detail. The most obvious example is the way he returns repeatedly to the subject of the priesthood of Christ, developing his argument a little further each time.

So it is with the ordinances of the tabernacle, to which he has already made reference in 8:5. That verse reminded us that Moses had to 'make all things [in the tabernacle] according to the pattern shown ... on the mount'. The Writer now elaborates this brief reference, describing in some detail the provisions made for priestly service under the old covenant: **'Then indeed, even the first covenant had ordinances of divine service and the earthly sanctuary'** (9:1).

His purpose, of course, is not to reinstate the old covenant in any way, but to illuminate further the ministry of Christ. The 'divine service' rendered by the priests of old is a picture of the infinitely greater service rendered by Christ under the new covenant — first to his Father and then to his people.

Symbols of salvation (9:1-2)

Although the Levitical system lacked the power to save, it was nevertheless rich with the symbols of salvation. As Calvin says, 'The sanctuary was in itself earthly and is rightly included among the elements of the world, and yet it was heavenly in what it signified.'[1] The 'earthly' provision of tabernacle, priesthood and sacrifice were 'the copy and shadow of the heavenly things' (8:5). They were, Paul tells the Colossians, 'a shadow of things to come, but the substance is of Christ' (Col. 2:17). And this is exactly what the Writer to the Hebrews is driving at in 9:1-5. For every shadow there is a substance. The shadows vary, but the substance is always Christ.

Brown warns against over-spiritualising the tabernacle services: 'That, generally speaking, the Levitical service was a type and shadow, there can be no doubt. That everything in it was emblematical, is much more than Scripture warrants us to assert.'[2] But he is, perhaps, too severe at this point. A preferable approach is that of John Owen who writes, 'The grace and glory of the new covenant are much set off and manifested by comparing it with the old ... and [this device] is greatly made use of in this epistle.'[3] And again: '... the tabernacle, with all the parts, furniture and services of it, and the design of God therein ... were all representative of Christ, in the discharge of his office, and by them God did instruct the church as unto their faith in him and expectation of him.'[4] Let us consider, then, how the priestly ministrations of the old covenant foreshadowed the work of Christ.

The Writer continues, **'For a tabernacle was prepared: the first part, in which was the lampstand, the table, and the shewbread, which is called the sanctuary'** (9:2). Throughout the epistle the Writer refers only to the tabernacle (or tent), never to the temple. Some have speculated that this is because Hebrews was written after the destruction of the temple in A.D. 70. However, there is a simpler explanation, namely, that the Writer was determined to reason only from Scripture, not from contemporary religious practice.

Although structures like Solomon's temple and the temple of the restoration are described in the Old Testament, the tabernacle in the wilderness receives by far the most detailed attention. Furthermore, unlike the later temples, its design was given by God himself at Sinai. It thus became a prototype — the original and definitive embodiment and focus of Israel's religion. The various temples that followed over the course of time were, at best, reproductions of the tabernacle.

The tabernacle was divided into two unequal parts. The first or outer chamber was called the 'sanctuary' or 'holy place' and only priests were allowed to enter it. Measuring some thirty feet long by fifteen feet wide, it occupied two-thirds of the tent.

However, the Writer's concern is not for architecture but for 'divine service', that is, the service the priests rendered to God in the tabernacle. He therefore focuses attention on the furniture — the lampstand and the table with its shewbread — rather than the holy place itself, because these articles were the focus of priestly activity within the holy place.

The seven-branched lampstand had to be filled with oil, and its lamps trimmed, on a daily basis so that the holy place would be lit continually (Exod. 27:20-21). This priestly service provides our first picture of Christ and his ministry. He is himself 'the light of the world' (John 8:12) and it is he who supplies to his people the 'oil' of his Holy Spirit so that the light of their testimony, though it may flicker, never fails.

Believers are to be lights that shine, 'blameless and harmless, children of God without fault in the midst of a crooked and perverse generation, among whom you shine as lights in the world'. How do we shine? By 'holding fast the word of life', replies the apostle (Phil. 2:15-16). Likewise, Jesus instructs us: 'Let your light so shine before men that they may see your good works and glorify your Father in heaven' (Matt. 5:16). These verses teach us a very practical lesson — believers 'shine' when they proclaim the gospel, the message of life, and demonstrate the power of that gospel by their works (James 2:18). But we can do neither of these things without 'the supply of the Spirit of grace' (10:29; Phil. 1:19) who enables us in every aspect of the Christian life. It is Christ's work to provide that supply, for he said, 'Without me you can do [i.e. accomplish] nothing' (John 15:5).

It is most important that we understand this. Too many Christians try to serve God in the power of the flesh (human nature), believing that success will be obtained by adopting the world's agenda. Nothing could be further from the truth. Zechariah saw a vision of the seven-branched lampstand fed with oil from two olive trees. 'Do you not know what these are?' asked the angel. 'This is the word of the LORD to Zerubbabel: Not by might, nor by power, but by my Spirit, says the LORD of hosts' (Zech. 4:1-6). This is a lesson we all need to learn and remember.

The shewbread (9:1-2 cont.)

The 'shewbread' or 'presence bread', consisted of loaves (probably unleavened) prepared afresh by the priests every Sabbath (1 Chr. 9:32). The bread was to be present continually, 'shown' or displayed openly before the Lord (2 Chr. 2:4). It was placed on a special table, made of acacia wood but overlaid with gold, along with a cloth and various utensils such as pans, pitchers and pouring bowls (Exod. 25:23-29). Bread removed from the holy place was food for the priests alone (an exception is related in 1 Sam. 21:6).

What does the table of shewbread signify? The fact that the bread was displayed along with utensils suggests that it represented a meal-table spread in the presence of God. Christ, the bread of life, provides sustenance to his people in the sight of God. This sustenance is ever-fresh and it imparts eternal life to those who 'eat' it by believing in Jesus (John 6:32-59). This reminds us that the table of salvation set before the believer in the presence of his enemies (Ps. 23:5) is also set in the presence of God. Christ is our food and drink, our sustenance and our joy, but he provides these inestimable gifts to us for the service and glory of his Father in heaven.

The altar of incense (9:1-2 cont.)

In reviewing the outer chamber, the Writer makes no mention of the altar of incense which stood in front of the second veil and on which incense was burned morning and evening (Exod. 30:1-10). We do not know why the Writer omits to mention this altar (though see comments below), but we can recognise its symbolism — it speaks to us of the prayers of God's people.

It was probably in reference to this 'golden altar' that (in John's vision) 'the smoke of the incense, with the prayers of the saints, ascended before God from the angel's hand' (Rev. 8:4).

Although believers offer their prayers directly to God the Father, they can only do so in the name, and by the Spirit, of Jesus Christ. There is an important sense, therefore, in which our prayers are offered by Christ on our behalf. Ephesians 2:18 says, 'For *through him* we ... have access by one Spirit to the Father' (emphasis added). Romans 8:26 tells us that '... the Spirit also helps in our weaknesses. For we do not know what we should pray for as we ought, but the Spirit himself makes intercession for us with groanings which cannot be uttered.' Again, in Romans 8:34 we read, 'It is Christ who died, and furthermore is also risen, who is even at the right hand of God, who also makes intercession for us.'

This is a great encouragement. As the priests of old offered daily incense, so Christ offers 'the prayers of the saints' to his Father. At the same time his Spirit, who alone knows the mind of God, empowers them to pray according to God's will (1 Cor. 2:10; 1 John 5:14). We are not alone when we pray — in our weakness and ignorance, we have divine assistance!

The holiest-of-all (9:3-4)

Moving on swiftly, the Writer brings us to the inner chamber, the 'most holy place' or 'holiest-of-all'.

Hebrews continues: '**... behind the second veil, [lay] the part of the tabernacle which is called the Holiest of All, which had the golden censer and the ark of the covenant overlaid on all sides with gold'** (9:3-4).

When the Writer refers to the 'golden censer', does he mean the altar of incense discussed above and omitted in the description of the outer chamber? Or is he referring to a small, hand-held censer used by the high priest to take coals from the altar of incense into the holiest-of-all on the Day of Atonement? Both explanations have their problems. If he means the altar of incense, he seems to locate it on the wrong side of the veil. If he means a censer, he omits any mention of the altar of incense while commenting on a minor object that goes unmentioned in Exodus.

The solution to this puzzle may lie in the way Exodus sets out the design of the tabernacle. Notably, no mention is made of the altar of incense when the contents of the holiest-of-all and the holy place are being described in Exodus 25:10-40. It is only mentioned after many other things have been described, including the construction of the tabernacle itself, the priestly garments, the consecration of the priests and the daily offerings. Furthermore, when it is eventually described in Exodus

30:1-10, its proximity to the ark and the mercy seat is what is emphasised (Exod. 30:6). Finally, the altar of incense served a dual function. On a daily basis, the high priest burned incense on it morning and evening. But also, once a year, he had to 'make atonement upon its horns ... with the blood of the sin offering of atonement' (Exod. 30:10). No doubt, this was done on the Day of Atonement when the high priest entered the holiest-of-all.

It is possible, therefore, that by saying that the holiest-of-all 'had' the altar of incense (not just a censer), the Writer intended to focus on what was happening during the annual act of atonement, when the inner veil was drawn aside to allow the high priest to enter the inner sanctuary. This would be entirely consistent with his emphasis, just three verses later, on the one offering Christ made to atone for the sins of his people (9:7; 10:12). As Hagner remarks, 'So vital was the burning of incense on the Day of Atonement ... that the author automatically associates the altar of incense with the Holy of Holies. It is after all the Day of Atonement that is his real concern as we see from verses 6-10.'[5]

The ark of the covenant (9:4-5)

The last article of furniture mentioned here is **'the ark of the covenant'** (9:4). It was so called because it contained **'the tablets of the covenant'**, that is, the two stone tablets bearing the Ten Commandments. Although, in his anxiety to proceed, the Writer adds, **'Of these things we cannot now speak in detail'** (9:5), we should again note that the ark represents Christ. It does so firstly with regard to his person — it was **'overlaid on all sides with gold'**. Gold is the symbol of royalty and durability. It speaks to us of Christ's divine majesty and eternity. And in so far as the ark was covered 'on all sides', it reminds us that 'he is altogether lovely', perfect in all his attributes and ways.

But again it is the 'divine service' of Christ that the Writer is concerned to emphasise. He takes time to mention the contents of the ark, namely **'the golden pot that had the manna, Aaron's rod that budded, and the tablets of the covenant'** (9:4). The typology is immediately apparent. Christ is the true manna, the 'living bread that came down from heaven' to give 'everlasting life' to those who believe on him (John 6:47-51). He, uniquely, is the 'rod that budded', the dead branch that came to life (see Num. 17). He 'was dead' but is now 'alive for evermore' and has 'the keys of Hades and of death' (Rev. 1:18). Jesus was raised from the dead, declares the apostle, 'for our justification' (Rom. 4:25, AV). That is, the resurrection of Christ is a declaration that all who trust in his atoning work are righteous in the sight of God.

Above all, however, the contents of the ark speak of the *work* of Christ in keeping the law on our behalf. The first tablets were broken when Moses threw them to the ground on seeing the people's idolatry. Their destruction symbolised man's inability to keep the law of God (Exod. 32:19). God then wrote a second set of tablets to replace the first, and these were committed to safe-keeping in the ark (Exod. 34:1).

As the tablets of the law were preserved in the ark, so God's righteous demands were fully met in the life of the man, Christ Jesus. It is his obedience to the law *as a man* that is imputed to believing sinners, constituting their justification before God. For 'God sent forth his Son, born of a woman, born under the law, to redeem those who were under the law, that we might receive the adoption as sons' (Gal. 4:4-5).

Finally, the Writer reminds us that the ark was covered by a slab of gold, the 'mercy seat' surmounted by **'the cherubim of glory overshadowing the mercy seat'** (9:5). The golden cherubs and the mercy seat were wrought of one piece, the wings of the cherubim forming an arch over the golden slab. They were 'cherubim of glory' because it was here, specifically, that the Shekinah glory rested, signifying the presence of the Lord. There also God promised to commune with Moses: 'There I will meet with you, and I will speak with you from above the mercy seat, from between the two cherubim ... of all which I will give you in commandment to the children of Israel' (Exod. 25:22).

The mercy seat and cherubim, as shadows of the true, typify several things concerning Christ. Firstly, God reveals his true majesty in his Son, not in the representative glory of the Shekinah, awesome though that was. As Paul writes, 'God ... has shone in our hearts to give the light of the knowledge of the glory of God in the face of Jesus Christ' (2 Cor. 4:6). Secondly, as we have seen, he communicates with man through the person of his Son (1:2). Thirdly, in Christ, God powerfully manifests his presence among his people: 'The Lord reigns; let the peoples tremble! He dwells between the cherubim; let the earth be moved! The Lord is great in Zion ...' (Ps. 99:1; see also Ps. 80:1). Needless to say, it is Christ Jesus who is 'the power of God and the wisdom of God' to his church (1 Cor. 1:24).

Lessons from the tabernacle

What, then, does the tabernacle teach us regarding the 'divine service' or ministry of Christ? Surely, that this new-covenant ministry surpasses anything foreshadowed under the Mosaic order. It is easy to envy the people of the old covenant for the access they had to such glorious and awesome manifestations of God as were witnessed in the tabernacle. If only we could see that visible glory and hear God's audible voice!

Yet the New Testament corrects our thinking. The administration of the law was 'the ministry of condemnation', declares Paul. If *that* had glory, he argues, then 'the ministry of righteousness [the new-covenant gospel of Christ] exceeds much more in glory' (2 Cor. 3:9). That which, under the old covenant, was *made* glorious has no glory, he continues, in comparison with that which is *intrinsically* glorious, namely, the person and ministry of Christ, who 'excels in glory' (2 Cor. 3:10).

26.
A symbol of Christ (II)

Please read Hebrews 9:6-10

Having outlined the tabernacle contents in verses 1-5, the Writer arrives at the truth he *really* wants to drive home — that **'the way into the Holiest of All was not yet made manifest while the first tabernacle was still standing'** (9:8). This is where it is all leading and why he was loath to linger over the details (9:5).

The tabernacle, he contends, pointed to a holy and glorious God whose presence had to be veiled from the people by a double curtain (and from the priests themselves by a single one). There was only one exception — the entry of the high priest into the holiest-of-all once a year on the Day of Atonement. But even that access was only permitted as a symbol, foreshadowing the work of Christ. Otherwise, the tabernacle proclaims that God is unapproachable by sinful man.

This reminds us that the Mosaic covenant prefigures Christ both positively *and* negatively. In positive terms, for example, the animal sacrifices establish the forensic nature of the death of Christ as 'the Lamb of God' (that is, Christ died as the sinner's substitute, bearing the punishment demanded by God's righteous law). Negatively, the provisions of the law could never open a way into the presence of God. That was something only Christ could do.

Preparation (9:6)

The tabernacle furniture was provided, says the Writer, by way of *preparation*: '**… when these things had been thus prepared, the priests always went into the first part of the tabernacle, performing the services**' (9:6). The contents of the tabernacle ('these things') were not an end in themselves but were means that enabled the priests to do their work. We need to remember this ourselves. The 'trappings' of service and worship are not important in themselves. Whether they be creeds, confessions, forms of worship, music, surroundings, traditions, organisations, structures, offices, aids, or anything else — they must never be allowed to usurp the primacy of *spiritual* worship and service. Properly employed, such things may help us worship God 'in Spirit and in truth' (John 4:23). But our focus must be upon Christ, not means, necessary though these sometimes are.

The word 'prepare' means to furnish, equip, or make ready. Of necessity, it points forward to some significant action or use that is to follow. In the tabernacle, the immediate action involved was the 'divine service' rendered by the priests in the outer 'sanctuary'. We have already considered how this service symbolises both Christ's own work for us, and our response to it (in terms of light-bearing, feeding on Christ, and praying in his all-prevailing name). But the priestly service in the holy place was only preparatory to something greater. The tabernacle was ultimately designed for another and higher act of service — one rendered by the high priest alone.

The Day of Atonement (9:7)

The Writer describes this greater service: '**But into the second part the high priest went alone once a year, not without**

blood, which he offered for himself and for the people's sins committed in ignorance' (9:7). This annual service — rendered on the Day of Atonement — is detailed in Leviticus 16 and involved sacrifices for both the high priest himself and for the people. Brown elaborates: 'When the high priest entered into the holy place, he entered "not without blood". These words convey two ideas — that he entered *with* blood, and that he could not enter lawfully *without* blood ... atonement was not completed till ... the blood was sprinkled seven times before the mercy seat.'[1]

It is clear from Leviticus that the atonement accomplished was 'for the children of Israel for all their sins' (Lev. 16:30,34). So comprehensive was this atonement that it covered not only the sins of the priests and the people but also atoned 'for the Holy Sanctuary ... for the tabernacle ... and for the altar' (Lev. 16:16,34). Lane remarks, 'The formulation of Leviticus 16:16 is significant because it describes sin as defilement and specifies that blood may act as the purging medium.'[2] That the earthly tabernacle was itself in need of cleansing signifies that it was imperfect — a prototype that pointed to a 'greater and more perfect tabernacle' (9:11). That, as we shall see, is heaven itself.

If the atonement made was indeed comprehensive, why does the Writer say that the blood-offering was only for 'sins committed in ignorance'? It would appear from Numbers 15:22-31 that there was a category of sins (sins of presumption or pride) for which no forgiveness was available under the old covenant. A distinction was made, therefore, between sins committed in ignorance (see Lev. 4) and those committed in deliberate defiance of God.

By including this detail, the Writer is no doubt repeating his warning against such defiance. But we must be careful not to read into it any limitation of Christ's ability to forgive sin. Paul clarifies the matter for us when, referring to his unconverted days, he explains that he sinned 'ignorantly in unbelief' (1 Tim. 1:13). He clearly knew what he was doing, but he was blinded by unbelief. He was not ignorant of his actions, but did not understand that they made him 'a blasphemer, a persecutor, and an insolent man'. Even such sins did not disbar Paul from the mercy of God. In this sense, therefore, every sin committed in unbelief is done 'ignorantly' and is open to forgiveness.

However, even the New Testament speaks of a sin that cannot be forgiven. 'Every sin and blasphemy will be forgiven men', said Jesus, 'but ... whoever speaks against the Holy Spirit, it will not be forgiven him, either in this age or the age to come (Matt. 12:31-32). These words have created unnecessary anxiety in many minds, and need to be understood. The only sin that falls into this category is a deliberate rejection of the light of the gospel, *once it has been revealed to a person's understanding by the Holy Spirit*. It cannot be forgiven because it amounts to a rejection of the way of forgiveness! It is regarding just such a sin that the Writer warns his readers in Hebrews 6:4-6 and 10:26-31.

No entry (9:8-10)

While the high priest's entry into the holiest-of-all was gloriously symbolic of the work of Christ, it was *only* symbolic. In fact the Writer's declared purpose here is to emphasise the shortcomings of the old covenant. He says, '**... the Holy Spirit [was] indicating this, that the way into the Holiest of All was not yet made manifest while the first tabernacle was still standing**' (9:8). Lane comments, 'The old sanctuary consisted of a system of barriers between the worshipper and God',[3] while A. W. Pink points out that '...under the Mosaic dispensation the people were barred from the very presence of God. Such a state of affairs could not be the ultimate and ideal.'[4] As

Pink implies, 'still standing' is not a reference to the physical structure of the tabernacle, which disappears from the biblical record on the completion of Solomon's temple (2 Chr. 5:5), but to the existence of the old covenant itself. There is, of course, an implied contrast with the new covenant, under which, in Christ, the believer is granted unhindered access to the presence of God. This glorious privilege is worked out explicitly in 9:11-15 which we shall consider in the next chapter.

Notice that 'the Holy Spirit' was **'indicating'** (or testifying) through the ordinances of the old covenant. This refers not only to the provisions of the law themselves but also, necessarily, to the Scriptures in which we read about these things — Scriptures that were 'written for our learning' (Rom. 15:4; 1 Cor. 10:11). In short, the Spirit testified in Scripture to the unapproachable holiness of God. The Mosaic covenant provided no way by which sinners could approach such a God. Forgiveness depended on the mediation of a priest who must offer atonement for his own sins before he could act on behalf of others. Sins *were* forgiven, but at a distance — the sinner still could not draw near to God. God's wrath *was* averted, but men's consciences were not cleansed. The ceremony **'was symbolic for the present time in which both gifts and sacrifices are offered which cannot make him who performed the service perfect in regard to the conscience'** (9:9).

We can make the mistake, even today, of thinking that various 'gifts and sacrifices' can make us 'perfect' (that is, complete in holiness and thus acceptable to God). We would not dream of offering old-covenant sacrifices, but we can easily offer our services in the *slavish spirit* of the old covenant rather than the liberty of the new. Paul exhorts his readers to 'stand fast ... in the liberty by which Christ has made us free and do not be entangled again with a yoke of bondage' (Gal. 5:1). His reference is to the Galatians' desire to bring themselves under the old covenant through circumcision. But, as he points out elsewhere, 'The letter [of the law] kills, but the Spirit gives life' (2 Cor. 3:6). Our service to God must not be rendered in bondage to external rules but in the strength of the indwelling Spirit, for (as we saw in Hebrews 8:10) God has put his laws in our minds and written them upon our hearts.

Any preoccupation that is **'concerned only with foods and drinks, various washings, and fleshly ordinances'** (9:10) — or the equivalent outward rituals and observances of our own day — is mistaken and endangers our spiritual lives. 'Fleshly ordinances' cover anything done in the strength of human nature ('the flesh'), whether religious observances, good works, or living by rules. These things cannot help us, simply because anyone who is 'in the flesh cannot please God' (Rom. 8:8). Guthrie observes: 'No doubt many of the restrictions were beneficial to the body, but they did not bring liberty to the spirit.'[5] Only those who are 'led by the Spirit' in their thinking and their living are 'the sons of God', for only they have received, 'not the spirit of bondage ... but ... the Spirit of adoption' (Rom. 8:14-15).

The time of reformation (9:10 cont.)

These outward ordinances, continues the Writer, were **'imposed until the time of reformation'** (9:10). That is, they were temporary and pointed forward to a new era. The Greek word translated 'reformation' signifies a 'thorough straightening out' and is used nowhere else in the New Testament. Its significance is best judged by reference to the words that follow in 9:11: 'But Christ came as high priest of the good things to come...' The time of reformation, therefore, must refer to the coming of the new covenant in Christ (cf. Gal. 4:4: 'When the fulness of the time had come, God sent forth his Son'). The New Testament — and Hebrews especially — sees the

Old Testament era as probationary. Of the Old Testament saints we read that '… they should not be made perfect apart from us' (11:40). That era was one, firstly of promise and secondly of law, both of which pointed forward to Christ who would set all things in order. He would accomplish this 'reformation' by fulfilling both the promise and the law (Gal. 3:16; Matt. 5:17). Like Paul in Galatians, the Writer is anxious that his readers should understand their faith from this 'reformed' perspective. New-covenant believers neither wait for the promise nor revert to the law — for Christ has come and has made all things new! (Rev. 21:5; note that the context relates this statement to the present era, not just the time of Christ's return).

In the next chapter we will explore what Christ's inauguration of 'the time of reformation' means.

27.
An eternal redemption

Please read Hebrews 9:11-15

The Old Testament tabernacle, with all its glory and ceremony, was only a faint picture of **'the greater and more perfect tabernacle'** (9:11). This 'true tabernacle' has already been referred to in 8:2 and represents the heavenly environment in which the ascended and glorified Christ now serves and reigns.

Among other things, this environment involves the actual presence of the Father (instead of the representational Shekinah glory); the all-powerful throne of heavenly grace (in place of a golden mercy seat); the worship of the angels (not the mere images of cherubim above the mercy seat); and the eternal efficacy of Christ's atoning work (rather than the blood of bulls and goats which cannot take away sin).

The Writer explains, therefore, how this heavenly sanctuary, where Christ ministers, transcends the earthly tabernacle of Moses and Aaron. In doing so he again underlines the *spiritual* character of the 'the time of reformation', that is, the new-covenant era. Importantly, he also applies his conclusions in a supremely practical way — to the consciences of his readers.

A spiritual tabernacle (9:11)

The first contrast between the two tabernacles (old-covenant and new) is that **'Christ came as High Priest of good things**

to come, with the greater and more perfect tabernacle not made with hands, that is, not of this creation' (9:11). Aaron and his descendants could offer atonement for past sins, but could promise nothing for the future. Christ's ministry, however, has promise of 'good things to come', being designed to bring 'many sons to glory' (2:10). Some translators render the words 'things to come' as 'things that have already come', referring to the new era inaugurated by Christ.[1] Either way, the new-covenant believer receives a blessedness that is both present and future.

In our eagerness to proclaim the death of Christ for the forgiveness of sins, we must not overlook the primary truth that Christ's atonement is not an end in itself. It is the means to a greater end, namely, **'that those who are called may receive the promise of the eternal inheritance'** (9:15). To 'receive the promise' means here 'to receive the things promised'.

This is further clarified in Galatians 4:5 where we are told that Christ came 'to redeem those who were under the law *that we might receive the adoption as sons'* (emphasis added). Furthermore, Romans 8:17 points out that, as adopted children, believers are necessarily also 'heirs of God and joint heirs with Christ'. So glorious is the future God has prepared for those who love him, that John is constrained to cry out: 'Beloved, now we are children of God, and it has not yet been revealed what we shall be' (1 John 3:2; see also 1 Cor. 2:9-10).

Secondly, the new covenant introduces a 'greater and more perfect tabernacle' which is 'not made with hands'. That is, it does not belong to 'this [material] creation' at all. It is a spiritual entity, the heavenly dimension in which Christ now ministers.

There is a certain tension in Hebrews between the idea that Christ still labours in the heavenly sanctuary as our great High Priest (see, for example, 7:25) and the fact that he rests from his labours, having 'sat down at the right hand of God ... waiting till his enemies are made his footstool' (10:12-13). The problem only arises because the Writer (and ultimately the Holy Spirit) is seeking to illustrate spiritual truths by using pictures comprehensible to the human mind. The priesthood, the ministry, the tabernacle, the throne, the serving and the resting — all are metaphors for different aspects of a glorious spiritual reality.

Perhaps we can understand it in this way. Christ's work is finished as regards atonement and satisfaction, but his work as our intercessor and the 'great Shepherd of the sheep' (13:20) will only be complete when every elect soul has been delivered from sin and death and gathered safely into the heavenly fold. Both facts should be a source of immense comfort to every believer. However, to perform this intercession, even now, requires of Christ no active labour, but only his *presence* in heaven as the 'slain' Lamb (Rev. 5:6).

His own blood (9:12)

The Writer continues to explain why the heavenly tabernacle is 'greater and more perfect'. Not only does it offer 'good things to come' and transcend the physical realm, but its sacrifices are of a completely different order.

Our great High Priest **'entered the Most Holy Place ... not with the blood of goats and calves, but with his own blood'** (9:12). In biblical thinking, a creature's blood represents its life — 'the life of the flesh is in the blood' (Lev. 17:11). In the same way, the blood of Christ represents his life — the life of the incarnate God. It was this divine yet human life that was sacrificed, an offering of infinite worth.

The psalmist tells us that no man 'can by any means redeem his brother, nor give to God a ransom for him ... that he should continue to live eternally and not see the pit'. He also tells us why — 'for the redemption of their souls is costly and it shall cease for ever' (Ps. 49:7-9). The sin of man is such that not even a human sacrifice can atone for another human soul, let alone the blood of bulls and goats. The redemption price is simply too high.

But the life of the God-man, Jesus Christ, is of such unimaginable value that a single, one-time offering ('it ceases for ever') is sufficient to atone for 'the sins of the whole world' (1 John 2:2; this does not signify that he made atonement for the sins of all men without *exception*, but for all men without *distinction*, having 'redeemed us to God by [his] blood out of every tribe and tongue and people and nation' — Rev. 5:9).

We further read that Christ **'entered the Most Holy Place once for all'** (9:12). In contrast to the high priests of the old covenant, who made atonement every year afresh, Christ made one sacrifice for ever. So complete was the satisfaction he offered to God for the sins of his people, that to repeat it was neither necessary nor possible. Here lies the fundamental error of the Roman Catholic 'mass' in which their priests claim in some way to offer Christ anew, repeating the sacrifice of Calvary. Such repetition (indeed, any repetition) is impossible.

Redemption obtained (9:12 cont.)

The *reason* why repetition is impossible is given in the words that follow — Christ entered the holy place **'having obtained eternal redemption'** (9:12). There could be no purpose in his *returning* to the work of atonement because it had been fully and perfectly completed — for time and eternity! Firefighters will enter a burning house at the risk of their lives if they know that people are trapped inside. They will go back again and again if necessary to rescue victims from the fire.

But once they have brought everyone to safety, and have accounted for each and every person, the work of rescue is complete. They will not re-enter the burning building, for there is no purpose in doing so.

Similarly, by his one offering of himself, Christ 'obtained' for his elect a redemption that was both complete and final. The Greek word used can mean 'find' or 'obtain'. It is used, says Owen, not only in the sense of 'to find' but also 'to obtain by our endeavours' (Rom. 4:1; Heb. 4:16).[2]

This verse demonstrates the miserable poverty of the idea that Jesus died on the cross merely to make salvation possible for those who choose to accept it. Such a view flatly contradicts this Scripture. If I *obtain* (or even 'find') something, it means that I possess it from that moment onwards. So Christ *obtained* eternal salvation for his people.

He possessed it, grasped it, and held it firm. Only if this were the case could he speak with such awesome confidence about the eternal security of his flock — 'My sheep hear my voice', he declares, 'and I know them, and they follow me. And I give them eternal life, and they shall never perish; neither shall anyone snatch them out of my hand. My Father, who has given them to me, is greater than all; and no one is able to snatch them out of my Father's hand' (John 10:27-29).

If the death of Christ only made salvation *possible*, then no atonement was actually accomplished when he died. No one was justified when he rose from the dead (Rom. 4:25). No one ascended with him to the heavenly places (Eph. 2:6). No one can be sure of eternal life. But if he has truly *obtained* eternal salvation, he has firmly secured it — not for himself, but for those whose faith and trust are in him, who are 'saved ... and called with a holy calling ... according to his own purpose and grace which was given to us in Christ Jesus before time began' (2 Tim. 1:9).

The conscience cleansed (9:13-14)

The Writer's argument reaches its climax in the verses that follow: **'For if the blood of bulls and goats and the ashes of a heifer, sprinkling the unclean, sanctifies for the purifying of the flesh, how much more shall the blood of Christ, who through the eternal Spirit offered himself without spot to God, cleanse your conscience from dead works to serve the living God?'** (9:13-14). The comparison and contrast made here bring us to the heart of the matter, namely the cleansing of the conscience. This is accomplished by the voluntary self-offering of a man who, uniquely, was both morally perfect ('without spot') and 'endowed with divine Spirit'.[3]

We note first that under the old covenant various cleansing rituals were provided, some of which the Writer mentions here by way of example. 'The blood of bulls and goats' is a direct reference to the Day of Atonement. During this annual ritual, the high priest first atoned for his own sins (and those of his household) by offering a bull and sprinkling its blood in the holy place. He then atoned for the sins of the people by offering a goat in the same way (Lev. 16:1-19).

Similarly, the 'ashes of a heifer' refer to a special provision described in Numbers 19. The animal was killed 'outside the camp' and burned to ashes. These were stored in a 'clean place' for use whenever anyone became ceremonially unclean (for example, by touching a dead body). Such people were to be cleansed by adding water to some of the ashes and sprinkling the concoction on the unclean person.

Of course, both types of sacrifice foreshadow the atoning work of Christ on the cross. Hebrews itself refers obliquely to the heifer towards the end of the epistle: 'Jesus ... suffered outside the gate [of Jerusalem]. Therefore let us go forth to him outside the camp, bearing his reproach' (13:13).

But the Writer's concern here does not lie in the detail. Rather, it is to point out that the sprinkling, whether of blood or ashes, effected only a ceremonial cleansing (a purifying of the flesh). It was a ritualistic purification that affected a man's relationship with the community — with God's people rather than with God himself (see, for example, Num. 19:13). In spiritual terms, it left the sinner inwardly unchanged.

That being so, '**how much more**' effective is the offering of Christ! For, by glorious contrast, the blood of Christ achieves a twofold purpose. Objectively, it purifies, not the flesh, but the soul, so that the sinner is accepted by a holy God. Subjectively, it cleanses the sinner's conscience, that is, his inner self (literally, the faculty of self-knowledge).

In turn, this inward cleansing also means two things. Firstly, it means that we have direct awareness or assurance of our cleansed condition. Secondly, it means that the soul cleansed by the blood of Christ is *truly* cleansed — for we could not *know* ourselves to be clean unless we were indeed so.

These are powerful, life-changing experiences — to be made *clean*, through and through, in the all-seeing eyes of the holy God whom we have offended constantly by our sin; and to be *sure* that we are clean! These are fundamental benefits of the new-covenant gospel, from which all other blessings flow. For unless we are truly, fully and finally cleansed from sin, we are unfit for adoption by God, unfit for heaven, and unfit for fellowship with Christ. But being cleansed '**from dead works**' (that is, our sins and transgressions) by the blood of Christ, we are qualified to '**serve the living God**'.

Believers are not, of course, without sin. 'If we say we have no sin', warns John, 'we deceive ourselves.' Yet 'if we confess our sins, he is faithful and just to forgive us our sin and to cleanse us from all unrighteousness' (1 John 1:8-9). We are constantly in danger of performing 'dead works' —

thoughts, words and actions that befit those who are spiritually dead rather than those who are 'risen with Christ' (Col. 3:1). But present-tense cleansing through the blood of Christ is ever available, so that even our sins (once confessed and repented of) cannot prevent us from walking with and serving the living God. For, 'If we walk in the light as he is in the light, we have fellowship one with another and the blood of Jesus Christ his Son cleanses us from all sin' (1 John 1:7; note the present tense of 'cleanses').

The eternal Spirit (9:14 cont.)

The Writer takes pains to emphasise the spiritual nature of the work of Christ. He tells us that when Christ **'offered himself without spot to God'** he did so **'through the eternal Spirit'** (9:14). The animal sacrifices of the old covenant had to be 'without spot', that is, free of physical blemish. But Christ's spotless purity was of a different order, being his moral and spiritual perfection before God. And just as his perfection was spiritual, so also was his offering, being made 'through the eternal Spirit'. Pink explains it as follows: 'He took upon him the "form of a servant", and therefore he was filled and energised by the [Holy] Spirit in all that he did... As he was subject to the Spirit in going into the wilderness (Matt. 4:1), so the Spirit led him a willing victim to the cross.'[4]

Other commentators believe that 'eternal Spirit' here refers not so much to the Holy Spirit as to the eternally divine nature of Christ himself. For example, John Brown says, 'Had it not been for our Lord's divine nature, he could not have yielded acceptable and effectual substituted obedience and satisfaction.'[5] On this understanding, 'through the eternal Spirit' could be paraphrased: 'in his own divine nature and thus in a manner acceptable to God'.

But there is more to it than that. The Writer adds, **'for this reason he is the Mediator of the new covenant, by means of death, for the redemption of the transgressions under the first covenant'** (9:15). Because his offering was acceptable to God and effectual in removing transgression, the Lord Jesus Christ has become the Redeemer of his people. He mediates a new order — the new covenant — under which sinners (through no merit or action of their own) are cleansed, accepted and adopted by the Father, being endowed with eternal life in Christ.

Furthermore, our verse alludes to the *effects* of Christ's atonement upon the sinner, namely, that it provides inner cleansing of the conscience rather than external (ritualistic) purification of the flesh. His offering avails to renew the inner man, for the essence of the new covenant, as we have seen in 8:10, is the inward transformation of the soul — God's laws are impressed upon the mind and written on a heart set free from sin.

These effects are brought about, of course, by the regenerating work and indwelling of the Holy Spirit — what the Scottish scholar Henry Scougal called 'the life of God in the soul of man'. The Lord Jesus Christ, 'by means of death', has secured 'the redemption' of those who transgress the law. He has thus cleared the way for the Holy Spirit to apply the work of atonement to individual sinners, bringing them to spiritual birth and taking up his residence in their souls.

An eternal inheritance (9:15)

Once again the Writer reminds us that Christ's atoning work is a means to a greater end. What is that end? **'That those who are called may receive the promise of the eternal inheritance'** (9:15). The beneficiaries of God's efficacious call and saving grace immediately receive 'the promise' — and, with equal certainty, they enter into 'the eternal inheritance' when their earthly pilgrimage is done. They possess, says Brown, 'that state of holy happiness, rising out of the enjoyment of the divine favour and fellowship, into which a man enters by believing, and which will be consummated in the heavenly world'.[6]

Indeed, the same Holy Spirit who brings us to life spiritually gives us assurance of this inheritance. Ephesians 1:14 tells us that the indwelling Spirit 'is the guarantee of our inheritance until the redemption of the purchased possession' (that is, until we actually enter into the inheritance). We have already considered the *nature* of this inheritance (the 'good things to come') in 9:11. But we notice further here that the inheritance can be obtained *only* through the new covenant. There is a *causal* connection between Christ mediating the new covenant (9:15a) and our position as heirs (9:15b) — 'heirs of God and joint heirs with Christ' (Rom. 8:17).

The Hebrews needed to grasp this, just as we do today. Many continue to place their faith in the ordinances of the old covenant, at least in the sense of believing that religious observances and rules for living can somehow bring them near to God. Paul berates the Colossians for holding such opinions: 'If you died with Christ from the basic principles [elements] of the world, why ... do you subject yourselves to regulations — "Do not touch, do not taste, do not handle" ... according to the commandments and doctrines of men?'

Some Christians claim, of course, that such regulations help them live a holy life, but this contradicts Paul, who continues: 'These things ... are of no value against the indulgence of the flesh' (Col. 2:20-23). We conquer sin as the indwelling Spirit applies the Word of God in the believing heart and mind. This process is not available under the old covenant, but is intrinsic to the new.

Finally, Christ mediates the blessings of the new covenant to 'those who are called' (9:15). They are called outwardly by the gospel (2 Thess. 2:14) and inwardly (and efficaciously) by the Spirit of Christ (John 10:27). As God's elect, they are called 'according to his purpose' (Rom. 8:28). They are the objects of mercy, called 'in the grace of Christ' (Gal. 1:6). They are called 'out of darkness into his marvellous light' (1 Peter 2:9). They are called to be 'saints' and to live in holiness (1 Cor. 1:2; 1 Peter 1:15).

28.
A better sacrifice

Please read Hebrews 9:16-24

Having returned to the subject of the new covenant, the Writer warms to his theme. As we have seen, it was *through his death* that Christ became the Mediator of the new covenant. His death was essential, **'for where there is a testament, there must also of necessity be the death of the testator'** (9:16). Moreover, although the covenant is eternal in its design, it could not be implemented until Christ had died for our sins, **'for a testament is in force after men are dead, since it has no power at all while the testator lives'** (9:17).

Thus the Writer drives home the one-to-one relationship between the death of Christ and the new covenant. Christ's atoning work *necessitates* a new covenant, while a new covenant *requires* his death — as mediator or 'testator'. That is why Paul preached 'Jesus Christ *and him crucified*' (1 Cor. 2:2, emphasis added), for **'without shedding of blood there is no remission'** (9:22).

This being the case, our passage demonstrates that the sacrifices and purification rites of the old covenant had no power in themselves, but were specifically given by God as pictures of the new. It made no sense, therefore, for the Hebrews to cling to the law now that Christ had come with 'the greater and more perfect tabernacle' (9:11).

God's covenants (9:16)

The Greek word translated 'testament' in verse 16 is the same word previously rendered 'covenant' in verse 15. This word *(diatheke)* means 'an arrangement' and normally signifies something having legal force or standing. Thus it can mean a will or testament (as is clearly intended here) or a more general agreement, covenant or contract between two (or more) parties.[1] Delitzsch comments: 'That the Mosaic dispensation is really to be regarded as being strictly such a covenant between two parties, is evident from the representation of it as a marriage contract ... which repeatedly meets us in the Old Testament.'[2] The NKJV translators have used different English words in verses 15 and 16 respectively to convey this flexibility of meaning.

In Galatians 3:20, Paul appears to make a play on the double meaning of the word. Enlarging on the fact that Moses was the mediator of the old covenant ('the law'), he points out that such mediation implies the assent of two parties ('Now a mediator does not mediate for one only'). He then adds, by way of contrast: 'but God is one'. What does this mean?

It refers back to the covenant of promise (which was the new covenant in anticipation). This was 'the covenant that was confirmed before by God in Christ' and which gives rise to 'the inheritance' (Gal. 3:17-18). In this context, therefore, the statement that 'God is one' indicates that 'God is alone' in establishing the new covenant, which is consequently more like a will or testament than a contract between two parties. Gooding puts it thus: 'What the Lord Jesus has put into operation by his death is a one-party covenant, a testament, a will. And we are not party to that testament in the sense that we have no conditions to fulfil in order to earn its benefits.'[3]

This distinction is important. The old covenant could not justify men, being 'weak through the flesh' (Rom. 8:3). It could only bring blessing if men were perfectly obedient to God's law. But because men are sinners by nature they are incapable of such obedience. The law is revealed, therefore, as that which exposes sin and drives us to Christ for free salvation (Rom. 3:20-24; Gal. 3:24).

This unmerited salvation is bestowed by grace under the new covenant, in which God acts alone, himself performing all things necessary for the redemption and reconciliation of the sinner. Those to whom God's mercy is thus extended contribute nothing to their salvation. Even the repentance and faith they must exercise has to be imparted by God's grace (Acts 5:31; Eph. 2:8). Christ's mediation is therefore of a wholly different kind from that of Moses. Whereas Moses arbitrated between God and Israel, Christ obtains 'the promise of the eternal inheritance' for his people and hands it down to them.[4]

Not without blood (9:17-18)

However, for this great inheritance to be passed down to men, Christ must die, **'for a testament ... has no power at all while the testator lives'** (9:17). Although God put the covenant of promise in place before time began (2 Tim. 1:9), and articulated it to Abraham, Isaac and Jacob, it could not be implemented as the *new* covenant until Christ had suffered and been glorified. 'It is his death alone', says Delitzsch, 'which, in accordance with the terms of the covenant, releases the inheritance for us.'[5] As a specific example of this, the Holy Spirit could not be sent to indwell believers in his fulness until this had occurred (see John 7:37-39).

But did not the Spirit also indwell Old Testament believers? Yes, indeed, but not in the new-covenant sense. Under the new covenant, the believer is 'filled with all the fulness of God' as Father and Son come to 'make [their] home with him' (Eph. 3:19; John 14:23). But before the new order could dawn, Jesus must shed his blood. This has important implications for our understanding of the old covenant, as the Writer proceeds to show.

'**Therefore**', he continues, '**not even the first covenant was dedicated without blood**' (9:18). The word 'therefore' is significant because it implies that whatever was ordained under the old covenant had *the single purpose of anticipating and illustrating the new*. Why were blood sacrifices required by the 'first covenant'? Because God's eternal plan was that his incarnate Son should die to redeem the elect. The ordinances of the old covenant were designed both to reflect and foreshadow that fact.

Because, in historical terms, the Mosaic system came first, many wrongly assume that Christ's saving work was somehow modelled on the old covenant. This gives the latter a priority it does not, in reality, possess. To accord it such priority was the error of the Judaisers, a mistake perpetuated today by sacerdotal, ritualistic and legalistic churches. But the very opposite is true — the provisions of the old covenant were preliminary models of the 'greater and more perfect tabernacle' that was yet to come. The New Testament utterly subordinates the old covenant to the new.

Nevertheless, once this is understood, the old covenant is powerfully illustrative of the new. That, indeed, is why the Mosaic covenant was instituted in the first place — to expose human sin and direct men to Christ (Rom. 3:19-26). It is to illuminate the work of Christ, therefore, that the Writer continues his description of the tabernacle and its ordinances.

Sprinkled with blood (9:19-22)

He reminds his readers that '**... when Moses had spoken every precept to all the people according to the law, he took the blood of calves and goats, with water, scarlet wool,** and hyssop, and sprinkled both the book itself and all the people, saying: "This is the blood of the covenant which God has commanded you." Then likewise he sprinkled with blood both the tabernacle and all the vessels of the ministry' (9:19-21). The Writer here augments the historical record in Exodus 24:3-8 in several respects,[6] but specially by adding 'the book' to the things sprinkled. This may be an oblique reference to the imperfection of the law, since the sole purpose of sprinkling was to make something clean in the sight of God. By way of further application, this passage tells us that the death of Christ is foundational to all acceptable proclamation of the Word ('the book'), to all worship ('the people'), and to all Christian service ('the vessels of ministry').

Once again we see why Paul 'determined not to know anything ... except Jesus Christ and him crucified' (1 Cor. 2:2). If our preaching, our worship, and our service have any other focus, they are misdirected. If we have any other trust than Christ, our confidence is false. Conversely, if our message majors on 'the precious blood of Christ' (1 Peter 1:19), and if we rely upon the efficacy of that blood to redeem both ourselves and those to whom we preach, then we are on solid ground indeed. For '... according to the law almost all things are purified with blood, and without shedding of blood there is no remission [of sin]' (9:22).

Copies of the true (9:23-24)

Without the death of Christ there could be no remission of sin. All forgiveness, whether granted to men before or after the time of Christ, is attributable to the one timeless sacrifice he made. This is the conclusion to which the Writer's logic drives us. 'Therefore', he continues, 'it was necessary that the copies of the things in the heavens should be purified with these' (9:23). *Necessary*, because without the sprinkling of blood the earthly sanctuary would not have been a copy of Christ's ministry at all! It would merely represent another false religion.

However, although animal sacrifices sufficed to illustrate the atoning work of Christ, that was all they could do; **'the heavenly things themselves'** could only be sanctified by **'better sacrifices than these'** (9:23). These 'better sacrifices' are, of course, the self-offering Jesus made upon the cross to save his people from their sins (Matt. 1:21). The use of the plural 'sacrifices' does not contradict the statement that Christ made 'one sacrifice for sins for ever' (10:12). It underlines, rather, the fact that his *single* sacrifice achieves in reality all that the *many* sacrifices of the old covenant accomplished typologically.[7]

Similarly, the 'heavenly things' that are 'purified' by his blood are the various elements of his saving work, from revelation to regeneration to glorification. All contribute efficaciously to the salvation of sinners because they are linked to the cross of Christ, being aspects of the new covenant in his blood.

The Writer is, of course, repeating here things that he has taught earlier in the epistle, but he does so for a reason. He seeks to drive home the lesson that the provisions of the old covenant were only 'copies of the true'. He says, **'Christ has not entered the holy places made with hands, which are copies of the true, but into heaven itself, now to appear in the presence of God for us'** (9:24). He wants his readers to understand that the Mosaic system was no more than a representation of the true gospel, and had no other purpose than to foreshadow the priestly work of Christ.

An original work of art may be immensely valuable, but copies can be bought for a few pence. These picture postcards derive their significance from the original, and serve only to remind us of the masterpiece they represent. So it is with the work of Christ and its representation in the types of the old covenant. If the Hebrews could only grasp this fact, their infatuation with rituals and legalistic practices would be cured.

29.
A sufficient offering

Please read Hebrews 9:25-28

The Writer now begins to rehearse, with growing emphasis, another aspect of the work of Christ, namely, that it was accomplished 'once for all'. He has, of course, already stated this in 9:12, but now he enlarges on the theme, not only here but also in the first eighteen verses of Hebrews 10. The epistle is moving towards the climax of its argument concerning the contrast between the two covenants, a culmination that will be reached in 10:18. As it does so, the Writer deems it necessary to underline the finality of the work of Christ on the cross. This is the pinnacle of his argument, the jewel in the gospel crown.

The conquest of sin (9:25-26)

The Writer uses repetition with great effect. Having stated his case first in 9:12, and rested it for a while, he now returns to it with renewed insistence: **'Not that [Christ] should offer himself often, as the high priest enters the Most Holy Place every year with blood of another. He then would have had to suffer often since the foundation of the world; but now, once at the end of the ages, he has appeared to put away sin by the sacrifice of himself'** (9:25-26).

Why did the 'copies' of heavenly things involve frequent and repeated sacrifices, while the reality they foreshadowed involved only one offering for ever? Does this not blur the typology and diminish the old covenant as a symbol of the new? Perhaps so, but the difference is inevitable.

The symbols could never take away sin, nor were they intended to do so. They were, in fact, a deliberate reminder that no final answer to sin had yet appeared (see 10:3). Their repetition thus gave notice of a better covenant and a better hope — 'for the law made nothing perfect [but pointed to] the bringing in of a better hope, through which we draw near to God' (7:19).

Contrariwise, it was impossible for Christ to suffer more than once. He certainly could not 'suffer often since the foundation of the world'. Why not? Because then *his* sacrifice would be demonstrably imperfect and not the final satisfaction for sin! Yet it is just that, for 'now, once ... he has appeared to put away sin by the sacrifice of himself' (9:26). Calvin remarks, 'Although we must daily seek for pardon, just as we daily provoke the wrath of God, yet because we are reconciled to God only by the pledge of the one death of Christ it is true to say that by it sin has been destroyed.'[1] We should not miss the full implication of this argument, namely, that Christ's single atoning sacrifice has settled the sin question once for all. And this means several things.

Firstly, it means that *the redemption of Christ's people is complete*. It requires no further meritorious or beneficial act — either on his part or on theirs. It is true that men must repent and believe the gospel if they are to be saved, but both repentance and faith are gifts imparted by the Holy Spirit in the process of regeneration, so that salvation is all of grace. The saved are God's 'workmanship' alone (Eph. 2:8-10).

Secondly, the uniqueness of Christ's death shows that *sin really has been conquered*. If it were not so, something more would be required of him. But no such thing is needed. Believers are 'dead indeed to sin, but alive to God in Christ Jesus our Lord' (Rom. 6:11). This is (and must be) an accomplished fact if Christ's atoning work is complete. 'Sin shall not have dominion over you', declares Paul, 'for you are not under law [the old covenant with its impotent offerings] but under grace [the new covenant in Christ's all-availing blood]' (Rom. 6:14).

But Christians still sin, you may respond. Yes, indeed they do. But this is because they still inhabit the flesh (the fallen body and mind) with its 'passions and desires' (Gal. 5:24). But those who are Christ's have crucified this fleshly nature and now live in the Spirit. They are, therefore, to walk in the Spirit as those who have been liberated from the power and the guilt of sin by the death of Christ (Gal. 5:24-25). In other words, the believer's victory over sin depends on his recognising the finality of Christ's death. It depends on his understanding that sin has no power over him and that he has 'put on the new man ... created by God in righteousness and true holiness' (Eph. 4:20-24). He has put on Christ (Gal. 3:26-27).

Thirdly, that Christ died once means that *Satan has been conquered.* Christ came that 'through death he might destroy him who had the power of death, that is the devil ...' (2:14). Through his death and resurrection, Christ has robbed the devil of his control over the destinies of men. At his second coming, he will complete the destruction of Satan. But the thing to notice is that Christ's death has *already* accomplished all that is necessary for Satan's current and ultimate defeat. There is simply nothing left for Christ to do in this regard. Although, therefore, we are ever conscious of the present activity of the enemy (1 Peter 5:8), we must always remember that he is a beaten foe and be ready to cry, with the apostle, 'Thanks be to God, who gives us the victory through our Lord Jesus Christ' (1 Cor. 15:57).

The finality of death (9:27-28)

The Writer caps his argument with an analogy. Men die but once: **'... it is appointed for men to die once, but after this the judgement'** (9:27). The Buddhist dream of reincarnation, of cycles of existence, is an illusion. So is the Roman Catholic doctrine of purgatory which seems to offer another chance to remedy our lives. Death is final and to die in our sins doubly so. There is nothing after death except judgement and that which follows it — heaven for those who trusted Christ or hell for those who did not.

Although we often quote this verse to emphasise the reality of judgement, the Writer's purpose is somewhat different. He invokes the judgement to emphasise the finality of death — the one death we all must die. He then draws his analogy: **'so Christ was offered once to bear the sins of many'** (9:28). If our death is final, and seals our future, how much more did the death of God's Son finalise and seal his life's work of saving his elect?

But within the analogy there is also a contrast. Quite properly, men fear judgement after death because they are sinners. If we are without Christ, we must die and bear our sins in the judgement. So Christ also died and also bore God's judgement upon sin. But whereas unforgiven men bear their own sin, Christ bore the sins of others. Specifically, he bore the sins 'of many'. He did not bear the sins of all men, either actually or potentially. This rules out both universalism in salvation, and the Arminian notion that anyone can be saved if they so choose. Only the 'many' (clearly, his elect) whose sins Christ bore are delivered.

Furthermore, since Christ *did* bear their sins it follows that they cannot be held responsible for those same sins in the judgement. Unlike those who must face the judgement of their sin, the elect have been delivered from condemnation by the blood of Jesus.

Great anticipation (9:28 cont.)

How may we recognise these beneficiaries of Jesus' death? They are identified as **'those who eagerly wait for him ... [to] appear a second time'** (9:28). These words refer back, of course, to verse 26: 'but now, once at the end of the ages, he has appeared to put away sin by the sacrifice of himself'. Christ's first coming occurred 'at the end of the ages' in the sense that it ushered in the final chapter of human history — the age of grace. During this age 'God is long-suffering towards us, not willing that any should perish but that all should come to repentance' (2 Peter 3:9-10). And, indeed, none of his elect *shall* perish — they will all come to repentance and faith in Christ. But, continues Peter, 'The day of the Lord will come as a thief in the night ... both the earth and the works that are in it will be burned up.'

However, those who are Christ's do not fear this cataclysm. Rather, they 'eagerly wait for him', looking for 'the blessed hope and glorious appearing of our great God and Saviour Jesus Christ' (Titus 2:13). With great anticipation, they 'look for new heavens and a new earth in which righteousness dwells' (2 Peter 3:13). They do not dread the judgement, for Christ has delivered them from condemnation.

On the contrary, they look forward eagerly to 'the day of the Lord', when Christ will 'appear' again. There might be a reference here to the high priest of old emerging from the tabernacle having completed the act of atonement. So Christ, having entered the true tabernacle with his own blood, and having once for all made efficacious atonement for sin, will reappear at his return in glory.

And he will do so **'apart from sin, for salvation'** (9:28). He will not come this time as a sacrificial lamb, destined to bear the sins of men, but 'apart from sin' as 'King of kings and Lord of lords', to finalise the salvation of his people — as the one who has vanquished death and hell and will wipe all tears away (Rev. 19:16; 20:14; 21:4). 'He appears not for expiation but for salvation', says John Brown, who continues: 'When he appears it will be ... for their complete and eternal deliverance from evil in all its forms and degrees, and for their being made happy ... up to their largest capacity of enjoyment, and during the entire eternity of their being.'[2]

30.
A body prepared

Please read Hebrews 10:1-5

The earthly sanctuary was cleansed by the blood of animal sacrifices, but 'the heavenly things themselves' had to be purified 'with better sacrifices' (9:23). The verses to which we now come expand and elaborate this statement. The 'better sacrifices' refer to Christ's atoning work; the superiority of that work over the shadows of the old covenant is now spelled out, with the help (and on the authority) of Scripture (Ps. 40:6-8).

It is instructive that Hebrews draws so heavily on Old Testament Scripture to substantiate its arguments. The Writer is never content just to state his case. He wants us to know that his exaltation of Christ and his rejection of the old covenant rest firmly on the law and the prophets *themselves*. Thus in verses 1-4 he first develops the logic of his contention and then in verses 5-10 seals his argument from Holy Writ. Thus this chapter and the next form a single unit, but they have been divided to keep each of them to a reasonable length.

A reminder of sin (10:1-4)

The Writer summarises his conclusions to date: **'For the law, having a shadow of the good things to come, and not the**

very image of the things, can never with these same sacrifices, which they offer continually year by year, make those
who approach perfect' (10:1). These things have all been
said before. The law is a shadow of heavenly things (8:5),
whereas the new covenant brings 'good things to come' (9:11).
The sacrifices of the law, though offered frequently, cannot
make men 'perfect' in the sight of God (9:9). But the Writer is
not afraid of repetition, for it is a powerful means of driving
home the truth. It also demonstrates the consistency of his
argument throughout this long epistle.

Neither should *we* fear to repeat ourselves when we teach
and preach the doctrine of Christ. While we must always strive
for freshness in presenting the gospel, the basic truths remain
unchanged. Freshness should never be confused with novelty
which, in striving to interest the hearers, introduces doctrines
and methods that have no scriptural warrant. Like Paul, we
must be willing to 'know nothing ... except Jesus Christ and
him crucified', for we shall never exhaust 'the unsearchable
riches of Christ' (1 Cor. 2:2; Eph. 3:8).

The use of the word **'shadow'** is significant. Kistemaker
says, 'What the Writer actually means is this: these [heavenly]
realities bask in the heavenly light and cast a shadow ... upon
practices stipulated by Old Testament law.'[1] Perhaps we can
make it even more specific. Just as a solid object casts an insubstantial shadow, so the new covenant consisting of 'good
things to come' projects a shadow backwards in time. The
result? The old covenant itself!

Looked at in this way, the new covenant is the solid eternal
reality and the old covenant is the shadow that it casts. Take
away the new and the old would disappear, just as a shadow
vanishes if the solid object is removed. Because, in time, the
old covenant came before the new (though not before the promise), we tend to think of it as having substance in itself. Like
the Hebrews, we may even give it precedence over the new.
But this is an illusion. The Mosaic 'shadow-covenant' only

existed because the new 'substance-covenant' was already in place (though 'not made known' until the appointed time — Eph. 3:3-5).

One consequence of this is, of course, that the old-covenant sacrifices were ineffectual. If they *could* have made men perfect, **'would they not have ceased to be offered?'** asks the Writer. Of course, **'for the worshippers, once purified, would have had no more consciousness of sins'** (10:2). That is, they would have no remaining sense of guilt or defilement. Delitzsch declares, 'The incapacity of the sacrifices of the day of atonement to perfect the worshippers is ... proved ... simply by the fact of their perpetual repetition.'[2]

The Writer's logic is impeccable, but we should not miss the implication. After all, it could be argued that the animal sacrifices *did* make men 'perfect' as regards their *past* sin but had to be repeated because there were always new sins to deal with. But this is inadmissible. The Writer's argument only makes sense if a perfect atonement is one that cleanses from *all* sins, past, present and future — one that deals with our *sinfulness* rather than our sins and requires no repetition.

Christ's atoning death is just such an offering for, says the Writer, it cleanses us from the very 'consciousness of sins'. This does not mean that believers are no longer aware of any sinful behaviour, for 'If we say that we have no sin, we deceive ourselves' (1 John 1:8). But it does mean that sin does not linger on the conscience of those who look to Jesus for cleansing, for 'If we confess our sins, he is faithful and just to forgive us our sins and to cleanse us from all unrighteousness' (1 John 1:9). The term 'consciousness of sin', says Lane, 'connotes the Hebrew sense of a burdened, smitten heart, which became most pronounced on the day of atonement when it was necessary to confront the holiness of God'.[3]

The old covenant offered no relief, since **'in those sacrifices there is** [not a removal of sin but rather] **a reminder of sins every year. For it is not possible that the blood of bulls**

and goats could take away sins' (10:3-4). Sacrifices were offered in the tabernacle daily, of course, but the reference here is, once again, to the Day of Atonement. The epistle concentrates on this annual rite because it most perfectly pictures the work of Christ as our great High Priest.

The annual repetition of the sacrifices, argues the Writer, in no way removed sin — whether in respect of its guilt or its power. On the contrary, it exacerbated the problem of sin by *reminding* the people of their sinful condition.

This was (and remains) the purpose of the law; for 'it was added', declares Paul, 'because of transgressions, till the seed [i.e. Christ] should come' (Gal. 3:19). Therefore, he concludes, '... the law was our tutor to bring us to Christ, that we might be justified by faith. But after faith has come, we are no longer under a tutor' (Gal. 3:24-25). And again: '... by the deeds of the law no flesh will be justified in his sight, for by the law is the knowledge of sin' (Rom. 3:20). Hebrews demonstrates that this oft-quoted statement applies not only to the moral aspect of the law, but also to its ceremonial aspects. The law in its *entirety* is designed to expose sin and point us to Christ as the only remedy.

A better sacrifice (10:5)

The Writer now turns to Psalm 40:6-8. His purpose is to show that the Old Testament itself supports his contention, testifying to the inadequacy of the law and pointing to the need for some better provision. This superior provision is found in the person of the incarnate Son of God. **'Therefore'**, continues the Writer, **'when he [Christ] came into the world he said: "Sacrifice and offering you did not desire, But a body you have prepared for me"'** (10:5). The Writer puts the words of Psalm 40:6 into the mouth of Christ. In so doing, he expresses both a negative truth and a positive one.

Christ declares first that the 'sacrifices and offerings' made under the old covenant were not desired by the Father. How can that be, seeing that God himself prescribed those same sacrifices and offerings? The answer is that he no longer requires them *now that Christ has come 'into the world'*. The idea here is that a new era has dawned, and what was once required has now become redundant. Shadow has been replaced by substance. And what is that substance? The positive statement gives the answer — 'a body you have prepared for me' (10:5).

Hebrews here, as elsewhere, follows the Septuagint Greek translation of the Old Testament, saying, 'a body you have prepared for me', instead of 'my ears you have opened [or pierced]', as in the original Hebrew. There have been many attempts to explain this deviation from the Hebrew text, the simplest being that the Writer always used the Septuagint, much as today we might work from an English translation of the original. This leaves unexplained, however, why the Septuagint deviates so markedly from the Hebrew in the first place.

Owen offers an alternative and better explanation. He suggests that the Septuagint was altered during the early centuries A.D. to conform to Hebrews. He cites other cases where New Testament readings seem to have been written back into the (earlier) Septuagint.[4] On this view, the Writer, under the guidance of the Holy Spirit, deliberately changed the words of the psalm to convey more clearly the meaning of David's prophecy. That is, he was not only quoting the psalm but interpreting it as well.

When the psalmist wrote, 'My ears you have pierced', he was probably referring to the ear-piercing ritual in which a slave, on the threshold of freedom after seven years' service, could voluntarily bind himself to his master for life (Exod. 21:1-6). This act of total commitment pictures the obedience of the incarnate Christ to his Father, an obedience to which the Writer has previously drawn our attention (5:7-8) and to which he will soon return (see 10:7). By altering the psalmist's words to 'A body you have prepared for me' the Writer links the idea of submissive obedience presented in the psalm to that of a bodily sacrifice. He thus expands on the original Hebrew of the psalm by implying that Christ's obedience was such as to lead him to the cross, where he offered himself bodily as a sacrifice for sins.

Preparation (10:5 cont.)

This thinking is in perfect harmony with Philippians 2:7-8: 'He made himself of no reputation, taking the form of a servant, coming in the likeness of men. And being found in appearance as a man, he humbled himself and became obedient [unto] death, even the death of the cross.'

The 'preparation' of Christ's body referred to in 10:5, involved several things. Firstly came *the incarnation*. Though he was 'in the form of God' he took the 'form of a servant, coming [to earth] in the likeness of men'. The incarnation is, perhaps, the greatest mystery of all. How was it possible for the eternal Son of God, while retaining his power and authority over all creation, to assume a truly human form with all its physical limitations? Well might Charles Wesley cry in wonder:

My God contracted to a span,
Incomprehensibly made man!

Yet Hebrews rightly insists on the coexistence in Jesus Christ of full deity and full humanity. This alone can fulfil God's eternal purposes of grace and fully meet the sinner's need.

Secondly, Christ's preparation involved *his life* — 'being found in appearance as a man'. He was truly man but unlike any other man he alone was without sin (4:15). His perfection *as a man* was essential, for the offering had to be without blemish. It is the righteousness of Christ *as a man* that is imputed to human sinners for their salvation.

The third and final preparation was *his obedience* as he faced the cross: 'For the joy that was set before him [he] endured the cross, despising the shame' (12:2). He humbled himself — 'as a sheep before its shearers is silent, so he opened not his mouth'. There was no bitter complaint over the way he was treated — no fury as his own creatures nailed him to a cross. He humbled himself because he had come to suffer vicariously for the 'transgression of [God's] people' (Isa. 53:7-8).

It is appropriate, therefore, that when we celebrate the Lord's Supper we specifically remember the 'breaking' of Christ's body and not simply his death as such. The sinless human body of Christ was an essential element in the logistics of redemption.

31.
A purpose fulfilled

Please read Hebrews 10:6-10

In the last chapter we began to consider the Writer's citation
from Psalm 40. We saw that the sole reason why the bodies of
animals were offered under the old covenant was to foreshadow
the bodily offering of the Son of God. Those animal sacrifices
meant nothing in themselves and provided no satisfaction to
the Godhead. That is why the psalmist continues: **'In burnt
offerings and sacrifices for sin you had no pleasure'** (10:6;
Ps. 40:6). However, the offering they *typified* is a different
matter altogether. For Jesus says, **'Behold, I have come —
in the volume of the book it is written of me — to do your
will, O God'** (10:7; Ps. 40:7-8).

The will of God (10:6-7,10)

Notice first how the psalmist emphasised the role of Old Testament Scripture in preparing for the coming of Christ — he
says, **'In the volume of the book it is written of me...'** The
word 'volume' refers to a scroll, while 'book' means anything
written. Although this is a clear reference to the Scriptures,
we do not know exactly *which* scriptures David had in mind.
However, it is a reasonable inference that he was speaking of
the law itself (particularly the priesthood and sacrifices) as
predictive of the work of Christ.

How difficult it would have been to understand the meaning of the death of Christ without the preparation provided by the old covenant! That would be true even for us today, but doubly so for Christians of the first century. A prophet arises, performs miracles of healing, claims to be the Son of God and is put to death by the Romans. What would his followers make of it all? But the law of Moses (along with other Scriptures) gave them a paradigm (a pattern) — one within which they could both interpret the death of Christ for themselves and proclaim it to others, especially their fellow Jews.

Above all, scriptural prediction implies that Christ came to do the will of God, for what is *prophesied* in advance must be *prepared* in advance. To the casual observer, Christ's death may have seemed an accident of history, the fortuitous outcome of human envy and intrigue. But Peter puts our thinking straight as he tells the Jews, 'Him, being delivered by the carefully planned intention and foreknowledge of God, you have taken by lawless hands, have crucified, and put to death' (Acts 2:23). Let us be clear — it was God's will that Christ should suffer and die for our sin. It was all planned in meticulous detail by a sovereign God. We can therefore be assured that 'God has called us ... not according to our works, but according to his own purpose and grace which was given to us in Christ Jesus before time began' (2 Tim. 1:9). Christ was 'the Lamb slain from the foundation of the world' (Rev. 13:8; see also 1 Peter 1:19-20).

The death of Christ was God's eternally ordained means for the salvation of the elect, whose names are written in the 'book of life of the Lamb' (Rev. 13:8). It was thus in obedience to the will of the Father, and in fulfilment of his timeless purpose, that Christ came bodily into the world to offer himself — 'a full, perfect and sufficient sacrifice' for sin. For, says Calvin, 'Christ alone ... is fully fitted to do the will of God.'[1]

The unprotesting animals sacrificed under the old covenant were merely pictures, preparing men's understanding for the

reality that would follow. It was this reality that Isaiah proclaimed, long before Christ came, when he wrote, 'He was led
as a lamb to the slaughter, and as a sheep before its shearers is
silent, so he opened not his mouth ... he was cut off from the
land of the living; for the transgression of my people he was
stricken' (Isa. 53:7-8).

The self-giving of the Saviour to redeem us from our sins
ought to be a constant source of comfort and thanksgiving for
every believer. Both the purpose and the means of our salvation were ordained before we existed, and represent not just
the *desire,* but the unchangeable *will* of our sovereign God!

Passing by verses 8-9 for the moment, we find the consequence of God's pre-ordained will and purpose stated in verse
10: **'By that will we have been sanctified** [consecrated]
**through the offering of the body of Jesus Christ once for
all.'** Lane comments, 'The immediate ground of consecration
is the totally new offering of the body of Jesus Christ as the
inaugural act of the new covenant. The ultimate source is the
will of God.'[2]

Note that 'sanctified' is in the perfect tense (indicating a
completed work) and the passive voice (indicating a work of
God, not man). Just as Christ's offering was once for all, so is
the setting apart (consecration) of God's elect. Kistemaker writes,
'The verb [been sanctified] indicates that at a given moment, someone acted on our behalf to sanctify us, and we have become
pure.'[3] Delitzsch adds, 'In [God's] will, we are or have been
once for all sanctified.'[4] What does this mean in practice?

Invariably in Hebrews, sanctification is the once-for-all act
of consecration by which God 'sets aside' the believer from a
profane and empty way of life to serve and glorify the living
God. Peter describes the sequence of God's saving work in
the soul of man. We are, he says, (1) 'elect according to the
foreknowledge of God the Father,' (2) 'in sanctification of [or
by] the Spirit, (3) 'for obedience [to the gospel] and' (4)
'sprinkling of the blood of Jesus Christ' (1 Peter 1:2).

The New Testament writers usually thought of sanctification as that work of the Holy Spirit in which he delivers an individual from the authority of darkness and translates him into the kingdom of Christ (Col. 1:13). For example, Paul reminds the Corinthians that they had once lived in rebellion against God, then adds, 'Such were some of you. But you were washed, but you *were sanctified*, but you were justified in the name of the Lord Jesus Christ and by the Spirit of our God' (1 Cor. 6:11, emphasis added). The believer's sanctification is not so much a thing that he must strive towards, as an accomplished work of grace by which he is obligated to live for God (1 Cor. 6:19-20).

Sanctification, in this sense, can therefore be thought of as the sum and outcome of four things. Firstly, the eternal purpose of the Father ('by that will we have been sanctified'). Secondly, the atoning work of Christ ('through the offering of the body of Jesus'). Thirdly, the effectual operation of the Holy Spirit, implementing and applying the first two means at the time of regeneration. And fourthly, the outworking of an *accomplished* sanctification in the daily life of the believer, causing him to walk in the ways of God. (The doctrine of sanctification is greatly impoverished if we restrict it to only the fourth of these points.)

What an amazing confluence of divine works! What pains God has taken to sanctify us! How important it must be, therefore, that we have been set apart in Christ for God's glory. Well might Paul instruct the Thessalonians: '... this is the will of God, your sanctification' (1 Thess. 4:3).

The two covenants cannot coexist (10:8-9)

We return, finally, to verses 8-9. Here the Writer draws a further lesson from Psalm 40, namely that the coming of the new covenant in Christ necessitates the extinction of the old covenant. He writes, **'Previously saying, "Sacrifice and offering, burnt offerings, and offerings for sin you did not desire, nor had pleasure in them" (which are offered according to the law), then he said, "Behold, I have come to do your will, O God." He takes away the first that he may establish the second'** (10:8-9). The sacrifices made according to the law are no longer acceptable to God. He has no pleasure in them at all — they have lost both their significance and any efficacy they once possessed. Why? Because God deliberately 'takes away the first'. Although, technically, 'the first' refers to the old-covenant sacrificial system, commentators generally agree that the sacrifices here stand for the arrangement or covenant from which they derived their validity.[5]

Under the first covenant, sacrifices were essential to man's approach to God. Only through those sacrifices was it possible for people to draw near to a holy God and find pardon and cleansing. Of course, as we have seen, such cleansing was ceremonial, not affecting the heart or conscience. But nevertheless, it was sufficient to restore a formal peace between God and the sinner. But now, suddenly, the first covenant is annulled and its sacrifices and other ordinances become meaningless. Again, why has God done this?

The Writer provides the answer: 'He takes away the first *that he may* establish the second' (10:9, emphasis added). The 'second' sacrifice — the new covenant in Christ — could not be established without the annulment of the old. That is, the two covenants cannot coexist. This is a fundamental tenet of Paul's theology and underlies his argument in the epistle to the Galatians (see, e.g., Gal. 4:21-31).

Paul does, of course, teach that the 'covenant of promise', which had its fulfilment in the new covenant, existed historically *alongside* the old covenant (Gal. 3:15-18). But there was never any blending or admixture of the covenants of promise and law; they remained separate and distinct. It was the basic error of the Judaisers to teach that the work of Christ could somehow be grafted on to the Mosaic covenant.[6]

But the new covenant in the blood of Christ, which is the culmination and full flower of the covenant of promise, not only stands separate from the old covenant — it necessitates its removal. Guthrie explains: 'The verb [take away] generally has the sense of "kill". There is a finality about the passing of the old. If there had not been, the second could never have been established.'[7] The law remains only as 'our tutor to bring us to Christ, that we might be justified by faith. But after faith has come we are no longer under a tutor' (Gal. 3:24-25).

Many who claim to follow Christ still make the same mistake as the Judaizers. They teach that the works of the law are necessary for salvation (legalism — Gal. 5:1-6). They make faith itself a work, believing it to be a capacity of the unregenerate human mind, whereas it is in fact God's gift by grace (Eph. 2:8-9). They perpetuate a human priesthood, still offering sacrifices for fellow sinners — when Christ has abolished human priestly orders and made the final sacrifice for sin (10:13-14). Yet others, more mildly, are confused about the role of old-covenant law in the Christian life.

Let us heed Paul's appeal to the Galatians: 'Stand fast therefore in the liberty by which Christ has made us free and do not be entangled again with a yoke of bondage' (Gal. 5:1). Some accused Paul of antinomianism, which teaches that because we are no longer 'under the law' we may live as we like, free of all moral constraint. Paul nails this lie. 'Shall we continue in sin that grace may abound?' he asks. 'Certainly not! How shall we who died to sin live any longer in it?' (Rom. 6:1-3). As we saw in Hebrews 8:7-13, the essence of the new covenant in Christ is that the ineffective externality of the Mosaic law is replaced by an efficacious inward principle, namely, of the law of Christ written in the mind and heart of every believer.

32.
An eternal perfection

Please read Hebrews 10:11-18

These verses represent a second pinnacle in the 'theological' part of Hebrews. The epistle reached a first climax as it unveiled the nature of the new covenant in Hebrews 8:7-13. The Writer then returned to garner yet deeper lessons from the symbolism of the Mosaic system, finding both parallels and contrasts between the two covenants. But now there is a new crescendo, as he begins to declare the ultimate achievement of Christ's atoning work — the eternal perfection of those for whom he died.

In the previous chapter we saw that believers have been 'sanctified' by the death of Christ according to the will of God (10:10). This sanctification is a completed work ('we have been sanctified') and refers to God's 'setting aside' of the elect for his own glory — in fulfilment of his eternal purpose (2 Tim. 1:9). The passage to which we now come enlarges on this theme, showing us the destiny of those who are thus sanctified. Under the new covenant, they have been 'perfected for ever'. Accordingly, there is no further need of offerings for sin.

Complete and perfect (10:11-12)

The Writer returns to the theme of Christ's 'once-only' offering, a theme previously developed in 7:23-27; 9:25-28 and

10:1-3. Clearly, this is a subject worthy of repetition, something the Hebrews needed to grasp. However, as always, the Writer does not just restate his earlier teaching, but elaborates it. He continues: **'And every priest stands ministering daily and offering repeatedly the same sacrifices, which can never take away sins. But this Man, after he had offered one sacrifice for sins for ever, sat down at the right hand of God'** (10:11-12).

The futility of the old covenant is first underlined. 'Every priest ... stands ... daily ... repeatedly ... the same sacrifices which can never take away sin.' Why ever did God institute such a system? We have already seen the answer in Galatians, where Paul asks, 'What purpose then does the law serve? It was added because of transgressions, till the Seed should come to whom the promise was made ... the law was our tutor to bring us to Christ' (Gal. 3:19-25). In pointing to Christ, and to our need of him, the law is rich with the holiness of God, the sinfulness of man and the typology of Christ. But as a means of cleansing sin and reconciling sinners to God, it was bankrupt. The Hebrews had failed to grasp this distinction.

The Writer deftly uses the redemptive poverty of the old covenant as a background against which to display the surpassing excellence of Christ's atoning work. This Man has offered 'one' sacrifice, not many. Its efficacy lasts 'for ever' so that it needs no repetition. He no longer stands ministering daily, but has 'sat down' — his labours ended and his work complete. 'A seated priest', says Bruce, 'is the guarantee of a finished work.'[1] And where is he seated? At 'the right hand of God', the place of glory, eminence, accomplishment and satisfaction.

The completeness and perfection of Christ's saving work should be a continual comfort to us, beset as we are with sin and frailty. Like Paul, every true believer is at times constrained to cry, 'O wretched man that I am! Who will deliver me from this body of death?' Who will liberate my soul from 'the sin that dwells in me'? (Rom. 7:24,20). We are conscious daily of our failure to live up to our high calling in Christ.

Under the old covenant we might have sought relief in the daily offerings made in the temple courts — but our *consciences* would have remained unclean (9:9). What are we to do? We are to turn to Christ, whose once-shed blood *does* cleanse the conscience from every dead work! It restores our souls to fellowship with the Lord, that we might serve the living God (9:14). 'If we walk in the light as he is in the light', declares John, 'we have fellowship with one another, and the blood of Jesus Christ his Son cleanses us from all sin' (1 John 1:7). 'Cleanses' here is in the simple present tense and can be understood to mean 'keeps on cleansing'. That is, just as walking in the light is the continuous enjoyment of a relationship with God, so cleansing is the continuous experience of those who do so walk.

Enemies vanquished (10:13)

Christ's 'session' (his being seated) at his Father's right hand not only denotes a finished work, but also anticipates a final victory — **'from that time [he is] waiting till his enemies are made his footstool'** (10:13). The enemies are still active, even as Christ reigns. Who are those enemies? They are, first of all, rebellious mankind, portrayed so graphically by the psalmist: 'The kings of the earth ... and the rulers take counsel together against the LORD and against his Anointed [Christ], saying, "Let us break their bonds in pieces and cast away their cords from us"' (Ps. 2:1-3). It was to this verse that the first disciples turned for comfort and encouragement as they faced the rising tide of persecution (Acts 4:23-27). They saw it fulfilled in the way Herod, Pilate, the Romans and the Jews, each for their own reasons, sought to exterminate the infant church of Christ.

But they also knew that the God who inspired David to pen the psalm was sovereign over the affairs of men. Their enemies 'were gathered together', they told their almighty Father, 'to do whatever your hand and your purpose determined before to be done' (Acts 4:28). This sublime confidence in the sovereignty of God was characteristic of the early church. Should it not also characterise the church today?

Jesus shares his Father's throne of omnipotence, and all authority has been given to him in heaven and on earth. It is in this confidence that we speak God's Word 'with all boldness', and seek to 'make disciples of all the nations' (Acts 4:29; Matt. 28:18-19). Because the enemies are still *there*, this will involve conflict. Men still resist the claims of Christ and determine to destroy his kingdom. But their wrath will be turned to the glory of God. Some of them will be saved despite themselves. The gates of hell will not withstand the onslaught of the gospel. God's purpose in Christ will be fulfilled.

Secondly, of course, Christ has an enemy in Satan. Ultimately, 'We do not wrestle against flesh and blood, but against principalities, against powers, against the rulers of the darkness of this age, against spiritual hosts of wickedness in the heavenly places' (Eph. 6:12). The devil and his hosts may employ men in their warfare against the church of Christ, but the strength of evil is ultimately a *spiritual* strength.

It is most important that we should understand this. Otherwise we shall try to use *natural* means to overcome the enemy, when only spiritual weapons will avail. Christians today seem shy of admitting the reality of Satan and his hosts, and are correspondingly slow to take up the necessary arms. Let us heed Paul's teaching here. 'Though we walk in the flesh', he declares, 'we do not war according to the flesh. For the weapons of our warfare are not carnal but mighty in God for pulling down strongholds, casting down arguments and every high thing that exalts itself against the knowledge of God, bringing every thought into captivity to the obedience of Christ' (2 Cor. 10:3-5).

There is something important for us to notice here. Although elsewhere the apostle exhorts us to *defend* ourselves with spiritual weapons, he is here speaking of *attack*! Satan's strongholds are reduced to rubble, ungodly arguments are undermined and those who oppose the gospel are abased. The philosophies of men are overwhelmed by the truth of God and led captive, as it were, by Christ. This was Paul's experience and it can be ours also.

What are these spiritual weapons? Not social involvement, political manipulation, ecclesiastical entertainment, or enticements offered to the natural man — as some appear to think. Rather, our weapons are the gospel of God's grace, the Word of truth, the proclamation of Christ and him crucified, the fruit of the Spirit, prevailing prayer and fellowship in the gospel. These are the means by which Christ's victory over the powers of darkness will be expressed and implemented.

When Christ disarmed principalities and made an open show of Satan — when he ascended on high and led captivity captive — what were his throne-gifts to the church? They were men raised up to minister the Word of God, the gospel of his grace (Col. 2:15; Eph. 4:8-12). We shall only experience the victory of Christ if we employ spiritual weapons in the battles that must still be fought.

However, the victory is assured. Indeed, it is already accomplished in the annals of heaven. Christ is at rest, seated — waiting for the time when his enemies will be finally subdued and will 'become his footstool'.

Perfected for ever (10:14)

There is one further enemy. Paul writes, concerning the general resurrection, 'Then comes the end, when [Christ] delivers the kingdom to God the Father, when he puts an end to all rule and all authority and power. For he must reign till he has put all enemies under his feet. The last enemy that will be destroyed is death' (1 Cor. 15:24-26). Christ's victory over death is implicit in his own death and resurrection, but it is made explicit in the Writer's next statement: '**... by one offering he has perfected for ever those who are being sanctified**' (10:14). The beneficiaries of God's saving grace, being 'perfected for ever', will no longer be subject to death.

This perfection requires that they should *live*, and do so in the fullest sense of that word ('perfection' means 'completeness'). Believers already have eternally saved *souls*, but one day they will also have redeemed and spiritual *bodies*, like Christ's own resurrection body (Rom. 8:23; 1 Cor. 15:22-23). The Writer can speak of this eternal perfection as already accomplished because, in terms of what is needful for it to occur, nothing remains to be done. The outcome is assured by Christ's 'one offering'.

What does it mean to be 'perfected for ever'? The primary meaning relates to a never-to-be-repeated cleansing or purging from sin.[2] The basis (though not the whole) of eternal perfection lies in the removal of sin. If this seems an anticlimax it is because we have a restricted view of sin and its consequences. Once we understand how profoundly sin has altered the very structure of the creation (see Rom. 8:18-25), and the relationship of God to man, we shall also understand the glory of our deliverance from sin. This deliverance, wrought by the once-for-all offering of our great High Priest, lies at the heart of all that God has purposed for his people. As Henry F. Lyte sings:

Ransomed, healed, restored, forgiven;
Who like me his praise should sing?

But there is more to it than that. The context links 'perfection' to the fulfilment of the new covenant. Bruce argues: 'That the "perfection" of which our author speaks is bound up with the new covenant is made plain by his repetition [in 10:16-17] of the words of Jeremiah 31:33 ff.'[3] The apostle John bears witness to the significance of this fulfilment: 'Beloved, now we are children of God; and it has not yet been revealed what we shall be, but we know that when he is revealed, we shall be like him, for we shall see him as he is' (1 John 3:2). Just as Christ 'has been perfected for ever' (7:28), so his elect will also be perfected (indeed, from heaven's perspective, have already been perfected).

In its fullest sense, then, this perfection is nothing short of eternal likeness to Christ. John freely admits that '... it has not yet been revealed what we shall be.' He does not mean that the believer's future involves something apart from likeness to Christ, but simply that we cannot yet begin to comprehend what it will *mean* to be like Christ.

We next notice that perfection attaches to 'those who are being sanctified'. What does this mean? It can be taken in one of two ways. It might refer to a *process* of sanctification ('progressive sanctification') in which the believer grows more Christ-like with the passage of time; or it could simply mean that Christ makes perfect those whom he first sanctifies or sets apart ('positional sanctification'). The words translated 'those who are being sanctified' (NIV and NKJV) or 'them that are sanctified' (AV and others; almost all older translations use this simple present tense) mean literally 'the sanctified'. Young's Literal Translation renders it: '... he hath perfected to the end those sanctified.'

Because 'sanctified' is a present participle in the original Greek, many authorities today represent sanctification as an ongoing process rather than an accomplished fact. However, it would be more consistent with general New Testament usage if the Writer is employing the present tense to signify 'those who *are now in a state of sanctification*'.

This, I believe, is the correct interpretation. Only four verses earlier (10:10), Hebrews clearly refers to the believer's sanctification as a completed work, accomplished by Jesus' death upon the cross. It is unlikely that the Writer now wishes to teach that sanctification is an ongoing and as yet incomplete process. Indeed, the idea that believers are being made more holy with the passage of time would sit uncomfortably with the primary statement of this verse, namely, that the elect *have been* perfected for ever by the death of Christ.

Brown puts it thus: 'The "sanctified", or separated, or consecrated ones, are the same persons who in other parts of the epistle are represented as those who shall be "heirs of salvation" — the "many sons" of God to be "brought to glory" — the "brethren" of the Messiah.'[4] Calvin agrees: 'When he says "them that are sanctified" he includes in this phrase all the sons of God and reminds us that we shall only seek in vain if we look elsewhere for the grace of sanctification.'[5]

The New Testament teaches that Christians must 'grow in the grace and knowledge of our Lord and Saviour Jesus Christ' (2 Peter 3:18). Many other Scriptures make it plain that the followers of Christ are to mature and not remain 'babes in Christ' — they must 'put off' the old man and 'put on' the new man. They are to 'add to [their] faith virtue, to virtue knowledge, to knowledge self-control ...' and so on, making their 'calling and election sure' (2 Peter 1:5-10). But the word 'sanctification' is seldom, if ever, used in the New Testament to describe these things.

No further offering (10:16-18)

The Writer now draws together his two climactic themes —
the new covenant and the eternal perfection of the believer.
He first reminds us of the nature of the new covenant — that
it produces an inward transformation whereby God's laws are
written in the heart and mind of the believer: **'But the Holy
Spirit also witnesses to us; for after he had said before,
"This is the covenant that I will make with them after
those days, says the LORD: I will put my laws into their
hearts, and in their minds I will write them"'** (10:16).
Notice how he attributes the prophetic word to the Holy Spirit
rather than to Jeremiah. Not only is the original prophecy from
God but the *written record* of that prophecy, the Scripture, is
here identified as the work of the Spirit.

Next, he states the judicial and enabling cause of God's
gracious new-covenant work in the heart of man. The prophecy continues: **' "Their sins and their lawless deeds I will
remember no more"'** (10:17). God 'forgets' the sins of his
people as a direct consequence of Christ's atoning work — he
remembers them no more. This does not mean that God has
amnesia! He knows all things — past, present and future. It
does mean, however, that he no longer *holds us to account* for
our sins. Paul puts it thus: 'You, being dead in your trespasses
... he [God] has made alive together with him [Christ], having
forgiven you all trespasses, having wiped out the handwriting
of requirements that was against us ... and he has taken it out
of the way, having nailed it to the cross' (Col. 2:13-14).

Finally, the Writer draws his conclusion: **'Now where there
is remission of these, there is no longer an offering for sin'**
(10:18). This can be viewed in two complementary ways. On
the one hand, it tells us that Christ's saving work, and the
remission of our sins, is complete and final. Since Christ will
not die again ('there is no longer an offering') the deliverance

of the believer from sin must, of necessity, be total and absolute. Our sins, past, present and future, have been forgiven for eternity. We have been delivered from the power of sin and death and set apart (sanctified) for the praise of the glory of God (Eph. 1:6-7). All this is an accomplished fact, for Christ '*became* for us ... righteousness, sanctification and redemption' (1 Cor. 1:30, emphasis added).

On the other hand, we can view it in reverse. Because the elect have been perfected for ever, and their sins obliterated by the death of Christ, there is no *need* of any further offering for sin. Meritorious works, religious cleansing rituals, exorcisms, the so-called 'sacrifice' of the Roman Catholic mass, and all similar devices, are alike pointless and inadmissible. They are *unnecessary* for the believer and *unavailing* for the unbeliever.

Some fear that such a complete exoneration of the believer from sin will encourage lawlessness, but the reverse is true. How am I, as a follower of Christ, to overcome 'the sin that [still] dwells in me'? (Rom. 7:20). Let Paul supply the answer: '... reckon yourselves to be dead indeed to sin, but alive to God in Christ Jesus our Lord. Therefore do not let sin reign in your mortal body, that you should obey it in its lusts ... present yourselves to God as being alive from the dead, and your members as instruments of righteousness to God. For sin shall not have dominion over you, for you are not under law but under grace' (Rom. 6:11-14).

33.
An entry to the holiest

Please read Hebrews 10:19-21

Having unveiled the twin pinnacles of his message — the new covenant and the eternal perfection of the believer — the Writer feels it appropriate to summarise and apply his conclusions. These verses are therefore a watershed in the epistle, marking its transition from theology to practice.

This is not to suggest that the first ten chapters of Hebrews lack practical application. An outstanding example is the exhortation in 4:14-16 that we should 'come boldly to the throne of grace that we may obtain mercy and grace to help in time of need'. Again, in 5:12 – 6:12, the Writer chides his readers for their immaturity and sounds a solemn alarm against apostasy. Nevertheless, the previous chapters have been predominantly didactic or instructional, setting forth in great detail the doctrine of Christ and the new covenant. Now the time has come to apply these great truths to the life of the believer and the church — by way of warnings, examples and encouragements. In beginning to do so, the Writer provides a brief but arresting summary of his message. We shall consider this summary in the present chapter, and its application in the next.

Boldness (10:19)

In summarising the work of redemption and the benefits of the new covenant, the Writer highlights three things that the believer possesses in Christ. The first is *boldness*, the second is *access*, and the third is *representation*: **'Therefore, brethren, having boldness to enter the Holy Place by the blood of Jesus, by a new and living way which he consecrated for us, through the veil, that is, his flesh, and having a High Priest over the house of God ...'** (10:19-21). We have boldness in the blood of Christ, access through the life of Christ and representation by the priesthood of Christ. Let us consider these in turn.

It is difficult for modern readers to grasp the radical nature of the first of these statements: 'having boldness (or authorisation[1]) to enter the Holy Place'. To a first-century Jew, the idea that anyone other than the high priest might seek to enter the holiest-of-all — even in thought or imagination — would be profoundly shocking. As we saw in 9:7-8, this awesome privilege was reserved for the high priest, and that but once a year. And even he would have entered fearfully, knowing the fate that awaited any who dared approach the presence of God with less than perfect obedience. How, then, can the Writer claim that *all* who believe in Christ may enter the inner sanctum *boldly*, without fear or trepidation? It is one thing to 'come boldly to the throne of grace' (4:16), amazing as that is. It is an entirely different matter to enter the presence of one who dwells 'in unapproachable light, whom no man has seen or can see' (1 Tim. 6:16). Yet, insists the Writer, believers have boldness to do exactly that.

The solution to this paradox is that we have 'boldness ... by the blood of Christ' (10:19). When the high priest of old entered the holiest he did so under the protection of the shed blood of animal sacrifices. The law taught him that God accepted their death in place of his own. But even so, since his conscience was not cleansed by those sacrifices, he must have entered with dread, not boldness. There was a further problem. He was only safe as long as he followed perfectly the detailed instructions God had given. How could he be sure that his obedience was perfect?

Under the new covenant, everything is different. Firstly, the believer enters the holiest — the presence of the living God — not alone but 'in Christ'. We are *accepted*, not in and of ourselves, but 'in the Beloved' (Eph. 1:6). Secondly, and more objectively, we come authorised and protected by the blood of Christ, the eternal Son of God, whose perfect self-offering *guarantees* our acceptance in a way that animal sacrifices never could. Thirdly, and subjectively, the blood of Jesus Christ cleanses our *consciences*, so that we come before God in the happy awareness of being truly clean in his sight. As we saw in 10:14, we have been 'perfected for ever' by the shedding of that blood, and perfection makes us bold. Fourthly, our confidence lies not in our own obedience but in Christ's perfect conformity to the will of God (10:7). Our boldness, therefore, derives from our understanding of what Christ has achieved for his blood-bought people, and from our faith in the perfection of his offering.

If this is so, then it underlines the importance of the doctrine of the atoning and vicarious death of Christ. Today, that doctrine is seldom taught in its fulness but is sadly fudged, romanticised or compromised. Yet unless we know, with crystal clarity, what was actually accomplished when Jesus died and rose again, we cannot come with boldness before a holy God. Let us, then, both understand and teach the glorious doctrine of Christ's atonement — how he died for our sins, rose again for our justification, and perfected for ever those whom he has set apart in sovereign, electing grace (Rom. 4:25; Heb. 10:14; 2 Tim. 1:9).

Access (10:20)

The second element of the Writer's summary is that we have access **'by a new and living way which he consecrated for us, through the veil, that is, his flesh'** (10:20). We learn here that our approach to 'the Majesty on high' is not only through the death of Christ, but also through his life — 'by a new and living way'. Owen expounds the significance of the 'new' way in the following terms: 'It is new (1) because it was but newly made and prepared; (2) because it belongs unto the new covenant; (3) because it admits of no decays but is always new, as unto its efficacy and use ...'[2]

It is a new way, firstly, because it differs profoundly from the way people came to God under the old covenant. They came to an earthly tabernacle with dead and ineffective sacrifices (9:11-12). They came through a sinful human intermediary, the high priest, who must atone for his own sins before he could account for theirs (9:7; cf. Lev. 16:11,15). They came with consciences which had not been cleansed, and in their coming were *reminded* of their sin, not *relieved* of it (9:14; 10:3-4).

Sadly, there are many today whose coming to God is equally marred. They trust in earth-bound institutions; in their own works rather than Christ's. They rely on human priesthoods, not on his high-priestly office. They know little of the sanctifying work of the Spirit or the cleansing of the conscience by the blood of Christ. Consequently, they know little of that 'access by faith into this grace in which we stand, and rejoice in hope of the glory of God' (Rom. 5:2).

Secondly, we come by a *living* way, for Jesus himself is 'the way, the truth and the life. No one comes to the Father except through [him]' (John 14:6). We often apply these words to the unsaved, urging them to put their trust in Christ. But the statement applies equally to the believing soul. He does

not just *show* us the way, or *open* the way — he *is* the way
into communion with the Father. When we approach God we
do so in Christ, that is, by virtue of our union with him in his
death, resurrection and exaltation. We come also by virtue of
his indwelling Spirit (John 17:23; Rom. 6:4-8; Gal. 2:20; Rom.
8:9-11).

That he has **'consecrated'** (or opened) this way 'for us'
means that he has pledged himself and undertaken to be our
eternal access to the Father. 'He is able to save to the uttermost those who come to God through him', just because 'he
ever lives to make intercession for them' (7:25).

The new and living way has been created **'through the
veil, that is, his flesh'**. The veil referred to here is the curtain
that separated the most holy place — and the Shekinah glory
— from the remainder of the tabernacle. Anyone entering the
holiest-of-all must, of course, pass through this curtain. It was
this same veil (albeit in the temple of Herod) that was 'torn in
two from top to bottom' when Jesus died, signifying that the
way into the holiest had at last been laid open (Mark 15:38; cf.
Heb. 9:8). All this rich symbolism is encapsulated in the Writer's
brief allusion.

The traditional interpretation of 10:20 is that the veil represents Christ's flesh. Calvin writes, 'His flesh ... conceals like
a veil the majesty of God.'[3] But many commentators reject
this idea, maintaining that the words 'his flesh' relate back to
'the new and living way', in which case the veil is only mentioned to remind us that Christ has entered the holiest-of-all.[4,5]
We shall follow the traditional view.[6,7]

The veil represents Christ's flesh in several ways. Firstly, it
is the incarnate Christ who reveals the Father while yet hiding
or veiling the sinner from God's burning holiness. To look on
the Shekinah was death, but to gaze upon God's glory 'in the
face of Jesus Christ' is life and health (2 Cor. 4:6).

Secondly, the rending of the veil, giving access to the holiest, pictures the breaking of Christ's body ('his flesh') on the cross. Delitzsch declares, 'The veil which was rent by the Lord's death in order to [permit] our entrance was that pierced body of humiliation.'[8] This is graphically portrayed every time we take the Lord's Supper, reminding us that our access to God was (and is still) made possible only by the death of Christ (1 Cor. 11:24). Thirdly, although the veil was a barrier to man, it was also a doorway. The man Christ Jesus has, by the offering of his flesh, removed the barrier and opened the door.

Representation (10:21)

Not only do we have boldness and access — we also have representation in the form of **'a High Priest over the house of God'** (10:21). The epistle has had so much to say about the high-priesthood of Christ that little more can, perhaps, be added. However, the Writer's purpose here is not to augment what he has already told us, but to remind us of it. Our boldness and access can (and must) be traced back to the person of Christ and the priestly role he has graciously undertaken. We dare not enter the holy place alone.

As High Priest, Christ is uniquely privileged to enter the presence of God's burning holiness. If we also are to enter, it can only be 'in him' that we do so, as we have already seen. We are 'accepted in the Beloved', not on our own account. Even our election and predestination do not qualify us to meet with God. Christ alone is our means and right of access.

He is also our representation before the throne of God — he is **'over the house of God'**. Although this expression can signify his rule and ownership over his household (3:6), its force here is probably that Jesus is the one who *represents* his people before God's ineffable holiness. Either way, it is not just individual believers that are in view, but rather his people corporately — the church of the living God. This is the church for which he gave himself, 'that he might sanctify and cleanse it ... [and] present it to himself a glorious church ... holy and without blemish' (Eph. 5:26-27).

Under the old covenant, the high priest 'carried' the tribes of Israel into the presence of God. How? By bearing their names inscribed on gemstones sewn into the breastplate and epaulets of his robes. These engraved stones served as 'a memorial for the sons of Israel' before the Lord (Exod. 39:6-7,8-14). This gloriously pictures the way Christ represents his new-covenant people before the Father. As regards their weakness, he bears them on his shoulders. As regards their value in his sight, he carries them on his heart. As our great High Priest, he dwells in the presence of Almighty God with our names upon his shoulders and our needs upon his heart. Like the jewels in the ephod and the breastplate, we are precious in the eyes of God the Father and of God the Son.

34.
An approach to God

Please read Hebrews 10:22-25

Having given a threefold summary of his teaching, the Writer now matches it with a fervent, threefold exhortation — let us draw near to God; let us hold fast our hope; and let us not forsake assembling. In launching these precepts, he anticipates the strong, hortatory character of the remainder of the epistle. Here is the watershed mentioned at the start of the previous chapter. The heights of doctrine have been scaled. Now the application of that doctrine gathers momentum as we descend into the valley of practical experience and life.

Drawing near (10:22)

The first exhortation comes as no surprise: '... **let us draw near with a true heart in full assurance of faith, having our hearts sprinkled from an evil conscience and our bodies washed with pure water'** (10:22). 'This drawing near', says Owen, 'containeth all the holy worship of the church, both public and private, all the ways of our access unto God by Christ.'¹

In the previous chapter we saw that the believer has 'boldness' to enter the holiest. Why, then, do we need this exhortation? Because 'having boldness' to enter, and actually entering with boldness, are not necessarily the same thing! The first indicates that we *may* come to God without fear; the second that we *do* so come. It is all too easy to leave our spiritual privileges and opportunities unused. The problem arises when we become theoretical in our religion. We go through the motions of corporate worship. We learn and approve the great doctrines of the faith, seeing how they fit together to create a splendid theological system. Or, if we are less intellectual in our approach, we simply sit back and enjoy the 'feel-good factor' imparted by the promises of God. But there is a great danger that we remain hearers, not doers of God's Word.

The Lord warned Ezekiel: '... they sit before you as my people, and they hear your words, but they do not do them; for with their mouth they show much love but their hearts pursue their own gain. Indeed you are to them as a very lovely song of one who has a pleasant voice ... for they hear your words but they do not do them' (Ezek. 33:31-32). Unfortunately this analysis applies all too often to Christians today — they appear to love God's Word and stoutly defend its truth, yet seem unable to grasp that we are meant to *practise* it and *live* by it.

What, then, is involved in 'drawing near'? Firstly, to 'draw near' means to approach the living God. We do not enter a physical sanctuary with its *representation* of glory, but the very presence of the Almighty. We must do so without fear, but not without reverence and awe, recognising who he is. We must also come with anticipation, for we insult God if we expect nothing from our meeting with him.

Secondly, we must come with **'a true heart in full assurance of faith'**. This is best understood as comprising a single requirement — a true heart *is* one that is fully assured through faith. Lane comments, 'The phrase evokes the relationship of heart-obedience to God that Jeremiah envisioned in terms of the "new heart" God would create in his people (Jer. 31:33)' under the new covenant.[2] Question: what *is* the assurance of such a heart? Answer: that a gracious reception awaits those who draw near.

It is not presumption to believe that the everlasting God will receive us graciously, for we come by his own appointed means, that is, through 'Jesus Christ the righteous [who] is the propitiation for our sins' (1 John 2:2). Indeed, to come to him *doubting* the sufficiency of Christ's provision is to dishonour God. After all, it was God himself who commanded Ephraim to 'take words with you, and return to the LORD. Say to him, "Take away all iniquity; receive us graciously"' (Hosea 14:2). As we shall see in 11:6, '... he who comes to God must *believe* that ... he is a rewarder of those who diligently seek him.'

The word **'faith'** occurs only three times previously in the epistle, but this does not mean that the Writer minimises its importance. In 4:2 faith is presented as the antidote to unbelief; in 6:1 as a foundational principle of the kingdom of God; and in 6:12 as essential if we are to inherit the promises. Although the subject of faith has not been prominent up to this point, it will shortly occupy centre-stage as we come to Hebrews 11. The apparent neglect of the subject in the earlier part of the epistle is due to fact that the Writer has hitherto been taken up with the *objects* of faith — Christ himself, his atoning work, and the new covenant in his blood — rather than with faith itself. The nature and exercise of faith provide much of the substance of the practical and hortatory content of the remainder of Hebrews.

Thirdly, we draw near **'having our hearts sprinkled from an evil conscience and our bodies washed with pure water'**. The Writer employs two metaphors borrowed from the old covenant. The first echoes the teaching of 9:14 and reminds us that the blood of Christ cleanses the believer's conscience that he might serve the living God. The second picture likens the inner cleansing of mind and spirit effected by the blood of

Christ to the washing that made men ritually pure under the former dispensation (e.g. Lev. 14:9; 15:11,13; 16:4,24,26).

That our 'bodies' are washed may further indicate that our actual sins, committed 'in the flesh', have been forgiven — not only is our *conscience* cleansed but our *whole person*. The Writer may also have in mind the new-covenant sign of water-baptism, which represents (among other things) the renewal of the soul by the symbolic act of immersing the body in water.[3] Calvin, however, prefers a spiritual interpretation: 'The body washed with pure water is taken by most people as referring to baptism, but to me it seems more likely that the apostle is alluding to the old ceremonies of the law and by the word "water" means the Spirit of God.'[4]

Whatever its detailed symbolism, this verse assures us that we enter the presence of God as those who have been made clean and fit for his presence by the atoning work of Christ on our behalf. The filthy rags of our iniquity have been removed, and we stand before God clothed in the rich robes of the righteousness of Christ (Zech. 3:1-5).

Holding fast (10:23)

As the first exhortation relates to faith, so the second invokes our common hope: **'Let us hold fast the confession of our hope without wavering, for he who promised is faithful'** (10:23). 'Hold fast' implies that we must both *possess* and *retain* this hope (cf. 4:14). In the New Testament, 'hope' means 'future expectation'. It does not carry the sense of uncertainty implied by modern usage ('I hope it won't rain but it probably will'!) There is nothing tentative about the Christian's 'great hope' — a hope that embraces all God's 'exceedingly great and precious promises' through which we are 'partakers of the divine nature, having escaped the corruption that is in the world through lust' (2 Peter 1:4). Paul's message was 'Christ in you, the hope of glory' as he laboured to 'present every man perfect [complete] in Christ Jesus' (Col. 1:27-29). 'This hope we have', adds the Writer himself, 'as an anchor of the soul, both sure and steadfast, and which enters the inner part behind the veil' (6:19-20).

Hope is an integral part of the gospel of grace. It is securely based upon the faithfulness of God, who has promised eternal salvation to all who trust in Christ. As a result, believers may look forward with confidence and expectation to the consummation of God's saving work in them. This hope sustains, enlivens and anchors the soul during our pilgrimage here on earth. It is strange, therefore, that we hear so little about it today. It is seldom preached, nor are many books written about it. Perhaps the comforts of life in this present world dim our expectations for the world to come.

A more likely cause, however, is the undue stress placed today on work, responsibility and witness here on earth, to the neglect of our heavenly future. Both are important, but we need to adjust our emphasis if we are to imitate those who embraced the promises — for they 'confessed that they were strangers and pilgrims on the earth' and 'desire[d] a better, that is, a heavenly country' (11:13-16). Hebrews 11 will teach us, in fact, that only those who *do* embrace the heavenly hope are likely to serve God effectively on earth.

However, it is not just hope itself that the Writer wants us to 'hold fast', but the *profession* (or confession) of that hope. In fact, the words **'without wavering'** translate an adjective that agrees with 'confession'[5] — suggesting that it is not only our inward hope that must not waver, but also our public profession of that hope.

Furthermore, the word **'profession'** carries the idea of 'speaking the same thing' and implies that our profession of faith and hope is a mutual and corporate activity. This is the significance of the great historical 'Confessions' — they were summaries and expositions of Christian doctrine agreed upon by men acting in concert and fellowship. We must never regard such confessions as infallible, of course, since they are the work of man. But they do emphasise the existence of a body of doctrine that is true to Scripture and that is held by the church corporately, not just by individual believers. The Writer is here appealing to his readers to remain in fellowship with the early church in their 'common salvation'— by holding fast to the 'faith once for all delivered to the saints', and to the personal hope engendered by that faith (Jude 3). The verse also teaches us that 'fellowship in the gospel' (Phil. 1:5) is a characteristic of the true church and that isolation is not a scriptural option (see 10:25 below).

Considering one another (10:24)

This leads naturally to the third exhortation: **'And let us consider one another in order to stir up love and good works'** (10:24). That the three exhortations appeal in turn to faith, hope and love is not accidental, bearing in mind the structural elegance of Hebrews. It may well reflect the Pauline influence discernible elsewhere in the epistle (cf. 1 Cor. 13:13). Although the mutuality of the Christian faith has not been emphasised up to this point, it has been implicit throughout. The Writer sees believers as the community of 'those sanctified' (see comment on 10:14). They are the children of one family (2:12,16); members of a single household (3:6); the people of God (4:9) represented by one great High Priest (4:14) — and together they are heirs of a better covenant based on better promises (8:6,11). All these benefits in Christ are enjoyed by believers *mutually* and bring with them commensurate responsibilities. What are these responsibilities? The Writer brings some of them to our attention.

Firstly, we are to 'consider one another'. It is a strong expression. According to *Strong's Concordance*, 'consider' means '(1) to perceive, remark, observe, understand; (2) to consider attentively, fix one's eyes or mind upon'. This, then, is no trivial or casual activity. It is much more than just considerate behaviour towards others. It is an ongoing, outgoing, sympathetic, empathetic, compassionate, caring and loving consideration for every fellow member of the body of Christ, whatever their need or condition. Although it is not limited to the sphere of the local church, that is where it will most actively be practised and observed.

The Writer is specific about what this entails. It is all too easy to utter kindly platitudes yet do nothing to help our believing 'neighbour'. Our consideration should have a particular aim, namely, 'to stir up love and good works' (10:24). How can this be done? The answer must surely be 'by example'. We are not told just to exhort one another to walk in love, with its resulting good works, but to *stir up* one another (the word means 'provoke', 'incite' or even 'irritate'!) Talking about it is not sufficient — there must be action, example and leadership. We all know that love begets love, and that a good example often shames men into imitation. Each of us, therefore, should set out upon such a course of persistent, practical and active good, so that others will be constrained to follow. Do not wait for them to lead in this matter. Do not say, 'I will show love when I see it in others.' If we were deliberately to imitate Christ, who 'went about doing good' (Acts 10:38), we might soon see a change in mood and atmosphere within our churches.

Assembling together (10:25)

This 'exemplified love', says the Writer, is specially displayed when we gather together in worship and fellowship. This may be a novel idea to us — is it *really* an act of love, a display of good works, to attend the midweek meeting, for example? It is indeed, for if we love our fellow believers, and seek their greatest good, we will **'not** [be found] **forsaking the assembling of ourselves together, as is the manner of some'** (10:25). Hywel Jones remarks, 'What is in view here includes all meetings for worship and fellowship, whether on the Lord's day or not.'[6]

We do not know what exactly lay behind this particular emphasis on regular attendance, except that the early church seems to have had no less a problem in this respect than we do today! Kistemaker comments, 'The *Didache*, a church manual for religious instruction from the latter part of the first century, gives this exhortation: "But be frequently gathered together seeking the things which are profitable for your souls."'[7] Citing another ancient document, Lane adds: 'It is sobering to discover that in the early second century in Rome it was simply preoccupation with business affairs that accounted for the neglect of the meetings of a house church.'[8]

Gathering together in the name of Jesus Christ invites his presence (Matt. 18:20), encourages pastors and teachers (13:7,17), strengthens the brethren (Col. 3:16), nurtures our souls (Acts 2:41-42) and proclaims the gospel (Acts 2:47). King David loved to gather with God's people. He wrote, 'My soul longs, yes, even faints, for the courts of the LORD; my heart and my flesh cry out for the living God' (Ps. 84:2; read the whole psalm!). How much more should we desire to assemble in the name of Christ — we who enter not an earthly but a heavenly tabernacle.

Therefore, concludes the Writer, we should consort together with our fellow believers at every opportunity, **'exhorting one another, and so much the more as you see the day approaching'** (10:25). The 'day' in question is the 'day of the Lord' — the time when Christ returns to gather his redeemed people and judge the world in righteousness. The early church lived in constant anticipation of this great event, even though (like us) they had no idea when it would occur. 'Be ready', said Jesus, 'for the Son of Man is coming at an hour when you do not expect him' (Matt. 24:36-44). Many of the parables express this same need for the church of Christ to be watching and waiting.

God has deliberately kept his people in this attitude of expectancy for two millennia. Why? Because it is helpful and spiritually healthful for us to live in the light of eternity — recognising that in this world we have 'no continuing city, but we seek the one to come' (13:14). This is why we should exhort one another to 'seek first the kingdom of God and his righteousness' and not be entangled with the affairs of this life to the detriment of our eternal welfare (Matt. 6:33). Of these things we need to be reminded constantly.

35.
A fearful thing

Please read Hebrews 10:26-31

As the epistle continues, the exhortations of the previous verses are suddenly revealed in a more sombre light. They do not just express the Writer's hopes for his readers — they also embody a spiritual health warning. The warning is developed in verses 26-31 with much gravity. Yet this is not purely negative, for it leads on to strong encouragement and further exhortation in verses 32-39.

This is the fourth time in the epistle that such a warning has been given. In 2:1-4 the Writer points out that there is no escape for those who 'drift away' and 'neglect so great a salvation'. In 3:12 – 4:13 he utters an extended warning against 'an evil heart of unbelief in departing from the living God' (3:12). In 6:4-8 he makes it clear that those who fall away put 'the Son of God ... to an open shame' and cannot be renewed again to repentance. Now, once again, he raises the spectre of apostasy.

The implication is, of course, that those who fail to progress, who do not draw near to God with the assurance of faith, who let slip the confession of their hope, who cease to attend church gatherings and who neglect to stir others up to love and good works are not just lazy Christians — they may not be Christians at all! No wonder they give concern to their pastors, who 'watch out for [their] souls as those who must give account' (13:17). We do well to take these warnings to heart for, if heeded, they protect both church and individual from danger.

No remaining sacrifice (10:26-27)

The Writer continues, **'For if we sin wilfully after we have received the knowledge of the truth, there no longer remains a sacrifice for sins, but a certain fearful expectation of judgement, and fiery indignation which will devour the adversaries'** (10:26-27). The reference is not to sin in general but specifically to the sin of neglecting gospel obedience. This sin consists in a rejection of the foregoing exhortations and reveals itself in several ways — a careless attitude towards the means of grace, a poor appetite for the Word of truth, and a preference for the things of the world over the things of God. We are neither saved nor sanctified by obedience to rules or precepts, but there is a necessary obedience *to the gospel*, namely, the obedience of faith and obedience to the faith (Acts 6:7; Rom. 15:18; 16:26; 1 Peter 1:2,14). This 'gospel obedience' involves joyful submission to the truth of the gospel, to the teaching of Scripture, and to Christ as Lord. It will be manifested in faith, love, perseverance and good works — the very things the Writer insists on in his earlier exhortations.

The warning is directed to those who 'have received the knowledge of the truth'. Since these people are clearly not regenerate (see discussion on 6:4-8), how are we to understand this expression? It means that they have both heard and 'accepted' the gospel. More than that, they have become practising Christians, at least for a time. But now they are falling away, becoming indifferent to the salvation that is in Christ. In short, they represent the stony ground and the thorny ground described so graphically in the parable of the sower (Matt. 13:20-22).

What hope is there for such people? None, declares the Writer. The once-only offering of Christ has been spurned, and its unrepeatable nature means that 'there no longer remains a sacrifice for sins'. The fact that Christ's atoning work is finished and complete is an enormous comfort to the true believer, but to those who turn away it becomes a dreadful reality. Unlike the Israelites of old, they cannot return tomorrow, or next year, to find relief in a new sacrifice. Nothing remains but the one offering they have already chosen to despise. Like the foolish virgins, they succumb to spiritual sleep and are excluded for ever from the kingdom of God (Matt. 25:13).

All that remains to them is 'a certain fearful expectation of judgement, and fiery indignation which will devour the adversaries' (10:27). They would not see themselves as adversaries, of course — they are simply indifferent. But indifference to the gospel they once professed to believe is active enmity towards God. The Writer warns them to expect a fearful and inevitable judgement, which he proceeds to elaborate.

Insulting the Spirit of grace (10:28-29)

What is the Writer's purpose in driving home his warning in such dire terms? Is he seeking to frighten his readers? In one sense, yes, but not without cause. He wants to bring home to them that apostasy is *serious* — that the gospel is not something to be sampled, enjoyed for a while, and then discarded in favour of some new religious fad. The present-day 'anything-goes' attitude to matters of faith — with its syncretism and incitement to browse in the multi-faith 'supermarket' — calls for similar admonitions. Men cannot trifle with God and get away with it.

The Writer exemplifies his point: **'Anyone who has rejected Moses' law dies without mercy on the testimony of
two or three witnesses. Of how much worse punishment,
do you suppose, will he be thought worthy who has
trampled the Son of God underfoot, counted the blood of
the covenant by which he was sanctified a common thing,
and insulted the Spirit of grace?'** (10:28-29). The reference
is specifically to idolatry (compare Deut. 17:2-4 with Deut.
17:5-7). It is unlikely that Moses' law against idolatry was
enforced with this degree of severity in the Writer's day, but
he uses the present tense for dramatic emphasis — to remind
us that it *was* once so applied (Deut. 13:8; 17:6). The law
required only 'two or three witnesses' to determine guilt. By
contrast, the Writer already has in mind what he articulates in
12:1, namely, that 'Christian' apostates commit *their* sin in the
face of a 'great cloud of witnesses'! The assembly of true believers gives united testimony against those who turn away
from Christ.

Any such defector is an idolater, for he has turned away
from worshipping the living God. In doing so he has committed three crimes. He has, firstly, **'trampled the Son of God
underfoot'** — he has despised 'the first-born over all creation
... the head of the body, the church'. The apostate dishonours
Christ in both his cosmic and saving roles, neither recognising
the one nor being grateful for the other. The Writer's vehe-
mence speaks volumes for his high view of Jesus Christ, a
view displayed constantly throughout this wonderful epistle.
Even those who do not fall away need to be reminded continually that Jesus is indeed God's Son, 'the brightness of his
glory and the express image of his person' (1:3).

Secondly, the defector has **'counted the blood of the covenant by which he was sanctified a common thing'**. This
second error, says Kistemaker, is 'even more significant because it relates to the meaning and purpose of the new covenant'.[1] In effect, those who offend in this respect reject the

new covenant, for the blood of Christ provides both the essence and effectiveness of that covenant. In treating his blood as 'common' they deny the uniqueness of Christ's death and equate it to the death of animals under the old covenant. Such people 'draw back' (or timidly withdraw) from the new covenant and revert to the old. And that, avows the Writer, leads to perdition (10:39).

Most commentators discuss the problem of interpretation attaching to the statement, **'he was sanctified'**. Some conclude that the apostate can be said to have been 'sanctified' in the outward sense of being ritually purified by profession or baptism.[2] We must remember that apostasy, by scriptural definition, occurs only in those who remain unregenerate, despite their claim to be Christians (see, e.g., 1 John 2:19). Owen also argues, however, that the sanctification in question may well be that of Christ who, by analogy with the Aaronic priests, was consecrated to his saving office with his own blood (cf. Lev. 8:30). Brown concludes that the one sanctified is neither Christ nor the apostate person. Rather, he suggests, the verse should be understood impersonally as 'the blood by which there is sanctification'.[3]

The third charge against such people is that they have **'insulted the Spirit of grace'**. Not only does the apostate reject the person of Christ and the atonement; he also spurns the testimony of the Spirit to the truth of the gospel. This, of course, is 'blasphemy against the Spirit' — the 'unforgivable sin' of Matthew 12:31-32. The fact that he rejects *grace* both adds to the offence and cuts off every remedy — for only grace can save us (Eph. 2:8).

A fearful thing (10:30-31)

Concerning the apostate, therefore, the Writer asks, 'Of how much worse punishment, do you suppose, will he be thought worthy?' Worse, that is, than the ignominious execution of the idolater under Moses' law. Although the question is rhetorical, it does raise questions as to the *nature* of this 'punishment worse than death'. The answer is, of course, that there is judgement *after* death: **'For we know him who said, "Vengeance is mine, I will repay," says the Lord. And again, "The LORD will judge his people." It is a fearful thing to fall into the hands of the living God'** (10:30-31). The quotations are from Deuteronomy 32:35-36, and the context is that of Israel's departure from the living God. The words are appropriately applied, therefore, to apostates, in whatever era. Concerning the final sentence ('It is a fearful thing ...'), Bruce reminds us: 'These words have no doubt been used frequently as a warning to the ungodly ... but their primary application is to the people of God.'[4] Even true believers need to be warned of the potential dangers of neglecting the pursuit and practice of their faith.

It is often wrongly claimed that the Old Testament presents a God of wrath and judgement, while the New Testament reveals a God of compassion and grace. But no one who actually reads his Bible will fall prey to such a false distinction. God is consistent as to his nature and his purpose through all Scripture — that is why Old and New Testaments together constitute the Word of God. Even the old covenant, though it could not save, was altogether gracious in pointing men to Christ, that they might be justified by faith (Gal. 3:24). Equally, the God of the New Testament is the same holy God who is 'of purer eyes than to behold evil, and cannot look on wickedness' (Hab. 1:13). Christ's message is one of grace and hope. But to those who 'do not obey the truth [of the gospel]' there remains only 'indignation and wrath, tribulation and anguish, on every soul of man who does evil'. Such people 'treasure up for [themselves] wrath in the day of wrath and revelation of the righteous judgement of God' (Rom. 2:5-9).

It is, indeed, 'a fearful thing to fall into the hands of the living God'. But this will be the fate of those who turn away from the new covenant in Christ — for all such people 'despise the riches of his goodness, forbearance, and long-suffering' (Rom. 2:4).

36.
A need to endure

Please read Hebrews 10:32-39

Following each of the earlier 'warning passages' in the epistle, the Writer offered comfort, pointing his readers away from spiritual shipwreck and towards Jesus Christ, who alone can save them. Now he repeats that strategy.

In Hebrews 6, having spelled out the danger of apostasy, he continued: 'But, beloved, we are confident of better things concerning you, though we speak in this manner' (6:9). Here, in similar vein, he earnestly counsels them to recall their 'first love' and take a new grip on their confidence in Christ — 'which has great reward' (10:35).

However, if they are to reap that reward, they will have to exercise faith in the promises of God, and patience under persecution. Christians, in other words, must take the long view. Their reward lies in the future, not the present — in the kingdom of heaven, not the kingdoms of this world. As Paul succinctly puts it, 'We were saved in this hope, but hope that is seen is not hope' (Rom. 8:24). This element of patience and 'future expectation' is central to the new covenant, but is sadly neglected today. People are taught to look for their rewards in this present world rather than in heaven.

This has several causes. One is the fear of being considered 'too heavenly minded to be of any earthly use'— which is a satanic lie if ever there was one! It is the person whose heart is set on things above who lives most usefully and fruitfully in this life (Col. 3:1-4,12-17). Another cause is the undue emphasis in many churches on social and political issues at the expense of biblical attitudes to these things. Of course, Christians are to 'do good to all men', but we need to get our priorities right. The greatest service we can render to our fellow men is to bring them to Christ, that they might have eternal life. A third problem is that 'the three Es' of modern evangelicalism (experience, excitement and entertainment) focus people's minds on the existential 'now' rather than the eternal future.

The Writer sets out to concentrate his readers' minds (and ours!) upon the patience and endurance needed on the road to heaven.

Remember (10:32)

He first invites them to remember: **'But recall the former days in which, after you were illuminated, you endured a great struggle with sufferings'** (10:32). 'Illuminated' here means 'enlightened' or 'imbued with saving knowledge'. By using this word the Writer emphasises that it is God who alone gives spiritual light — 'It is the God who commanded the light to shine out of darkness who has shone in our hearts to give the light of the knowledge of the glory of God in the face of Jesus Christ' (2 Cor. 4:6).

This enlightenment led them not only into the joy of the Lord, but also into 'a great struggle with sufferings'. Such is the animosity towards Christ — from the world, the flesh and the devil — that believers inevitably find themselves engaged in spiritual warfare. Moreover, this is no mere 'sideshow' but 'a great struggle' — calling for much fortitude and impregnable spiritual armour. The apostle Paul enlarges on this, of course, in Ephesians 6:10-20. He bids his readers to 'be strong in the Lord and the power of his might', and to put on 'the whole armour of God'. But although we must be strong and protect ourselves, it is ultimately on God that we rely. Our strength is *in the Lord* and our security in the armour *of God*. Thus we are not alone in this fight because, as David told Goliath, '... the battle is the Lord's' (1 Sam. 17:47).

Because they fought the fight of faith, the Hebrews successfully 'endured' their struggle and their sufferings. This does not mean that they simply experienced these things, nor that they just 'put up' with them. Their endurance was both joyful and triumphant, as the following verses testify. But before we consider those verses we need to return to the injunction in verse 32 that bids us 'remember' these things. Such recollections, suggests the Writer, would help them endure their present trials and temptations. Calvin remarks, 'Whenever the things we have done or suffered for Christ come to mind they should urge us on and incite us to higher attainment.'[1] But just how does remembrance help?

Firstly, in remembering their early tribulations, they would also remember the peace and joy that filled them when they first believed — and they would be encouraged (Rom. 15:13; Gal. 4:15). Secondly, they would recall that God had led them safely through *those* difficult days and had delivered them from their enemies. If God had done so then, would he not do so again? Paul had no doubt about the consistency of the Almighty in this matter. 'Thanks be to God', he declares, 'who *always* leads us in triumph in Christ' (2 Cor. 2:14, emphasis added; see also Rom. 8:37-39).

Thirdly, as they remembered 'the years of the right hand of the Most High', they would, like the psalmist, take courage in the Lord when downcast or distressed. They would find their hearts lifted to a contemplation of his greatness and glory (Ps. 77:1-3,10-20). The ministry of memory is just as effective today as it was then. Let us make good use of it!

An enduring possession (10:33-34)

Accordingly, the Writer prompts their collective memory, describing some of the difficulties they endured in those early days. He continues: '**... partly while you were made a spectacle both by reproaches and tribulations, and partly while you became companions of those who were so treated; for you had compassion on me in my** [or, "on those in"] **chains, and joyfully accepted the plundering of your goods, knowing that you have a better and an enduring possession for yourselves in heaven'** (10:33-34). The reading 'me in my chains' is doubtful and most commentators prefer 'those in chains'.[2]

The Greek verb translated 'made a spectacle' has given us the English word 'theatre'. These believers were 'set on a stage' and 'exposed to contempt'.[3] The persecution of the early church is normally remembered in terms of stoning, imprisonment and lions. But the forms of persecution we experience in Western society today, such as ridicule and vandalism, were clearly not unknown to our New Testament forerunners. They also were held up to public ridicule and 'treated like dirt'. Their possessions were plundered, leaving them destitute of this world's goods. But in spite of their afflictions, the Hebrews had given public support to those imprisoned for their faith — a stand that could have brought even greater calumny upon their heads. They had the courage of their convictions even though it cost them dearly.

Persecution has dogged the true church of Christ down the ages, as Jesus himself promised it would (Matt. 5:11-12). But Peter reminds us that all such suffering glorifies God: 'If you are reproached for the name of Christ, blessed are you, for the Spirit of glory and of God rests upon you. On their part he is blasphemed, but on your part he is glorified' (1 Peter 4:14).

Moreover, the glory that rests upon the suffering saints is not only for the present life. They are also strengthened by the hope of future glory, 'knowing that [they] have a better and an enduring possession ... in heaven' (10:34). Earthly reputations and belongings are like rubbish compared with the privilege of being found in Christ, possessing his righteousness, and hearing his 'upward call' to glory (Phil. 3:7-14). Heaven and Christ — enduring possessions indeed — are an overwhelming compensation for the sufferings of earthly life.

All this the Hebrews had once understood, and this understanding had made them not only patient but even *joyful* in the face of adversity. If they could rejoice under such draconian persecution, how much more should we, whose lot is mostly easier, rejoice in God and his salvation! James admonishes us: 'My brethren, count it all joy when you fall into various trials, knowing that the testing of your faith produces patience' (James 1:2).

The perfect work of patience (10:35-37)

But those days lay in the past, and the patience they had once displayed had grown threadbare. They were in danger of throwing away all that they had once suffered to obtain, namely, their confidence in Christ. Neglecting to 'let patience have its perfect [i.e. complete] work' (James 1:3), they stood in danger of losing their assurance of salvation. **'Therefore'**, urges the Writer, **'do not cast away your confidence, which has great reward. For you have need of endurance, so that after you have done the will of God, you may receive the promise'** (10:35-36).

Endurance is a mark of reality, a characteristic of true spirituality. Christ himself 'endured the cross, despising the shame,

and has sat down on the right hand of the throne of God'
(12:2) — and this same quality of endurance will mark the
lives of the elect. 'You will be hated by all for my name's sake',
warned the Saviour. 'But he who endures to the end will be
saved.' And again: '... because lawlessness will abound, the
love of many shall grow cold. But he who endures to the end
shall be saved' (Matt. 10:22; 24:13). In the parable of the sower,
the stony-ground hearer 'endures only for a while', whereas
the one who 'hears the word and understands ... bears fruit'
(Matt. 13:21-23).

This last reference makes it clear that endurance is not a
meritorious condition for salvation. We are not saved because
we endure to the end. Rather, true believers endure to the end
because they are saved. The soil of their hearts is good ground
because they are Christ's elect. They are the sheep that the
Father has given him, and from his safe keeping they can never
be removed (John 10:27-29).

Confidence in Christ holds out promise of **'great reward'**,
declares the Writer. In speaking thus, he prepares the ground
for his famous dissertation on faith in Hebrews 11. Not only
will those who hold fast their confidence to the end be saved
— they will also inherit 'the kingdom prepared for [them] from
the foundation of the world' (Matt. 25:34). We shall see more
of this kingdom (and of this endurance) when we come to
Hebrews 11.

The Writer adds further encouragement: **'For yet a little
while, and he who is coming will come and will not tarry'**
(10:37). According to Brown the reference here is not to
Christ's second coming, which lay far in the future, but to his
imminent coming in judgement upon their persecutors — something fulfilled terribly by the destruction of Jerusalem by Titus
in A.D. 70.[4] The words, 'Yet a little while', may be a free
rendition of Habakkuk 2:3, or may be borrowed from the
Septuagint version of Isaiah 26:20, where God's people are

counselled to hide themselves away until 'the Lord comes out of his place to punish the inhabitants of the earth for their iniquity'.[5] The difficulty here is that any idea of 'hiding' from persecution is foreign to Hebrews which teaches, rather, that we should 'go forth to [Christ] outside the camp, bearing his reproach' (13:13).

Whatever its source, most commentators apply the verse to the Second Coming of Christ. Owen has it both ways, suggesting that the promised coming has a variety of fulfilments, including both of the above options.[6] The New Testament writers commonly appealed to the Lord's second coming as a source of encouragement to persecuted believers (see e.g. James 5:7-8; 1 Peter 4:12-13; Rev. 19-21). Jesus the forerunner has gone before his disciples 'to prepare a place' for them in his 'Father's house' where 'there are many mansions'. And he has promised: 'If I go and prepare a place for you, I will come again and receive you to myself, that where I am, there you may be also' (John 14:2).

But can 'a little while' refer to the indefinite interval before Christ returns? (No one knows when that will be — Matt. 24:36). Yes, because Peter says, 'Beloved, do not forget this one thing, that with the Lord one day is as a thousand years' (2 Peter 3:8). Not only is time flexible in the mind of God, but our first-century brethren *knew* this. Although they had to be reminded of it, therefore, they would not have assumed that the words predicated the imminent return of Christ. Rather, they would have seen them as implying a delay, during which their patience and faith would be tested and purified.

Introducing faith (10:38-39)

The Writer drives home his application with a further Old Testament citation, this time from Habakkuk: **'Now the just shall**

live by faith; But if anyone draws back, my soul has no pleasure in him' (10:38, quoting Hab. 2:4). He then pours in the oil of comfort, adding, **'But we are not of those who draw back to perdition, but of those who believe to the saving of the soul'** (10:39).

These words — 'The just shall live by faith' — serve to introduce the famous eleventh chapter of Hebrews, often referred to in such terms as 'the faith gallery' or 'the parade ground of faith'. The 'downside' is that this eminent chapter is usually considered out of context, as a dissertation in its own right. It will be helpful, therefore, to remind ourselves that we only possess Hebrews 11 because faith plays a central role in the new covenant.

In its first ten chapters, the epistle contains only five references to 'faith' including the one in our present verse. By contrast, Hebrews 11 uses the word twenty-three times, while there is just one further example in each of the remaining two chapters.

Why does the Writer use the word so sparingly in his first ten chapters? One reason may be that he takes for granted the foundational nature of faith as the bedrock of the new covenant. In 6:1 he declines an opportunity to lay again 'the foundation of repentance from dead works and *faith towards God'*. He obviously considers his readers to be fully aware of these things. In support of this view, the earlier references to faith in 6:12 and chapter 10 are all made in the context of exhortation rather than instruction.

However, in the light of Hebrews 11, it is more likely that the Writer has been 'saving up' his exposition of faith until he has fully established the nature and implications of the new covenant in Christ. That is, he devotes the first ten chapters to a presentation of the *objects* of faith (Christ's person and atoning work) before turning to the *nature and experience* of faith. This is consistent with the Writer's methodology — he likes to prepare the ground before launching his major themes. He follows the same strategy with the new covenant itself, which receives no explicit mention until verse 6 of Hebrews 8, even though it is the central theme of the whole epistle.

Living by faith (10:39 cont.)

Returning to the Writer's quotation from Habakkuk, we are presented with a clear-cut choice — 'live by faith' and please God, or 'draw back' in unbelief and displease him. There is no middle way, for '... without faith it is impossible to please [God]' (11:6). The whole epistle testifies to the fact that this was a real choice facing the Hebrews and, by implication, ourselves. In spiritual terms, we must go forward because there is no way back. The Writer has already put this choice before his readers several times and does not apologise for repeating it.

Today we are often afraid to call on people to choose between God and mammon, between true religion and false. The very distinction is blurred in our syncretistic age. We tolerate a 'Christianity' that is barely recognisable as the New Testament product. Many professing believers can barely stir themselves to attend one service on the Lord's Day, and bring forth little recognisable 'fruit of the Spirit' (Gal. 5:22). Human nature has not changed, of course. But are we willing to address the subject as openly as the Writer to the Hebrews? Or are we so fearful of offending people that we soft-pedal the truth? May God give us the boldness of the early church to declare all his counsel (Acts 4:29; 20:26-27).

However, our exhortations must be patterned on Scripture. There is a tendency for preachers to tell us how to live in terms of works and duties without sufficiently emphasising the role and necessity of faith. But the New Testament majors on the life of faith — 'The just shall live by *faith*.' Of course, duties are to be fulfilled and works done — but the whole message of Hebrews 11, as we shall see, is that nothing of value can be accomplished in the practical realm without faith. Paul declares, 'The life I now live in the flesh, I live by faith in the Son of God, who loved me and gave himself for me' (Gal. 2:20). What faith is, and exactly how it achieves God's ends by 'working through love' (Gal. 5:6), we shall see in Hebrews 11.

So then, '**... we are not of those who draw back to perdition, but of those who believe to the saving of the soul**' (10:39). Graciously, the Writer includes his errant readers among those whose faith holds firm. The use of 'we' does not signify 'we as distinct from you' but 'we together with you'. He thus repeats the 'carrot and stick' tactic that we have previously noted in 6:6-9: 'But, beloved, we are confident of better things concerning you, yes, things that accompany salvation, though we speak in this manner.' His dire warnings are not inconsistent with his optimism concerning their spiritual state. Indeed, the warnings are designed to alert them to danger and so confirm them in a walk of faith.

Part 4:
Faith and its fruits

37.
Defining faith

Please read Hebrews 11:1-3

Every mountaineer, or even serious hill-walker, has had the experience. You surmount what you thought was the highest point, only to find that further and higher peaks lie before you. Hebrews is a little like that. In 8:7-13 we reached the pinnacle of the Writer's theological argument, the unveiling of the new covenant. But a further peak appeared as we considered the outcome of that covenant — the believer has been 'perfected for ever' (10:12-18). We then discovered an even higher point in 10:19-25, which sets out the implications of the covenant in terms of our approach to God, our eternal hope and our relationship to our fellow believers. Can there be further heights to scale? The answer is 'Yes', and Hebrews 11 is just such — a spiritual massif.

But what has this greatly loved passage on faith to do with the new covenant? Does the Writer set off on a new tangent in Hebrews 11? Not at all. As we have seen, the subject of faith is introduced in the closing verses of Hebrews 10. There we read, 'You have need of endurance, so that after you have done the will of God, you may receive the promise' (10:35-36). Clearly, 'the promise' is that which accrues to believers under the new covenant in Christ. But how can we endure in such a way as to obtain it? The Writer has already answered the question — we endure by faith. Hebrews 11 shows us how it works.

Faith and the new covenant (11:1)

Although there is no explicit mention of faith in 8:7-13, where Jeremiah's prophecy of the new covenant is presented, there can be no doubt that faith is integral to the enjoyment of this covenant. On God's part, we enter the new covenant through election, effectual calling and regeneration. But on our part we both enter and endure through God's gift of faith. It is by faith in Christ, says Paul, that 'we have *access* into this grace in which we *stand* and rejoice in hope of the glory of God' (Rom. 5:1-2, emphasis added).

This emerges clearly in the opening verse of chapter 11, where we read, '... **faith is the substance of things hoped for, the evidence of things not seen'** (11:1). These words are normally seen as a definition of what faith *is*, and we shall consider them in this way presently. But before doing so, notice how the Writer here links faith to two essential aspects of the new covenant — hope and invisibility! In fact, of course, these two aspects are themselves related, for Paul tells us that 'we were saved in this hope, but hope that is seen is not hope; for why does one still hope for what he sees?' (Rom. 8:24).

Unlike the old covenant, with its manifest glory and public ceremonies, the new covenant is invisible. As Paul declares, '... we do not look at the things which are seen, but at the things which are not seen. For the things which are seen are temporary, but the things which are not seen are eternal' (2 Cor. 4:18). Gone is the visible earthly tabernacle — replaced by a heavenly sanctuary which is 'not of this creation' (9:11). Gone are the animal sacrifices, with their annual (and indeed daily) reminder of sin and atonement. They are replaced by a once-for-all satisfaction that occurred historically two millennia ago (10:3,12). Gone is an all-too-human high priest, richly arrayed, esteemed by men, conducting endless and complex rituals in the sight of all the people. The great High Priest of the new covenant is invisible, for he has passed through the heavens into the presence of the unseen God (4:14).

It was, perhaps, the loss of this visible element in religion that troubled the Hebrews and tempted them to return to their former ways. The same is often true today. People seek reassurance in what is tangible, visible and ritualistic. Many churches pander to this desire, adorning their so-called priests in special robes, elevating them above the laity and glorying in their priestly powers. Their church buildings are ornate, a celebration of human artistry — earthly tabernacles that delight the sensibilities of man but are irrelevant to the worship of God in Spirit and in truth.

Even in evangelical churches there is often a tendency to dress up; to create 'atmospheres'; to provide spectacle of one sort or another; to capture the eye and focus the mind on visible religion. But our hearts and minds ought rather to be set on the invisible Christ who ministers in the heavenly sanctuary — and for that we need faith!

Similarly, just as we cannot 'see' the invisible entities of the new covenant without faith, neither can we entertain hope concerning them. Men may have vague and tentative 'hopes' about such matters as righteousness and heaven, but without faith such hopes are groundless. A person suffering from a terminal disease may still 'hope' to be cured, but this may be no more than wishful thinking.

But the hope that believers have in Christ is altogether different, because 'faith is the substance [foundation] of things hoped for' (11:1). When we hope our hopes *in faith*, we do so with assurance — for they are grounded in certainty.

Defining faith (11:1-2)

So our verse demonstrates the essential link between faith and new-covenant hope. But it also tells us something about the nature of faith itself. This is important, for there is much confusion over this matter. **'Now faith'**, avers the Writer, **'is the substance of things hoped for, the evidence of things not seen'** (11:1).

Some commentators do not see the verse as a definition of faith. For example, Hywel Jones, in his excellent *Let's study Hebrews*, argues that 11:1 is deficient as a definition because Christ is not mentioned as the object of faith.[1] Others, like Kistemaker,[2] prefer to read the verse subjectively — 'faith is being sure of what we hope for and certain of what we do not see' — rather than as an objective definition of faith (though he does not rule out the latter). Bruce also favours the subjective sense but helpfully adds: 'Physical eyesight produces conviction or evidence of visible things; faith is the organ which enables people ... to see the invisible order.'[3] However, Lane insists that 'Faith is something objective that bestows upon the objects of hope ... a substantial reality.'[4]

Who is right? Perhaps an illustration will help us understand what the Writer is telling us here about the nature of faith. If I ask you to define the word 'bicycle' you could reply that a bicycle is a machine consisting of a frame, two wheels, pedals, handlebars, and so on. You would have defined the bicycle *objectively*, that is, as an object.

Alternatively, if you are a keen cyclist, you might simply say that a bicycle is something you enjoy riding. This tells me nothing about a bicycle as such, but only about your subjective experience of it. It is a fully *subjective* definition.

However, there is a third possibility. You could define the bicycle as 'a man-powered means of transport'. This would be neither an objective nor a subjective definition, but a *functional* definition. Hebrews 11:1 is best understood in this way — as a functional definition of faith.

On this view, the verse means: 'Faith *gives* substance to things hoped for and *provides* conviction or evidence concerning things not seen.' In other words, the verse tells us what faith *does* for us. In harmony with this view, Owen comments, '[Things] hoped for ... have a present subsistence given unto them; as they are unseen they are to be made evident: both which are done by faith.'[5] And again: '[Faith] is the cause and means giving them a subsistence.'[6]

Although, therefore, this verse does not amount to a fully objective definition of faith, it necessarily implies that faith is an objective reality — a faculty by which believers apprehend the unseen realities of God. In short, faith is spiritual 'eyesight' or discernment (1 Cor. 2:14). It was 'by faith' that Moses 'endured as *seeing* him who is invisible' (11:27, emphasis added).

Because faith enables us to discern spiritual realities, it also allows us to trust in them. Because by faith we *behold* Christ's glory, 'full of grace and truth' (John 1:14), we are able to *receive* the grace and believe the truth that reside in him. Because we discern by faith the efficacy of the blood of Christ to cleanse our consciences from sin, we are enabled to trust savingly in the atoning work he has performed. As William Cowper wrote:

E'er since by faith I saw the stream
Thy flowing wounds supply,
Redeeming love has been my theme,
And shall be till I die.

This element of trust is vital. Spiritual discernment alone is not saving faith. The devils are fully cognisant of spiritual truth, but their knowledge of that truth does not save them — they 'believe and tremble' (James 2:19). When someone is 'born again' by the work of the Holy Spirit (John 3:3-8) they not only receive the gift of spiritual sight, but *by it* are caused to love and know 'the only true God and Jesus Christ whom [he has] sent' (Rom. 5:5; John 17:3). As a result, the faith-endowed soul is 'not disobedient to the heavenly vision' (Acts 26:19). It *trusts* its Saviour and *worships* its Lord. But without the faculty of faith it could do neither.

This is why the Writer can continue: **'For by [faith] the elders obtained a good testimony'** (11:2). More literally, they 'had witness borne to them', that is, they 'received the divine commendation'.[7] God could hardly commend them for the faith he had provided as a gift — but he could do so for the way they *used* it to demonstrate their trust and confidence in his wondrous person and divine purpose.

The 'elders' here are not leaders of synagogues or churches as is usual in the New Testament writings, but simply those who believed and trusted God 'of old'. They were elders, not on account of age or eminence (some of this chapter's heroes were young and obscure) but because they were mature in faith.

Faith and understanding (11:3)

So far we have learned three things. Firstly, we need a new faculty — faith — to apprehend the invisible spiritual realities of the new covenant. We need it because 'the natural man does not receive the things of the Spirit of God, for they are foolishness to him; nor can he know them, because they are spiritually discerned' (1 Cor. 2:14).

Secondly, this discernment, or 'spiritual sight', is imparted to the soul during regeneration, for 'unless one is born again he cannot *see* the kingdom of God' (John 3:3, emphasis added). Faith is thus the gift of God. It is not a natural faculty that resides in human nature and can be awakened by appropriate means. Paul reminds the Ephesians: '... by grace you have been saved through faith, and that not of yourselves; it is the gift of God' (Eph. 2:8). The whole of salvation, including the faith that saves, is God's gift.

Thirdly, we have seen that faith involves not only a knowledge of spiritual things but trust in, and obedience to, the things revealed — specifically, obedience to the gospel of Christ (1 Peter 1:2).

But this by no means exhausts the meaning of faith, for we are next told that **'By faith we understand that the worlds were framed by the word of God, so that the things which are seen were not made of things which are visible'** (11:3). The assertion that 'by faith we understand ...' is most important.

Commonly, faith is considered to be the antithesis of reason or understanding. Even Isaac Watts wrote, 'Where reason fails with all her powers, there faith prevails and love adores.' While we understand what Watts is saying, he does give the impression that faith is somehow contrary to, or independent of, rational thought.

Many Christians hold erroneous views of faith as something irrational. But if this were so, we could not 'understand' anything by faith! The problem here is a confusion of categories — faith and reason are not alternative routes to knowledge, any more than physical sight and reason are alternatives.

Sight provides information — 'sense-data' if you like. Then reason operates on these data to provide an understanding or interpretation of the things observed. There is no conflict between sight and understanding — they are complementary. Indeed, without sight (or other senses, of course) there would be nothing to understand, for we would remain ignorant of the world around us.

This analogy with physical sight helps to clarify the way in which faith facilitates understanding. Faith, as spiritual sight, reveals unseen spiritual realities. These are the data on which reason then operates to reach an understanding of spiritual truth.

We all know this from experience, if we are believers. Our minds are *active* as we read the Scriptures — as we hear them expounded or meditate upon them. The idea that we can receive valid spiritual impressions without the involvement of the mind is cultic and dangerous. It lies at the root of charismatic excesses, mysticism and many other errors. Genuine Christian experience involves the whole person, including the emotions and the will — but it never bypasses the mind and understanding.

This is well demonstrated by a single example. In Romans 12:1-2, Paul makes the transition from his doctrinal treatise to the application of the doctrines. In the light of 'the mercies of God', he calls on his readers to 'present [their] bodies a living sacrifice, holy and acceptable to God'. Why should they do that? Because, says the apostle, it is their 'reasonable service'.

He is, in effect, asking them to consider the great salvation that is theirs in Christ and to reason out what response is appropriate on their part. There can be only one answer, of course, as he tells them. But it is a *rational* response that he seeks, through the 'renewing of your mind' (Rom. 12:2), rather than one that is merely emotional or volitional.

Understanding creation (11:3 cont.)

To illustrate how faith leads to understanding, the Writer chooses the largest topic imaginable — the creation of the universe! **'By faith we understand that the worlds were framed by the word of God'** (11:3). The word translated 'worlds' is literally 'ages', that is, all things that exist in space and, particularly, time. 'Framed' means established or created, and the agency of this creation is identified as 'the word of God'. Although creation is unambiguously attributed to Christ in 1:2 — as well as in other places such as John 1:3 and

Colossians 1:16 — the Writer nowhere describes Christ as 'the Word', nor is the Greek word *logos* used here. His reference is, rather, to God's spoken word in Genesis 1 — 'God said let there be ... and there was ...' (Gen. 1:3,6,9,11 etc). This reminds us that faith feeds upon God's self-revelation in the Bible. When Scripture says God formed the worlds by his word, faith believes it and understands it to be so.

What exactly is it that we understand concerning creation? **'That the things which are seen** [the visible universe] **were not made of things which are visible'** (11:3). The Writer may here be correcting the theory, advanced by Plato, that God's 'all-powerful hand created the world out of formless matter'.[8] On the contrary, asserts the Writer, the universe was made *without* material (visible) precursors. This is the doctrine of *creatio ex nihilo* — creation from nothing.

Careful commentators point out that the Writer simply states a negative — the universe was *not* made from visible precursors. With the hindsight of modern science, for example, we might see this as an inspired insight into the fact that all matter is composed of invisible entities such as atoms, protons, neutrons, electrons, quarks and so on. However, this is a little too ingenious. The most obvious interpretation is the simplest, namely, that the verse teaches a straightforward *ex-nihilo* creation by divine *fiat*. God spoke, and space, time, matter and energy sprang into being at his command. This is wholly consistent with the Writer's assertion in 1:3 that Christ is, even now, 'upholding all things by the word of his power'.

This has implications for the modern debate on origins. Those who believe the plain meaning of Scripture find themselves at loggerheads with others who promote the doctrine of evolution. It is sometimes tempting for creationists to seek 'proofs' of creation by appeal to scientific observations — such as evidences for a young earth or against the random evolution of complex biological systems. Such arguments are important as a means of refuting the claims of evolutionists, but they can never amount to a *proof* of 'special' (i.e. miraculous) creation. Why not? Because our understanding of God's work of creation derives ultimately from faith, not from scientific exploration or theorising. If it were possible to 'prove' special creation by scientific tests or philosophical arguments, the Writer could never have made the statement he does in 11:3.

38.
Pleasing God

Please read Hebrews 11:4-7

Having defined faith, the Writer now begins to draw out its major characteristics. Two such features are presented in verses 4-7. Firstly, faith is the means by which righteousness is obtained and, secondly, it pleases God. These two aspects are related, of course — faith pleases God just *because* it leads to righteousness, and that through a personal relationship with God ('Enoch walked with God'). Faith thus glorifies Christ, through whom alone true righteousness can be secured.

This underlines an important feature of Hebrews 11 that can easily be overlooked. The chapter is not just a catalogue of Old Testament saints and their works. It is, rather, a dissertation on the nature of faith (an 'anatomy of faith' if you like) presented *through* examples. The people and events cited are not the most important things. It is what they illustrate concerning faith that we need to understand. This is why the list of faith's heroes is not exhaustive; the Writer is content to present each facet of the jewel of faith using just one or a few 'case studies'.

A more excellent sacrifice (11:4)

The Writer presents his witnesses chronologically. He does not choose an aspect of faith to expound and then illustrate it randomly from Old Testament Scripture. His method is *biblical* rather than *theological*, and this lends freshness and vitality to his teaching. We can learn from this approach. Truth is more readily taken to heart when it is seen to arise naturally from Scripture. This is the secret of true expository preaching.

The Writer begins with that great and glorious new-covenant theme, justification by faith. This statement may raise some eyebrows. How can the justifying faith of these *Old Testament* saints be a manifestation of the new covenant, which was not inaugurated till Christ died? The answer is that the new covenant and its precursor — the age-old covenant of promise — are all of one. Paul makes this clear in Galatians 3:16-18, emphasising the continuity between the promise made to Abraham (and which preceded the law) and the new-covenant inheritance. By contrast, he shows that the Mosaic law has no part in transmitting the inheritance: 'For if the inheritance is of the law, it is no longer of promise; but God gave it to Abraham by promise.'

Accordingly, the Writer begins by demonstrating that a person is accounted righteous in God's eyes, not through works but through faith in the atoning work of Christ. Abel is his first witness to this fact. **'By faith Abel offered to God a more excellent sacrifice than Cain'** (11:4). The story, told in Genesis 4:1-7, is well known — and at first sight it presents a problem. Cain was an arable farmer, while Abel was a shepherd. When they brought their respective offerings, therefore, they were both doing what came naturally. Cain brought grain, fruit or vegetables, the product of his labours, while Abel sacrificed lambs — the product of *his* labours! How, then, did they differ? Why did God accept Abel's offering but reject Cain's?

The answer is that Abel's offering was a blood sacrifice, involving the death of living creatures. This is clear from the fact that he also offered their fat, regarded as the choicest part of the animal. Like all the animal sacrifices of Old Testament times, Abel's offering represented the death of Christ, and Abel's faith looked forward to that greater atonement. Abel was not just lucky in his choice of offering — he understood that his animals pictured 'the Lamb of God who takes away the sins of the world' (John 1:29). How do we know? Because if this were *not* the case, there would have been no faith and no acceptance by God.

Cain, on the other hand, had no such faith or understanding. He did what men habitually do — they bring to God the work of their hands and seek acceptance thereby. But such offerings are of no avail, since salvation is 'by grace through faith ... not of works lest anyone should boast' (Eph. 2:8-9).

Owen explains the difference thus: 'Cain considered God only as a creator and preserver, whereon he offered the fruits of the earth... The faith of Abel was fixed on God, not only as a creator, but as a redeemer also ... who ... had appointed the way of redemption by sacrifice and atonement...'[1]

By offering a blood sacrifice, Abel **'obtained witness that he was righteous, God testifying of his gifts'** (11:4). This witness was twofold. Firstly, of course, the pages of Scripture bear witness. Abel is *on record* as one who was accepted by God on the basis of his faith in atoning blood. But even more significant is the fact that God *himself* testified to the acceptability of Abel's sacrifice at the time it was offered. This must be so, because Cain became angry when his own sacrifice procured no such witness (Gen. 4:5). We are not told what form this witness took — perhaps some visible sign was given in response to Abel's offering. Some even suggest that fire from heaven consumed the sacrifice.[2,3] But the important thing is that God *did* bear witness to the righteousness of faith — and he still does!

How does God testify today to the righteousness of those who believe? By his Holy Spirit, replies the New Testament:

'The Spirit himself bears witness with our spirit that we are children of God' (Rom. 8:16). Before arriving at this statement, of course, Paul expounds the doctrine of justification by faith in great detail in Romans 3:21 – 5:5. It is those who are thus justified that receive the Spirit (compare Rom. 5:1 and 5:5).

This is a matter of great practical importance. Justification by faith can easily be misrepresented as the acceptance of certain doctrines. This can lead to 'easy-believism', which requires nothing of the 'convert' but to sign a decision card or accept a series of Bible texts. Or it can give rise to intellectualism, in which 'faith' is no more than mental assent to the facts of the gospel. These abuses, in turn, may cause a backlash in which Christians seek to avoid the barrenness of 'believism' by joining works to faith as justifying means. This is understandable but dangerous; works are the *fruit* of justification but never its *cause* (Eph. 2:8-10).

In contrast to these false ideas, genuine faith is distinguished by the witness of the Spirit — a witness borne both by inward assurance (Rom. 8:16) and visible fruit (John 15:16; Gal. 5:22).

Finally, concerning Abel's offering, we are told that **'through it he being dead still speaks'** (11:4). Although, in one sense, all the witnesses in Hebrews 11 still speak to us, only Abel is described in these terms. Why is this? Probably because the Writer sees spiritual lessons not only in the offering that Abel made but also in the manner of his death. This emerges in 12:24: 'You have come ... to Jesus the mediator of the new covenant, and to the blood of sprinkling that speaks better things than that of Abel.'

Firstly, just as Abel was slain by his religious brother, so Christ was put to death by his own religious society. 'Abel's death', says Pink, 'was ... a pledge and representation of the death of Christ himself — murdered by the religious world.'[4]

Secondly, Abel's death speaks of Christ by way of contrast. His blood cried out for vengeance (Gen. 4:10), but Jesus' blood proclaims forgiveness! Such is the nature of the new covenant (12:24).

Pleasing God (11:5)

Next, in 11:5-6, we discover that the faith that justifies the sinner also pleases God, for it glorifies his Son. So the Writer moves on to consider this second aspect of faith. His example is Enoch: **'By faith Enoch was taken away so that he did not see death, "and was not found, because God had taken him"; for before he was taken he had this testimony, that he pleased God'** (11:5). Genesis tells us that 'Enoch walked with God and was not, for God took him' (Gen. 5:24). Clearly, then, the Writer equates 'walking with God' to 'pleasing God'. Philip Eveson writes, 'Walking with God is associated with those who experience God's favour and blessing. It refers to those who are in a right relationship with God.'[5] Of course, Enoch's case was unique. But that does not mean that we cannot imitate him. We too can please God by walking with him.

Believers 'walk by faith, not by sight' (2 Cor. 5:7). Interestingly, Paul makes this statement in the context of death and glory: '...we are always confident, knowing that while we are at home in the body we are absent from the Lord.' In this life we 'groan, being burdened', but God 'has given us the Spirit as a guarantee' that we shall inherit 'a house [body] not made with hands, eternal in the heavens ... that mortality may be swallowed up by life' (2 Cor. 5:1-7). The first aspect of walking by faith, therefore, is living with an expectation of, and longing for, the presence of God in glory. We are citizens of heaven and 'seek a homeland' prepared by God for those who love him (11:14). Faith focuses on heaven, and this focus results in a certain character of life. Such things please God.

Walking with God by faith also means that we 'walk in the light as [God] is in the light'. If we do, says John, 'we have fellowship with one another [and with God] and the blood of Jesus Christ his Son cleanses us from all sin' (1 John 1:7). The reference is not just to living a moral and upright life. Moral obedience is important — 'See ... that you walk circumspectly ... redeeming the time because the days are evil' (Eph. 5:15-16). But morality can never be the source of fellowship and cleansing from sin. Rather, John is speaking here of an ongoing faith in the atoning work of Christ. This is what brings us cleansing from sin and fellowship with God and with our fellow believers. Lose sight of the cross of Christ and you will stumble. But live in the light of God's gracious provision in Christ and, like Enoch, you will walk with God.

Thirdly, to walk by faith is to 'walk in the Spirit' (or 'keep in step with the Spirit'), bearing the fruit of the Spirit 'against [which] there is no law' (Gal. 5:22-26). This too is pleasing to God.

Expectant faith (11:6)

Not only does faith please God — nothing *but* faith pleases God, at least as far as human beings are concerned! **'Without faith'**, asserts the Writer, **'it is impossible to please him, for he who comes to God must believe that he is, and that he is a rewarder of those who diligently seek him'** (11:6). Paul likewise testifies that 'those that are in the flesh cannot please God' (Rom. 8:8). Faith is indispensable.

The exclusivity of faith as a means of pleasing God is something we need to ponder in a day when legalism and works-based religion hold so much sway. Even evangelicals can fall into this error, believing that we are somehow 'sanctified' (and made pleasing to God) by our works. But the 'work of faith' (1 Thess. 1:3) does not bring about sanctification. Rather, it flows from and demonstrates sanctification, for sanctification is God's work, not ours (1 Thess. 5:23). Believers' good works, ordained as they are by God, bring us no merit, for when we have done everything God commands we remain 'unprofitable servants' (Eph. 2:10; Luke 17:10). Only faith in Christ pleases God — but that faith, being a dynamic principle, will always be evidenced by its fruit and by its works.

In amplifying his statement the Writer begins with a surprisingly basic statement: '**... he who comes to God must believe that he is** [exists]' (11:6). Scripture always *assumes* the existence of God. It is not something the Bible ever sets out to prove. When preaching to polytheistic people, Paul had much to say concerning the *nature* of the true and living God (Acts 14:15; 17:24), but he still assumes his existence. Surely the Hebrews already accepted this fundamental fact? Why, then, does the Writer seem to question their belief in the existence of God?

Perhaps the Writer is making a different point altogether. We could read the complete sentence thus: 'He who comes to God must [not only] believe that he exists [but also] that he rewards those who seek him diligently.' That is, mere belief in God's existence is not enough — there must also be trust and confidence in God, and diligence in seeking him. If this is the Writer's meaning, everything falls into place. He is questioning, not their basic belief in God, but the nature and efficacy of that belief. James makes the same point when he reminds his readers that 'faith without works is dead', for 'the demons believe — and tremble!' (James 2:19-20).

In short, we do not please God by acknowledging the fact of his existence. That is not what the Writer means by faith.

We must also believe that he 'is a rewarder of those who diligently seek him'. True God-pleasing faith approaches the throne of grace frequently, confidently and diligently. It comes in joyful anticipation, *expecting* to 'obtain mercy and find grace to help in time of need' (4:16). Too often our churches and our personal spiritual lives are blighted by a lack of this spiritual anticipation. There is no pleasure or excitement in our approach to God. We go through the motions of prayer and worship, but our hearts are not in it. We expect nothing from God as we go dourly about our spiritual exercises. We need a new understanding of the generosity of God — that he really does reward those who seek him diligently and with their whole heart. Let us set ourselves to this task afresh, for only then shall we please God!

Godly fear (11:7)

Pursuing the subject of justifying faith, the Writer now brings forward a second witness — Noah. What can Noah teach us concerning justification by faith?

We read, **'By faith Noah, being divinely warned of things not yet seen, moved with godly fear, prepared an ark for the saving of his household, by which he condemned the world and became heir of the righteousness which is according to faith'** (11:7). Essentially, Noah believed things that were 'not yet seen'. He was able to see them in advance because he possessed faith, and faith is spiritual discernment — the sight of the soul. Noah was 'divinely warned'; that is, God revealed his intentions to Noah's 'eyes of faith'. The Lord told him, 'The earth is filled with violence through [its people] and behold I will destroy them with the earth' (Gen. 6:13).

But Noah teaches us things about justifying faith that go beyond the basics. Firstly, we are told, he was 'moved with godly fear'. Calvin comments, 'Noah paid such respect to the word of God that he turned his eyes from the contemporary view of things and went in fear of the destruction which God threatened as though it were present to him.'[6]

God had shown him a fearful prospect and he was genuinely afraid. Today, few of us manifest this aspect of saving faith, namely, an appropriate response to the prospect of God's judgement upon sin. The Writer himself reminds us that 'It is a fearful thing to fall into the hands of the living God' (10:31), while Revelation 6:16 pictures the terror of those who will cry out 'to the mountains and rocks: "Fall on us and hide us from the face of him who sits on the throne and from the wrath of the Lamb!"'

Noah trembled with godly fear at the prospect of God's judgement. Do we? Paul wrote, 'We must all appear before the judgement seat of Christ that each one may receive the things done in the body, whether good or bad. Knowing therefore the terror of the Lord, we persuade men ...' (2 Cor. 5:10-11). The apostle not only felt this terror in his own soul, but was motivated by it to preach the gospel to others — with new persuasiveness and urgency.

Secondly, being moved with fear, Noah 'prepared an ark for the saving of his household' (11:7). Of course, this was no 'self-help' salvation. God himself provided the concept, plan and detailed design of the ark. Only in this way could the ark be a picture of Christ's saving work (1 Peter 3:20-22). Noah was not justified by the 'work' of building the ark, but because he trusted in God's provision for his safety.

Furthermore, Noah's faith moved him *to act in obedience to God's instructions.* That is how 'he condemned the world and became heir of the righteousness which is according to faith' (11:7). Justifying faith is not passive. It does not sit back and wait for God to save us if he will. That is fatalism, not faith. Genuine faith fears God and obeys his instructions to seek refuge from judgement. This is what Noah did in building the ark. For us, the work of faith is to repent and believe on the Lord Jesus Christ (John 6:29). Faith *strives* to enter by the narrow gate (Luke 13:24).

'*Obedience* to the gospel' was a familiar concept to the apostolic church, but is little spoken of today (see 1 Peter 1:2). Such obedience is not to be confused with human 'works'. Noah's faith did not *consist* in his obedience, but was *expressed* by it. James clarifies the matter: 'Show me your faith without your works [if you can!] and I will show you my faith by my works' (James 2:18).

39.
Waiting for a city

Please read Hebrews 11:8-12

Nobody features more frequently in the annals of faith than Abraham. The patriarch commands such prominence in Hebrews 11 that we shall spend the next three chapters with him and his family. Both Romans and Galatians appeal at length to the faith of Abraham, because it epitomises the new covenant in Christ over against the 'works of the law' (Rom. 4; Gal. 3).

But how could Abraham know about the new covenant so far in advance? Paul explains: 'The Scripture, foreseeing that God would justify the nations by faith, preached the gospel to Abraham beforehand, saying, "In you all the nations shall be blessed"' (Gal. 3:8). Of course, Abraham had no written Scripture. But God's word, now *recorded* as Scripture, came to him with just this promise and effect. Accordingly, says Jesus, 'Abraham rejoiced to see my day, and he saw it and was glad' (John 8:56). Abraham's faith, therefore, was faith in Christ. This must always be the case with saving faith.

Hebrews takes over where Romans and Galatians leave off, emphasising the practical consequences of Abraham's faith (and Sarah's too). As a result, in verses 8-12, the Writer unveils three aspects of faith. The first — obedience — we have met already. The other two — patience and strength — break new ground.

The obedience of faith (11:8)

The Writer starts at the beginning, with Abraham's call: **'By faith Abraham obeyed when he was called to go out to the place which he would receive as an inheritance. And he went out, not knowing where he was going'** (11:8). The verse tells us several things concerning the obedience of faith.

1. Faith hears God's call.
2. Faith obeys God's command.
3. Faith trusts God's providence.
4. Faith inherits God's promise.

Firstly, faith 'hears', or otherwise discerns, the call of God: **'Abraham ... was called...'** This call, says Owen, was 'the foundation of the faith and obedience of Abraham',[1] and had 'two parts: a command ... "Get thee out of thy country" etc. [and] a promise ... "And I will make of thee..."'[2] Without the call, Abraham would have lived out his life in Ur of the Chaldees and we would never have heard of him. Everything began when God spoke to the patriarch. The same is true of others, like Paul, who 'was not disobedient to the heavenly vision' (Acts 26:19). There had to *be* a vision, a self-revelation of God, before Paul could obey.

God's call is just that — a divine self-revelation — and it is inextricably bound up with faith. In Galatians 3:2 Paul speaks of 'the hearing of faith' — indicating that those to whom faith has been imparted by the Spirit heed the gospel call to repent and believe. Jesus said, 'My sheep hear my voice, and I know them' (John 10:27). From Romans we learn that those whom God has predestined to be like Christ, and has justified by faith, are 'the called according to [God's] purpose' (Rom. 8:28-30). Other scriptures tell us that believers have been called 'in the grace of Christ' and 'out of darkness into his marvellous light' (Gal. 1:6; 1 Peter 2:9). Many similar references could be given. Faith always responds, but God in grace takes the initiative — he reveals himself in his call. Without it we remain in darkness.

God's call comes to us as it came to Abraham — through the Scriptures (or, in the case of Abraham, what would later *become* Scripture). It comes to us personally, for example, as the Bible is preached or read. It is just *because* the Scriptures are God's self-revelation to man that they are precious to believers. By the same token, the virility of our faith can be measured by our appetite for God's Word. Do I (like David) find God's 'testimonies ... my delight and my counsellors', and cry, 'How sweet are your words to my taste ...'? (Ps. 119:24,103). How important to us is the midweek Bible Study? How diligently and expectantly do we attend the preaching of God's Word?

But hearing is not enough. Faith delights not only to hear but to obey. Secondly, therefore, faith *responds* obediently to God's Word — **'Abraham obeyed when he was called.'** This is true whether the command is to 'repent and believe the gospel' or to follow Christ subsequently, in general or particular ways. Jesus said, 'My sheep hear my voice ... *and they follow me*' (John 10:27). Ezekiel received a salutary warning from the Lord: '... they sit before you as my people, and they hear your words, but they do not do them; for with their mouths they show much love but their hearts pursue their own gain' (Ezek. 33:30-33; see also James 1:22-25).

Sadly, this same problem is often discernible in our churches. People proclaim their love for the Word of God and profess submission to it. But when Monday morning arrives, their conformity to God's Word is nowhere to be seen. In their attitudes, preoccupations, motivations and behaviour, they are indistinguishable from the world around them. The problem can run deep. Those who gather for a contentious church business meeting may be unrecognisable as the congregation that worshipped together the previous Sunday. As James wryly observes, 'Out of the same mouth proceed blessings and cursing. My brethren, these things ought not to be so. Does a spring send forth fresh water and bitter from the same opening?' (James 3:10-12). If we are to 'be renewed in the spirit of [our] mind' (Eph. 4:23) we must not only hear the Word of God, we must heed it!

Inheritance (11:8 cont.)

Thirdly, although the call to Abraham was specific and accompanied by a promise, it left Abraham completely in the dark concerning his destination: **'... he went out, not knowing where he was going'** (11:8). His obedience necessarily involved trusting the providence of God. 'Where am I going? What will happen to me? How will I cope? These are things he might well have asked, and we often have similar questions as we face uncharted waters. How does God reply? 'Trust me', he says; 'I will show you everything in due course; but for now you have to trust.' The great 'proof text' is, of course, Romans 8:28: 'We know that all things work together for good to those who love God, who are the called according to his purpose.'

Nor does the apostle stop there. He continues, 'If God is for us, who can be against us? He who did not spare his own Son, but delivered him up for us all, how shall he not also with him freely give us all things?' (Rom. 8:31-32). Jesus rebukes our 'little faith'. He counsels: 'Do not worry, saying, "What shall we eat?" or "What shall we drink?" or "What shall we wear?" ... For your heavenly Father knows that you need all these things' (Matt. 6:31-32). Faith has total confidence in God's eternal purpose and providential care.

Fourthly, just as God called Abraham **'to the place which he would receive as an inheritance'** (11:8), so our own faith will also inherit what God has promised. It is both our calling and our privilege, says the Writer, to 'imitate those who through faith and patience inherit the promises' (6:12). As we shall see presently, faith always has a goal. 'I press on', declares Paul, 'that I may lay hold of that for which Christ Jesus has also laid hold of me... I press towards the goal for the prize of the upward call of God in Christ Jesus' (Phil. 3:12-14). There is a prize, an inheritance of glory, to be possessed. This is God's ultimate purpose for his redeemed people. Faith sees it and pursues it with diligence, vigour, fortitude and patience.

The patience of faith (11:9-10)

Although Abraham had to trust God for the future, his faith was by no means 'blind'. Rather, he looked forward to the fulfilment of God's promise, a city-home in heaven. The Writer continues: **'By faith he dwelt in the land of promise as in a foreign country, dwelling in tents with Isaac and Jacob, the heirs with him of the same promise; for he waited for** [looked forward to] **the city which has foundations, whose builder and maker is God'** (11:9-10). God did not implement his promise immediately — and seldom does. It is part and parcel of God's eternal purpose that we are 'saved in this hope', namely, the hope of 'the adoption, the redemption of our body'. And, continues the apostle, 'if we hope for what we do not see [have], we eagerly wait for it with perseverance' (Rom. 8:23-25). Faith waits patiently for God to unfold his purposes, knowing that his promises cannot fail.

Abraham displayed patience on two distinct levels. First, he waited for the promise of an earthly inheritance, the land of Canaan. He and his immediate descendants saw this land with their own eyes. They even dwelt in it, but only 'in tents', as strangers and nomads. Full possession of the land followed centuries later, long after their death. This, of course, is a parable for ourselves. In this life believers are 'sojourners and pilgrims', and as such must 'abstain from fleshly lusts that war against the soul' (1 Peter 2:11). 'Our citizenship is in heaven' (Phil. 3:20) and we should 'seek those things which are above where Christ is, sitting at the right hand of God'. We must 'set [our] mind on things above, not on things on the earth' (Col. 3:1-3). Pink observes, 'Abram's "dwelling in tents" also denoted the disposition of his heart... A little would serve Abraham on earth because he expected so much in heaven.'³

There is much emphasis today on 'relevance', 'community service' and 'practicality' in Christian circles. This is fine as long as these things flow from faith in Christ and a desire to imitate him who 'went about doing good' (Acts 10:38). But too often Christians betray an impatience with biblical priorities, which always put spiritual concerns before material ones. Let us never forget that here believers 'live in tents' — this world is not our true home.

The second level on which Abraham exercised patience immediately follows. He not only pictures the Christian's hope for heaven — he shares it! Although he 'waited for' an earthly inheritance, he also looked forward to an eternal city. Lane comments, 'Abraham continued to accept an unsettled mode of existence in the promised land ... "for he was looking forward with certainty to the city which has foundations". Both the nuance and the tense of the main verb ... "to wait for", "to look forward to", are significant. The verb is intensive in force, connoting "to expect with absolute confidence" ... while the imperfect tense expresses continuous expectation.'⁴

'The city which has foundations' contrasts dramatically with the 'tents' in which the patriarchs lived out their earthly lives. They sought no earthly metropolis, designed and constructed by men, but a heavenly city **'whose builder and maker is God'** (11:10).

Notice first that this city **'has foundations'**. It is 'a kingdom which cannot be shaken', a 'continuing city' (12:28; 13:14). Calvin remarks, 'He calls heaven the city which hath foundations because it is fixed for all eternity.'[5] Cities have always been seen as places of permanency — solid, safe and lasting. Kings and emperors have built cities to preserve their fame and secure their dynasties. In modern times we still lavish vast sums on the design and construction of cities, seeking to make them prestigious, pleasant, earthquake-proof, efficient in function, and so much else. And if the result is pleasing to our eyes and comfortable to our needs, how much more the city that God has constructed for his glory, eternal in the heavens!

Nothing on earth lasts for ever. Cities that were once the glory of the ancient world now lie in ruins. Many have vanished without trace. In contrast, the city of God remains, eternally secure, for it is the eternal bride of the eternal Son. John saw 'the holy city, new Jerusalem, coming down out of heaven from God, prepared as a bride adorned for her husband' (Rev. 21:2). This city is not simply 'bricks and mortar', or even their spiritual equivalent. It is a people, 'the city of the living God, the heavenly Jerusalem ... the general assembly and church of the first-born' (12:22-23).

Note secondly that God is its **'builder'**. The word (from which we get our own word 'technician') is used in the New Testament only here, and means 'designer' or 'craftsman'. Speaking through Isaiah, God promises, 'He [Christ] shall build my city and let my exiles go free, not for price or reward' (Isa. 45:13), while Jesus himself declares, 'Upon this rock I will build my church' (Matt. 16:18). Christ is, at one and the same time, its foundation and the one who crafts it with infinite skill. This city, then, is still being built. One by one, the elect are being called and, as living stones, incorporated into the household and city of God (1 Peter 2:5).

Furthermore, the work of building is God's work, not ours. This is important for us to grasp. Unless we do, we shall see the task of building the church as our own, and will employ whatever short-term means seem to serve the end. We shall be preoccupied with methods and forms; we shall endeavour to please men rather than God; we shall offer experiences, entertainment and excitement to attract people into our churches, thinking that thereby we do God's work. But, in reality, only God can build his church, and he does so as his Holy Spirit calls lost sinners into the fellowship of the gospel. Our task is to preach the unsearchable riches of Christ, for his gospel alone 'is the power of God to salvation' (Eph. 3:8; Rom. 1:16).

Thirdly, God is also the **'maker'** of this city. Plato, Philo and other contemporary authors used the same Greek word to denote the prime originator of the physical universe.[6] The Writer borrows this concept but applies it to a structure whose creation *preceded* that of the universe. For although this city is still under construction, it already exists in its full perfection in the mind and purpose of God. Its ultimate inhabitants are all known by name, having been chosen in Christ 'from before the foundation of the world' (Eph. 1:4). So supreme is this city that it overshadows the ephemeral physical world, for Christ is 'head over all things to the church, which is his body, the fulness of him who fills all in all' (Eph. 1:22-23).

But above all, the city is that which God has *promised*. Hebrews is replete with references to the promises of God, which are mentioned eighteen times in the epistle (compared with nine times in Romans). This emphasis serves to underline the radical nature of new-covenant religion, namely, that it designs to provide an eternal inheritance rather than satisfy mere temporal needs. The recipients of Hebrews were seeking present comfort in visible religious symbols, but they should rather have endured discomfort and persecution on earth to 'obtain a better resurrection' (11:35). The Writer encourages them to follow Abraham's example and look beyond this life to the 'solid joys and lasting pleasures' of the eternal city of God.

The strength of faith (11:11-12)

Faith is not only obedient and patient — it is also strong. Abraham 'did not waver at the promise of God through unbelief, but was [inwardly] strengthened in faith, giving glory to God' (Rom. 4:20). Likewise, **'By faith Sarah herself also received strength to conceive seed, and she bore a child when she was past the age, because she judged him faithful who had promised'** (11:11). Various commentators point out that the language used in the original makes Abraham, rather than Sarah, the more likely subject of this sentence. Bruce translates it: 'By faith he also, together with Sarah, received power to beget a child...'[7] But, either way, the significant thing is that the strength was *received*. 'Through faith ... out of weakness [they] were *made* strong' (11:34, emphasis added). This is important for us to understand. The strength that comes through faith is not born of human effort, determination or will-power. It is 'not by might nor by power, but by my Spirit, says the LORD of hosts' (Zech. 4:6). It is the strength of Christ himself, *imparted* to the believer by the indwelling Holy Spirit. As Paul explains, 'My grace is sufficient for you [says the Lord] for my strength is made perfect in weakness.' Paul responds, 'Most gladly I will rather boast in my infirmities that the power of Christ may rest upon me... For when I am weak, then I am strong' (2 Cor. 12:9-10). He was 'strengthened with might through [God's] Spirit in the inner man' (Eph. 3:16).

The divine origin of this power is evident, of course, from Abraham and Sarah's experience. Their particular 'strength' was to do the impossible — conceive a child in their old age! Only God can do things like that. Nevertheless, there is a balance here between the faith that the believer must exercise and the divine power that attends such exercise. God 'gives power to the weak ... [for] those who wait on the LORD shall renew their strength' (Isa. 40:29-31). To know this strength for ourselves we too must wait on God, looking to him expectantly and counting him faithful to his promise.

Faith brings divine strength, and that in turn has consequences. In Sarah's case these consequences were immense: **'Therefore from one man, and him as good as dead, were born as many as the stars of the sky in multitude — innumerable as the sand which is by the seashore'** (11:12). Again, let us learn the lesson of this verse. When the power of Christ comes upon a believer or a church, there are always consequences that redound to God's glory. Christ's power is not bestowed for our selfish enjoyment, or that we might have experiences, ecstasies or spiritual 'highs'. This seems to be the preoccupation of many today for whom worship is all about man's pleasure and has little to do with God's glory.

When believers are truly empowered by God, however, the results are of eternal value. Peter details some of them in his first epistle (2:9-10). People are called out of darkness into the marvellous light of Christ; they live holy lives; their intercession is efficacious; they proclaim his praises; and they confess themselves the unworthy objects of God's mercy and grace. These things always happen. But sometimes, in the sovereign purpose of God, there is more. Just as Sarah, through faith, gave birth to a great nation so, in times of revival, multitudes may be born of the Spirit. As Christ is preached, weak human vessels become the means by which the Lord makes known the treasure of his glory in the face of Jesus Christ (2 Cor. 3:5-7). Faith demonstrates its strength.

40.
Seeking a homeland

Please read Hebrews 11:13-16

There is considerable overlap between this passage and the previous one. Both portray believers as 'strangers and pilgrims', having no 'continuing city' in this world (see also 13:14). Both speak of the eternal city that God has prepared for those who love him, and of their heartfelt desire to reach it. But new aspects of faith are none the less laid before us here. What are they? That faith embraces the promises of God and actively pursues their fulfilment.

In our dealings with men we are often constrained to cry in frustration: 'Promises, promises!' We are tired of promises that go unfulfilled. We want action, not words. But things are different when we deal with God for, unlike men, 'he is faithful who ... promised' (11:11). This passage, therefore, directs our attention to the faithfulness and promises of God — a God who keeps his covenant with his Son, and thus with the beneficiaries of that covenant, the heirs of salvation.

Embracing the promises (11:13)

The Writer continues, **'These all died in faith, not having received the promises, but having seen them afar off were assured of them, embraced them and confessed that they**

were strangers and pilgrims on the earth' (11:13). 'These' refers, of course, to Abraham, Sarah, Isaac and Jacob. They died in faith, we are told, without receiving the promises of God. What, then, were those promises?

They are recorded for us in Genesis and contained three elements. First, Abraham and his sons were promised a land; secondly, they were promised descendants without number; and thirdly, they were promised that their seed would become a blessing to all the nations of the earth (Gen. 12:1-3; 13:14-17; 15:4-6; 17:1-8; 22:16-18; 26:3-5; 28:13-15; 35:11-12).

The promises were fulfilled, physically and historically, long after the patriarchs had died. Israel *did* possess the promised land of Canaan in the days of Joshua, and Israel *did* become a mighty nation. Even more importantly, the seed of Abraham, Jesus Christ, invaded human history to bring the blessing of his kingdom to every tongue and tribe and kindred and people.

But even a cursory reading of the New Testament shows that the promises had a spiritual fulfilment far more important than the historical one — and this is what the Writer seeks to show in these verses. Although their descendants would receive the land as a natural inheritance, this would be of little value to the patriarchs after their death! Rather, in pursuit of the promises, they looked for things they *would* eventually experience and enjoy. Delitzsch observes, 'The shell of their longing might be of earth, [but] its kernel was heavenly and divine.'[1]

What were their future expectations? Firstly, a spiritual homeland and a heavenly city. Secondly, spiritual descendants without number — people who would share both their faith in God and the eternal inheritance he has prepared for those that love him (Gal. 3:29). Thirdly, the blessing of personal salvation through Abraham's own ultimate Seed, namely Christ (Gal. 3:16; John 8:56). These were the things they saw 'afar off' and concerning which they 'were assured'. And it was in this sense that they 'died in faith', still anticipating these eternal blessings — blessings now being fulfilled through the gospel of Jesus Christ.

Notice once again how the Writer equates faith to spiritual sight — having *seen* the promises, Abraham and his family were assured of their truth and reliability. They did not *infer* the promises, or *deduce* anything relating to them. Their assurance did not flow from speculation or intellectual exercises. On the contrary, it was based on *revelation* — what God showed them directly by his words. The same holds true for us today. God speaks to us through his written Word, the Bible, and faith discerns both the import and the truth of what he says. This is the experience of every true believer and the basis of all our assurance.

We are further told that they **'embraced'** the promises in faith. The verb is normally translated 'salute' or 'greet' but 'embrace' is appropriate here because it underlines the warmth of the action. As Pink writes, 'They who really embrace the promises of God are suitably affected and influenced by them: their delight in heavenly things is manifested by a weanedness from earthly things ... [the patriarchs] had such a satisfying portion in the promises of God that they publicly renounced … a concern in the world ...'[2] Owen adds succinctly, 'This embracing of the promises is the heart's cleaving to them with love, delight and complacency.'[3]

It is not enough merely to 'see' God's promises, nor even to be assured of them; faith's work is not complete until we have embraced them. It is this final step of grasping and holding the promises to our heart that generates the kind of positive action and achievement recorded in Hebrews 11.

'Believism' is a common problem in the church today. Christians both understand and believe the teaching of Scripture, but many do so in a merely intellectual manner, engaging the mind but not the heart and will. There is no commitment, no

passion, no sacrifice, no abandonment to that which God reveals. As a result, there is no fruit, no 'work of faith', no 'labour
of love' no 'patience of hope' (1 Thess. 1:3). Let Hebrews
teach us not only to *approve* what God reveals and commands,
but to *embrace* it!

Making a statement (11:13-14)

Abraham and his family not only believed inwardly, they also
vocalised and evidenced their faith — they **'confessed that
they were strangers and pilgrims on the earth'** (11:13).
This confession was twofold. Firstly, they did not hesitate to
tell others where their allegiance lay. For example, Abraham
refused to accept gifts from the King of Sodom saying, 'I have
lifted my hand to the LORD, God Most High, the possessor of
heaven and earth, that I will take nothing ... lest you should
say, "I have made Abram rich"' (Gen. 14:23). Abraham made
it clear that he looked to God for his supply and sustenance,
not to man. Secondly, the patriarchs confessed their desire for
a heavenly country by their actions as well as their words.
Thus Abraham allowed Lot to choose the richest land for himself, disdaining the earthbound self-interest that motivated his
nephew (Gen. 13:9-12). By both their words and actions, therefore, these men and women of faith made the clearest of statements — **'For those who say such things declare plainly
that they seek a homeland'** (11:14).

Genuine faith has an unmistakable impact on the life of the
believer. 'Show me your faith without your works, and I will
show you my faith by my works', challenges James (James
2:18). True faith is never invisible, for it prompts the faithful
to confess where their confidence lies, both in speech and lifestyle. 'If ... you were raised with Christ', says Paul, 'seek those
things which are above, where Christ is, sitting at the right

hand of God. Set your mind on things above, not on things on the earth' (Col. 3:1-2). These words of exhortation launch one of Paul's most trenchant statements on the practical implications of the Christian life, including sins to be avoided, graces to be cultivated, ministries to be exercised, and relationships to be honoured (Col. 3:3 – 4:6). Faith *works*, in every sense of that phrase!

Furthermore, the work of faith spells out one message in particular — heaven is our homeland. That is why we are to set our minds on things above, not on things on the earth. We have died to this world and our 'life is hidden with Christ in God. When Christ who is our life appears, then [we] also [shall] appear with him in glory' (Col. 3:3-4). Believers engage in the affairs of this world that they might serve Christ, testify to his grace, preach his gospel and glorify his name. But they do so as 'strangers and pilgrims', not entangling themselves with the issues of this life (11:13; 2 Tim. 2:4). As beneficiaries of the new covenant, they have an altogether higher calling than unbelievers — and must recognise it.

No looking back (11:15-16)

Jesus once told a would-be disciple, 'No one, having put his hand to the plough, and looking back, is fit for the kingdom of God' (Luke 9:62). Severe words, perhaps, but necessary. The Writer has already raised the issue of those who cast longing glances behind them: 'But we are not of those who draw back to perdition, but of those who believe to the saving of the soul' (10:39). He now underlines the lesson by reference to the pilgrim patriarchs.

He writes, **'And truly if they had called to mind that country from which they had come out, they would have had opportunity to return'** (11:15). 'They might easily have returned to Chaldea', writes Brown. 'The distance was no obstacle. There does not seem to have been any external obstruction. But they gave clear evidence that they were not disposed to return.'[4] No doubt their country of origin had much to offer that was not available in Canaan: civilisation, for one thing; a settled existence, for another. But the patriarchs embraced a nomadic existence because **'they desire[d] a better, that is, a heavenly country'** (11:16). Their example must surely challenge us today, accustomed as we are to the comforts and attractions of the world around us.

In the West at least, many Christians have grown 'soft'. To 'endure hardship as a good soldier of Jesus Christ' is just not on our agenda (2 Tim. 2:3). We find it hard to imitate the one who 'pleased not himself' (Rom. 15:1-3, AV). Should we not review our lifestyles and priorities, including the use of our time, money and possessions? Should we not display more of the love, compassion and sacrificial self-giving that characterised the Lord Jesus Christ on earth? In short, should we not live as citizens of the heavenly country that God is giving us, rather than squander our lives on the affairs and preoccupations of this world? We should indeed, if we truly 'desire' the heavenly country.

Their God (11:16 cont.)

The words, 'I will be their God and they shall be my people,' are definitive of the new covenant (8:10). The Writer now recalls and underlines this gracious provision. The faith of the patriarchs had an immediate reward, not just the distant prospect of one. What was this instant reward? Nothing less than the favour of God! **'Therefore God is not ashamed to be called their God, for he has prepared a city for them'** (11:16). Although they suffered privations and hardship, these 'people of faith' are not to be seen as stoical individuals, clinging grimly to the unseen promise of God. Rather, they rejoiced in God and knew his smile.

Their relationship with the Almighty under the covenant of promise was deeply experiential, for God drew near to them in intimate and dramatic self-revelation. To give but one example: 'The LORD said, "Shall I hide from Abraham what I am doing, since Abraham shall surely become a great and mighty nation, and all the nations of the earth shall be blessed in him?"' (Gen. 18:17-18). These people walked with God by faith, and he in turn was not ashamed — it was not beneath his dignity — to declare himself 'their God'. He bound himself to them in glorious and compassionate condescension.

This is an amazing thing. Isaiah teaches the same remarkable truth: 'Thus says the high and lofty One, who inhabits eternity, whose name is Holy. I dwell in the high and holy place with him who has a contrite and humble spirit, to revive the spirit of the humble and to revive the heart of the contrite ones' (Isa. 57:15). Shall God indeed dwell with men? Yes, he is not ashamed to do so, and has demonstrated this fact once and for all by sending his Son into the world 'to seek and to save that which was lost' (Luke 19:10). And for the redeemed 'he has prepared a city' (11:16) where 'there shall be no more curse, but the throne of God and of the Lamb shall be in it, and his servants shall serve him. They shall see his face and his name shall be on their foreheads' (Rev. 22:3-4).

41.
Believing God

Please read Hebrews 11:17-22

In the previous chapter we saw that Abraham and his family 'died in faith' — that is, they continued to believe up to (and in) the moment of their death. In the present passage the Writer brings home the full implication of these words. His unspoken question here is: 'How does faith face death?' The answer reveals yet another aspect of faith, namely, that it triumphs in trials, even over death itself.

Each of the cases cited in verses 17-22 confronts us with death or the prospect of death. In verses 17-19, God commands Abraham to sacrifice his only son Isaac. How does he react to this terrible trial? In verses 20-22 we meet Isaac, Jacob and Joseph facing their own impending deaths. What are their thoughts at such a solemn hour? The answers Hebrews gives to these questions are full of instruction, comfort and support. They will strengthen us as we ourselves face the end of a life on earth, whether our own or that of a loved one.

Tested (11:17-18)

Once again, Abraham is our first example: **'By faith Abraham, when he was tested, offered up Isaac, and he who had received the promises offered up his only begotten son, of**

whom it was said, "In Isaac your seed shall be called"' (11:17-18). The testing Abraham endured was threefold. Firstly, he was called to give up his beloved and 'only begotten' son. That in itself would be an enormous loss, as any parent will understand. The Writer deliberately calls Isaac 'only begotten' in spite of the fact that Abraham had another son, Ishmael. Isaac was the only child of Abraham's marriage to Sarah, and thus the only *legitimate* son. But the term 'only begotten' also signifies that Isaac is a picture of Christ, of whom John writes, 'God so loved the world that he gave his only begotten Son, that whoever believes in him should not perish but have everlasting life' (John 3:16). Abraham's heart-rending decision to part with his son is an apt parable of God's great love to a lost world.

Secondly, the patriarch was tested in that he himself must wield the knife to kill his own son. What a dreadful prospect this must have been! Yet this is exactly what the Father did when he caused Christ to die to bear the sins of his people. The Almighty God cries, '"Awake, O sword, against my Shepherd, against the Man who is my companion," says the LORD of hosts' (Zech. 13:7). Only by striking his Son — an innocent substitute — could the Father punish sin and set the sinner free.

Thirdly, and perhaps hardest of all, Abraham was called to yield up the very promises that bound him to God! Lane comments, 'When Abraham obeyed God's mandate to leave Ur, he simply gave up his past. But when he was summoned to Mount Moriah to deliver his own son to God, he was asked to surrender his future.' His promised posterity depended on the life of his son ('in Isaac your seed shall be called'). In like manner, 'the riches of the glory of [the Father's] inheritance in the saints' depended on the life of Christ (Eph. 1:18). If Jesus remained dead, none would be justified and the inheritance would be void (Rom. 4:25).

Before we see how these dilemmas were resolved, let us notice one thing — testing is an intrinsic part of the believer's experience. Indeed, James goes as far as to say, 'My brethren, count it all joy when you fall into various trials, knowing that the testing of your faith produces patience' (James 1:2-3). Peter adds his own words of comfort: '... now, for a little while, if need be, you have been grieved by various trials, that the genuineness of your faith, being much more precious than gold that perishes, although it is tested by fire, may be found to praise, honour and glory at the revelation of Jesus Christ' (1 Peter 1:6-7). As a precious metal survives the fire that purges it of dross, so faith survives testing and is purified thereby. God takes pains with his believing children.

The solution (11:19)

But how exactly did Abraham cope with this threefold trial? 'By faith', says Hebrews. James concurs, adding that genuine faith results in works — works that both please God and vindicate its nature as justifying faith. He writes, 'Faith without works is dead. Was not Abraham ... justified by works when he offered up Isaac...? Do you see that faith was working together with his works, and by works was made perfect [complete]? And the Scripture was fulfilled which says, "Abraham believed God and it was accounted to him for righteousness"' (James 2:21-23).

Abraham did indeed believe God, **'concluding that God was able to raise [Isaac] up, even from the dead'** (11:19). The word 'conclude' means 'reckon (as on a fact)' and is related to our English word 'logic'. When the bombshell struck, and Abraham was commanded to sacrifice Isaac, his faith was immediately engaged. But he also wrestled *mentally* with the huge problem that confronted him and reached a clear *conclusion* — that God could and would raise the slain Isaac from the dead.

This is an important point because faith is so often viewed, even by Christians, as the negation of reason or logic. But, as we saw earlier (see comment on 11:3) there is neither conflict nor valid comparison between faith and reason, for they are quite different kinds of faculty. Faith provides spiritual information, to which we can and should apply our rational minds.

It is both right and proper, then, that we should *reason* on the basis of what faith reveals. This is exactly what Abraham did. He asked himself how it was possible to reconcile the death of Isaac with the promise of God. One possible answer was that God had withdrawn the promise or changed his mind about it. But that could not be, for faith knows that 'the gifts and calling of God are irrevocable' (Rom. 11:29). What was the alternative? It was that God would demonstrate his acceptance of the sacrifice by raising Isaac from the dead!

Here lay not only the resolution of Abraham's anguish but also an amazing insight into the redeeming work of Christ. For it is the resurrection of God's Son that declares the sufficiency of his offering to justify the ungodly (Rom. 4:25). And, having taught Abraham one lesson concerning redemption, God gave him another! He restrained Abraham from slaying Isaac and provided a *substitute* in the form of a ram (Gen. 22:11-14). Perhaps this was the point at which, in particular, Abraham 'saw' Christ's day and rejoiced (John 8:56).

Of course, Isaac did not die. But nevertheless, Abraham **'received him** [from the dead] **in a figurative sense'** (11:19) — 'meaning, probably', suggests Bruce, 'in a manner that prefigures the resurrection of Christ'.[2] Abraham's faith was rewarded in a most remarkable way. Not only was Isaac spared, but that which Abraham had surrendered in faith was restored to him abundantly. Consider the outcome. Abraham's faith had stared death in the face and had triumphed. It had been vindicated and strengthened. Isaac also (who must have been a willing participant in the intended sacrifice) was also taught that God saves through the sacrifice of a substitute, even 'the Lamb of God who takes away the sin of the world' (John 1:29). The promise of God, which had seemed under such dire threat, was renewed and reinforced (Gen. 22:16-18). And Abraham learnt the glorious truth that 'The LORD will provide' (Gen. 22:14).

It would be difficult to imagine a more severe trial than Abraham and Isaac together suffered through this event. Yet they both believed God and proved him worthy of their trust. So may we, in all our own trials, including the test that death itself presents. For we have the promise of God that those who die in Christ will rise again to everlasting life and glory: 'Thanks be to God, who gives us the victory through our Lord Jesus Christ!' (1 Cor. 15:49-57).

Old age (11:20-22)

The three verses that follow may seem something of an anti-climax after the drama on Mount Moriah. But life's inevitabilities outnumber life's dramas! One of those inevitable events is the onset of old age and the approach of death. How does faith react to these things? With confidence concerning the future — a future revealed by God. The Writer's examples are Isaac, Jacob and Joseph. All three were enfeebled and approaching death, but rather than indulge in self-pity — or even reminiscences — they all looked forward to things that were yet to come. In doing so they blessed and encouraged those they would shortly leave behind.

'**By faith Isaac blessed Jacob and Esau concerning things to come**' (11:20). Remarkably, though he had been tricked into blessing Jacob as the first-born, Isaac did not retract his benediction. He saw by faith that even Jacob's deceit lay within the sovereign providence of God, whose purposes would be fulfilled despite man's perfidy. He saw that Jacob, sinner that he was, would be changed and become God's instrument to carry forward both the lineage and faith of Abraham. Had not God so promised when he said, 'The older shall serve the younger'? (Gen. 25:23). Owen writes, 'We may see herein the infinite purity of the divine will, effectually accomplishing its own purpose and designs through the failings and miscarriages of men, without the least mixture with or approbation of their iniquities...'[3]

For all his failings, Isaac understood that God's purpose does not change: 'God is not a man that he should lie, nor a son of man that he should repent. Has he said and will he not do it? Has he spoken and will he not make it good?' (Num. 23:19). Remarkably, Isaac blessed Esau also 'concerning things to come' — in spite of the way the latter had despised his birthright (12:16-17; Gen. 27:37-40). For Isaac's sake, perhaps, God would graciously provide for the material well-being of Esau.

In course of time, it was Jacob's turn. **'By faith Jacob, when he was dying, blessed each of the sons of Joseph, and worshipped, leaning on the top of his staff'** (11:21). Just as Isaac had unwittingly blessed his younger son above the older, so now Jacob knowingly repeats the action, laying his right hand on the younger Ephraim rather than the first-born Manasseh (Gen. 48:14-20). He knew from his own experience that God's choice prevails over man's, and that his purposes are irreversible. He 'worshipped' in that he ascribed ultimate worth or value to his covenant-keeping God — not just to the promises but to the one who made them. In his frailty, Jacob leaned upon his staff — but in his faith he leaned on the sovereign God. As Lane remarks, 'Jacob's faith consisted in the conviction that God's designs were invincible and that the promises were being worked out under God's care.'[4]

The final example of dying faith is provided by Joseph: **'By faith Joseph, when he was dying, made mention of the departure of the children of Israel, and gave instructions concerning his bones'** (11:22). This man, who had experienced such remarkable providences throughout his life, remembered God's promise to his great-grandfather and knew it would be kept: 'Know certainly that your descendants will be strangers in a land that is not theirs, and will serve its people and be afflicted by them four hundred years. And also the nation whom they serve I will judge; afterwards they shall come out with great possessions' (Gen. 15:13-14). Joseph had no intention of missing the Exodus to the promised land (Gen. 50:24-26), even though only his bones would make the journey!

What do these vignettes of dying patriarchs tell us about faith? They reveal men who saw a future for themselves, even beyond death, because of the promises of God. That future lay, firstly, in their descendants, who would play a vital role in the fulfilment of God's plan of redemption and the outworking of his gracious purposes in human history. Even detailed things, like the ascendancy of one son over another, were significant to them, for God had shown it to them. Their progeny, along with the prophecies and benedictions they bestowed on them, would perpetuate their testimony and so imbue their brief lives with eternal meaning.

But their faith saw even further. Not only would their descendants carry forward the purposes of God, but those purposes would culminate in Christ, through whom they also would inherit the 'promised land' of personal salvation. As we have seen, they sought a city in heaven, not upon earth. They anticipated Jesus' words: 'Let not your heart be troubled... In my Father's house there are many mansions... I go to prepare a place for you' (John 14:1-2). And this faith-born knowledge energised their souls, even as their bodies weakened and died. For the dying believer, 'The path of the just is like the shining light, that shines ever brighter unto the perfect day' (Prov. 4:18) — for the best is yet to be.

42.
Seeing the invisible

Please read Hebrews 11:23-31

The Writer turns from death to life. The patriarchs in our previous chapter did not fear death, but now we are introduced to people who did not fear life — including what it can bring by way of threats, dangers, hazards and enemies. In other words, these verses tell us that *faith is not afraid*. Thus Moses' parents were 'not afraid of the king's command'; Moses himself was not afraid of 'the wrath of the king'; and Rahab dared to protect Joshua's spies from her countrymen.

Although all the characters were Old Testament believers, they teach a thoroughly new-covenant message — one which combines the awesome power of God with his tender mercies. Jesus himself teaches the balance between the two: 'Do not fear those who kill the body but cannot kill the soul. But rather fear him who is able to destroy both soul and body in hell... Are not two sparrows sold for a copper coin? And not one of them falls to the ground apart from your Father's will... Do not fear, therefore; you are of more value than many sparrows' (Matt. 10:28-31). In this passage Jesus reminds us that faith *does* fear — but it fears only God. Seeing the invisible, faith fears neither man nor circumstance, for it knows they are under God's sovereign control.

Refusing to conform (11:23-25)

The passage begins with believing people who refused to be cowed by an evil regime. The example is that of Moses' parents: **'By faith Moses, when he was born, was hidden three months by his parents, because they saw he was a beautiful child; and they were not afraid of the king's command'** (11:23). Rejecting Pharaoh's edict to surrender their baby to be drowned, they hid him for three months from their Egyptian neighbours. Furthermore, when they could hide him no longer, they conceived a bold plan to save their child. The rest, as they say, is history (Exod. 1:22 – 2:4).

The Bible teaches that we should 'submit ... to every ordinance of man for the Lord's sake, whether to the king as supreme or to governors ... ' (1 Peter 2:13). But Peter makes it clear that '... this is the will of God, that *by doing good* you may put to silence the ignorance of foolish men' (1 Peter 2:15, emphasis added). If our rulers command us to do evil rather than good, we are no longer bound to obey. Indeed, faith will vigorously resist any such ordinances, putting the fear of God before the fear of man. Thus the apostles, when ordered to cease preaching Christ, refused, saying, 'Whether it is right in the sight of God to listen to you more than to God, you judge. For we cannot but speak the things which we have seen and heard' (Acts 4:19-20).

Clearly, we must not make this an excuse for law-breaking or making martyrs of ourselves, and should do everything we can to obey our civic leaders. Paul reminds us that rulers are ordained by God to preserve an orderly, peaceful and law-abiding society, in which good is rewarded and evil punished (Rom. 13:1-7; 1 Tim. 2:1-3). But there are limits beyond which believers cannot go when the laws of men conflict with their clear moral and spiritual duty to God and their fellow men.

Where evil must be resisted, faith is ready to act fearlessly, whatever the physical consequences may be. The multitude of Christian martyrs, both past and present, bear abundant testimony to this fact.

The Writer's next example, Moses himself, offers a related lesson: **'By faith Moses, when he became of age, refused to be called the son of Pharaoh's daughter, choosing rather to suffer affliction with the people of God than to enjoy the passing pleasures of sin'** (11:24-25). Unlike his parents, Moses was not resisting an unjust edict — but he was rejecting an ungodly lifestyle! Owen understands the 'pleasures of sin' as things that 'might ... in themselves be enjoyed and used without sin; and so they were by him until the appointed time came when he was called from them'.[1] Other commentators agree that the sin in question was the apostasy that Moses *would* have committed, had he refused to obey God's call.[2]

Alternatively, however, the words could imply that to live in Pharaoh's household meant a life of pleasurable sin — no doubt involving the indulgence of materialistic and fleshly appetites. Certainly, the latter view is more relevant to our own age, when the large majority of people are motivated by a desire for personal pleasure and satisfaction, with no regard for the commandments and counsel of God's Word. Like Moses, we also have to make a choice.

Consider the sacrifice that Moses made. As 'the son of Pharaoh's [only?] daughter' he may even have been in line for the throne of Egypt.[3] He certainly enjoyed both riches and status. How much good might he have done had he remained at court and used his influence to assist God's people? Such arguments are often used to justify compromise with the world, whether by individuals or by the church itself. Involvement with worldly methods, alignment with worldly thinking, and the enjoyment of worldly esteem, too often characterise 'Christians' and their churches. But stripped of sophistry, it all comes down to compromise — and compromise usually stems from the fear of man.

Greater riches (11:26)

At the age of forty, Moses made a deliberate and courageous choice — and he did it 'by faith'. No one in his right mind would choose affliction rather than pleasure, slavery rather than dominion — unless he knew something that others could not see. This was the case with Moses. By faith he saw that Israel were 'the people of God' (11:25), and there lay the secret of his extraordinary decision. In truth he did not see it as a choice between hardship or affluence, wealth or poverty, slavery or mastery, but as a choice between God and Mammon. The material consequences were incidental, because he esteemed **'the reproach of Christ greater riches than the treasures in Egypt; for he looked to the reward'** (11:26). Like his faithful forebears, he sought 'those things which are above, where Christ is, sitting at the right hand of God' (Col. 3:1).

Many commentators find problems with the expression 'the reproach of Christ', doubting that it implies any knowledge on Moses' part of the promised Messiah.[4] Suggestions include the idea that the word 'Christ' or 'anointed one' here signifies Israel, as God's anointed people. Alternatively, the Writer may have chosen to describe Moses' self-humiliation as 'the reproach of Christ' because it pictured the condescension involved in the incarnation.

But these explanations seem unnecessarily cautious.[5] Why should Moses not have had the same intimation of the coming Christ as did Abraham? (John 8:56). And was it not specifically *Christ* that he saw as the one 'who is invisible? (11:27 — see below). And what was the 'reward' to which he looked, if it was not the same spiritual promise concerning the saving work of Christ that sustained the patriarchs in Canaan? To suggest that Moses knew nothing of the promised Messiah is to diminish his faith. Remember that *all* the heroes of faith in Hebrews 11 sought 'a better resurrection' (11:35) — and *that* can only be obtained through the work of Christ.

Towards the end of the epistle, the Writer himself illuminates the term 'the reproach of Christ'. He exhorts: 'Jesus also, that he might sanctify the people with his own blood, suffered outside the gate [of Jerusalem]. Therefore let us go forth to him, outside the camp, bearing his reproach. For here we have no continuing city, but we seek the one to come' (13:12-14). 'Reproach', therefore, signifies rejection, such as Christ himself suffered at the hands of his own people. It was largely through fear of such rejection by their fellow Jews that the Hebrews were drawing back into the shadows of the old covenant. But faith is not afraid. It is willing to suffer loss and forfeit the friendship of the world.

Indeed, it counts 'the treasures in Egypt' of little value in comparison with 'the unsearchable riches of Christ' and the glory of the city that is to come. Let Paul tell it his way: 'What things were gain to me, these I have counted loss for Christ. But indeed I also count all things loss for the excellence of the knowledge of Christ Jesus my Lord ... that I may gain Christ ... [and] the righteousness which is from God by faith ... [that] I may attain to the resurrection of the dead' (Phil. 3:7-11).

The Exodus (11:27)

The Writer passes over much of Moses' life and particularly omits his first departure from Egypt. This is significant because we read that after killing the Egyptian, 'Moses *feared* and said, "Surely this thing is known!"' Consequently, when

Pharaoh sought to kill him, he fled to Midian (Exod. 2:14-15; see also Acts 7:29). Since Moses was afraid, this cannot be the occasion referred to in our next verse: **'By faith he forsook Egypt, not fearing the wrath of the king'** (11:27). His forsaking Egypt must here refer to the later Exodus. The Writer's concern, of course, is to emphasise that faith is *not* afraid. The Exodus fits this purpose while the flight to Midian does not. But this does remind us that even the heroes of faith were not perfect in faith. Hard on the heels of Moses' courageous decision to identify with downtrodden Israel comes the killing of the Egyptian, leading to a fear of retribution and the flight to Midian (Acts 7:23-25). Did Moses' faith falter at this point? If so he is in good company!

Abraham himself stumbled when he fathered Ishmael, fearing that God's promise of a son would go unfulfilled. Jacob also failed, using deception to obtain a birthright that God had already promised him. But while faith is never perfect, its imperfections are overruled by perfect providence. In each case where faith was wanting, the sovereign Lord used even failure to further his ends and bring his counsel to pass (Eph. 1:11). This reminds us that it is not so much faith that overcomes, as the one in whom our faith is placed.

At the time of the Exodus from Egypt, Moses' faith allowed him to lead the people out, enriched and triumphant. The unarmed multitude was no match for the armies of Pharaoh, and Moses knew that the angry king would pursue them, but he was not afraid. Sheer bravery? No, clear faith — **'for he endured as seeing him who is invisible'** (11:27). If further proof were needed that faith is equivalent to spiritual sight, here it is. Moses, like Paul, did 'not look not at the things which are seen' (by physical sight) but he *did* look by faith 'at the things which are not seen. For the things which are seen are temporary, but the things which are not seen are eternal' (2 Cor. 4:18).

Gazing at invisible spiritual realities, Moses was able to endure both the anger of Pharaoh and the unbelief of Israel — and that without fear of what would transpire. Here lies the secret of spiritual endurance, the ability to be strong and steadfast in the face of threats, trials and discouragement. How important this is to Christians everywhere and at all times! We all know believers who display rock-like stability in their faith and service, while others waver and faint. The difference does not lie in our personalities but in our faith.

But what exactly did Moses see by faith? Not the outward manifestation of God's presence — the pillar of cloud and fire — for that was visible to the naked eye. He saw a person, '*him* who is invisible'. Owen writes, 'A double act of the faith of Moses is intended herein: (1) A clear distinct view and apprehension of God in his omnipresence, power, and faithfulness. (2) A fixed trust in him on that account, at all times and on all occasions.'[6] Clearly, Moses looked by faith, not only on the promises and instructions God gave, but on the divine person himself. And this person was surely the one who had met Moses so fatefully at the burning bush, namely, 'the Angel of the LORD' — a title that normally attaches to the eternal Son, the Second Person of the triune God (Exod. 3:1-6).

It is significant that Moses' faith looked to *Christ*, and not just to God, vaguely conceived. For the climax of Hebrews 11 is the exhortation of Hebrews 12: 2 — to look to 'Jesus, the author and finisher of our faith'. The application is self-evident. If we are to endure and accomplish God's work, we too must look to Christ and fix our attention on the unseen verities of God. Then we also will be without fear.

The Passover (11:28-29)

For his next example, the Writer turns to the Passover. The Israelites might well have feared the very plagues that prefaced their deliverance. There could be no greater dread than the prospect of the final plague — the death of 'all the first-born in the land of Egypt' (Exod. 12:12). Admittedly, God promised the Israelites protection from this judgement — through the blood of the Passover lamb (Exod. 12:13). But could God be believed? What difference would lambs' blood make amid the impending catastrophe?

Moses, however, did believe — and led his people to do the same: **'By faith he kept the Passover and the sprinkling of blood, lest he who destroyed the first-born should touch them'** (11:28). Moses' absolute trust in God drove out all fear of judgement. The blood of the lamb *would* suffice to save all who sheltered in faith beneath its stain! Here is a dramatic type and picture of 'the Lamb of God who takes away the sin of the world', and removes all fear of judgement for those who trust in his atoning blood (John 1:29; 1 Cor. 5:7; 1 Peter 1:19-20).

One last frightening situation faced Moses and the people as they departed from Egypt. Behind them were the armies of Pharaoh, bent on revenge. Before them lay the equally implacable waters of the Red Sea. Had they come so far only to perish on its shores? Not at all, for God had provided a way of safety through the sea. And it was **'by faith'** that **'they passed through the Red Sea as by dry land, whereas the Egyptians, attempting to do so, were drowned'** (11:29).

When the people saw the Egyptian chariots approaching, we read, 'They were very afraid.' In their panic they cried, 'It would have been better for us to serve the Egyptians than that we should die in the wilderness' (Exod. 14:10-12). But Moses, moved by faith rather than by fear, 'said to the people, "Do not be afraid. Stand still and see the salvation of the LORD ... the LORD will fight for you, and you shall hold your peace"' (Exod. 14:13-14). Only then did they trust God's word, obey his instructions and walk dry-shod between the waters.

We see here how Moses' faith set an example to the people. They were fearful and panic-stricken, but he was at peace, for he already knew what God would do (Exod. 14:1-4). Not only would God deliver the Israelites from Pharaoh, but would do so permanently. The very obstacle they feared became their way of escape and the destruction of their enemies! So often for us, God in grace and providence turns something we dread into a pathway for our feet and a graveyard for our fears.

The Writer to the Hebrews graciously attributes faith to all the Israelites, not just Moses. If he is right, it implies that Moses' example was the human means by which the people also acquired faith. So today also, the lack of fear that faith bestows is a powerful witness to fearful, unbelieving souls around us.

Faith overcomes the fear of man (11:30-31)

Arguably, there is no greater fear than the fear of man. We may fear sickness, poverty, danger and many other things. But no fear is more pervasive than the fear of what others will think of us (or do to us) if we fail to conform. Such fear is a blight on the lives of many Christians, whose witness is muted and whose example goes unseen. It dulls the clarity of much preaching and teaching, that fears to offend people by proclaiming biblical doctrines such as election and sovereign grace. The Writer's final examples in this passage relate to two people who overcame such fears through faith.

Immediately they entered the promised land, Joshua was confronted by a walled fortress, the city of Jericho (Josh. 5:10; 6:1). Forty years earlier such cities had struck fear into the hearts of the hand-picked warriors that Moses sent to spy out the land (Num. 13:17-20,28). But now things were different and Joshua could cry, 'Shout, for the LORD has given you the city!' (Josh. 6:16).

What made the difference? Faith, declares the Writer: **'By faith the walls of Jericho fell down after they were encircled for seven days'** (11:30). Once again, we find that faith rested on a self-revelation by God, this time in the form of a 'theophany' in which God manifested himself in human form. As Joshua surveyed the city from afar, he was met by one who called himself 'the Commander of the army of the LORD' (Josh. 5:13-15). It is evident that this 'man' was God — for Joshua worshipped him. Almost by definition, a theophany must involve the pre-incarnate Christ, for 'No one has seen God at any time. The only-begotten Son, who is in the bosom of the Father, he has declared him' (John 1:18).

Joshua received detailed instructions from the Commander, who declared, 'See! I have given Jericho into your hand, its king and the mighty men of valour' (Josh. 6:1-7). Joshua's faith, and the outcome of the campaign, rested alike on what God had shown him through Christ. By what mechanism the walls were destroyed, we cannot tell. Nor could Joshua. What if they had encircled the walls for seven days and nothing had happened? Did Joshua fear humiliation if things went wrong? Not at all. He trusted God to fulfil his promise miraculously — using means that were, in and of themselves, incapable of achieving such an outcome. Thus God chooses 'the weak things of the world to put to shame the things which are mighty ... and the things which are not, to bring to nothing the things that are, that no flesh should glory in his presence' (1 Cor. 1:27-29). We should take this to heart, and be encouraged.

Finally, and not without purpose, the Writer introduces the faith of a non-Jew, as if to emphasis that the new covenant is for all nations and all manner of sinners. **'By faith the harlot Rahab did not perish with those who did not believe, when she had received the spies with peace'** (11:31). The full story is told in Joshua 2. Where did she put her faith? In God alone, declaring, 'The LORD your God ... is God in heaven above and on earth beneath' (Josh. 2:11). Though her profession of faith may seem mundane to us, it was an extraordinary statement for a Canaanite. And because she had such a high view of the God of Israel, she was not afraid to defy the king and his minions (Josh. 2:1-6). Her action was traitorous and she would have died without mercy had it been discovered. But she had formed a higher allegiance, and trusted a great and sovereign God. Her faith saved her and her family from destruction, and so will ours if we look to Christ alone for deliverance from 'the wrath to come' (Matt. 3:7). She believed and, consequently, she was not afraid.

43.
Shaming the world

Please read Hebrews 11:32-40

The Writer gets no further than the book of Joshua in his detailed chronology of the heroes of faith. He has hardly begun, he suggests, and so much more could be said. But he has already achieved his main purpose — to delineate the chief *characteristics* of faith.

Accordingly, he summarises in general terms: **'And what more shall I say? For the time would fail me to tell of Gideon and Barak and Samson and Jephthah, also of David and Samuel and the prophets'** (11:32). However, the brief summary that follows in verses 32-37 fulfils an important second purpose, namely, to underline the *consequences* or achievements of faith.

Clearly, the Writer assumes that his readers have a thorough knowledge of the Old Testament. Otherwise the brief allusions employed in these verses would mean nothing to them. But the whole epistle testifies to the fact that although they *knew* the Scriptures, they did not *understand* them.

This remains a common problem today, even among Christians, when people fail to recognise that the purpose of Old Testament Scripture is to reveal Christ — it is 'our tutor to bring us to Christ, that we might be justified by faith' (Gal. 3:24). Jesus himself emphasised this truth, claiming 'these [Old Testament Scriptures] are they which testify of me' (John 5:39) and expounding 'in all the Scriptures the things concerning himself' (Luke 24:27). Of course, the epistle to the Hebrews perfectly exemplifies this principle, displaying Christ in a multitude of Old Testament references.

Yet all too often the Old Testament is used in a *Christless* way to teach such things as origins, history, ethics, morality, theology, ecclesiology — even the attributes of God, forgetting that these attributes are most perfectly revealed in God's only begotten Son (see 1:1-4). If Hebrews teaches us anything, it is that 'Christ is all and in all' (Col. 3:11). Let us not exclude him from the very Scriptures that testify to him!

Faith overcomes (11:33)

We can summarise the consequences of faith set out in 11:33-35 by saying that faith *overcomes*. It overcomes political power, evil, doubt, physical danger, violence, deadly persecution, weakness, fear, hostile armies and death itself. Let us consider these briefly in turn.

Firstly, **'through faith [they] subdued kingdoms'** (11:33). That is, faith's heroes overcame political forces and powers to attain God's purposes. Moses overcame the Egyptians, Joshua the Canaanites, Samson and David the Philistines, and so on. But these historical victories are also pictures of the way faith triumphs over *all* political adversity. The early church 'overcame' the power of Rome by its witness to Christ amid bitter persecution and suffering. Similar victories have been repeated throughout history by martyrs, reformers, Puritans, pioneer missionaries and others like them. They knew what it means to be 'counted as sheep for the slaughter' — but they were also 'more than conquerors through him who loved [them]' (Rom. 8:36-37).

Today we often face more subtle political foes — not the naked sword of persecution but the pressure to conform and compromise. Like the Hebrews before us, we fear to be different. We find it hard to resist the tides of liberalism, ecumenism, inclusivism and pluralism (such as the modern emphasis on 'churches together' and multi-faith religion). It is more comfortable to defer to the perceptions of a godless society, 'dumbing down' the gospel and Christ's claim to exclusivity.

But whatever the consequences, faith does not, indeed cannot, compromise — 'We cannot but speak the things that we have heard and seen' (Acts 4:20). And faith overcomes the obstacles. The gospel of God's sovereign grace in Christ is not silenced; the church is not destroyed; the gospel continues to flourish — and all because of faith.

Secondly, they **'worked righteousness'** (11:33). Brown sees this as *judicial* righteousness — that is, they executed judgement on the unrighteous[1] — while Owen and Bruce believe it refers to *political* righteousness, the persons named being rulers who established godly nations or societies.[2,3] However, the expression allows for a broader interpretation, and one that is more relevant to ourselves. While favouring the political interpretation, Lane admits that 'The idiom is used in Scripture of doing what is right in the sense of personal integrity.'[4]

On this view, to 'work righteousness' is to 'overcome evil with good' and to 'live soberly, righteously and godly in this present age, looking for the blessed hope and glorious appearing of our great God and Saviour Jesus Christ' (Rom. 12:21; Titus 2:12-13). The latter verse again emphasises that faith looks *at* and *for* things as yet unseen. True believers are those who 'by patient continuance in doing good, seek for glory, honour and immortality' (Rom. 2:7). By so doing, they overcome the evil around them in the world and testify to Christ, the Righteous One.

Thirdly, these people of faith **'obtained promises'** (11:33). When the promises of God seemed improbable or unattainable, they overcame their own doubt and unbelief. We have already seen how this worked in the lives of Abraham and Sarah, but it applies equally to such as Gideon (Judg. 6:12-16; 7:7), Barak (Judg. 4:6-7,14), Samson (Judg. 13:5) and David (2 Sam. 7:11). Furthermore, the Writer has already urged his readers not to 'become sluggish, but [to] imitate those who through faith and patience inherit the promises' (6:12; see also 10:35-36).

All who trust Christ have 'been given ... exceedingly great and precious promises, that through these [they] may be partakers of the divine nature, having escaped the corruption that is in the world through lust' (2 Peter 1:2-4). Although Peter's words apply to all God's promises in Scripture, his reference to 'the divine nature' relates specifically to the indwelling of the Holy Spirit in the believer. That is, faith obtains 'the promise of the Spirit' — a promise fulfilled when we trust in Christ (Gal. 3:14; 4:4-7). And that is not all. The 'promise of the Spirit' garners the *further* promise of eternal glory. For believers are 'sealed with the Holy Spirit of promise, who is the guarantee of our inheritance until the redemption of the purchased possession' (Eph. 1:13-14). God's promises in Christ are truly 'great and precious' and should be a source of daily strength.

Valiant in conflict (11:33-34)

The conquests of faith continue. Fourthly, we are told that by faith our predecessors **'stopped the mouths of lions, quenched the violence of fire, [and] escaped the edge of the sword'** (11:33-34). In other words, they overcame physical danger — violence and deadly persecution. The allusions are transparent. Daniel survives the lion's den (Dan. 6:10-23). His three friends are delivered from the fiery furnace (Dan. 3:19-30). David escapes the sword of Goliath (1 Sam. 17:45-46; other such escapes are also recorded).

In each case there was explicit trust in the living God. David confronted the giant with the words: 'This day the LORD will deliver you into my hand.' Shadrach, Meshach and Abed-Nego testified: 'Our God whom we serve ... will deliver...' And such was Daniel's testimony that his faith was actually enunciated by his reluctant persecutor: 'Your God, whom you serve continually, he will deliver you.'

Of course, not all such events issue in miraculous deliverance. Those who died for their faith are celebrated in a later verse. But this does not alter the fact that faith *always* overcomes violence, whether by life or by death. It is worth noting the full statement of Shadrach and his companions: 'Our God ... will deliver us... *But if not*, let it be known to you, O king, that we will not serve your gods' (Dan. 3:17-18, emphasis added). The italicised words remind us that these men of faith submitted their fate to a sovereign God, who was well able to save them physically, but for whom they were prepared to die if that were necessary (see 11:35 below). Either way, their faith held firm.

The Writer continues. Through faith, some **'out of weakness were made strong'**, overcoming natural weakness. Others **'became valiant in battle [and] turned to flight the armies of the aliens'** (11:34). They overcame both their fears and their enemies. A host of examples could be given, from Joseph to Joshua, from Moses to Mordecai, from David to Daniel. Brief though the statements in 11:34 may be, they open up a rich vein of biblical truth and consolation.

Isaiah testifies, 'The everlasting God ... gives power to the weak, and to those who have no might he increases strength.

Even the youths shall faint and be weary, but those who wait on the LORD shall renew their strength; they shall mount up with wings like eagles, they shall run and not be weary, they shall walk and not faint' (Isa. 40:28-31). Paul adds his testimony as he suffers the pain and perplexity of his 'thorn in the flesh': 'The Lord ... said to me, "My grace is sufficient for you, for my strength is made perfect in weakness" ... for when I am weak, then I am strong' (2 Cor. 12:9-10). Furthermore, we remember that 'God has chosen ... the weak things of the world to put to shame the things which are mighty ... that no flesh should glory in his presence' (1 Cor. 1:27-29).

What an amazing strategy the Lord has adopted! He deliberately uses the human frailty of his children to accomplish the most mighty victories of faith. Thereby he comforts his people, encourages his servants, defeats his enemies, accomplishes his purposes, and gets all the glory to himself. Let us also, in faith, draw deeply from the wells of our own weakness!

Lastly in the catalogue of overcoming faith, we are told that **'women received their dead raised to life again'** (11:35). The Writer clearly has in mind the widow of Zarephath who fed Elijah (1 Kings 17:17-24), and the Shunammite who ministered to Elisha (2 Kings 4:8-37), both of whose sons were brought back to life. Some suggest that the faith involved here was that of the prophets rather than the mothers. But Delitzsch counters this idea: 'Both women showed their faith in the appeal which they made to God's servants, as [also] in their previous kindness to them as messengers of God.'[5] In support, we may note that the Shunammite could bring herself to say, 'It is well', even in the midst of her distress.

The lesson for us is not so much that 'the prayer of faith will save the sick' (James 5:15), though under the sovereignty of God that is true. It is, rather, that faith looks forward to the sure resurrection and glory of those who die trusting in Christ. Our earthly grief, though real, is not to be compared with 'the

things which God has prepared for those who love him' (1 Cor.
2:9).

Faith suffers (11:35-38)

The focus now changes. Whereas in 11:33-35a we read of
those who escaped the edge of the sword, verses 35b-38 speak
of those who 'were slain with the sword'. The message is unchanged, namely, that faith overcomes. But now its victories
are won *through* suffering, rather than through *deliverance*
from suffering. In terms of faith there is no change, but the
human experience is a different matter.

The Writer continues: **'And others were tortured, not
accepting deliverance, that they might obtain a better resurrection. Still others had trial of mockings and scourgings,
yes, and of chains and imprisonment. They were stoned,
they were sawn in two, were tempted, were slain with the
sword. They wandered about in sheepskins and goatskins,
being destitute, afflicted, tormented — of whom the world
was not worthy. They wandered in deserts and mountains,
in dens and caves of the earth'** (11:35-38). We shall not
attempt to illustrate these statements by detailed Old Testament references, since a multitude of cases could be cited. We
can, however, draw from these verses three principles that
pertain to faith and those who exercise it.

Firstly, and most obviously, *faith suffers*. This is a general
fact of spiritual life. 'All who desire to live a godly life in Christ
Jesus', declares Paul, 'will suffer persecution' (2 Tim. 3:12).
Paul and Barnabas 'strengthened the souls of the disciples,
exhorting them to continue in the faith, and saying, "We must
through much tribulation enter the kingdom of God"' (Acts
14:22). Jesus himself taught, 'Blessed are you when they revile and persecute you, and say all kinds of evil against you

falsely for my sake. Rejoice and be exceedingly glad, for great is your reward in heaven, for so they persecuted the prophets who were before you' (Matt. 5:11-12). Jesus consoles his disciples with the words: 'In the world you will have tribulation; but be of good cheer, I have overcome the world' (John 16:33).

All these references, and many more, remind us that believers unavoidably live in a hostile environment. As 'strangers and pilgrims', they do not 'belong' in this present world, and the world is quick to recognise it. The people of this world do not have to be taught to ridicule and persecute those who owe allegiance to the living God — such behaviour comes naturally. Peter makes the application for us: 'Beloved, do not think it strange concerning the fiery trial which is to try you, as if some strange thing happened to you; but rejoice to the extent that you partake of Christ's sufferings, that when his glory shall be revealed, you may also be glad with exceeding joy' (1 Peter 4:12-13).

Secondly, *faith both seeks and obtains a 'better resurrection'* and will not, therefore, compromise or recant in order to escape the trials and hardships of this life. The term 'better resurrection' denotes final or 'eschatological' resurrection to eternal life — as opposed to the temporary resurrection of those restored to this present life and referred to in 11:35.[6] Those whose faith is celebrated here had this in common with Abraham — they looked forward to a bodily resurrection and an eternal future in the city of glory. The hope of bodily resurrection and eternal blessedness in the presence of Christ is one of the outstanding benefits of gospel faith (see, for example, 1 Cor. 15:19-20,50-58). Well might Paul cry in this context, 'Thanks be to God, who gives us the victory through our Lord Jesus Christ' (1 Cor. 15:57).

Thirdly, *faith puts the world to shame*, for 'the world was not worthy' of those the Writer honours in this passage. This is important to grasp, because the design of those who persecute believers is to put *them* to shame. But even in man's estimation the murderer is more shamed by his crime than the victim, the bully than the one harassed. How much more in God's sight does the world debase itself when it mocks and injures innocent and godly people!

Jesus comforts his persecuted flock from heaven's perspective: 'Rejoice and be exceedingly glad, for great is your reward in heaven, for so they persecuted the prophets who were before you' (Matt. 5:12). Likewise, writing to his persecuted brethren, Peter can say, 'If you are reproached for the name of Christ, blessed are you, for the Spirit of glory and of God rests upon you. On their part he is blasphemed, but on your part he is glorified' (1 Peter 4:14).

Faith expects (11:39-40)

So faith overcomes, both in life and death. But to what purpose? The Writer tells us, **'And all these, having obtained a good testimony through faith, did not receive the promise, God having provided something better for us, that they should not be made perfect apart from us'** (11:39-40). This final declaration is in no way negative, though it may appear so at first sight. The point being made here is that the trailblazing heroes of the Old Testament era, revered as they deserve to be, still had to wait for the dawning of the new covenant in Christ before their expectations could be realised. They lived in the era of promise, but we live in a time of fulfilment.

Yet this was the very time in which the Hebrews had been born and born again! Could they not see how privileged they were — how little, in terms of faith, was being asked of them in comparison with the demands made upon their forebears? The Old Testament saints had 'endured as seeing him who is invisible'. But they possessed 'something better', that is, the final revelation of God in Christ — the new covenant revealed in all its satisfying fulness. The faith of the fathers had shamed the world — let it not also shame the Hebrews! Rather, let it both inspire and strengthen their faith, teaching them patience under their 'light affliction, which is but for a moment'. Such endurance will produce 'a far more exceeding and eternal weight of glory, while we do not look at the things which are seen, but at the things which are not seen' (2 Cor. 4:17-18).

The words 'something better' do not refer to the final state of blessedness under the new covenant, which will be the same for all believers of whatever era. They refer, rather, to the clarity of revelation enjoyed by believers since God spoke to us in Christ (1:2). Although these Old Testament saints 'shall not be made perfect apart from us', they *will* be made perfect *along with* us! No other outcome is possible, for the God in whom they believed is the God in whom we also trust. The substitute on whom they cast their sins is the Christ who 'bore our sins in his own body on the tree' and 'by whose stripes [we are] healed' (1 Peter 2:24). The faith by which they believed is the same spiritual sight by which we too 'behold the Lamb of God' (John 1:29,36). The faith that saved them is the same gift of grace that God bestows on sinners still. They have 'obtained a good testimony through faith' — the commendation of God in Scripture. The Writer urges his readers to follow in their train.

44.
Looking to Jesus

Please read Hebrews 12:1-2

If you have ever watched or experienced white-water rafting, you will know what it is to be borne through rapids as if by an irresistible force! Hebrews 11 is rather like that — a veritable cataract of teeming images, coruscating exploits, towering achievements, compelling stories and breathtaking testimonies to the power of faith. The rafter takes a deep breath when he emerges from the maelstrom into quieter waters! So we must also, as the tumult and exhilaration of this extraordinary chapter die away.

Where does Hebrews 11 leave us? What is its application, its final conclusion? The answer is provided in the opening verses of Hebrews 12.

Racing to glory (12:1)

The Writer arrives at his conclusion: **'Therefore we also, since we are surrounded by so great a cloud of witnesses, let us lay aside every weight, and the sin which so easily ensnares us, and let us run with endurance the race that is set before us, looking unto Jesus...'** (12:1-2). At first sight these verses urge three distinct actions. We are (1) to run the race, (2) lay aside weights and sin, and (3) look to Jesus. But although we shall consider each of these in turn, they cannot really be separated. We cannot run without looking to Jesus. We cannot run unless we divest ourselves of weights and sins. And we cannot cast off these hindrances unless we look to Christ.

The metaphor is of athletes striving for victory before a 'cloud' (vast crowd) of spectators. The Writer probably had in mind the Greek 'footrace' — a test of fitness and endurance. Lane writes, 'The footrace was one of the five contests of the pentathlon in the great panhellenic games and always came first. At the Olympic games the footrace was the only athletic contest [that lasted] for an extended period.'[1]

This race is **'set before us'**, says Hebrews. We have not stumbled into the competition by accident, nor have we joined it of our own volition. We are *called by God* to participate — and that on account of 'his own glory and virtue' (Rom. 1:6; 2 Peter 1:3).

The witnesses are, of course, the people who populate Hebrews 11. The word **'witnesses'** implies two things. Firstly, they are those commended by God and Scripture — 'they obtained a good testimony through faith' (11:39). Because of this, they bear effective witness to Christ and the promise of the new covenant.[2] They stand as examples to be followed. Even more, they speak to us from the pages of Scripture to encourage us and urge us on.

Secondly, their 'witness' as *spectators* suggests that we ourselves are under observation as we pursue our own 'work of faith, labour of love and patience of hope in our Lord Jesus Christ' (1 Thess. 1:3). Lane points out that 'The participle ... "surrounded by" particularly suggests that they are witnesses to our efforts',[3] while the Living Bible's paraphrase reads: 'since we have such a huge crowd of men of faith watching us from the grandstands' (apparently forgetting that women also feature in Hebrews 11!).

However, we must not take this too literally. While our own 'work of faith' is most certainly performed 'in the sight of our God and Father' (1 Thess. 1:3), we need not assume that the faithful dead are actually watching our every action (a somewhat alarming idea). Rather, it is *as if* they were spectators — people whose expectations would be disappointed if we failed to emulate their exploits in the arena of faith.

Because their example is ever before us, declares the Writer, certain responsibilities rest upon us. We are like runners selected to represent their country at an international event, and must do our utmost to fulfil our privileged role. 'I press on', declares Paul, 'that I may lay hold of that for which Christ Jesus *has also laid hold of me*' (Phil. 3:12, emphasis added).

To complete our appointed task, therefore, we must **'run with endurance the race that is set before us'** (12:1). The prize we seek is not a transient gold medal or laurel wreath, but the everlasting glory of the redeemed. Here is something of a paradox. Christ has already won that glory for all his elect — yet only if we run well shall we attain it. Paul confirms the paradox. 'Not that I have already attained ...', he writes, but 'reaching forward to those things which are ahead, I press towards the goal [finishing tape] for the prize of the upward call of God in Christ Jesus' (Phil. 3:12-14).

Paul also helps us resolve the paradox. He instructs the Corinthians at length: 'Do you not know that those who run in a race all run, but one receives the prize? Run in such a way that you may obtain it. And everyone who competes for the prize is temperate in all things. Now they do it to obtain a perishable crown, but we for an imperishable crown. Therefore I run ... not with uncertainty ... but I discipline my body and bring it into subjection, lest when I have preached to others, I myself should become disqualified' (1 Cor. 9:24-27).

Neither the Writer nor the apostle is teaching salvation by self-effort. If they were, there would be no need for faith — the whole discussion would be pointless! What they *are* saying is that saving faith is demonstrated, recognised and vindicated by its supreme effort and endurance. That, surely, is the lesson of Hebrews 11, and the Writer is not afraid to drive it home. If we *do* run with endurance, we shall prove that we are called of God. But if we fail this test we reveal our lost condition, whatever profession we may make. The test is just as valid now as it was then.

Weights and sins (12:1)

To run successfully, adds the Writer, we must **'lay aside every weight, and the sin which so easily ensnares us'** (12:1). This double exhortation contains, perhaps, a spark of humour. A runner is pictured struggling down the racetrack encumbered by superfluous clothing and other burdens ('weights'). His progress is further hindered by obstacles ('sin') strewn in his path that 'ensnare' or deflect him from his purpose. But what do these images represent, and what is the difference between a 'weight' and a 'sin'?

Some suggest that 'weight' refers specifically to moral hindrances or vices,[4] but it seems more likely that it covers anything that hinders a Christian's progress *without in itself being sinful*. Owen singles out earthly riches as foremost among such weights, citing 1 Timothy 6:9-10: 'those who desire to be rich fall into temptation and a snare... For the love of money is a root of all kinds of evil, for which some have strayed from the faith ... and pierced themselves through with many sorrows.'[5] Riches in themselves are not sinful, nor is the possession of them (Abraham was a wealthy man). But if they are made the objects of desire and love, they become a millstone round our necks.

Other examples spring readily to mind. To follow Christ we must often forfeit the approbation of men. There is nothing wrong with being popular, but if popularity takes precedence over Christ, we stumble. To desire peace is not sinful, but to seek 'peace at any price' and thereby deny Christ is a weight we dare not carry. Again, it is healthy to be ambitious, but ambition that distracts us from following Christ is a weight that has to go. If we 'seek first the kingdom of God and his righteousness', God himself will care for our every need (Matt. 6:33).

The 'sin which so easily ensnares us', being sinful in itself, is clearly something different from a 'weight'. Some see this sin as the sin of apostasy — which certainly concerns the Writer elsewhere. Thus Kasemann claims: 'For the people of God, [this] sin can only be apostasy.'[6] But this can hardly be the case, since apostates are not engaged in this race at all! The sin in view here is either sin in general or, more probably, the 'indwelling sin' that troubles all true believers. The Writer is concerned here with sin itself (singular) rather than sins (plural). It is just *because* indwelling sin lurks within our own nature that it ensnares us 'so easily'.

But what exactly is 'indwelling sin'? The apostle Paul explains. Bemoaning the 'sin that dwells in me', he continues: 'For I know that in me (that is, in my flesh) nothing good dwells; for to will is present with me, but how to perform what is good I do not find' (Rom. 7:17-18). He is referring to the fact that even after regeneration the believer retains his old sinful nature ('the flesh') alongside the new nature acquired through the indwelling of Christ by the Spirit (Gal. 2:19-20). This indwelling sin, Paul continues, constitutes 'a law [principle], that evil is with me, the person who wills to do good. For I delight in the law of God according to the inward man. But I see another law in my members, warring against the law of my mind, and bringing me into captivity to the law of sin which is in my members' (Rom. 7:21-23; see also Gal.5:17). Owen comments: 'Sin doth not only still abide in us, but is still acting, still labouring to bring forth the deeds of the flesh.'[7] Every true believer will know what he means.

To run effectively, therefore, we must 'lay aside' these weights and sins. We must divest ourselves of them, just as athletes discard excess clothing before a race. What spiritual action is indicated here, and how can it be carried out? The New Testament provides clear answers to these questions. Paul instructs the Ephesians to 'put off, concerning your former conduct, the old man which grows corrupt according to the deceitful lusts, and ... put on the new man which was created according to God in righteousness and true holiness' (Eph. 4:22-24). Put simply, this means that although the believer possesses two natures — the old and the new — he nevertheless has the power to choose which of them will run his life!

How does he do this? By faith, replies the Scripture. We are to 'reckon' ourselves dead to sin but alive to God. Paul's full statement is as follows: 'Knowing ... that our old man was crucified with [Christ] ... knowing that Christ, having been raised from the dead, dies no more ... reckon yourselves to be dead indeed to sin, but alive to God in Christ Jesus our Lord' (Rom. 6:6-11).

We begin with things we *know* by faith — we are crucified with Christ and raised to 'newness of life' in him (Rom. 6:4). Then we 'reckon' on these things, that is, we count them to be true. As we do, we find that the weights and sins are powerless to hinder us. Moreover, since our newness of life consists in the indwelling of the Holy Spirit (Rom. 8:9-11), we shall 'walk in the Spirit and not fulfil the works of the flesh' (Gal: 5:16).

This 'laying aside' of hindrances has to be a continuous process. The weights of this life are never far away and, most certainly, we are never free from indwelling sin. We have a lifetime's work, therefore, in mortifying the flesh and denying its ungodly desires. This is a battle that never ends until we go to glory. If Hebrews 11 teaches us anything, it is that the victory can only be won by faith, never by will-power. Many seek to subdue the old nature by 'self-imposed religion, false humility, and neglect of the flesh [i.e. body]', but such things 'are of no value against the indulgence of the flesh [i.e. the old nature]' (Col. 2:23). No — faith in Christ is the only way to overcome.

Faith's craftsman (12:2)

Because faith in Christ is the only way, we must run the race **'looking unto Jesus, the author and finisher of our faith'** (12:2). This is a most important statement. Indeed, scholars struggle to interpret it. 'It resists facile translation', says Lane, and 'must be given precision in the light of the larger development in Hebrews.'[8]

Clearly, to run looking to Jesus can signify several things. Firstly, Christ is the greatest of all examples — 'the exemplar, the champion of faith'.[9] The Writer exhorts us to imitate the witnesses of Hebrews 11, for they testified to the faithfulness of God and the certainty of his promises. They are rightly held up to us as people to emulate. But if this is the case, how much more is Christ himself an example to be followed! 'Imitate me', urged the apostle Paul, 'just as I also imitate Christ' (1 Cor. 11:1). The Greek word translated 'imitate' (AV, 'follow') gives us our English word 'mimic'. If the Spirit of Christ dwells in us, it is by no means beyond our power to emulate Christ's actions and attitudes here on earth. Indeed, it is our duty and privilege to do so, for Jesus himself urged his disciples to imitate him (see, e.g., John 13:14-15).

But Christ is much more than an example to follow. He is the **'author** [originator] **and finisher** [perfector] **of faith'**. In a most profound sense, Jesus is the divine craftsman who originates and shapes our faith, and brings it to perfection. Brown sees various possible interpretations.[10] It could mean that Christ is the author of *the* faith — that is, the gospel; or that he is the originator of the *faithful* — that is, his redeemed people. However, the whole subject of this part of the epistle is *personal* faith — that which is exercised by the believing soul as it seeks to obey the living God. It is more likely, then, that the Writer is here thinking of such personal faith. That is, we must look to Jesus because he supplies the very faith by which we run!

Firstly, he is the 'author' of our faith because he gave it to us in the first place: 'By grace you have been saved through faith, and that not of yourselves: it is the gift of God... For we are his workmanship' (Eph. 2:8-10). Secondly, Christ alone can perfect our faith — that is, bring it to its full fruition and reward. The words 'author' and 'finisher', declares Owen, 'express an efficiency, a real power and efficacy, with respect unto our faith'.[11]

In practice, this means that Christ is far more than a role-model or source of inspiration. It means that through the agency of the Holy Spirit he is continually *providing* help and sustenance as we run the race of faith. Paul tells us that 'the Spirit also helps in our weaknesses' (Rom. 8:26) and prays that his readers might be 'strengthened with might by his Spirit in the inner man, that Christ may dwell in your hearts through faith' (Eph. 3:17). Significantly, that same prayer ends with a doxology — to 'him who is able to do exceeding abundantly above all that we ask or think, according to his power *that works in us*' (Eph. 3:20, emphasis added).

To put it simply, Paul teaches that the life of faith is one indwelt and empowered by the Holy Spirit. How may we access this power in our own lives? By looking to Christ for 'the supply of the Spirit of Jesus Christ' (Phil. 1:19) — just as a small child trusts its parents to supply its every need.

Christ our example (12:2 cont.)

Christ is not *just* our example — but he *is* an example. Thus
the Writer returns to the theme in which he juxtaposes the
example of Christ with that of the Old Testament saints. We
are to look to Jesus **'who for the joy that was set before him
endured the cross, despising the shame, and has sat down
at the right hand of the throne of God'** (12:2). The heroes
of faith endured hardship; they despised indignities; they looked
forward to a future and eternal reward; and they will assuredly 'sit down in the kingdom of God' (Luke 13:28-29). But
how much greater is the pattern that Jesus provides! He endured not only death, but death on a cross — rejected by man
and judged by God — as he suffered vicariously for the sins of
his people. The creator and sustainer of all things was mocked
and scorned by his pathetic creatures — yet he despised such
mind-shattering shame. How could he do it? Because of 'the
joy that was set before him', replies the Writer. Lane points
out that the joy referred to could be either the joy he laid aside
in undertaking his mission to earth, or the joy with which he
was rewarded when he returned to heaven.[12] We adopt the
second alternative.

What was that joy? The joy of a shepherd over his sheep;
the joy of a farmer over his harvest; the joy of a warrior over
his conquests; the joy of a king over his kingdom; the joy of a
father over his children; the joy of a bridegroom over his bride!
We have noticed before that Paul wants us to understand 'what
are the riches of the glory of [Christ's] inheritance in the saints'
(Eph. 1:18). The Writer to the Hebrews wants us to grasp it
too. 'The joy of the Lord' is not just our joy in him, but also
his joy in us!

Having endured the cross and despised the shame, Christ
'has sat down at the right hand of the throne of God'. Because

he humbled himself to die on a cross for our salvation, the Father 'has highly exalted him and given him the name which is above every name, that at the name of Jesus every knee should bow ... and every tongue should confess that Jesus Christ is Lord, to the glory of God the Father' (Phil. 2:9-11). So Hebrews again picks up the theme, launched in its opening verses, of Christ transcendent — exalted to the place of supremacy, honour, privilege, power and glory. By implication, the Writer holds out to his readers the amazing prospect that the redeemed will share Christ's glory as his eternal bride (Rev. 21:9-11). But they will *only* do so if they prove they are truly his — by their joyful, enduring and forward-looking faith. This is no time to turn back.

45.
Facing hostility

Please read Hebrews 12:3-4

We have considered how Jesus 'endured the cross, despising the shame', but the Writer now reminds us that Christ's crucifixion was the culmination of a whole life of endurance. We cannot suffer as he did in his vicarious death — that would be impossible. But the children of the new covenant *can* identify with the ordeals and indignities that marked his life. Indeed, they must do so, for 'The servant is not greater than his master', said Christ — 'If they persecute me, they will also persecute you' (John 15:20). The apostle Paul derives much comfort from the thought that, in his own trials, he was experiencing 'the fellowship of [Christ's] sufferings' and being thereby 'conformed to his death' (Phil. 3:9-11).

This being so, the Writer calls upon the Hebrews to look to Christ in yet another way, that is, to **'consider him who endured such hostility from sinners against himself, lest you become weary and discouraged in your souls'** (12:3). Thus these verses both diagnose their condition and prescribe the remedy. Let us look first at their problem.

Weary and discouraged (12:3)

The first readers of this epistle were 'weary and discouraged in their souls' — or, at least, stood in serious danger of becoming so. Spiritually speaking, they were tired, sick at heart and ready to give up the unequal struggle. What was the cause of their trouble? The same **'hostility from sinners'** that the Lord himself endured during his time on earth.

Earlier in the epistle we learned that they had 'endured a great struggle with suffering', being made 'a spectacle both by reproaches and tribulations' and suffering 'the plundering of [their] goods' (10:32-34). They had been treated shamefully by the society in which they lived. Yet, significantly, they had received these trials 'joyfully' at the time (cf. James 1:2-4). But now the selfsame afflictions produced weariness and discouragement — because they had taken their eyes off Christ.

We should not be unsympathetic. Their sufferings were far greater than most Christians experience today. At the human level, therefore, it was no surprise that they were weary and discouraged. They were not the first to be so, nor would they be the last. The psalmist Asaph, contrasting his lot with that of the ungodly rich, complained, 'Surely I have cleansed my heart in vain, and washed my hands in innocence [foolish simplicity]. For all day long I have been plagued and chastened every morning' (Ps. 73:13-14). Inadvertently, however, Asaph provides his own answer — by using the word 'chastened'. For chastening comes not from our enemies but from God. The idea of chastening is one that the Writer takes up and develops in the following verses, as we shall shortly see.

It is inevitable that contestants in a long-distance race get tired. So we also can grow weary and discouraged in the Christian race. But God both understands and cares: 'As a father pities his children, so the LORD pities those who fear him. For he knows our frame; he remembers that we are dust' (Ps. 103:13-14). How does he help us? The answer lies in another question. How do athletes overcome *their* physical weariness? In four ways. Firstly, by proper training; secondly by focusing on their goal; thirdly by overcoming the 'pain barrier' and getting the mysterious 'second wind'; and fourthly by keeping their eyes on the front runner (perhaps a 'pace-maker'). There are spiritual parallels to all these things.

Proper training, firstly, reminds us that *we must be diligent in our Christian life.* No athlete can succeed unless he trains with single-minded thoroughness. Since, as believers, we have 'escaped the corruption that is in the world through lust', says Peter, we should '[give] all diligence [to] add to our faith virtue, to virtue knowledge, to knowledge self-control, to self-control perseverance, to perseverance godliness, to godliness brotherly kindness, and to brotherly kindness love'. Then he adds: 'If these things are yours and abound, you will be neither barren nor unfruitful in the knowledge of our Lord Jesus Christ... Therefore, brethren, be even more diligent to make your calling and election sure, for if you do these things you will never stumble' (2 Peter 1:5-10).

Here is spiritual training — a runner's manual if ever there was one! Those who are diligent in the Christian life, and equip themselves with the graces listed by Peter, will be forearmed against weariness. To this end, we must consistently use the *means* of grace that God provides — reading and hearing the Word, corporate worship, prayer, fellowship and witness. If we do, we shall have the resilience to conquer discouragement (see 2 Cor. 4:1,16).

Secondly, we overcome weariness and discouragement by *focusing on our goal.* This is what the patriarchs did when they looked towards 'a better, that is, a heavenly country' (11:16). We shall shed our weariness, and press on with new resolution, if we remember that we are racing to glory.

Thirdly, we defeat weariness and discouragement by the *gracious strength of the Spirit of God.* Our 'second wind' is no physiological mystery, but the indwelling of Christ by his Spirit. The Spirit teaches us, quickens us, leads us, bears witness with us, helps our infirmities, strengthens us and guarantees our inheritance in Christ (John 14:26; Rom. 8:11,14,16,26; Eph. 3:16; 1:14).

Fourthly and finally, *we fix our gaze on the 'forerunner ... Jesus'*, our great High Priest, who has entered through the veil into the presence of the living God (6:20). If we run 'looking unto Jesus', our weariness and discouragement, though oft-times burdensome, will melt away. The old chorus puts it well:

> Turn your eyes upon Jesus,
> Look full in his wonderful face,
> And the things of earth will grow strangely dim,
> In the light of his glory and grace.

Consider him (12:3-4)

To protect themselves against discouragement, therefore, the Writer urges the Hebrews to **'consider him who endured such hostility from sinners against himself'** (12:3). They should not only to *look* to Jesus, but *consider* him. The word carries the nuance of 'weighing' or 'calculating' — of making a proportionate judgement.[1] They must take a long look at Christ, not a cursory glance. In other words, they should meditate and dwell upon (1) the patient manner in which he endured his own prior sufferings, and (2) the reason why he did so.

The hostility Jesus faced was greater than anything they could imagine: 'He was in the world, and the world was made through him, and the world did not know him. He came to his own, and his own did not receive him' (John 1:10-11). Were the Hebrews rejected by their fellow men? Then Christ was rejected by those he had created! Were they persecuted by the Jews? Then he was murdered by the very nation he had so graciously chosen as his special people! Were they ill-treated by fellow sinners? Then he, the Holy One, was accused of insurrection and blasphemy! The Writer asks them a question. Could they not follow Christ's example and *despise* the shame? He had paid an incalculable penalty for their sakes, to bring them to glory (2:10). Was it too much to ask them to endure their lesser trials for him? When John the Baptist cried, 'Behold the Lamb of God!' he was not thinking of a cuddly animal but of a sacrifice.

We too must 'consider him'. Indeed, our faith must be Christ-centred in every respect. This has implications for our worship, our preaching, our fellowship, our evangelism and our daily walk. If Christ was 'all and in all' to the apostle Paul, he should not be less to us (Col. 3:11). These words from Colossians fall in a passage which reminds us that 'Christ is our life' and exhorts us to 'seek those things which are above, where Christ is'. We are to forgive as Christ forgave, to 'let the word of Christ dwell in [us] richly', and to 'do all in the name of the Lord Jesus' (Col. 3:1-17). New-covenant faith and life is saturated with Christ. How far do our lives match up to this?

If we are anything like the Hebrews, the sad answer is, 'Not very well'. For, chides the Writer, **'You have not yet resisted to bloodshed, striving against sin'** (12:4). This could be a reference to martyrdom since, in detailing the Hebrews' sufferings in 10:32-34, he makes no mention of anyone dying for their faith. More likely, however, the Writer is using further imagery from the arena, switching from running to armed boxing — a vicious sport in which the spectators expected blood to flow.

According to the Stoic philosopher Seneca, the true athlete was one 'who saw his own blood'.[2] Whatever the allusion, one thing is clear. In distinct contrast to Christ — who gave his life to *conquer* sin — the recipients of this letter had not striven to the limit in *resisting* it. The sin of unbelief is particularly in view. Like a modern boxer who 'throws in the towel', they were opting out of the contest when they were barely scratched. The Writer's disapproval is obvious. Is he being too hard on them? Surely not, when we consider what is at stake — their eternal security and the glory of God.

We live in easygoing days, and 'striving' is not a word we often use. Yet the new-covenant life of faith calls us to strive against sin, while at the same time resting in Christ. There is no contradiction.

46.
Enduring chastening

Please read Hebrews 12:5-11

The Writer now introduces another arresting analogy — the trials that his readers are suffering can and should be viewed as 'chastening' from a loving heavenly Father. This emphasis brings out and applies yet another aspect of the new covenant — the doctrine of adoption. Those who believe in Christ are God's people in the profound sense that they are his children and his heirs (Rom. 8:17).

The word 'chastening' signifies 'instruction' or 'child-training'. Affliction may take many forms, and come through many agencies — but it is masterminded by God for the eventual good of his children. Needless to say, when Christians embrace this perspective, it transforms their outlook on the problems and hardships of life.

Training (12:5-6)

Sadly, although the Hebrews had once understood these things, they no longer remembered: '... **you have forgotten the exhortation which speaks to you as to sons: "My son, do not despise the chastening of the LORD, nor be discouraged when you are rebuked by him; for whom the LORD loves he chastens, And scourges every son whom he receives"'**

(12:5-6). The word translated 'exhortation', says Lane, 'combines the notions of exhortation and comfort ... the note of encouragement appears to be dominant.'[1]

The Scripture quotation is from Proverbs 3:11-12. We may compare it with Job 5:17: 'Happy is the man whom God corrects; therefore do not despise the chastening of the Almighty. For he bruises, but he binds up; he wounds, but his hands make whole.'

We find similar teaching in many places in Scripture. In Deuteronomy 8:5 the Lord is said to chasten his people 'as a man chastens his son', while Psalm 94:12 declares, 'Blessed is the man whom you instruct [chasten], O Lord, and teach out of your law.' In the New Testament, Paul declares that 'Our light affliction, which is but for a moment, is working for us a far more exceeding and eternal weight of glory' (2 Cor. 4:17). Both James and Peter classify the trials and persecutions of this life as 'the testing of ... faith' (James 1:3; 1 Peter 1:6-7). Hebrews develops the idea of 'child-training' or chastening to its logical conclusion.

Although the Writer scolds his readers for their forgetfulness, his words are actually full of comfort. The expression, 'every son whom he receives', signifies 'favourable reception' or 'love' on the part of God. It implies the glorious doctrine of adoption.

Testing (12:7-8)

In harmony with this doctrine, the afflicted believer is a 'son'. God's 'rebuke' is designed to help, not discourage, and chastening is a token of his love towards (and acceptance of) his child. The Writer elaborates with tender logic: **'If you endure chastening, God deals with you as with sons; for what son is there whom a father does not chasten? But if you are**

without chastening, of which all have become partakers, then you are illegitimate and not sons' (12:7-8). Owen points out that 'deals with' is a weak translation and that the force of the words is better rendered: 'He [God] offers himself to you in the ... 'habit' of a father to his children... He proposes himself to you as a father and acts accordingly.'[2] Thus trouble is a sign, not of God's disfavour, but of his fatherhood; not of his remoteness, but of his closeness; not of his forgetfulness but of his devotion to the well-being of his children.

Human parents who fail to correct their offspring — or let them go unpunished when they misbehave — are actually doing them irreparable harm. Happily, many parents do respond appropriately to sinful and anti-social actions by their children; punishment is meted out and the child learns what is and what is not acceptable. But any widespread failure at this point corrupts the very fabric of society, causing destructive and amoral behaviour patterns to emerge. The Western world in our day is showing serious signs of such moral collapse, and it can be traced back largely to parental failure.

God will never be guilty of such failure towards his children. He has chosen them in Christ and redeemed them by grace, and they are infinitely precious in his sight. He is the perfect parent and fulfils his responsibilities to the full. Logic requires, therefore, that the believer must experience trials and discomforts in this life. The pattern is set in Deuteronomy 8:2-3: 'You shall remember that the LORD your God led you all the way these forty years in the wilderness, to humble you and test you, to know what was in your heart, whether you would keep his commandments or not. So he humbled you, allowed you to hunger, and fed you with manna ... that he might make you know that man shall not live by bread alone; but ... by every word that proceeds from the mouth of the LORD.'

If we lack such divine correction, declares the Writer, we are 'illegitimate' — not God's children at all. Delitzsch observes, 'He who lives without experience of this fatherly discipline is no genuine child but a *nothos* of doubtful parentage, of neglected education, left to himself.'[3] Although the Writer uses strong language, his statement is fully justified, for many who profess to follow Christ fail the test of reality (Matt. 7:23; 1 John 2:19). The Writer has warned his readers several times of the dangers of unbelief and apostasy, and his assertion must be read in that context. Far from being a cause of despair, their sufferings testified to the fact that they were truly God's children and not apostates.

Subjection (12:9-10)

The Writer presses his analogy: **'Furthermore, we have had human fathers who corrected us, and we paid them respect. Shall we not much more readily be in subjection to the Father of spirits and live?'** (12:9). The words 'Father of spirits' can be read as 'Father of *our* spirits',[4] contrasting God's transcendent spiritual fatherhood with the mundane physical fatherhood of our 'human' progenitors. Brown understands the closing word, 'live', as meaning 'be happy', and suggests that this provides 'a strong additional motive to ... subjection'.[5] It seems likely, however, that the Writer has 'eternal life' in mind as well as earthly happiness (see below).

In spite of rebellious interludes, most children respect their imperfect human parents. Under the law of Moses a 'stubborn and rebellious son, who will not obey the voice of his father or ... his mother, and who, when they have chastened him, will not heed them', could be put to death for his evil ways (Deut. 21:18-21). This serves to emphasise how rare and unusual such rebellion was, and how severely it was punished in times past.

Today, of course, parents neither possess nor desire such draconian sanctions. Indeed, the pendulum may have swung too far in our easygoing culture, where children frequently go unpunished for disobedience. But in spite of this, in the providence of God, respect and love for parents is the norm rather than the exception, and this is specially true where wholesome discipline has been consistently applied.

If this is so, then believers — 'as obedient children' of God (1 Peter 1:14) — ought to respect his heavenly wisdom when he chastens them. The words of Christ are germane to such situations: 'What I am doing you do not understand now, but you will know after this' (John 13:7). We may not understand why God allows us to suffer, but our respect for his judgement and integrity will enable us to submit ('be in subjection') to his divine providence.

By faith we shall accept that 'all things work together for good to those who love God' (Rom. 8:28) — whatever the appearances. We shall say with the psalmist, 'Surely I have calmed and quieted my soul, like a weaned child with his mother' (Ps. 131:2). Let Peter instruct us. If you 'suffer according to the will of God', he declares, you 'will commit [your] souls to him ... as to a faithful Creator'. You will 'humble yourselves under the mighty hand of God, that he may exalt you in due time, casting all your care upon him, for he cares for you' (1 Peter 4:19; 5:6-7).

Moreover, continues the Writer, God's chastening is altogether superior to that received from human parents: **'For they indeed for a few days chastened us as seemed best to them, but he for our profit, that we may be partakers of his holiness'** (12:10). The superiority of God's instruction is threefold. Firstly, its benefits are eternal rather than temporal ('for a few days'). This is the import of the preceding words: 'Shall we not ... be in subjection to the Father of spirits *and* *live*?' (emphasis added). Divine discipline leads on to eternal life, for those who are subject to it are thereby proven to be sons of God.

Secondly, while human parents have mixed and imperfect motives, God's actions are purely altruistic, designed wholly 'for our profit'. And what profit this is! For 'so an entrance will be supplied to you abundantly into the everlasting kingdom of our Lord and Saviour Jesus Christ' (2 Peter 1:10-11).

Thirdly, whereas human discipline fits us to live amicably in human society, the chastening of God makes us 'partakers of his holiness'. This is a breathtaking concept. It has both a current significance in the practical holiness of the believer[6] and implications for our eternal state. Well might Paul declare that 'The sufferings of this present time are not worthy to be compared with the glory that shall be revealed in us' — not *to* us, notice, but *in* us! (Rom. 8:18).

Fruitfulness (12:11)

Such is the believer's prospect of glory that the problems and hardships of life should seem as nothing in comparison. But God's work of child-training also bears fruit here on earth: **'Now no chastening seems to be joyful for the present, but painful; nevertheless, afterward it yields the peaceable fruit of righteousness to those who have been trained** [or exercised] **by it'** (12:11). Chastening, admits the Writer, is unpleasant. It always humbles us and can be humiliating. It brings pain, not pleasure. But this is evidence of its effectiveness. As a child, I was often told that the nastier the medicine, the more good it did. Not true, of course! But the idea is valid in the spiritual realm, for chastening produces altogether beneficial effects — 'the peaceable fruit of righteousness'.

The righteousness referred to here is not the imputed right-eousness of Christ, by which we stand perfect and complete before God. If it were, we would be saved by our suffering. Indeed, many have erred — sadly and seriously — in thinking that penances, privations and even martyrdom can earn men merit in the sight of God. But however noble and sacrificial our works may be, we can be saved only 'by grace ... through faith ... not of works' (Eph. 2:8-9).

What, then, is the **'righteousness'** inculcated by God's chas-tening? It is that *practical* righteousness so often enjoined and attested in Scripture (11:33; Acts 10:35; Rom. 6:13-19; 2 Cor. 9:10; Phil. 1:11; 2 Tim. 2:22; 3:16; James 3:18; 1 John 2:29). It is associated with the avoidance of sin, a humble walk with God, and a new determination to please him. Although such 'righteous living' cannot justify the sinner (since it is never perfect), it is intimately related to the imputed righteousness of Christ, because it is a fruit or *consequence* of justification.

See how Paul applies this truth in exhorting the Corinthians to abstain from sinful lifestyles. He writes, 'Do you not know that the unrighteous will not inherit the kingdom of God? Do not be deceived. Neither fornicators, nor idolaters ... nor thieves, nor drunkards ... will inherit the kingdom of God. And such were some of you. But you were washed, you were sanctified, you were justified in the name of the Lord Jesus and by the Spirit of our God' (1 Cor. 6:9-11). The remem-brance of what God has done for them, to them and in them — of what they *are* in Christ — will protect them from sin.

Commentators differ as to the overall meaning of the phrase, **'the peaceable fruit [or harvest] of righteousness'**. The fruit in question could be either the *result* of righteousness or the righteousness *itself*.[7] However, in either case the teaching is the same, namely, that chastening produces submission, sub-mission brings obedience, and obedience begets practical righteousness — which in turn either constitutes or produces a 'peaceable harvest'.

The 'cascade' interpretation — chastening leads to practical righteousness, which then produces fruit — is probably preferable. This emphasis is reflected in such Scriptures as 2 Corinthians 9:10-11: 'May [God] ... increase the fruits of your righteousness, while you are enriched in everything ...' (see also Phil. 1:11; James 3:18).

The harvest, then, consists of the blessings that flow from a life lived righteously, the enjoyment of an intimate walk with God. These blessings are 'peaceable' because they bring peace to heart and mind. 'Great peace have those who love your law, and nothing causes them to stumble' (Ps. 119:165).

47.
Running straight

Please read Hebrews 12:12-14

The exhortations now flow thick and fast. But exhortations *alone* are ineffective, and Scripture never dispenses them in a theological vacuum. The Writer has already laid a careful foundation of truth before he launches into these admonitions.

Broadly, this foundation comprises the whole epistle up to this point. More immediately, however, two things stand out. Firstly, we are joined to Christ (in that he both originates and perfects our faith) and, secondly, those who receive this precious gift of faith are adopted ('received') by the Father as his children. Only by perceiving these basic spiritual relationships can the Hebrews respond appropriately to the practical exhortations that follow.

The doctrine of adoption is not taught explicitly in Hebrews (as it is, for example in Romans 8:15-17 and Galatians 4:5-7). But it is everywhere implicit in the epistle and is a fundamental reality of the new covenant (see, e.g., 2:10; 3:6; 12:8; 8:10). In the light of this great provision and privileged relationship, the Writer calls for action.

This is important for us to bear in mind. Too often we put pressure on people to meet our expectations on the grounds of mere conformity. 'Why must we do this?' they ask. 'Because that is what Christians do', we reply. By contrast, Scripture always provides a theological basis for the attitudes, actions and practices it urges upon us — and that theology always brings us back to the person and the work of Jesus Christ. To put it another way, the Bible always provides us with Christ-centred motivations for the way we should live. We shall see this theme developed in what follows.

The highway of holiness (12:12-13)

'Therefore', demands the Writer, **'strengthen the hands which hang down, and the feeble knees, and make straight paths for your feet'** (12:12-13). Here are things that *we must do*, because no one else will do them for us. But equally, they are things *we can do* because God affords us every resource, support and encouragement.

The vivid image of the racetrack is still in the Writer's mind. The runner has begun to drag his feet. His arms, instead of pumping as they should, begin to sag. The knees fail to straighten after every stride. Instead of forging ahead in a straight line, the athlete weaves wearily from side to side like a drunken man. Quite literally, he needs to pull himself together. So it is in the spiritual race. We grow weary and disconsolate, our outlook becomes jaundiced. We complain and grow critical of others because we are unhappy in our souls. But almost always the problem lies within ourselves, not with those around us. Like the stumbling athlete, we need to take corrective action. Delitzsch writes, 'Out of this condition of collapse and infirmity they are to rouse, lift up, stretch out again the hands and knees of the inward man (1 Peter 1:15).'[1] But how are they to do this?

This answer becomes clear when we realise that the Writer's words are cited generally from two Old Testament passages — Isaiah 35:3 and Proverbs 4:25-27. The former says,

'Strengthen the weak hands and make firm the feeble knees. Say to those who are fearful-hearted, "Be strong, do not fear! Behold, your God ... will come and save you."' Ultimately, we can only strengthen ourselves by trusting in such promises as these. Faith in God, and in his Christ, is the answer to all our needs.

There is, of course, a paradox here. We are to strengthen *ourselves* but we cannot do so without God's assistance. However, there is nothing new about this. We have previously cited Isaiah 40:29-31: 'He gives power to the weak, and to those who have no might he increases strength... Those who wait on the LORD shall renew their strength.' We can only 'be strong' if we are strong 'in the Lord and in the power of his might' (Eph. 6:10). When we are weak in ourselves, we are strong in Christ (2 Cor. 12:10). Our responsibility is simply to count on this as true — to wait on God's enabling and rely upon Christ's strength, imparted to us by his Spirit.

The Writer's second reference, Proverbs 4:25-27, includes the words: 'Let your eyes look straight ahead... Ponder the path of [*or* make level paths for] your feet... Do not turn to the right or to the left.' It seems likely that the Writer had this passage in mind when he first directed his readers to 'run the race ... set before' them, looking to Jesus for strength, comfort and endurance. He may also still be thinking of Isaiah 35, where we read in verse 8: 'A highway shall be there, and a road, and it shall be called the Highway of Holiness ... whoever walks the road, although a fool, shall not go astray.'

How, then, do we make straight paths for our feet? 'Then are our paths straight', says Owen, 'when we walk uprightly in the paths of God.'[2] And in order to do so, we must let our eyes direct our feet. The ploughman of old made his furrows straight by fixing his eyes on a distant object. In the same way, we set our gaze upon Christ. Spiritually speaking, we are fools

— unstable, unreliable and prone to err, but even we 'shall not go astray' if our faith is set on him. We shall walk the Highway of Holiness because we look to Christ.

But what will this mean in practice? If we are to strengthen our hands, straighten our knees and pursue straight paths, we must make use of the resources that we have in Jesus Christ. What are they? Paul sets them out in Ephesians 6, using a totally different metaphor — that of armour. We have the chain-mail of truth — the truth of Scripture and the gospel; the breast-plate of the imputed righteousness of Christ; shoes of gospel peace with which to tread the stoniest pathways; the shield of faith 'above all', to quench temptation and unbelief; the helmet of salvation by grace, that protects our minds from 'other gospels' and all false teaching; 'the sword of the Spirit, which is the word of God'; and the power of 'all prayer'. In other words, we must fill our minds with Scripture and our hearts with Christ.

We must attend the preaching and teaching of the Word of God as it directs us unfailingly to him. We must reinforce our faith by fellowship with others in the gospel. We must meditate on the gospel of peace — the peace Jesus made in the blood of his cross (Col. 1:20); we must believe the promises of God, for he cannot lie; and we must persevere in prayer, saying with Jacob, 'I will not let you go unless you bless me' (Gen. 32:26). And weak as we are, the Spirit of God will help our infirmities (Rom. 8:26).

The purpose of it all is restoration, so **'that what is lame may not be dislocated, but rather be healed'** (12:13). These words may contain yet further echoes of Isaiah 35, where in verses 6-7 we read, 'Then the lame shall leap like a deer, and the tongue of the dumb sing. For waters shall burst forth in the wilderness and streams in the desert. The parched ground shall become a pool.' Whether this is the case or not, the prophet's words are apposite, for lameness and dryness are just different pictures of the same disabling problem — a lack of spiritual strength and vitality. Once again, God's answer to these things is 'the supply of the Spirit of Christ Jesus' (Phil. 1:19) for, throughout Scripture, water is a picture of the Spirit (John 4:14; 7:38-39).

Things to pursue (12:14)

In the race of faith, as we have seen, some things must be 'laid aside' and some things 'strengthened'. But there are also things that must be actively and positively 'pursued': **'Pursue peace with all people, and holiness, without which no one will see the Lord'** (12:14). The tone is both strong and urgent. The word 'pursue' is more forceful than 'seek' and suggests earnest striving. This is no mere nuance, for if we fail we forfeit nothing less than grace and glory (seeing the Lord).

These words, therefore, are not just sundry afterthoughts or random admonitions. Rather, they gather up and encapsulate all the exhortations the Writer has urged upon his readers throughout the epistle. Seen in this light, the directive to 'pursue peace with all people' takes on greater significance than at first appears. Although many commentators take these words at their face value, a clearer translation would be pursue 'peace *in company with* everyone' (Moffatt). The peace referred to is not so much harmony with our fellow believers, or with people in general, but that essential peace with God that characterises (and in one sense constitutes) our new-covenant relationship with Christ. 'Those who enjoy the blessings of the new covenant', says Lane, 'are to be united in earnestly pursuing the peace that is both sign [the sign of that covenant] and gift from God.'[3]

This explains the juxtaposition of 'peace' and 'holiness', which otherwise seems odd — even inept. The Writer wants the Hebrews to strive *together*, as a community, to grasp securely the peace that Christ has made in the blood of his cross. In other words, both as individuals and as a community of believers, they must return to the pure gospel of the grace of God in Christ. This is surely the thrust of the whole epistle. If they fail to rediscover that gospel, they will 'fall short of the grace of God' — that is, fail to attain the goal of salvation by grace through faith. Of course, the Writer is not suggesting that true believers can be lost. But he *is* warning them that some who *think* themselves believers may well be turned away.

The second thing to be pursued is **'holiness'**. The Greek word used here is sometimes translated 'sanctification', and many consider it refers to 'progressive sanctification'. Thus Kistemaker comments, 'The word in the original Greek refers to the sanctifying process that occurs in the life of the believer ... the believer ... becomes more and more like Christ.'[4]

However, we need to be cautious here. Of the five cases where this word is translated 'sanctification' in the New Testament (AV), most refer unambiguously to 'positional sanctification' — the believer's standing as one 'set apart' in Christ (for example, 1 Cor. 1:30; 2 Thess. 2:13; 1 Peter 1:2). Furthermore, if 'progressive sanctification' is intended here, salvation itself (seeing the Lord) becomes dependent on such sanctification. What, then, of those who repent on their deathbeds and have no opportunity to 'progress' in sanctification? And how *far* beyond justification by faith must we progress before we are qualified to 'see the Lord'? A theological quagmire confronts us!

The context, therefore, seems to rule out 'progressive sanctification' as an explanation of this exhortation — as other commentators have recognised. Lane declares, 'In Hebrews human endeavour is never the subject of sanctification. Christ alone is the one who consecrates others to God through his sacrificial death. Holiness is ... the objective gift of Christ achieved through his sacrificial death on the cross (10:29; 13:12).'[5]

Where does this leave us? It means that the injunctions to 'pursue peace' and to 'pursue holiness' are emphasising the same need — to strive to lay hold upon the gift of God, the pure promise of grace in Jesus Christ. He *alone* is our peace, our sanctification, our holiness, and we are 'complete in him' (Col. 2:10). To seek these things outside of him — in ceremonies, in shadows, in law-keeping, or anywhere under the old covenant — is to turn aside from the race that is set before us, to depart from the Highway of Holiness.

But are we not also to strive for practical holiness? Of course. That is what the Writer was teaching so earnestly in 12:1-2, where he urged us to divest ourselves of hindrances and sins. But the point to grasp is that an understanding of what we *are* in Christ, and what we possess in him, is the essential foundation for practical holiness. Boston puts it thus: 'The truth we are sanctified by is not held in the head, as in a prison; but runs with its sanctifying influences through heart and life.'[6]

48.
Looking carefully

Please read Hebrews 12:15-17

As together we pursue the gift of God and the benefits of the new covenant, we are to do so watchfully — **'looking carefully lest anyone fall short of the grace of God'** (12:15). There is a subtle change here, as the focus of concern turns from the assembly as a whole to the individual ('anyone'). Not only is the believer to examine himself (1 Cor. 11:28; 2 Cor. 13:5), but the believing community must also keep watch over its members.

A responsibility is here laid upon every member of the church to have concern for his fellow believers. Every one of us is, in a real sense, our 'brother's keeper'. True to character, Cain disclaimed responsibility for *his* brother, but this is not an option for the children of the new covenant. 'The members [of the body]', declares the apostle, 'should have the same care for one another' (1 Cor. 12:25).

Watching (12:15)

Although this applies to all of us, the elders or pastors of the assembly carry a particular responsibility to safeguard the flock. Referring to such elders, the Writer counsels, 'Obey those who rule over you, and be submissive, for *they watch out for your souls*, as those who must give account' (13:17, emphasis added). Clearly, this calls for great wisdom and patience. Peter warns elders not to act like 'lords over those entrusted to you' but rather be 'examples to the flock' (1 Peter 5:3). Again, Paul urges those 'who are spiritual' to 'restore [an offender] in a spirit of gentleness, considering yourself lest you also be tempted' (Gal. 6:1).

Nevertheless, with true motives and spiritual skill, the shepherds are to guard the flock — the parents are to watch over the children. When problems arise (as they surely will) they need to be recognised early and dealt with gently, firmly and appropriately. Why? Because those who stray do so at the risk of their eternal souls.

But exactly what must we look out for? The Writer begins by making a general point — beware **'lest anyone fall short of the grace of God'** (12:15). To understand this we must first be clear what is meant by 'grace'. Brown explains that 'In the Scriptures, the grace of God is the divine kindness, or some effect of the divine kindness.'[1] Under the new covenant, the *effect* of God's kindness is nothing short of salvation, heaven and glory. 'To fail of this grace', continues Brown, 'is just to come short of heaven.' We keep watch so that those who profess Christ might truly 'gain Christ' and not be cast away (Phil. 3:8).

The Writer illustrates his general point with specific examples. Firstly, the church must be watchful **'lest any root of bitterness springing up cause trouble, and by this many become defiled'** (12:15). The reference is to Deuteronomy 29:14-18. Moses states that God made a covenant with Israel 'so that there may not be among you ... [any] whose heart turns away today from the LORD our God, to go and serve the gods of these nations, and that there may not be among you a root bearing bitterness or wormwood'. Clearly, the Writer again has apostasy in mind.

The tendency against which the Writer forewarns them has two features. Firstly, it is a **'root'** and therefore lurks unseen until it **'springs up'**. Secondly, it becomes a plant that bears bitter fruit. This refers to the bitter *consequences* of sin rather than to bitterness in the heart of the offender. Once again, in these specific illustrations, the Writer has the 'big picture' in view. Thus the 'root' referred to here is not just some personal failing in a member of the assembly, but the sin of unbelief which has been the target of the epistle from the outset.

Unbelief in the sufficiency of Christ and the new covenant can be harboured in the heart of a person who seems outwardly to conform and be an active member of the body of Christ. When such unbelief eventually surfaces, however, consternation ensues. Many, sampling its bitter fruit, are **'defiled'**. That is, they cease to be holy or 'sanctified' (cf. 10:29, where some who belonged outwardly to the visible assembly proved they had no part among God's true children).

They call in question the basic tenets of the gospel. Grace is challenged ('man must do his part in salvation'); faith is devalued (it becomes a human attribute rather than the gift of God); Christ has not 'perfected the sanctified ones for ever' (10:14), but has merely facilitated their salvation. 'The sin of one individual can corrupt the entire community', says Lane, 'when that sin is apostasy.'[2] If we question the need for the Writer's warning, we should look around us. The bitter fruit of unbelief is everywhere apparent in the professing church.

Falling short (12:16)

The Writer's second illustration of the need to be watchful relates to 'profane' attitudes and behaviour. We need to be **'looking diligently ... lest there be any fornicator or profane person like Esau, who for one morsel of food sold his**

birthright' (12:16). The word 'fornicator' normally refers to sexual immorality (as in 13:4), and most commentators understand this verse to be condemning sexual immorality on the one hand, and godlessness ('profanity') on the other. Thus Kistemaker writes, 'What does the writer of Hebrews teach? Simply this: abstain from immorality and avoid godlessness.'[3] But this is surely too lame — given that the immediate context is the Writer's massive culminating argument (see especially verses 18-29 that follow). Furthermore, why should sexual immorality be singled out as uniquely damaging? There is no suggestion that the Hebrews had the same problems as the Corinthian church in this respect.

Of course, Scripture treats sexual sins seriously, and tells us that 'Neither fornicators ... nor adulterers ... will inherit the kingdom of God' (1 Cor. 6:9-10). Yet this is not a subject with which Hebrews concerns itself significantly. It is far more likely, therefore, that 'fornication' refers here to *spiritual* unfaithfulness or adultery — a concept widely applied to unfaithful Israel in the Old Testament and thus disturbingly familiar to the Hebrews (see, e.g., Isa. 1:10-11; Jer. 2:20-21; 3:8-9; Hosea 2:1-13; 3:1 and many other places). As far back as 3:12 the Writer warns: 'Beware, brethren, lest there be in any of you an evil heart of unbelief in departing from the living God.' Anyone who rejects the new covenant in Christ's blood — the only authentic gospel — thereby departs from the living God and embraces a false God, an idol of his own making. He is a spiritual fornicator.

This is why the Writer can drive home his point by reference to Esau. As far as we know, Jacob's twin brother was not sexually immoral. But he *was* a 'profane person', guilty of *spiritual* adultery — that is, he embraced his own appetites in preference to the blessing of God. Calvin writes, 'The profane are those in whom the love of the world so holds sway and prevails, that they forget heaven ... and give the spiritual kingdom of Christ either no place or the last place in their concerns.'[4]

Esau, we are told, 'sold his birthright' for 'one morsel of food' (12:16; cf. Gen. 25:29-34). In the Genesis account we read that 'Esau despised his birthright'. That is, in surrendering his rights as first-born to his younger brother, he placed no higher value on them that the price of a meal! The essence of his sin was to esteem lightly the privileges that attach to a son and heir.

This was exactly the crime committed by some among the Hebrews. They were spurning the new-covenant privileges to which they had access as members of a gospel community. Instead of laying hold upon the promises of God — as sons who esteem their inheritance above all — they were despising the grace of God and turning to what Paul calls 'the weak and beggarly elements' of old-covenant observations (Gal. 4:9-10).

The sin of Esau is 'alive and well' today. Professing Christians in their multitudes despise the gospel of grace — 'the manifold wisdom of God' and the 'unsearchable riches of Christ' (Eph. 3:8-12). Instead they follow 'profane', (that is, worldly) doctrines, hankering after human works, earthly rewards, financial benefit, human esteem, ceremonial superstitions and fleshly appetites. By contrast, the Writer points his readers to suffering and rejection, to a hunger for God — and to the heavenly sanctuary, the finished work of Christ, and a heavenly reward.

Finding no place (12:17)

If they persist in their course of unbelief, warns the Writer, they will suffer the same rejection as Esau, and for the same reasons. **'For you know that afterward, when [Esau] wanted to inherit the blessing, he was rejected, for he found**

no place for repentance, though he sought it diligently with tears' (12:17). The original story in Genesis 27:30-38 makes it clear that the 'repentance' that was not forthcoming was Isaac's, not Esau's. That is, having been tricked into blessing Jacob instead of Esau, Isaac refused to change his mind ('repent'): 'I have blessed him and indeed he shall be blessed ... your brother ... has taken away your blessing.'

Esau, belatedly appreciating his loss, wept and pleaded, but to no avail. At no time, however, did he repent of his sin or seek to do so. Indeed, insists the Writer, it is impossible to renew people like Esau to repentance, since they despise the very blessing and inheritance that Christ provides (6:4-6).

We all need to ponder these solemn words. Certainly, there can be no repentance after death — the parable of Dives and Lazarus makes that clear (Luke 16:19-31). But the Writer is warning here that the opportunity to repent can be lost even in the course of this present life. This is a repetition of his earlier warnings in 2:1-3; 3:7-15; 6:4-8; and 10:26-31. If we despise God's gracious provision in Christ — if we turn to other means for our 'wisdom ... righteousness, sanctification and redemption' (1 Cor. 1:30) — we are departing from the living God and will reap the consequences.

The message echoes like a drum-beat — 'today, if you will hear his voice, harden not your hearts'. To get right with God, and remain so, must be our daily priority. Only thus can we ensure that we do not fall short of the grace of God.

49.
Coming to Zion

Please read Hebrews 12:18-22

As Hebrews 12 draws to a close, the epistle reaches its final climax. It would be difficult to imagine a more explicit and majestic statement of the excellencies, glories and imperatives of the new covenant than we find here. This chapter and the next cover the climactic passage of verses 18-24, while chapters 51 and 52 will consider its trenchant application in verses 25-29. However, at the outset, it will help us grasp the awesome solemnity of these verses if we remember the closing statement of Hebrews 12: 'For our God is a consuming fire' (12:29).

The passage before us (in this chapter and the next) both summarises and dramatises the entire epistle. It reveals graphically the profound divergence between the old and new covenants. As Christian pilgrims, we have not come to earthly Sinai, but to heavenly Zion, the transcendent city of the living God. And that is just as well for, as Thomas Boston remarks, 'The law lays open the wound [of human sin] but it is the gospel that heals.'[1] Our hopes reside in Christ alone, not Moses or the law.

A terrifying sight (12:18-21)

We have heard the exhortations — run the race; discard the hindrances; look to Jesus; submit to chastening; strengthen resolve; straighten the path; lay hold on the peace and holiness that Christ has obtained for those who trust him; be watchful against unbelief. We have also seen how these injunctions are based on solid spiritual premises — that God is the Father of the faithful and Christ the author of their faith.

But the Writer is not yet content. He wants to provide further incentives to provoke obedience to the faith. And this he does, building exhortation on reason and adding reason to exhortation. In effect he says, 'Because of this, do that, because of this.' It is a simple formula but it launches him into a statement of immense grandeur and importance. **'For'**, he writes, **'you have not come to the mountain that may be touched and that burned with fire, and to blackness and darkness and tempest, and the sound of a trumpet and the voice of words'** (12:18-19).

The mountain was, of course, Mount Sinai. The Israelites had arrived there very shortly after their deliverance from Egypt, and there God made a covenant with them (Exod. 19:1-5). That covenant is often called 'the law' or 'the law of Moses' (because Moses was its mediator — Gal. 3:19). It is not to be confused with Old Testament Scripture generally, which is also sometimes called God's 'Law' (e.g., Ps. 119:97-105). The distinction is important because the Old Testament contains not only the Mosaic law but also the covenant of promise (which preceded the covenant of Sinai — Gal. 3:16-18) together with much that applies directly to the new covenant (such as Jeremiah's prophecy cited in 8:8-12).

The Writer borrows his description of the giving of the law from Deuteronomy 4:11, employing his considerable powers of imagery to sketch the scene indelibly, yet with a minimum of words. His account is deft and majestic.

But what is the Writer's purpose in verses 18-21? At first sight he describes only the *manner* in which the law was given, but there is more to it than that — the way it was given reflects the nature and character of the law. The key is found in the words, 'you have not come ...' (12:18). To what have the followers of Christ 'not come'? Surely, to the old covenant itself. As John Brown explains, 'Instead of saying in simple words, "ye are not under the law, that severe and wrathful economy", he says, "ye are not of the congregation of Israel who came to mount Sinai and from its cloud-capt summit received ... a fiery law.'[2] Lane adds, 'It should be recognised that the Writer compares two covenants under the imagery of two mountains in order to contrast the distance that separated the worshipper from God under the old covenant with the unrestricted access to God under the new covenant... Sinai and Zion are extended metaphors.'[3] What, then, do these contrasting metaphors teach us?

Firstly, the fact that Sinai **'may be touched'** — it was a real physical mountain — signifies that the covenant made there was couched in terms of outward observance. Hywel Jones says, 'The way in which God revealed himself to his people at Mount Sinai was sensual; it was visual, audible and even tangible.'[4] Of course, the law *embodied* spiritual and moral principles, especially the tenth commandment: 'You shall not covet ...' (Exod. 20:17). But under the old covenant these principles were applied chiefly to regulate *outward* conduct rather than as spiritual criteria affecting our relationship with God. For example, the law forbade and punished physical adultery, but the new covenant looks not only at physical behaviour but at inner motivation, and calls for purity of heart as well as body (Exod. 20:14 compared with Matt. 5:27-30). Again, idolatry and murder were forbidden under the law of Sinai, but the new covenant reveals that both are, first and foremost, matters of the heart (Matt. 5:21-22; Eph. 5:5).

Secondly, that the mountain **'burned with fire'** speaks of the holiness of God. When Moses besought the Lord to show him his glory, he replied, 'You cannot see my face; for no man shall see me, and live' (Exod. 33:18-20). In his very essence, 'our God is a consuming fire' (12:29). This reminds us that while the requirements of the law reveal God's holiness, they do so without clearly revealing God himself. *That* revelation could only be made under the new covenant, for only Christ is 'the express image of [God's] person' and 'the image of the invisible God' (1:3; Col. 1:15). And, said Jesus, 'He who has seen me has seen the Father' (John 14:9). Under the new covenant, God in his holiness is still 'a consuming fire' — but he has nevertheless 'shone in our hearts to give the light of the knowledge of the glory of God in the face of Jesus Christ' (2 Cor. 4:6).

Thirdly, that Sinai was enveloped in 'blackness and darkness', and was rent by a 'tempest', reminds us of God's anger against human sin. Enquiring as to the purpose of the law, Paul concludes that 'the law ... was added because of transgressions, till the Seed should come to whom the promise was made [that is, Christ]' (Gal. 3:19). In Romans 3:20 he further concludes that '... by the deeds of the law no flesh will be justified in [God's] sight, for by the law is the knowledge of sin.' Little wonder, then, that the Israelites quailed at 'the sound of a trumpet and the voice of words', since the words spelled out their sin and the trumpet heralded their condemnation. Although the mountain could be touched, to touch it meant death, even for an innocent beast (12:20). It has often been pointed out that the law was given to a redeemed people, and that is so. But their redemption involved a physical liberation from slavery in Egypt. It *typified* a spiritual redemption, but did not *constitute* such a redemption — it could never take away their sin.

The Writer continues: '**... those who heard it begged that the word should not be spoken to them any more, for they could not endure what was commanded: "And if so much as a beast touches the mountain, it shall be stoned or shot with an arrow"**' (12:20). Indeed, continues the Writer, '...

so terrifying was the sight that Moses said, "I am exceedingly afraid and trembling"' (12:21). Paul tells us in 2 Corinthians 3:7-11 that God's covenant at Sinai was an external enactment, a 'ministry of death, written and engraved on stones'. It ministered spiritual death because it was 'the ministry of condemnation' — not because of any deficiency in itself, but because man in his fallen state 'could not endure what was commanded', that is, they could never keep its requirements (12:20; Rom. 3:19-20). Furthermore, continues the apostle, it was 'passing away', a temporary provision until the new covenant in Christ would be inaugurated (2 Cor. 3:11; Gal. 3:19; Heb. 8:13).

Yet even this 'covenant of death' embodied the holiness and beauty of God. Accordingly, it was delivered amidst a terrifying manifestation of his power and glory. In the passage from 2 Corinthians cited above, Paul seizes on this demonstration of divine majesty to bring home the transcendent glory of the new covenant: 'If the ministry of death ... was glorious, so that the children of Israel could not look steadily at the face of Moses ... how will the ministry of the Spirit not be more glorious? For if the ministry of condemnation had glory, the ministry of righteousness [the gospel] exceeds much more in glory ... the glory that excels' (2 Cor. 3:1-10). The 'glory that excels' is the glory of Christ in the new covenant, as Hebrews amply testifies.

Of course, the law also unveils provision for the cleansing and forgiveness of the sinner. It goes on to provide a meeting place with God, an interceding priesthood and a sacrifice for sin. But most of Hebrews is devoted to showing that these provisions were *also* external and ceremonial, and incapable of actually removing sin (see, e.g., 9:12-15; 10:4). Only the death of Christ, and the new covenant in his blood, could remove 'the transgressions under the first covenant' (9:15). By revealing our sin, and God's wrath against it, 'the law was our tutor to bring us to Christ, that we might be justified by faith' (Gal. 3:24).

City of the living God (12:22)

What relief — to know that '... after faith has come, we are no longer under a tutor'! (Gal. 3:25). Sinai is no longer the object of our pilgrimage. On the contrary, declares the Writer, believers have been brought by grace to an entirely different mountain: **'But you have come to Mount Zion and to the city of the living God, the heavenly Jerusalem'** (12:22). Zion was the original Jebusite fortress which was overthrown by King David. It became his capital and the heart of the greater city of Jerusalem (2 Sam. 5:6-10). The terms 'Mount Zion', 'the city of the living God' and 'the heavenly Jerusalem', are therefore synonymous. They all refer, not to a place, but to a people — the people of God, the church of Jesus Christ. Whereas Sinai was rugged and inhospitable, Zion, though also high and lifted up, is a place of beauty and joy. It is likely that the Writer had in mind Psalm 48:1-3:

> Great is the LORD,
> And greatly to be praised
> In the city of our God,
> In his holy mountain.
> Beautiful in elevation,
> The joy of the whole earth,
> Is Mount Zion on the sides of the north,
> The city of the great King,
> God is in her palaces;
> He is known as her refuge.

Notice how the psalm brings together the same ideas as Hebrews. Zion (Jerusalem) is an elevated place, a 'holy mountain'. It is 'the city of God' and of his Christ ('the great King'). Sinai was uninhabitable, but Zion is a city of palaces where the righteous dwell with God in safety and delight. Here is a beautiful picture of the church of the new covenant. Let us consider it in more detail.

Firstly, both Sinai and Zion were holy mountains where God manifested his presence. But there the similarity ends. Sinai was forbidding and terrifying, but Zion is 'beautiful in elevation' — a breathtaking sight that lifts the eyes and attracts rather than repels those who approach it. Sinai begets fear, but Zion evokes joy — and that for peoples of 'the whole earth'. Delitzsch remarks, 'The antithesis is not that of drawing near under one covenant and remaining afar off under the other ... but that of the heaven-wide difference between the objects to which approach is made. These objects were, on the one hand, things dark and terrible ... on the other, they are things glorious and lovely, with a gracious and attractive charm.'[5] May the Lord help us to see his church in these latter terms — and to esteem its local manifestation (the local assembly of believers) accordingly.

Secondly, God came down upon Mount Sinai *temporarily* as the law-giver, but he dwells *permanently* in Zion as its King. Robertson writes, 'The exalted Christ now rules from the heavenly Jerusalem ... manifesting his sovereignty over all nations until the end of the age.'[6] Furthermore, it is the essence of the new covenant that a new and inward relationship exists between God and his people (8:10). This is pictured in the psalm by God's presence in Zion's palaces, that is, by his living in and among his people by the Spirit (cf. Eph. 2:22).

Thirdly, on Sinai there was no place to hide from the fearful presence of God. But in Zion God is 'known as her refuge'. Christ is not just King over the city but the people's place of safety — 'A glorious high throne from the beginning is the place of our sanctuary', cries Jeremiah (Jer. 17:12), while the hymn concurs:

> From sin and guilt and grief and shame,
> I hide me, Jesus, in thy name!

Fourthly, as no one could dwell on Sinai, so none can possess spiritual life under the law. Being 'the ministry of death' it is devoid of life-giving power. By contrast, the palaces of the heavenly Jerusalem are thronged with spiritual children. Paul writes, 'The Jerusalem above is the mother of us all. For it is written: "Rejoice O barren, You who do not bear! ... For the desolate has many more children than she who has a husband"' (Gal. 4:26-27; see also Zech. 14:8-11). Through the regenerating power of the Holy Spirit, the gospel begets children without number 'of all nations, tribes, peoples and tongues' (Rev. 7:9).

Fifthly, 'The LORD ... is greatly to be praised in the city of our God.' It is the church's task and privilege to praise God, for he is great and his mercy in Christ is everlasting — 'O give thanks to the LORD, for he is good! For his mercy endures for ever. Let the redeemed of the LORD say so, whom he has redeemed from the hand of the enemy, and gathered out of the lands ... for he satisfies the longing soul, and fills the hungry soul with goodness' (Ps. 107:1-3, 9). Praise should be the daily portion of those who inhabit the new Jerusalem.

Sixthly, although the heavenly Jerusalem has already been attained by every believer ('you *have* come'), the full realisation of its glory is yet future. 'The images chosen by the writer in vv. 22-24 have apocalyptic overtones', comments Lane.[7] In his vision, John saw 'the holy city, new Jerusalem, coming down out of heaven from God, prepared as a bride adorned for her husband', and heard a voice proclaiming: 'Behold, the tabernacle of God is with men, and he will dwell with them, and they shall be his people and God will ... be their God' (Rev. 21:2-3). Note how the new covenant relationship between God and his people is repeated here (cf. 8:10).

The hosts of God (12:22 cont.)

If the children of the new Jerusalem cannot be numbered, it follows that the angels who attend to their welfare are also innumerable. These angels, we are told in Hebrews 1:14, are 'ministering spirits sent forth to minister for those who will inherit salvation'. Thus those who have come to Mount Zion have also come **'to an innumerable company of angels'** (12:22). There is a parallel here, since on Sinai God was accompanied by angels who were involved in some manner with the transmission of the law (2:2; Deut. 33:2, where 'saints' or 'holy ones' can be interpreted as angels — Gal. 3:19). But while the angels of Sinai handed down the law, the angels of new Jerusalem uphold the saints!

The Bible has little to say about the role of angels under the new covenant, and this makes the references in Hebrews specially valuable. In the gospel era, angels are for the most part invisible, unseen and unheard (for exceptions see Acts 5:19; 12:7). Normally, we are simply not aware of their presence or even their existence. But this cannot alter the fact that they are *there* and that they continue to fulfil the ministry described in Hebrews 1:14.

Superstitions abound, of course, and the term 'guardian angel' has passed into common usage as a nervous, half-flippant, recognition of an unseen world. But abuses should not blind us to the solid spiritual realities spoken of here. The people of God are, even now, surrounded and assisted by angelic hosts. Elisha's experience at Dothan helps to crystallise the matter for us. Surrounded by Syrian troops, the prophet's servant was distraught. 'Alas, my master! What shall we do?', he cried. Elisha answered, 'Do not fear, for those who are with us are more than those who are with them.' Then Elisha prayed that God would open his servant's eyes — 'and he saw ... the mountain full of horses and chariots of fire all around Elisha' (2 Kings 6:15-17).

Mount Zion also is populated by the hosts of God, and those who dwell there are surrounded by powerful beings whose purpose is to minister to them. This is a glorious concept, and one that should encourage us continually. For example, it is easy for a minister to become discouraged when preaching to small congregations — but it helps enormously to remember that the visible audience is swelled by an unseen host of angels, who rejoice to hear Christ proclaimed! 'Christians in their worship', says Pink, 'unite with all the holy hosts of heaven in blessing and adoring the Triune God.'[8]

50.
Mediating the new covenant

Please read Hebrews 12:23-24

The Writer's exploration of Mount Zion continues. He has already described it under the figure of the heavenly Jerusalem, the city of the living God. The city teems with life, not least with the angelic hosts of the Lord. But the purpose of the city is to accommodate not angels, but redeemed sinners — the heirs of God's new covenant in Christ.

In these verses, therefore, we meet the inhabitants of Zion — the assembled 'first-born' and 'the spirits of just men made perfect'. But above all, we meet God, the Judge of all, and Jesus, the Mediator of the new covenant.

Heirs of the new covenant (12:23)

Abandoning metaphor, the Writer unveils another aspect of Mount Zion. It is, he says, **'the general assembly and church of the first-born who are registered** [permanently inscribed] **in heaven'** (12:23). 'First-born' is a plural word, referring not to Christ (as in 1:6; Col. 1:15,18) but to believers. It may denote those who were first to believe, such as the apostles (cf. 2:3). More likely, however, it signifies that *every* believer is so privileged to be a child of God and an inhabitant of Zion that the honorific term 'first-born' is appropriate to describe them.

'General assembly' clearly denotes a corporate gathering. More recent commentators apply it to the angels rather than the church,[1,2,3] but Owen gives good reasons for following the translators in referring it to the church.[4] He points out that in Greek culture 'assembly' denoted a joyful and festive gathering, while the word 'church' signified a more formal meeting of citizens at which business was conducted. Both can properly be applied to the church, the body of Christ, and we shall follow Owen.

Concerning this assembly we are told that God 'put all things under [Christ's] feet, and gave him to be head over all things to the church, which is his body, the fulness of him who fills all in all' (Eph. 1:22-23). The assembly is 'general', therefore, because it is universal in scope and influence, and also because it embraces believers from all eras (including the 'cloud of witnesses' from Old Testament days) and from all nations. Clearly, the Writer is not here speaking of some human organisation like certain 'churches' that falsely claim universal authority on earth. This assembly, remember, is in heaven, and consists only of those who come to God through faith in Jesus Christ. These are also the elect, for their names are 'permanently inscribed' in heaven, and have been since before time began (Eph. 1:4; 2 Tim. 1:9). Bruce writes, 'Probably the reference is to the whole communion of saints, including those who, while "militant here on earth", are enrolled as citizens of heaven. To this community believers have come — not merely into its presence ... but into its membership.'[5]

To be members of such an august assembly, suggests the Writer, is an inexpressible privilege. They are heirs of salvation and glory — 'heirs of God and joint heirs with Christ' (Rom. 8:16-17). But let us not forget that the only manifestation we have of this assembly on earth is the local church! Imperfect as it is, with no visible glory and little visible strength, the local gathering of believers is nevertheless where the heavenly Jerusalem intrudes into space and time. We should remember this and hold the local church in high esteem.

Made perfect (12:23)

The inhabitants of the new Jerusalem have also come **'to God the Judge of all'** and **'to the spirits of just men made perfect'** (12:23). The two phrases are connected. The first would more naturally be translated 'to a judge who is God of all', emphasising God's right to judge those he has created.[6] Although the city of God is a place of festivity and joy to those who dwell there, the Writer never lets us forget that we can enjoy its blessings only if we have been justified, and our spirits 'made perfect', through the atoning work of Christ. The one whom Abraham calls 'the Judge of all the earth' (Gen. 18:25) is still the Judge of all; nothing in the new covenant has changed that eternal fact. It is still a 'fearful thing to fall into the hands of the living God' (10:31) and he is still 'a consuming fire' (12:29).

The glory of the new covenant emerges when the two phrases are taken together — setting God's judgement and the believer's perfection in juxtaposition. Those who trust Christ, who are 'the called according to his purpose' (Rom. 8:28), have had their sins judged fully and finally in Christ. 'He was wounded for our transgressions, he was bruised for our iniquities; the chastisement for our peace was upon him and by his stripes we are healed' (Isa. 53:5). Every member of the city of God has therefore been made 'just' through the grace of God and faith in Christ. In stark contrast, the Writer warns those who despise the grace of God, and turn from faith to works and ceremonies, that they cannot escape the righteous judgement of God.

Believers are both 'just' and 'made perfect' in the sight of God. Does this mean that justification describes the believer's lifetime state while perfection describes his eventual heavenly condition? No, for 'made perfect' or 'complete' describes a finished state, and 10:14 tells us that Christ has *already* perfected his people. Such is the efficacy of the death of Christ that both justification and perfection describe the believer's present standing in the sight of God.

Better things (12:24)

The pinnacle and crowning glory of Mount Zion is that we have come **'to Jesus the Mediator of the new covenant, and to the blood of sprinkling that speaks better things than that of Abel'** (12:24). Though clear and simple, this statement is also profound. In a few short phrases it encapsulates the message of the whole epistle. We have come 'to Jesus' — and what a glorious person the Writer has shown him to be! Eternal Son, embodiment of the Father's glory, heir of all things, creator and sustainer of the universe, he nevertheless became a man and dwelt among us. He is our brother, priest and intercessor; our sin-offering and our meeting-place with God. Now, having perfected his elect for ever, he reigns on high, yet occupies a throne of grace and dwells among his people. And we have 'come' to him in such a way that we have entered with him into the presence of Almighty God. In Christ our privilege is unspeakable and our riches unsearchable! Could not the Hebrews grasp this fact?

But the Writer does not leave it there. We have not just 'come to Jesus' but rather to 'Jesus-the-Mediator-of-the-new-covenant'. As Moses mediated the old covenant, so Christ mediates the new and better covenant (8:6; 9:15). It is worth recalling the words of 9:15: 'He is the mediator of the new covenant, by means of death, for the redemption of the transgressions under the first [old] covenant, that those who are called may receive the promise of the eternal inheritance.'

The contrast between the two covenants could not be greater. The first marks and condemns transgression; the second redeems the transgressor. Those bound under the old covenant could look forward only to death, for it was 'the ministry of condemnation' (2 Cor. 3:9). But under the new covenant it is Christ who dies, atoning for our sin. The first covenant held promise only of an earthly homeland; but the new both promises and guarantees an eternal inheritance. To enter this amazing covenant of grace we must come to God through Christ, for he alone is its mediator.

The Christ to whom we come is not merely a glorious person who offers sundry benefits to those who care to seek them. Too often today men preach a lesser Jesus, or a Christ whose role in God's economy is ill-defined. The Writer is in no doubt about the matter. Christ is 'the Mediator of the new covenant'. That is what he *is* — what he came to be. Neither he nor his ministry towards sinners can be understood apart from the covenant he came to inaugurate and consummate. The everlasting purposes of God; the covenants of promise made with Noah, Abraham, David; the covenant at Sinai — indeed, his covenant of redemption made with his Son before time began — are all fulfilled in, and only in, the new covenant. That is why it is such immense folly to turn back from this covenant to the shadow-world of Mosaic law, to outward religion, to sanctification by moral or religious works, or to a 'holiness' found anywhere except in Christ.

But the Writer's argument goes one step further. We have come to Jesus. He is Mediator of the new covenant. But, in addition, the new covenant is *the 'new covenant in [his] blood'*

(Luke 22:20). This last step is spelled out in a striking analogy. We have come, says the Writer, **'to the blood of sprinkling that speaks better things than that of Abel'** (12:24). In this pregnant statement the Writer loops back to 11:4, employing an elegant stylistic device and one he uses constantly to underline and unite his arguments. The word 'sprinkling' identifies the death of Christ as an act of atonement — by analogy with the Levitical sacrifices where the blood was sprinkled to cleanse and purify.

But what can the blood of Abel teach us? Several things. Firstly, Abel was the first human being to die — in that sense he was representative of us all. This reminds us starkly of the curse of death, a curse Christ came both to bear and to abolish (Gal. 3:13-14). Secondly, Abel's unnatural death underlines the fact that death was not 'natural' for the sons of Adam, but the result of sin.

Thirdly, Cain could not hide his sin from the eyes of an all-seeing God, and neither can we. Genesis 4:10 reports God's accusation against Cain: 'The voice of your brother's blood cries out to me from the ground.' The law (in retrospect) declared Cain guilty, and it continues to serve that purpose today, for 'By the law is the knowledge of sin' (Rom. 3:20). Abel's blood was damning evidence against his brother.

Fourthly, Abel's blood cried out against Cain, not only in evidence, but also in accusation. It pleaded for vengeance and for recompense.

What **'better things'**, then, does the 'sprinkled' blood of Christ proclaim? Like Abel's blood, the blood of Christ is evidence — but no longer of the crime! Instead, it is the evidence of God's gracious intent. For 'God demonstrates his own love towards us, in that while we were still sinners, Christ died for us, [that] having now been justified by his blood, we shall be saved from wrath through him' (Rom. 5:8-9). Furthermore, the blood of Christ makes no accusation, nor does it cry for vengeance, but rather testifies to the justification of the sinner and his deliverance from wrath.

Better things indeed! And that is the heart of the new covenant. Elect sinners, saved by grace through faith, are called into the fellowship of Christ's suffering, that they may serve the living God and afterward obtain an inheritance of eternal glory. What could be simpler, yet more profound? What earthbound religion can approach its majesty and power? What love and compassion can match that which Christ, our Maker, Priest and King, extends towards us in the new covenant? Only the blind and foolish would despise it.

51.
Shaking the heavens

Please read Hebrews 12:25-27

God is articulate — indeed, eloquent. He has spoken and continues to speak. The foundational statement of the epistle is that God has *spoken* through the prophets down the ages and 'has in these last days *spoken* to us by his Son' (1:1-2). This idea of a vocal God permeates the whole of Hebrews. It is no surprise, therefore, that the Writer emphasises this very point as he applies the climactic statement of verses 18-24.

In the closing words of that passage we read that the blood of Abel and the blood of Christ 'speak'. Though mute in themselves, they convey *messages*, the messages, respectively, of God's judgement upon human sin and his forgiveness of sinners through Christ.

In the present passage the Writer picks up the theme of God's speaking and draws three further lessons from Sinai and Zion. Once again, they are lessons both of similarity and contrast. Firstly, as God spoke *on earth* to Moses and Israel at Sinai, so he now speaks *from heaven* in the gospel of Christ. Secondly, as God shook the *earth* in the desert, so he has shaken *both earth and heaven* by the advent and cosmic triumph of Christ. Thirdly, (see next chapter) as fire ignited on *earth* at Sinai, so will the fires of *celestial* judgement consume the ungodly in the day of visitation. In the midst of this cosmic conflagration, the children of the new covenant will not only survive, but will inherit a heavenly kingdom that cannot be shaken. Knowing this, they should serve God here on earth with reverence and godly fear.

Speaking from heaven (12:25)

Since God is speaking, we must listen — and respond appropriately: **'See that you do not refuse him who speaks'** (12:25). The fact that God still speaks should enliven our expectations, even today. When we preach the gospel of the new covenant in Christ, we are not simply reporting history or airing theology — we are not even just teaching truth. If our ministry is to be blessed, *God must speak through it* with power and persuasion (1 Cor. 2:4). Many of our problems today arise from a failure to understand that God is speaking through his Word whenever Christ is preached.

However, if we 'hear' but ignore what we hear, says the Writer, we 'refuse [or disregard] him who speaks'. Here lies great danger, for in refusing God's words we refuse God himself. Even when God speaks, professing Christians may hear and yet not *listen*. We can be 'hearers only', with minds informed but hearts unwarmed and wills unmoved. James urges: '... receive with meekness the implanted word, which is able to save your souls. But be doers of the word, and not hearers only, deceiving yourselves' (James 1:21-22; Ezek. 33:30-32).

Intellectual assent to the Bible (or even enjoyment of it) is not enough. There is such a thing as 'ritual evangelicalism', in which the Scriptures are esteemed, preached, heard, taught, discussed, defended and commended — all with skill, diligence and thoroughness. But no one thinks it strange when there is no impact on people's lives; when our hearing of the Word of God fails to change our attitudes, priorities or lifestyles; when our belief in Scripture yields no fruit of the Spirit — such as love, joy, peace and patience. God demands more than mere assent, for he declares, 'On *this* one will I look [with favour]: on him who is poor and of a contrite spirit, and who *trembles* at my word' (Isa. 66:2, emphasis added). If we are to avoid the sin of 'refusing him who speaks', we too must learn to tremble at his word.

Earlier in the epistle the Writer posed a rhetorical question: 'If the word spoken through angels [i.e., the law] proved stead-fast, and every transgression and disobedience received a just reward, how shall we escape if we neglect so great a salvation, which at the first began to be spoken by the Lord?' (2:1-4). In effect, he now repeats that early warning, but in even stronger terms. In Hebrews 2 it was God's gracious work ('so great salvation') that was being 'neglected'. In Hebrews 12 the danger is more sharply focused — it is God *himself* who is 're-fused' or disregarded if we reject his word. The punishment is correspondingly severe: **'For if they did not escape who re-fused him who spoke** [warned] **on earth, much more shall we not escape if we turn away from him who speaks** [warns] **from heaven'** (12:25).

At first sight two 'speakers' are mentioned here — one who warned 'on earth' and one who warned 'from heaven'. Commentators have variously identified the first as either Moses or God, at Sinai, and the second as Jesus, or the Father speaking through his Son. There is another interpretation, however, and one that fits better with the verses that follow. According to this view, there is only one speaker, God him-self, but two different occasions. At Sinai God spoke 'on earth' whereas in Christ he speaks 'from heaven' (since Christ both came from heaven and now reigns and ministers there). In other words, God has spoken in both covenants, but one con-cerns men on earth while the other *also* embraces eternity and heaven.

Those who **'did not escape'** under the old covenant may refer specifically to the generation of Israelites who perished in the wilderness because of their unbelief (3:16-19). Alternatively, the description could apply more generally to any who sinned under the law of Moses (as in 2:2). Either way, sin and unbelief were severely punished under the regime of law, because to break the law amounted to a rejection ('refusal') of God. Yet, for all its severity, the Mosaic law was only a shadow of what was to come. It was propagated on earth, it was given to a small and stateless people, and it was temporary in its intent. Moreover, it addressed chiefly the external behaviour of men rather than the 'thoughts and intents of the heart' (4:12), so that the apostle Paul could, at one and the same time, be the 'chief of sinners' and yet 'blameless' as regards 'the righteousness which is in the law' (1 Tim. 1:15; Phil. 3:6). Further, the provisions for atonement and cleansing under the old covenant were also earthly and external, offering ceremonial purification but no true forgiveness or cleansing of the conscience (9:14; 10:1-4).

So then, if rejection of the law — circumscribed as it was — brought swift judgement, how much more will rejection of the gospel be judged? For the new covenant is promoted not from earth but from heaven, being confirmed by God's own oath (6:17) and mediated by God's own Son. The specific sin envisaged here is a 'turning away' from truth once apparently embraced. Again, therefore, the Writer has apostasy in his sights.

These warnings, repeated with growing urgency throughout the epistle, are frighteningly relevant today. The term 'apostasy' has almost disappeared from the Christian vocabulary, but the reality it describes is rampant. I refer not only to those churches that have long ago turned their backs on biblical truth, but to many who suppose that their biblical credentials are intact. Remember Jesus' words: 'Many will say to me in that day, "Lord, Lord, have we not prophesied in your name, cast out demons in your name, and done many wonders in your name?" And then I will declare to them, "I never knew you: depart from me, you who practise lawlessness!"'

What is their sin? Simply this; they do not do the will of the Father in heaven (Matt. 7:21-23). And what is the will of the Father? 'This is the work of God, that you believe in him whom he sent' (John 6:29). Our religious works, no matter how zealous and apparently successful, can never bring us to know Christ, whom to know is eternal life. Faith in Christ alone avails.

Shaking the heavens (12:26)

The Writer introduces his second parallel and contrast. When God spoke at Sinai, his **'voice then shook the earth'**. Sinai was rocked by an earthquake (or something very much like it; Judg. 5:4-5). But the new covenant promises an altogether greater paroxysm: '**... but now he has promised, saying, "Yet once more I shake not only the earth, but also heaven"**' (12:26).

The words are cited from Haggai, and to understand them we need to consider their full context. The prophet writes, 'For thus says the LORD of hosts, "Once more (it is a little while) I will shake heaven and earth, the sea and dry land; and I will shake all nations and they shall come to the Desire of All Nations, and I will fill this temple with glory... The glory of this latter temple shall be greater than the former", says the LORD of hosts, "And in this place I will give peace..."' (Haggai 2:6-9).

The temple in question was the temple of the restoration, rebuilt by the Jews between 536-516 B.C. at the command of Cyrus, King of Persia, following the seventy-year Babylonian captivity (the book of Ezra tells the story). We must assume that the Hebrews were well-versed in the relevant Scriptures, including the prophecies of Haggai and Zechariah. They would have known the passage to which the Writer now draws their attention.

What is Haggai telling us? He is not saying that the temple of the restoration would be more glorious than its predecessor (Solomon's temple). The reverse was, in fact, the case — as is clear from Haggai 2:3. No, the future glory of which the prophet spoke was the glory of Christ, the Desire of Nations. He would bring glory to his temple — the church, 'built' not of hewn rock but of 'living stones' — people from all nations (1 Peter 2:5,10). It is in *this* temple that his people would be given peace.

This being the case, Haggai's future 'shaking' clearly refers to the coming of Christ. But is it his first or second coming that is in view? Owen is in no doubt: 'These things are spoken in the prophet expressly with respect unto the first coming of Christ, and the promulgation of the gospel thereon.'[1] Lane, however, sees a reference both to the new-covenant era and to its eschatological fulfilment,[2] while Bruce relates the cosmic shaking solely to 'the end of the present world order'.[3] Owen (as also Brown[4]) is probably right, since the Writer's purpose here is to contrast the old and new covenants, not to teach eschatology. Of course, the new-covenant era will have an eschatological consummation, but this is not the preoccupation of the epistle at this point.

The shaking of earth and heaven thus refers primarily to the changes and convulsions that resulted from the coming of Christ to inaugurate the new covenant. The earth (human society) was indeed 'shaken' — according to some, the world was turned upside down! (Acts 17:6). The gospel challenges all purely human philosophies and social structures. It was a revolutionary creed from the beginning and remains so today, especially in its radical analysis of the human condition and its transforming power in individuals and communities.

But the new order in Christ also shakes heaven. What does this mean (if it does not relate to the cosmic events at the end of time)? It could refer to the *physical* events surrounding the death and resurrection of Christ, such as the darkness, the rending of the veil, and the resurrection of believers — as reported in Matthew 27:45-54. Or, more persuasively, it could refer to the sweeping *spiritual* changes that took place when the veil was rent and Christ entered the *heavenly* tabernacle, bearing his own atoning blood. Favouring this interpretation, Brown comments: 'The law was added to the promise as a temporary appendage, and did not abrogate it; but the gospel takes the place of the law and thus abolishes it ... the gospel reaches both *the earth* and *the heaven* of the church, and "old things pass away, and all things become new".' [5] The new-covenant revolution has changed the geography of heaven as well as the societies of the earth.

Things being shaken (12:27)

The Writer makes his application. God's 'shaking' of heaven and earth will remove some things but leave others untouched. Human and earthly institutions ('things that are made') will succumb, but the kingdom of Christ will remain. Thus the text continues: **'Now this, "Yet once more," indicates the removal of those things that are being shaken, as of things that are made, that the things which cannot be shaken may remain'** (12:27).

'Yet once more' signifies *only* once more. There would not be a succession of shakings, resulting in a succession of changes. Once this cosmic transformation has been brought about — once the new era has been established — it will last for ever. We could, of course, apply this to the final eschatological event — the creation of 'new heavens and a new earth' (2 Peter 3:10-13). But again we must remember that the Writer's purpose is to emphasise the eternal validity of the *new covenant* rather than of the *new heavens*. The finality of the events in question, therefore, is better understood in terms of the 'stone cut out without hands' described by Daniel: '... in the days of these kings the God of heaven will set up a kingdom which shall never be destroyed ... it shall break in pieces and consume all these [other] kingdoms and shall stand for ever' (Dan. 2:44). This is Christ's kingdom, and it cannot be shaken.

It follows naturally that the **'removal of those things that are being shaken'** (note the present tense) refers to earthly institutions, including both the Mosaic system of religion and the secular kingdoms of the earth. All such entities are described as 'things that are made'. It must be admitted that the interpretation of this expression is easier for those who treat the passage eschatologically, for it would then simply refer to the entire created order. However, against this is the fact that the 'things that are made' were already '*being* shaken' as the Writer penned his epistle. What things were under threat in his day? Clearly, such institutions as Jewish nationhood and (in particular) the old covenant, which was 'becoming obsolete and growing old [and] ready to pass away' (8:13).

Any difficulty we may have in describing these institutions as 'things that are made' vanishes when we adopt the Writer's own perspective, as expressed in 8:2 and 9:11. In those verses he contrasts the tabernacle of the old covenant with the 'true tabernacle which the Lord erected, and not man', and with 'the greater and more perfect tabernacle not made with hands, that is, not of this creation'. The Writer obviously sees the old covenant as centred in a tabernacle that was, indeed, 'made' — being 'erected' by man, 'made with hands' and 'of this creation'. It is perfectly natural, then, for him to refer to the old covenant as something that has been 'made'. The same applies, of course, to man's earthly kingdoms over against the spiritual kingdom of God.

The lesson is clear. God's people must not trust in earth's transient, crumbling ordinances and institutions. Life itself demonstrates that they do not last, no matter how aggressively they strut across the stage of history. The same applies to religions in so far as they involve the efforts and accomplishments of man. They last for a while only. The fads and fashions of so much that passes for 'Christianity' in our own day are ample evidence of this. Only the spiritual kingdom of Christ can endure unchanged — God shakes all other confidence to destruction.

52.
Receiving a kingdom

Please read Hebrews 12:28-29

Hebrews is full of surprises — and this passage contains the epistle's first mention of the kingdom of God. The only other reference is the brief quotation from Psalm 45 found in 1:8, where the emphasis is on the kingship of Christ rather than the kingdom itself. Neither does the manifold description of the church in the preceding verses (12:22-24) make any mention of a kingdom, though references to the citadel of David might carry that implication. Why, then, does the Writer suddenly introduce 'the kingdom' at such a late stage in his epistle?

We can only speculate. He may be drawing a parallel between the two covenants. Just as the first covenant created the 'church-state' of Israel, and eventually a kingdom, so the new covenant can be presented in similar terms.[1] In words reminiscent of Jeremiah's new-covenant prophecy (8:10), Peter presents the church of Christ as 'a royal priesthood, a holy nation, his own special people'. He tells us that the purpose of this 'holy nation' or kingdom is to 'proclaim the praises of him who called you out of darkness into his marvellous light'. Peter continues: 'Once [you were] not a people, but are now the people of God, who had not obtained mercy but now have obtained mercy' (1 Peter 2:9-10). Certainly, the 'kingdom theme' is well developed in the New Testament — chiefly in the Synoptic Gospels, but also in Acts, Revelation and Paul's epistles (e.g., 1 Cor. 6:9; 15:24; Gal. 5:21; Col. 1:13, etc). But up to this point, Hebrews has been strangely silent on the matter.

There is a further possible reason for the sudden introduction of the theme. It could be that the Writer's presentation in 12:27 of the *impermanence* of earthly institutions, and the *permanence* of the new covenant, brought to his mind the passage we cited from Daniel in the previous chapter — which powerfully teaches this very truth. The various kingdoms represented by the great image in Nebuchadnezzar's dream are destroyed by the 'stone cut out without hands' (that is, not made by man). But the stone itself becomes a mighty and eternal kingdom that fills the whole earth (Dan. 2:29-45). This is certainly the new-covenant perspective on human history, as we look for the triumph of Christ, the heavenly Jerusalem, and the everlasting inheritance of his people.

An unshakeable kingdom (12:28)

Whatever his reason for introducing the kingdom at this late juncture, the Writer is concerned to make a positive application: **'Therefore, since we are receiving a kingdom which cannot be shaken, let us have grace ...'** (12:28). Unlike the kingdoms of time and space, Christ's kingdom 'cannot be shaken'. It has its foundations in eternity past — in God's eternal decrees. Its plenitude lies in eternity to come — in God's unchanging purpose. Its king is the eternal Son of God, whose 'years will not fail' (1:12), and its people are his eternal joy. 'His servants shall serve him. They shall see his face ... and they shall reign for ever and ever' (Rev. 22:3-5). Furthermore, since it is the *heavenly* Jerusalem, this kingdom cannot suffer the fate of 'things made' — which 'will all grow old like a garment' (1:12). Rather, as Daniel foresaw, 'the time came for the saints to possess the kingdom. Then the kingdom and dominion ... shall be given to the people, the saints of the Most High. His kingdom is an everlasting kingdom, and all dominions shall serve and obey him' (Dan. 7:22-27).

But what help is this to hard-pressed believers in this present world? The Writer is eager to explain — we are *already* in the process of 'receiving' this new-covenant kingdom. It is a present reality as well as a future hope! We see the gospel message spreading throughout the world. We see the elect being gathered in. But even more — by knowing Christ we are *already* enjoying the personal and corporate benefits of citizenship in the 'everlasting kingdom of our Lord and Saviour Jesus Christ' (2 Peter 1:11). 'Such a kingdom it is', says Owen, 'whose treasures and revenues consist in these things ... light, liberty, righteousness, peace, grace, and mercy.'[2] Most surely, '... the God and Father of our Lord Jesus Christ ... has blessed us with every spiritual blessing in the heavenly places in Christ' (Eph. 1:3).

Acceptable worship (12:28 cont.)

That being so, urges the Writer, we should be profoundly thankful. To be a citizen of a benign kingdom on earth is both a privilege and joy — ask any stateless person or asylum seeker! How much greater is the blessedness of belonging to Christ's unshakeable heavenly kingdom, with its promise of eternal security, felicity and rest! **'Therefore,'** continues the Writer, **'let us have grace, by which we may serve God acceptably with reverence and godly fear'** (12:28). 'Let us have grace' is better translated, 'let us be thankful or grateful'.[3,4] It is only when we are grateful to God for bringing us into his kingdom that we are able to 'serve' (the word means 'worship') acceptably. Thankfulness is an indispensable ingredient of spiritual worship.

We seldom recognise this as clearly as we ought. Worship has many dimensions, but Christians today often lack this element of gratitude to God for all his mercies. We come before God congratulating ourselves — when we should be congratulating him and humbling ourselves in 'reverence and godly fear'. There is a melting quality in thankfulness that, when experienced, transforms worship and pleases God. The psalmist points us in the right direction: 'What shall I render to the LORD for all his benefits to me? ... You have loosed my bonds. I will offer to you the sacrifice of thanksgiving and will call upon the name of the LORD' (Ps. 116:12-17).

Although public worship is probably the predominant issue here, Lane reminds us that 'The concept of worship is almost certainly to be expanded in v. 28b to include "a manner of life which is pleasing to God and which is sustained both by gratitude and by a serious sense of responsibility".' [5] 'Service' includes not only formal worship in a congregation but a life dedicated daily to the glory of God.

It is fitting that worship should emerge as the climax of this majestic twelfth chapter. The teeming blessings and unspeakable privileges of the new covenant have passed before our eyes. We, who once rebelled against the King of heaven, are in the process of receiving his glorious and eternal kingdom! The deepest gratitude is clearly called for, but gratitude alone is not enough. It must lead us higher — to reverential worship and godly fear. Nothing less is acceptable to God.

How we need to understand this today! We argue over the externals of worship — psalms or hymns, ancient or modern, vestments or casual wear, set liturgy or spontaneity — but neglect the 'weightier matters' of what God himself deems acceptable. Hebrews sets us right. What does God ask of us in worship? Gratitude, reverence and godly fear! Of course, these things will have a significant influence on the way we conduct our worship. But it is ultimately not the outward form but the *attitude* of heart and mind that the Lord approves or rejects.

A consuming fire (12:29)

Let us, therefore, remember who it is we worship, **'for our God is a consuming fire'** (12:29). Here is the Writer's third parallel between Sinai and the new covenant, referred to at the beginning of the previous chapter. The desert mountain burned with fire, but such is the holiness of the God and Father of our Lord Jesus Christ that he is *in himself* a consuming fire.

The words come from Deuteronomy 4:24: 'For the LORD your God is a consuming fire, a jealous God.' Pink observes, 'Though God has taken the redeemed into intimate nearness to himself, yet he requires that they always retain a due apprehension of the majesty of his person, the holiness of his nature, the severity of his justice, and the ardent jealousy of his worship.'[6] Our glorious God is 'the High and Lofty One, who inhabits eternity, whose name is holy' (Isa. 57:15), and we must approach him in reverential fear, remembering that he is holy beyond our comprehension.

But we shall also approach with joy, remembering also that, through Christ, God dwells 'in the high and holy place, *with him who has a contrite and a humble spirit*, to revive the spirit of the humble, and to revive the heart of the contrite ones' (Isa. 57:15, emphasis added).

To understand that God is 'a consuming fire' will most certainly purge our worship of unworthy things, but we cannot escape the fact that this statement *also* constitutes a final warning to potential apostates. In its original place, this description of God was given to caution Israel against idolatry (Deut.

4:23-28). Idolatry and apostasy are all of one, for both despise the living God and his gracious work of salvation. If any turn back when they are on the verge of receiving the kingdom, surely the fires of God's anger will destroy them without mercy. There are echoes here of the sin of Israel, who turned away on the very threshold of the promised land (3:16-19). Let the Hebrews beware! The Writer leaves his warnings ringing in their ears.

Part 5:
The law fulfilled by love

53.
Led by love

Please read Hebrews 13:1-6

It would be easy to regard Hebrews 13 as an appendix —
indeed some have done so. Others speculate that it was added
by another hand to change the character of the writing, transforming an original homiletic discourse or sermon into a letter.[1] These ideas arise because, as the chapter opens, there is
an abrupt transition from the high themes of Christ and the
new covenant to a sequence of apparently unrelated practical
exhortations.

But the discontinuity is more apparent than real. The integrity of Hebrews 13 with the remainder of the epistle is attested
in many ways. Lane points out that 'Attention has been called
to the character of the vocabulary, to lines of argumentation,
to the sustained appeal to texts from the Pentateuch and the
Psalms, to the recurrence of key concepts, and to considerations of structure, all of which tend to exhibit the basic ho-
mogeneity of chap. 13 with the rest of the document.'[2]

The key to this continuity is found in 12:28, where the
Hebrews are urged to offer thankful and reverential worship
for God's new-covenant mercies. Although this will be expressed in public worship, it is also a 'service' that must by its
very nature spill over into daily life. Indeed, worship in its
fullest sense *consists* in living our lives 'for him who died for
[us] and rose again'. Paul exhorts, 'Present your bodies, a

living sacrifice, holy and acceptable to God, which is your reasonable service' (2 Cor. 5:14-16; Rom. 12:1-2). It is just such holy and sacrificial living that constitutes the burden and import of Hebrews 13.

A new covenant demands a new lifestyle — one that flows from God's laws written in the heart and in the mind. As Jesus and his apostles frequently made plain, *that* means a life of love: 'You shall love the LORD your God with all your heart, with all your soul, with all your strength, and with all your mind, and your neighbour as yourself' (Luke 10:27). These two commandments, said Jesus, embody all the law and the prophets (Matt. 22:37-40) — and in obeying the law of love, adds Paul, the law of Moses is fulfilled (Rom. 13:8-10; Gal. 5:14; see also. John 15:9-14; 1 Cor. 13; 1 John 2:9-11). This reminds us that although Sinai's law is unfruitful, being 'weak through the flesh', its *intentions* are not set aside but rather *fulfilled* and *enabled* under the new covenant in Christ (Rom. 8:3-4).

We are going to look at Hebrews 13 from that standpoint. Although it mentions 'love' explicitly only once, it is a passage that exalts love, in all its aspects, as the believer's way of life.

Loving the brethren (13:1)

It is appropriate, therefore, that the chapter begins with the words: **'Let brotherly love continue'** (13:1). Writing to the Thessalonians, Paul observes that brotherly love (love for fellow believers) is something 'taught by God' (1 Thess. 4:9-10). This underlines the fact that, in true new-covenant style, such love flows not from an outward rule but from an inner principle — the 'love of God ... poured out in our hearts by the Holy Spirit who was given to us' (Rom. 5:5).

However, as always, there is a balance between God's work *in* the believer and its outworking *by* the believer. This balance is beautifully stated in Paul's injunction: '*Work out* your own salvation with fear and trembling, for it is God who *works in* you both to will and to act according to his good purpose' (Phil. 2:13, NIV, emphasis added). This is why an exhortation to 'continue' in the practice and exercise of mutual love is both permissible and necessary, even though the Hebrews were already active in this ministry (6:10). We need to be reminded frequently to bring forth the fruit of the Spirit ('which is love ...') and not the works of the flesh (Gal. 5:18-22).

But brotherly love has another dimension, and one that was highly relevant to the Hebrews' own situation — this grace is evidence of spiritual life. John explains: 'We know that we have passed from death to life, because we love the brethren. He who does not love his brother abides in death' (1 John 3:14; 4:12). Having been warned again and again of the dangers of apostasy, the Hebrews would be comforted concerning their spiritual state if they practised mutual love. And let us be clear — it *must* be practised to be real! John continues: 'My little children, let us not love in word or in tongue, but in deed and in truth. And by this we know that we are of the truth and shall assure our hearts before him' (1 John 3:18-19).

Loving strangers (13:2-3)

The Writer cites a second manifestation of the life of love — we are to show love well beyond the circle of our Christian friends. He continues: **'Do not forget to entertain strangers, for by so doing some have unwittingly entertained angels'** (13:2). The Spirit's fruitage of love reaches out to all people, especially those who are in need. If we are to be children of our heavenly Father, we shall display the same compassion as

the one who is 'a father of the fatherless, a defender of wid-
ows ... [who] sets the solitary in families [and] brings out those
who are bound into prosperity' (Ps. 68:5-6). Jesus warns us
against limiting our love to our own close circle: 'If you love
those who love you, what reward have you? Do not even the
tax collectors do the same? And if you greet your brethren
only, what do you do more than others? ... Therefore you shall
be perfect, just as your Father in heaven is perfect' (Matt.
5:46-48). Hospitality is frequently enjoined as a Christian responsibility in the New Testament (Rom. 12:13; 1 Tim. 3:2;
Titus 1:8; 1 Peter 4:9).

This is a very practical matter for the local church. All too
often it becomes a 'holy huddle' from which newcomers and
strangers feel excluded. Recently, an African believer began
attending a church known to the author — and expressed
amazement at being welcomed and treated like a brother in
Christ by a 'white church'! He had clearly had different experiences elsewhere. To 'entertain strangers' means to be hospit-
able towards them, and applies not only to the practice of hospitality but also, says Owen, to 'the disposition, readiness and
frame of mind which are required in it and unto it'.[3] It is a
spiritual duty which requires us to be on the lookout for those
in need. It is also a sobering thought that our activity in this
area will feature in the Day of Judgement — for Christ will
say, 'Come you blessed of my Father, inherit the kingdom prepared for you from the foundation of the world: for I was
hungry and you gave me food; I was thirsty and you gave me
drink; I was a stranger and you took me in' (Matt. 25:34-35).

Although hospitality often involves personal cost, it can
also be immensely rewarding — for in extending hospitality to
strangers 'some have unwittingly entertained angels'. The specific reference is to Abraham and Lot (Gen. 18:1-15;19:1-29).
In both cases, their hospitality resulted in signal blessing. For
Abraham and Sarah it brought the renewed promise of a son,

and an opportunity to intercede for Lot and his family. For Lot himself it brought nothing less than deliverance from destruction. Kistemaker suggests that the Writer also had Gideon and Samson's parents in mind (Judg. 6:11-23; 13:3-21),[4] but this is unlikely since *their* hospitality was hardly rendered in ignorance of the nature of their guests.

Another category of people needing love was that of prisoners. The Writer urges his readers to **'remember the prisoners as if chained with them — those who are mistreated — since you yourselves are in the body also'** (13:3). Guthrie points out that 'Prisoners are out of sight and apt to be forgotten, hence the exhortation to remember.'[5] The reference here is specifically to Christians imprisoned (and thus 'mistreated') for their faith. But it will also bear a wider application — to those whose crimes are receiving a just reward but who can still be reached by the gospel. In our own day, significant numbers are being converted in prisons throughout the world through 'prison ministries' of various kinds.

To **'remember'** these needy ones is not merely to think about them, but to pray for them (Acts 12:5), visit them (Matt. 25:36) and provide for their material needs (Phil. 4:10-20). By way of incentive, the Writer reminds them that they also are **'in the body'** and thus liable, potentially at least, to be 'chained with them'. Some have seen 'the body' as a reference to the church, but most commentators believe it refers to the physical body and thus, by implication, the physical vulnerability of believers. Nevertheless, this is a clear application of the Pauline teaching that 'If one member suffers all the members suffer with it' (1 Cor. 12:26).[6] Either way, the Writer suggests that all Christians were under threat of imprisonment in those days — and calls on the Hebrews to empathise 'as if you yourselves were suffering'.[7]

Again, we know that the Hebrews had not neglected this responsibility, for their faithfulness in this matter is referred to in 10:33-34. Nevertheless, the Writer does not hesitate to remind them to *continue* in their 'work of faith and labour of love' (1 Thess. 1:3). A church should never assume that its members are 'getting on' with the ministry of compassion without needing to be stirred up to their responsibility. It is all too easy to 'grow weary in well doing' and we need reminding constantly to practise what we preach (2 Thess. 3:13).

Love and sex (13:4)

The third area where new-covenant behaviour is both expected and required is that of sexual relationships: **'Marriage is honourable among all, and the bed undefiled; but fornicators and adulterers God will judge'** (13:4). Love between human beings reaches its highest expression in the marriage of a man to a woman. Their sexual union is both ordained and blessed by their Creator (Gen. 1:28; 2:24; Mark 10:5-9). Consequently, 'the bed is undefiled'. That is, the sexual union between marriage partners is pure. Indeed, it is beautiful — for the word 'undefiled' conveys not just a negative attribute — 'not defiled' — but has a strongly positive connotation, being applied in other contexts to pure religion (James 1:27), our heavenly inheritance (1 Peter 1:4) and even to Christ himself (7:26).

But there is a darker side to the Writer's statement. For when marriage is spurned or despised, dreadful consequences follow: '… fornicators and adulterers God will judge.' 'Fornication' refers to all kinds of sexual relationships outside marriage, including homosexual activity, while 'adultery' refers specifically to marital unfaithfulness.[8] All sexual sins will be judged by God, whether in this life or at the judgement or both, for they constitute a rejection of God's way of love and undermine his pattern for human relationships.

Sexual immorality has been a feature of the world from time immemorial. It would certainly have characterised society before the flood (Gen. 6:5) and is a focal point of Paul's denunciation of the ancient world in Romans 1:18-32. But it should be neither seen nor tolerated in the church, which consists of sinners who have been cleansed and delivered from all such wickedness (1 Cor. 6:9-11). Sadly, however, even true believers can succumb, as was the case in the Corinthian church (1 Cor. 5; 2 Cor. 2:3-11). The church at Thyatira also had a problem in this regard (Rev. 2:18-24) which required urgent action if serious judgement was to be avoided. Jude 1-4 suggests that the early church struggled to maintain sexual purity within its ranks in a society where promiscuity was the norm.

These things are relevant to our own age, when the constraints and conventions of a past Christian heritage have been swept away by a tide of sexual permissiveness. The institution of marriage is under renewed threat; casual sex is regarded as legitimate and harmless entertainment, even for children in their early teens; homosexuality is now 'respectable' and flaunted openly by leading politicians, entertainers and others; and any outcry against these things is roundly condemned as 'discrimination'.

Such is the world of our day, but what of the professing church? At the time of writing, the Anglican communion has just appointed as its leading archbishop a man who has knowingly ordained a practising homosexual to the ministry (and would do so again). A significant section of that church has decided that sexual immorality is no longer relevant, either to Christian profession or to Christian ministry. Again, the Roman Catholic Church is racked by scandals relating to child-abuse by 'priests'. And so we could continue. Of course, we may dismiss these denominations as 'apostate churches' and claim that things are different in the true church. But the New

Testament examples cited did occur in genuine apostolic churches, so that none of us can afford to be complacent.

That is why the Writer issues this warning. Sexual immorality is a denial of love — and love is what the new covenant both produces and requires.

Loving our neighbour (13:5-6)

All the injunctions in the first five verses of Hebrews 13 could be comprehended under the command: 'You shall love your neighbour as yourself' (Matt. 22:39; Lev. 19:18). Christian brethren, strangers and prisoners, wives and husbands, people susceptible to sexual pressure — all are in one sense or another our neighbours. As our fellow human beings they are worthy of respect, says the Mediator of the new covenant (Matt. 5:22-24,28-32). In harmony with this principle, the final injunction says, **'Let your conduct be without covetousness'** (13:5). As the Decalogue makes clear, covetousness is a sin against our neighbour — 'You shall not covet your *neighbour's* house, you shall not covet your *neighbour's* wife ...' (Exod. 20:17, emphasis added). Why is this? Because to covet is the first step on the road to theft. It is, at heart, the willingness to deprive others of what is rightfully theirs. But there is another side to this odious coin. According to Paul, covetousness despises not only our neighbour but God himself, for 'a covetous man ... is an idolater' (Eph. 5:5). The covetous person rates material possessions higher than the God who gives them — he worships and serves 'the creature rather than the Creator' (Rom. 1:25).

The new-covenant believer is no longer under the law of Moses, but that does not mean that the unchanging God has withdrawn his ancient requirements for holy living. Quite the reverse, in fact, for the law of Christ written in the heart is far more demanding than the law of Moses.

The inner constraint of the law of Christ is brought out beautifully in our verses. Contentment, the antithesis of covetousness, is based on the believer's possession of Christ! — **'Be content with such things as you have, for he himself has said, "I will never leave you nor forsake you." So we may boldly say: "The Lord is my helper; I will not fear. What can man do to me?"'** (13:5-6). The Writer employs two quotations. The first — 'I will never leave you nor forsake you' — is from Deuteronomy 31:6 and Joshua 1:5, and refers to God's presence with his people in conquering the promised land. This reminds us (as it should have reminded the Hebrews) that all the Writer's exhortations are based upon a single new-covenant theme — our entry into the 'promised land' of salvation in Christ. As Robertson observes, 'The old covenant appealed to the human longing for a sure and settled land; yet it could not compare with the realities of new covenant fulfilment.'[9]

The second quotation comes from Psalm 118:6, where the psalmist celebrates the enduring mercy of God towards his people when they are distressed and surrounded by enemies: 'The Lord is my strength and song, and he has become my salvation' (Ps. 118:14). The Lord is 'on our side', our helper indeed. What harm can we suffer at the hands of men?

What have these quotations to do with avoiding covetousness? What reasons do they provide for the believer not to covet? The answer is as follows. Under the old covenant the tenth commandment was a straightforward prohibition, designed to subdue greed and preserve an orderly society. But the new covenant (like the covenant of promise in Old Testament times) offers an entirely new reason for not coveting, namely, that Christ is the believer's portion and companion through life — he will never leave us or forsake us. Like Abraham, the new-covenant believer has heard God say, 'Do not be afraid ... I am your shield, your exceeding great reward' (Gen. 15:1). Again, he heeds and embraces Jesus' words: 'Seek first the kingdom of God and his righteousness and all these things shall be added to you' (Matt. 6:33). Very simply, those who follow Christ can say with Paul, 'I ... count all things loss for the excellence of the knowledge of Christ Jesus my Lord' (Phil. 3:8).

As a result, continues the Writer, we can face the world 'boldly' and without fear, and this applies in two ways. Firstly, we can retain our peace and equanimity when we are mocked by a world that despises Christians for their unworldliness. Covetousness is a way of life for the world, and they delight to ridicule those who reject it. This is something the Hebrews had experienced — they had been made 'a spectacle both by reproaches and tribulations' (10:33). Secondly, far from being allowed to indulge in covetousness, they had suffered the 'plundering of [their] goods'. Yet they had suffered this material loss 'joyfully', knowing that they had 'a better and enduring possession ... in heaven' (10:34). Unlike the worldling, who trusts in earthly possessions and status, believers look for a spiritual inheritance and heavenly glory. Since these things cannot be taken from them, they may well ask, 'What [harm] can man do to me?' The answer, of course, is, 'None'.

54.
Established by grace

Please read Hebrews 13:7-9

The life of love is now further described, but from a new perspective. The new-covenant lifestyle is characterised by love, not only for people but also for the things of God. What are these 'things'? They include the Word of God, the doctrine of Christ, grace, spiritual food, the reproach of Christ, a heavenly hope, the 'sacrifices' of praise and good works, obedience in the church and prayer. All these are found in 13:7-19 and will be covered in this and the next two chapters.

Remember your leaders (13:7)

The Writer exhorts his readers: **'Remember those who rule over you, who have spoken the word of God to you, whose faith follow, considering the outcome of their conduct'** (13:7). The words 'those who have the rule over you' actually translate a much simpler Greek expression — 'your leaders'. Delitzsch points out that Luke uses the same word in Acts 15:22 ('leading men') and Luke 22:26 ('he who leads').[1] Furthermore, the English translation conceals the fact that the leaders in question were those who had ministered (who 'spoke') to the Hebrews *in time past*. The Writer implies that these former leaders had finished their course and gone to their reward, leaving the 'outcome' of their conduct here on earth as a powerful example and testimony to the continuing local church. These leaders had been preachers — they had 'spoken the word of God' to them and, crucially, they had practised what they preached! Here is a challenge both for pastors and people.

Those who led the church (Paul would have called them pastors, elders, teachers) had 'spoken the word of God'. The verb 'speak' means just that, and is not the usual New Testament word for 'preach'. It implies that the ministry of these leaders had not been limited to pulpit preaching, but that on every possible occasion they had taught the Word of God — the Scriptures — to their people. This echoes Paul's charge to Timothy: 'Preach the word! Be ready in season and out of season. Convince, rebuke, exhort, with all long-suffering and teaching' (2 Tim. 4:2). In short, leaders have a responsibility to bring God's Word to bear on *all* aspects of life and at *every* opportunity, both public and private. It is all too easy to say one thing from the pulpit and another in personal conversation; to be bold in preaching generalities but timid when dealing with specific issues and specific people. But chief among the qualities of true spiritual leadership are transparency and consistency — both in message and life.

This brings us to a further responsibility laid on pastors and elders, implicit in the words **'whose faith follow'** — they are to be 'examples to the flock' (1 Peter 5:3). The Writer clearly had known (or known of) the former leaders in question, and could wholeheartedly commend their example to his present readers. Could he commend ours? Paul's words to Timothy are again pertinent: 'Be an example to the believers in word, in conduct, in love, in spirit, in faith, in purity' (1 Tim. 4:12).

Concerning the people, the Hebrews are challenged to 're-member' their former leaders and to 'consider' (study carefully) the outcome (end or achievement) of their manner of life. Like the aged Paul, their mentors had 'endured to the end', having 'fought a good fight ... finished the race ... [and]

kept the faith'. A crown of righteousness awaited them in glory (2 Tim. 4:7-8). Now the Hebrews must themselves 'follow' (mimic) their leaders' faith — exhibiting their love and appreciation for these men in three ways. Firstly, in embracing their doctrine; secondly, in sharing their faith and joy in Christ; and thirdly, in imitating their exemplary lives. The Writer is simply underlining the message of Hebrews 11, but using contemporary rather than historical examples to do so.

We can only do these things out of love — duty alone cannot provide sufficient motivation. To embrace our leaders' faith requires us to love the doctrine of Christ, 'in whom are hidden all the treasures of wisdom and knowledge' (Col. 2:3). To share their living faith in Christ we must love Christ himself, 'who is our life' (Col. 3:4). And to follow their example we must love his Word, letting it 'dwell in [us] richly with all wisdom' (Col. 3:16).

Sadly, many of us fail this challenge to imitate our leaders. We expect them to be consistent, dependable, patient, faithful and spiritual men. But we do not see any need to match this behaviour ourselves. A small but all-too-common example is this — as church members we would be shocked if our pastor failed to turn up to lead a service, but think nothing of absenting ourselves without notice for less-than-convincing reasons. What is the problem? It arises when we see ourselves as mere adherents rather than organic members of the body of Christ. Lacking the gifts and calling of ministers and elders, we fail to see that perhaps *our* appointed function in the body includes simply *being there* when the church gathers, to encourage our leaders and our brethren (cf. 10:25).

The unchanging Christ (13:8)

There follows one of the best-known verses in the epistle: **'Jesus Christ is the same yesterday, today, and for ever'**

(13:8). Needless to say, the statement is normally quoted out of context — but what exactly *is* the context? At first sight the verse seems to have no connection with either the preceding or the following text.

Some find a link to the foregoing verse in the contrast between their mortal leaders, who have passed on, and their heavenly leader, Jesus Christ, who is always present and never changes (cf. 13:5).[2] However, this would seem to diminish the importance of the very lives the Writer urges his readers to 'study carefully'.

The Greek word translated 'outcome' or 'end' in verse 7 occurs only twice in the New Testament — here and in 1 Corinthians 10:13, where it is rendered 'way of escape'. Literally it means 'a going-up-out-of',[3,4] and in classical Greek was used of disembarking from a ship, or of an egress or escape. Some see this as a reference to martyrdom,[5] but in the present context perhaps 'outcome' would be the most appropriate translation. But what was this outcome, if not a testimony to the unchanging grace of Jesus Christ himself?

Looked at in this way, the juxtaposition of verses 7 and 8 traces the outstanding testimony of these church leaders back to its source — to Christ, the 'author and finisher' of the faith they both lived and taught. They had indeed run their race 'looking to Jesus' (compare also Phil. 3:7-11). 'This is a notable passage', says Calvin, 'from which we learn that there is no other rule of true wisdom than to fix all our thoughts on Christ alone.'[6]

Turning to the statement itself, we see displayed the unchanging nature of Christ. This is not so much a reference to his eternal sonship as to his saving work and ministry. Calvin again writes, 'It is clear that the apostle is not discussing the eternal being of Christ but the knowledge of him which flourished among believers in every age and which was the lasting foundation of the church.'[7]

Jesus Christ was the same 'yesterday', that is, during Old Testament times, as he is today (and will for ever remain) under the new covenant. The importance of this statement cannot be exaggerated, for it tells us clearly that salvation has always been through faith *in Christ*. No act or attitude of faith, in itself, has saving power. It is the great end and object of our faith — Christ himself — who saves.

Similarly, Jesus Christ is 'the same ... today'. He alone is 'the way, the truth and the life' and no one comes to the Father except through him (John 14:6). This was the immediate lesson the Hebrews needed to learn. The shadows of the old covenant would avail them nothing. Only Christ could save and keep their souls amid the trials and temptations of this present life. Similarly today, unless I can say with the apostle, 'For me to live is Christ', I am at risk of being sidetracked into apostasy, whatever my religious experience or profession (Phil. 1:21).

Finally, he is 'the same ... for ever'. Again the Writer underlines his oft-repeated teaching of the eternal nature and finality of Christ's redeeming work, who 'is able to save to the uttermost those who come to God through him, since he ever lives to make intercession for them' (7:25). Whether we look back, around us or to the future, the Lord Jesus Christ fills the horizon of those 'who love his appearing' (2 Tim. 4:8, AV).

Shifting sands (13:9)

The constancy of Christ and his saving work stands in contrast to the shifting sands of human philosophy and doctrine. In common with all the early churches, the Hebrews were assailed by novel teachings that were 'according to the traditions of men' and not 'according to Christ' (Col. 2:8). The Writer therefore warns his readers, **'Do not be carried about**

**with various and strange doctrines. For it is good that the
heart be established by grace, not with foods which have
not profited those who have been occupied with them'**
(13:9). The false teaching referred to clearly involved certain
dietary requirements. In view of the following verses, the reference might be to old-covenant ritual practices, but this seems
unlikely because the Writer would hardly describe *them* as 'various and strange'. Delitzsch understands these 'doctrines' to
refer to 'misleading and self-willed speculations and interpretations of divine [old covenant] precepts'. He continues: 'Jewish asceticism in the apostolic age dealt largely in precepts and
injunctions concerning the use of, and abstinence from, various kinds of food.'[8] Owen adds, 'The things were many and
various, and so were the doctrines concerning them; which
are since multiplied in [the Jewish] Talmud and other writings,
into such a heap of confusion as is inexpressible.'[9]

We do not face these specific problems today, but the principle still applies. The church of Christ is still troubled by 'various and strange doctrines'. Perhaps the most obvious example
is seen in the sects that continue to rise up and flourish, drawing away disciples to themselves. Much of their attraction lies
in the claim to have received some new revelation that 'im-
proves' upon the biblical gospel in some way.

Evangelicals are not immune, for many dabble in doctrines
such as 'continuous revelation' through modern prophets, or
promote their leaders to iconic status. Others label themselves
'Neo-evangelicals' seeking to reinterpret ancient truths such
as the inspiration of Scripture, the meaning of the atonement,
and justification by faith alone. The charismatic movement is a
further example, with its successive 'waves' of 'new things'
and increasingly bizarre physical manifestations. Again, the
'Willow Creek' and 'church growth' movements have discovered new but dubious ways of winning adherents, while the

'contemporary Christian music movement' fills churches with rock music — and those intoxicated by its beat and rhythm.

Neither these 'foods' nor the doctrines that underlie them can profit spiritually 'those that have been occupied with them'. Instead, we should love and 'desire the pure milk of the word that [we] may grow thereby' (1 Peter 2:2). If we are 'carried about' with novel and unbiblical teachings, warns the Writer, we shall forfeit grace — and the righteousness, peace and joy that attend it. For 'the kingdom of God is not food and drink, but righteousness and peace and joy in the Holy Spirit' (Rom. 14:17).

There is a better way, says the Writer — 'for it is good for the heart to be established by grace'. This means, firstly, that genuine Christianity is inward and spiritual, and does not consist in outward rituals, observances, methods or displays of emotion. It has to do rather with internal things like 'the heart' and 'grace' — like 'righteousness, peace and joy'. This, of course, is the message the Writer has been drumming into his readers throughout the epistle. We look by faith to Jesus Christ — an *invisible* High Priest, who serves an *ineffable* God in a *heavenly* sanctuary and has made an *eternal* satisfaction for our sins. The Hebrews, like many today, lusted after visible religion, earthly security, tangible joys and emotional satisfaction. But this is not what the gospel is about, as Hebrews 11 testifies so eloquently.

Secondly, we learn that grace is able to 'establish' the heart. The word means 'confirm' or 'strengthen' and is significant in the context of the Hebrews' wavering and embattled faith. We are not only saved by grace, but continually helped and strengthened by it. God's generosity to sinners (which is what grace means) does not cease when we come to faith in Christ. The gospel does not, as some suggest, send the believer back, alone, to the law to learn how he should live. If God 'did not spare his own Son, but delivered him up for us all, how shall he not with him *also freely give us all things*?' (Rom. 8:32, emphasis added; see also 2 Peter 1:3). The same gospel and the same Spirit that gave us life in Christ are ever present to strengthen our resolve, help our infirmities and establish our faith — especially in the face of persecution, stress and difficulty (2 Cor. 4:1,16; Rom. 8:26).

55.
Sanctified by Christ

Please read Hebrews 13:10-14

Although rituals and regulations concerning 'foods' are of no spiritual profit (13:9), the believer must nevertheless feed — on Christ! This appears to be the train of thought that leads the Writer from the futility of dietary rules in verse 9 to the striking declaration that follows in verse 10. In this chapter, therefore, it is the believer's love for Christ that is brought into focus. This love is not without its consequences, as we shall see.

In New Testament times, a significant number of Christians had become entangled with such dietary rules.[1] The transition from man-made religion to the new covenant was difficult for many, and this included Gentiles as well as Jews. Paul has to reprove the Colossians, for example, concerning these matters. 'If you died with Christ from the basic principles of the world', he asks, 'why, as though living in the world, do you subject yourselves to regulations — "Do not touch, do not taste, do not handle", which all concern things which perish with the using — according to the commandments and doctrines of men?' (Col. 2:20-22).

But how can a believer be *liberated* from such scruples, rooted as they are in the age-old religions and philosophies of men? Paul and the Writer have a common strategy — each directs his readers to Christ.

Feeding on Christ (13:10)

In pointing us to Christ, they emphasise specifically the believer's participation in the Lord's death. Paul reminds the Colossians that they have 'died' to their former enslavement to works-based religion, having been crucified with Christ. The Writer also alludes to our participation in Christ's death, but uses a different metaphor. Just as the priests and Levites of the old covenant fed upon the animals sacrificed at the altar, so the believing soul feeds spiritually upon 'Christ and him crucified' (1 Cor. 2:2).

He writes, **'We have an altar from which those who serve the tabernacle have no right to eat'** (13:10). The words contain both a parallel ('we have an altar') and a distinction (some 'have no right to eat').

The children of the new covenant *do* follow a diet, but a very different one from that prescribed by human rules and regulations! They love and enjoy the food of the gospel. Spiritually, by faith, they eat the body and drink the blood of Jesus Christ — and doing so receive eternal life (John 6:53-58). The atoning death of Christ is the 'altar' from which the believer eats (the Greek word translated 'altar' means a 'place of sacrifice' and stands as a metaphor for the sacrifice itself). 'The altar which we now have is Christ alone and his sacrifice', declares Owen.[2]

When we eat physically, we draw enjoyment, nourishment and sustenance from what we ingest. It is the same when we feed spiritually on Christ. First, the indwelling Holy Spirit gives us an appetite for Christ — 'he will glorify me', said Jesus, 'for he will take of what is mine and declare it to you' (John 16:14). Then, as we 'consider him' and meditate on his glorious person and redeeming work, our faith is engaged, our hearts are quickened, and our souls are satisfied 'as with marrow and fatness' (Ps. 63:5).

Moreover, this 'eating' is an ongoing experience, as we are reminded every time we celebrate the Lord's Supper. We must not *equate* 'the altar' in this verse with the Lord's Table (as some do), for that would turn the latter into some kind of eucharistic offering. We must always remember that the Lord's Supper is a *remembrance* of Christ's once-for-all offering, not a *re-enactment* of it.[3] Nevertheless, the supper reminds us that spiritual life, and all the benefits of the new covenant, flow from an 'altar' from which we are privileged to feed continually. That altar is 'Jesus Christ and him crucified'.

In sad contrast, says the Writer, adherents of the old covenant have no part in Christ ('no right to eat'). This applies even to the priests and Levites, 'who serve the tabernacle', let alone the generality of those who continue under the old covenant. Why? Because by clinging to the shadows they reject 'the living bread which came down from heaven' (John 6:51).

Thus the Writer draws a stark distinction between the two covenants. They are mutually exclusive. 'No one can serve two masters; for ... he will hate the one and love the other' (Matt. 6:24). Jesus was speaking of God and mammon, of course, but the principle applies. We cannot, at one and the same time, 'serve the tabernacle' and obey Christ. Nor can we blend the old and new covenants into some kind of twilight gospel.

The application to our own day is clear. Works-religion (of whatever kind), ritualism, externalism, legalism, cultic practices, priestcraft, and all such things, are counter-productive deceptions. To think that we can add them to the gospel of pure grace is a delusion. Those who place their confidence in *anyone or anything but Christ alone* 'have no right' to the benefits of the new covenant. Only faith in him avails.

Outside the camp (13:11-12)

Elaborating his illustration, the Writer continues: **'For the bodies of those animals, whose blood is brought into the sanctuary by the high priest for sin, are burned outside the camp'** (13:11). This verse may relate to the previous statement about those who 'have no right' to eat the sacrifice. Clearly, the Mosaic priests had 'no right' to eat the *special* sacrifices offered on the Day of Atonement, because they had to be burned 'outside the camp'. ('Camp' is a reference to Israel pitching camp during their forty-year wanderings in the wilderness).

Is the Writer drawing a contrast between the priests' *inability* to derive nourishment from these special sacrifices, and the believer's *right and privilege* to do so — to feed on the one they typified? Calvin believes so: 'Christ ... was sacrificed on the condition that those who serve the tabernacle should not feed on him ... we must renounce the tabernacle in order to have a share in Christ.'[4] Delitzsch agrees: '... as the priests of the law were debarred from partaking of the sin offering of the day of atonement ... so also they have no right to partake of the antitypical sin offering of ... the cross.'[5] This subtle parallel would certainly be consistent with both the message and methodology of the epistle.

One thing is certain. The animals sacrificed on the Day of Atonement, whose blood was brought into the holiest-of-all, were not available as food for the priests (Lev. 6:30). Indeed, such was their uncleanness that (1) they were burned (not on an altar but as rubbish); (2) they were destroyed outside the camp; and (3) whoever burned them had to wash his clothes and bathe his body before he could return (Lev. 16:27-28). Hebrews presents this as a powerful — even disturbing — picture of the *totality* of Christ's sacrifice for sin. Such was the reproach and degradation suffered by the Son of God in

atoning for our offences, that the animal sacrifices that prefigured him had to be treated as loathsome and polluted. Perhaps
this gives us new insight into Paul's statement that Christ was
'*made ... sin for us*, that we might become the righteousness
of God in him' (2 Cor. 5:21, emphasis added).

The Writer continues, '**Therefore Jesus also, that he might
sanctify the people with his own blood, suffered outside
the gate**' (13:12). Christ was crucified outside the city gates
of Jerusalem, for to execute anyone *within* the city would have
defiled it. His rejection, both by man and by the Father, is
thereby shown to be utter and complete. He was forsaken of
God (Matt. 27:46; Mark 15:34). Yet the very completeness of
his rejection guarantees our salvation! He became 'a curse for
us' that he might redeem us from the curse of the law, namely,
God's wrath upon sin (Gal. 3:13-14). Christ was not spared.
He drank sin's cup to its dregs to make *full* atonement for
God's elect (Rom. 8:31-33). Only thus could he bear the totality of our sins and 'sanctify [his] people with his own blood'
— perfecting them for ever and saving 'to the uttermost'
(10:14; 7:25).

We are reminded once again that, for the Writer, 'sanctification' refers to the once-for-all separation of Christ's people
to eternal life — the beneficiaries of his death for the glory of
God. We are also reminded that the old-covenant shadows
were specifically designed to foreshadow Christ in the new
covenant. To this end, even their detailed provisions (such as
the burning outside the camp) were prophetic of his ministry
and work.

The reproach of Christ (13:13)

Where, then, is Christ to be found? 'Outside the camp', replies the Writer. Applying the foregoing verses to the Hebrews,

he designates the Judaism of the old covenant as 'the camp'
— a community they must be prepared to quit if they are to
keep company with Christ. Again, he brilliantly dramatises the
incompatibility of old and new covenants. In Jerusalem (rep-
resenting the old covenant; see Gal. 4:25) they had '**no continuing city**' (13:14; cf. 11:13). It had served them as a temporary abode, but they dare not linger *in that city* if they were
to '**seek the one to come**' (13:14; cf. 11:16). A clear-cut choice
has to be made. Accordingly, he exhorts: '**Therefore let us go
forth to him, outside the camp, bearing his reproach**'
(13:13). Just as Jesus suffered outside the camp, so must they,
for it is impossible to fellowship with Christ without *also* bearing his reproach. Raymond Brown comments, 'This verse calls
... reticent believers to heroism and courageous testimony. If
they are to follow Christ they must be prepared for hardship.'[6]

We should remember that Christ's death outside the city
wall was the climax of a *religious* excommunication. Evangelicals face just such an excommunication whenever they are
labelled 'cultic', 'extremist' and 'fundamentalist' by society,
the media and mainline denominations. Down the centuries,
Bible-believers have often had to suffer outside the 'camp' of
religious orthodoxy, and this remains true today. In this situation, the Writer's words are comforting and supportive.

Sharing the reproach of Christ is a constant theme of the
New Testament. 'A disciple is not above his teacher, nor a
servant above his master', said Jesus. 'If they have called the
master of the house Beelzebub, how much more will they call
those of his household!' (Matt. 10:24-25). The Beatitudes end
with the following words: 'Blessed are you when they revile
you and persecute you and say all kinds of evil against you
falsely for my sake. Rejoice and be exceedingly glad, for great
is your reward in heaven ...' (Matt. 5:11-12). Paul gloried in
the 'offence of the cross' (Gal 5:11) and counted 'all things
loss for the excellence of the knowledge of Christ Jesus',

desiring to know 'the fellowship of his sufferings' (Phil. 3:7-11). The Writer himself refers to the 'reproaches and tribulations' suffered by his readers, and reminds us that Moses chose 'rather to suffer afflictions with the people of God than to enjoy the passing pleasures of sin, esteeming the reproach of Christ greater riches than the treasures in Egypt; for he looked to the reward' (11:25-26).

We need to ponder these things in a day of ease and freedom. What do we know of bearing Christ's reproach? Are we willing to do so, even if not called upon to suffer indignities and hardships for his sake? Or do we compromise with the world — effectively denying Christ — to obtain an easier passage through life? And if we *do* so suffer for his name's sake, do we grow bitter, or bear it joyfully? Can we, with Joseph, profess to the world: 'You meant evil against me, but God meant it for good'? (Gen. 50:20). God does not expect us to *enjoy* reproach and suffering. Our joy, like Christ's, resides in the recompense (12:2). With Moses, we must look 'for the reward'.

Let Peter sum this matter up for us: 'Rejoice to the extent that you partake of Christ's sufferings, that when his glory is revealed, you may also be glad with exceeding joy. If you are reproached for the name of Christ, blessed are you, for the Spirit of glory and of God rests upon you. On their part he is blasphemed, but on your part he is glorified' (1 Peter 4:13-14).

56.
Well-pleasing to God

Please read Hebrews 13:15-19

Just as love for Christ was the theme of the previous verses, so the present passage explores the believer's love for God the Father. Once again, the word 'love' is absent, but the actions and attitudes enjoined reflect and crystallise just such a love. The word the Writer *does* use is 'sacrifice', and it is no accident that he employs a concept which is so ubiquitous in Hebrews. He has expanded on the sacrificial system of the old covenant. He has set forth the glories of Christ's unique high-priestly offering — 'one sacrifice for sins for ever' (10:12). And now he calls upon his readers to respond in love and gratitude to God by offering *bloodless* sacrifices of their own. What are these sacrifices? The sacrifice of praise (13:15), the sacrifice of good works (13:16), the sacrifice of obedience (13:17) and the sacrifice of prayer (13:18).

It is true that only the first two of these are designated 'sacrifices' in the text. But by referring in 13:16 to 'such sacrifices' the Writer makes it clear that *everything* we do in loving service to our heavenly Father is an acceptable sacrifice, well-pleasing to him through our Lord Jesus Christ. He thus echoes Paul's admonition: 'Whatever you do in word or deed, do all in the name of the Lord Jesus, *giving thanks to God the Father through him*' (Col. 3:17, emphasis added).

The sacrifice of praise (13:15)

Under the old covenant, every Israelite was privileged (and often obliged) to bring sacrifices to the altar of God. They would do so for cleansing from sin, for ceremonial purification, for thanksgiving, and in making vows (e.g., Lev. 6:6; 12:6; 7:12; 7:16). The Jews were accustomed, therefore, to the idea of bringing offerings and sacrifices on a personal level. But not only that — they were also familiar with the concept of a 'sacrifice of praise'. This is made clear, for example, in Hosea 14:2: 'Take away all iniquity and receive us graciously, for we will offer the sacrifices [literally, bull-calves] of our lips.' The psalms also bear witness to this idea: 'O that men would give thanks to the Lord for his goodness... Let them sacrifice the sacrifices of thanksgiving, and declare his works with rejoicing' (Ps. 107:21-22). And again: 'I will offer sacrifices of joy in his tabernacle; I will sing, yes, I will sing praises to the LORD' (Ps. 27:6).

It is possible, of course, that the 'sacrifices of praise' were actual sacrifices (whether animals or 'unbloody' offerings of meal etc.) brought as an act of praise to God. This is clearly the case in Jeremiah 17:26, for example. Nevertheless, Hosea's words undoubtedly embrace the idea that praise to God was *itself* an acceptable 'sacrifice', even when it involved no physical offering. The Hebrews would thus have had no problem with the Writer's next injunction: **'Therefore by him let us continually offer the sacrifice of praise to God, that is, the fruit of our lips, giving thanks to his name'** (13:15). However, there was one important difference — these 'sacrifices of praise' are to be offered 'by him', that is, by Jesus Christ.

In what sense can our praise be regarded as a **'sacrifice'**? Firstly, because it is offered 'by' or through a mediator, our great High Priest. Under the old covenant, people brought their personal offering to the priest, who alone was authorised to sprinkle its blood upon the altar and before the Lord. By analogy, indicates the Writer, our praise to God the Father is mediated by the Son. Under the new covenant, we praise God through (or 'in the name of') Jesus Christ, for he alone is qualified to bear that praise before the ineffable presence of the Father.

But how perfectly he does so, transforming our defective, stumbling worship into something worthy of God! This is a matter of great practical importance. How often do we feel unworthy and utterly incapable of discharging our duty of praise to God? Our hearts are dull and our words lifeless. But as we place these offerings in Jesus' hands to offer to the Father, they are graciously and gloriously transformed — into praise and worship that is both acceptable to God and commensurate with his glory.

This we are to do **'continually'** —a word we have met before in this epistle! The high priests of the old covenant offered blood sacrifices *continually* but ineffectively (10:1). The High Priest of the new covenant, on the other hand, lifts our praises to the Father *continually* and with maximum effect!

Secondly, praise can be regarded as a sacrifice because it is 'the fruit of our lips'. The allusion is to the verse cited earlier from Hosea 14:2, which refers to 'the bull-calves of our lips'. Owen explains: 'The Apostle therefore doth not only cite [Hosea's] words, but respects the design of the Holy Ghost in them, which was to declare the cessation of all carnal sacrifices, upon the deliverance of the church by the sacrifice of Christ.'[1] Since these carnal sacrifices have ceased, there remains nothing in their stead but the joy of praise to God for his gracious and redeeming love.

This praise is here called 'fruit' instead of 'calves', probably because the Writer is concerned to employ a new-covenant idiom — 'calves' recalls only the death of sacrificial beasts, whereas fruit is the product and evidence of inner spiritual life. 'I am the vine, you are the branches', declared Jesus. 'He who abides in me, and I in him, bears much fruit; for without me you can do nothing' (John 15:5). Of course, the fruit of which Christ speaks appears in every aspect of the believer's life, but the fruit of praise is an important element of that rich harvest.

Furthermore, since praise is the fruit of 'our lips', the Writer obviously has in mind vocal, audible and public praise. Clearly, true public praise must have its wellspring in a praising heart, but it should not stop there! Paul and Silas 'were praying and singing hymns to God' at midnight, we are told, 'and the [other] prisoners were listening to them'. The Lord responded with a liberating earthquake! (Acts 16:25-26). Note also 2 Chronicles 20:22: 'Now when they began to sing and to praise, the LORD set ambushes against the people of Ammon, Moab and Mount Seir, who had come against Judah; and they were defeated.' Vocal praise is a testimony to the world, a scourge to our adversaries, and an encouragement to our fellow believers.

The sacrifice of good works (13:16)

The second bloodless sacrifice we should offer is that of good works: **'But do not forget to do good and to share, for with such sacrifices God is well pleased'** (13:16). The Writer knows how easy it is for believers to neglect the simple but God-honouring activity of doing good. Yet such works are genuine sacrifices — acts of worship that please God! We need to be clear about what the Bible actually teaches concerning 'good works', for many are confused over this subject. Briefly, we should understand two things.

1. Man cannot earn salvation by good works for, as a sinner by nature, he can never perform such works in a manner pleasing to God (Isa. 64:6; Zech. 3:1-5; Rom. 3:20,23-24; 7:22-25). Only the sinless Jesus Christ was able to do that. Salvation for sinners is (as the Reformers taught) by grace alone, through faith alone, in Christ alone. 'By grace you have been saved through faith, and that not of yourselves; it is the gift of God, not of works, lest anyone should boast. For we are his workmanship ...' (Eph. 2:8-10).

2. However, Ephesians 2 does not stop there. Being God's workmanship, the *regenerate* soul is 'created in Christ Jesus for good works, which God prepared beforehand that we should walk in them' (Eph. 2:10). This important statement tells us that good works are *a necessary and preordained consequence of salvation.* By the same token, they constitute the evidence that such salvation has truly occurred. This is what James means when he says, 'I will show you my faith by my works ... faith without works is dead... Was not Abraham ... justified by works when he offered Isaac his son on the altar? Do you not see that faith was working together with his works, and by works faith was made complete?' (James 2:18-26).

James is making a most important point. 'Faith' can be misinterpreted as mental assent to the gospel — a mere acknowledgement that it is true. This error has re-emerged strongly in our own day, when much evangelism seems to imply that salvation can be obtained by an act of will, by mere intellectual assent to doctrine. But James points out that even the devils have that kind of faith! (James 2:19). By contrast, the faith that saves is a faith which gives rise to fruit — that is, good works — which bring honour to God. This is the message of Hebrews 11, as we have already seen at length. Jesus himself commanded his disciples, 'Let your light so shine before men, that they may see your good works and glorify your Father in heaven' (Matt. 5:16). Calvin observes, 'It is no common honour that God regards what we do for men as sacrifices offered to himself.'[2]

Among the good works that we should do, the Writer singles out 'sharing'. He does so, perhaps, because to share our time, energy, homes or possessions with others involves genuine and practical sacrifice. Yet costly as it is to share, there are also great rewards. Solomon expressed the spiritual truth beautifully when he wrote, 'There is one who scatters, yet increases more, and there is one who withholds more than is right, but it leads to poverty' (Prov. 11:24). God is no man's debtor.

The sacrifice of obedience (13:17)

The third 'sacrifice' indicated in this passage is obedience. Admittedly, the Writer does not actually use the word 'sacrifice' in relation to this grace, but it is not unreasonable to extrapolate from the term 'such sacrifices' in verse 16, which suggests that doing good and sharing are just examples of a wider spectrum of God-pleasing actions and attitudes. To include obedience (13:17) and prayer (13:18) among the sacrifices with which 'God is well pleased' has the advantage of unifying this portion of the chapter and explaining why the Writer returns to the subject of 'leaders', having already covered it in 13:7. Some commentators have proposed that the subject is revisited in 13:17 to fulfil a complex and subtle structural purpose,[3] but this seems somewhat contrived. The alternative idea that obedience to church leaders is a sacrifice pleasing to God, and thus forms a natural sequel to verse 16, has the merit of simplicity.

Thus the Writer continues: **'Obey those who rule over you, and be submissive, for they watch out for your souls, as those who must give account. Let them do so with joy and not with grief, for that would be unprofitable for you'** (13:17). Obedience to God and to the gospel is, of course, central to the new covenant (1 Peter 1:2). By grace and the enlightening power of the Holy Spirit, God's people are made willingly obedient to Christ — 'Thy people shall be willing in the day of thy power' (Ps. 110:3, AV; the person addressed is the one 'ordained a priest after the order of Melchizedek'). However, the obedience enjoined here is a *secondary* obedience, rendered to man, not God. The Hebrews were to obey and submit to their church leaders.

In our own confusing times, this exhortation needs careful evaluation. It cannot be employed, for example, to justify the mind-control techniques or draconian discipline practised by cult leaders. Nor, in evangelical circles, should it be used to allow leaders to behave as 'lords over those entrusted to [them]'. On the contrary, says Peter, elders should be humble shepherds and examples to the flock (1 Peter 5:1-3). Church leaders are not infallible, and their authority lies not in themselves but in the Word of God they minister to the people. Nevertheless, in so far as they faithfully discharge the responsibilities given to them, they are to be obeyed. Two questions arise. Firstly, what are these responsibilities? Secondly, what does it mean to 'obey' in this context?

The leaders (elders) of the church, we are told, 'watch out for your souls' and 'give account' to God. The first responsibility implies, says Lane, 'that they have been ... endowed with the gift of discernment and were prepared to exercise this gift in the service of the church'.[4] As under-shepherds appointed by Christ himself, their task is to guard the flock against spiritual dangers and attacks (1 Peter 5:1-4). This requires vigilance, devotion, patience, self-discipline, humility, consistency, compassion and love. It also involves feeding the flock with clear teaching of the truth 'as it is in Christ', so that error cannot gain a foothold in the spiritually nourished assembly.

Clearly, only those equipped and called by the Spirit of God can hope to fulfil this role with any chance of success. Even then they will be conscious of being inadequate 'earthen vessels' (2 Cor. 4:7). Theirs is an exacting and sacrificial life. It is reasonable, therefore, that those who benefit from their labours should also act sacrificially by heeding (obeying) their spiritual instruction.

However, the leaders' responsibility does not end with 'watching out', for they must also 'give account' to God for the eternal souls of those they lead. They must be able to testify before the judgement seat of Christ that they have obeyed their Master's orders to 'Preach the word! Be ready in season and out of season. Convince, rebuke, exhort, with all long-suffering and teaching ... be watchful in all things, endure afflictions, do the work of an evangelist, fulfil your ministry.' And they must be able to add, 'I have fought the good fight, I have finished the race, I have kept the faith' (2 Tim. 4:2-7). For this cause also, they are to be esteemed and obeyed. As Calvin remarks, 'Since they must give account of us to God, it would be a disgrace if they were held in no account by us.'[5]

But what does it mean to obey? Paul enlightens us: 'We urge you, brethren, to recognise those who labour among you, and are over you in the Lord and admonish you, and to esteem them very highly in love for their works' sake [and] be at peace among yourselves' (1 Thess. 5:12-13). It means to heed their words, honour their persons, and love the Christ whose bond-servants they are. It means to labour with them for the peace of the church, the glory of God and the proclamation of the gospel, even when this requires us to humble ourselves and subdue our natural impulses. Such 'sacrifices' are well-pleasing to God.

The sacrifice of prayer (13:18-19)

The fourth and final 'sacrifice' is that of intercessory prayer. It is no easy task. In a rare personal allusion, the Writer requests his readers to pray for him — not only in general terms but also specifically for his early restoration to them. He writes, **'Pray for us; for we are confident that we have a good conscience, in all things desiring to live honourably. But I especially urge you to do this, that I may be restored to you the sooner'** (13:18-19). The Writer has a twofold claim upon their prayers. Firstly, he is a servant of the Lord, having a good conscience concerning his work for Christ. Like the apostle Paul he could claim that 'by manifestation of the truth' he had commended himself 'to every man's conscience in the sight of God'. He could thus declare his *own* conscience clear concerning the discharge of his duty to God (2 Cor. 4:2). That the Writer lived 'honourably' is not just a reference to consistent Christian conduct, but relates specifically to the *example* he set as he went about his ministry. How important it is that those who preach the gospel should 'strive to have a conscience without offence towards God and men' (Acts 24:16). It is as a faithful bond-slave of Christ, therefore, that he has a special claim upon their prayers — for himself and for his ministry.

Secondly, they had good reason to pray for his speedy and safe return to their company. The epistle bears abundant witness to his deep pastoral interest in and concern for them, and his renewed presence could only bring them further benefit. Clearly, this verse tells us that the Writer was no stranger to them — he had visited them at least once before and may have worked among them for a period of time (he knew, or knew of, their former leaders — 13:7). His intimate knowledge of their circumstances and temptations adds considerable weight to his admonitions and exhortations. His concerns were not theoretical but real and intimate.

The 'sacrifice' of intercessory prayer will not be limited to a particular individual, of course. It will range freely over many persons, churches and situations, but these verses remind us that such prayer is effective only if it is *specific*. Our private and public prayers are too often taken up with generalities. We seem too timid to ask God for specific answers to specific needs (because, perhaps, we have too little faith and expectation as we approach our heavenly Father). The result? We 'do not have [receive] because we do not ask' (James 4:2). The Writer has previously bidden us 'come boldly to the throne of grace' on our own behalf (4:16). We should come with equal boldness when we intercede for others.

57.
Loved by the Shepherd

Please read Hebrews 13:20-21

Under the new covenant, the law is indeed fulfilled by love. We have seen how the final chapter of Hebrews — which at first appears to be a series of loosely connected exhortations — perfectly encapsulates this principle. But, true to style, the Writer has one last surprise for us. Having devoted his closing words to the *believer's* 'life of love', he suddenly turns the concept around and, with a parting flourish, exalts the love of God *for us*. In doing so he gives us not only a benediction of outstanding beauty, but a parting view of Christ as the 'great Shepherd of the sheep' — the one who 'is himself our peace' (Eph. 2:14). And peace is what the benediction is all about. It begins with 'the God of peace' and (as we shall see) develops this idea to embrace every aspect of the new-covenant life.

But the benediction is also a prayer (Lane calls it a 'prayer-wish'), expressing the Writer's conviction that what God had begun in his readers he would continue and perfect. 'The fact that the prayer-wish takes up again central themes from the homily, indicates that the formulation was not simply taken over from some pre-formed liturgical expression ... but is organically related to the development of the sermon.'[1] Not only are old themes remembered — new ideas are introduced. The Writer's parting gift is to leave us with an appetite for more of Christ.

The God of peace (13:20)

In many ways, Hebrews is a fighting epistle. It was written to oppose dangerous trends in both doctrine and practice — trends that, if allowed to develop, would negate the gospel. While the Writer urges his readers to enter into the *rest* of faith (4:11), he makes it plain that this requires diligence, watchfulness and strenuous effort (4:11; 12:1-15). Yet, of course, at the heart of the new covenant lies a profound peace — a peace between God and man made 'through the blood of his cross' (Col. 1:20). It is appropriate, therefore, that the epistle's parting benediction should begin: **'Now may the God of peace ...'** (13:20). The Writer desires above all that the Hebrews should know both the peace of a once-for-all atonement *and* the God who ordained that peace before the world began. The two things go together, of course. It is because Christ has 'perfected for ever' those he has sanctified (10:14) that they have access into the holy presence of the God of peace (10:19). It is because Christ has an unchangeable priesthood (7:24) that we may ever 'come to God through him' (7:25).

The ascription 'God of peace' was widely used by the early church, and emphasises that peace is first and foremost an attribute of God himself (Rom. 15:33; 16:20; 1 Cor. 14:33; 2 Cor. 13:11; Phil. 4:9; 1 Thess. 5:23; 2 Thess. 3:16). There is, perhaps, a conscious contrast here with the revelation of God in 12:29 as a 'consuming fire'. The Hebrews needed to understand that God is, at the same time, a God of judgement and a God of grace and peace. We too must be careful to maintain a balanced view of the divine nature, not cancelling out one attribute by another, as some do, but embracing *all* that Scripture shows us of God's unfathomable glory. What, then, does it mean that he is 'the God of peace'? It means:

1. That the triune Godhead is eternally at peace within itself.

2. Accordingly, God's purpose is to bring peace to rebellious sinners through the gospel message — 'the word which he sent ... preaching peace through Jesus Christ; he is Lord of all' (Acts 10:36).

3. In consequence, the hearts and minds of those who trust in Christ are guarded by 'the peace of God that surpasses understanding' (Phil. 4:7).

4. Finally, peace then becomes 'fruit' borne by the indwelling Spirit, so that it is normative for Christians to 'be at peace among [themselves]' (Gal. 5:22; 1 Thess. 5:13).

This gracious and glorious 'cascade' of peace originates within the nature of God himself; it flows *to* us in the gospel; is bestowed *upon* us by the atoning work of Christ; works *in* us by the Holy Spirit; and issues *from* us in our relationships with others.

Peace through the blood (13:20 cont.)

The God of peace, we read, **'brought up our Lord Jesus from the dead ... through the blood of the everlasting covenant'** (13:20). More literally, the Father was 'leading up Jesus from the dead by virtue of the blood of the everlasting covenant'. The Writer weaves together in this brief statement three powerful ideas, ascribing God's great work of peace-making to (1) the death of Christ, (2) the resurrection of Christ, and (3) his new, yet everlasting, covenant of redemption. As we look at the separate strands we must not forget that they constitute a single threefold cord.

Firstly, God has made peace through the blood of Christ. The key verse is one we have already cited: 'It pleased the Father that in [Christ] all the fulness should dwell, and by him to reconcile all things to himself—by him, whether things on earth or things in heaven, having made peace through the blood of his cross' (Col. 1:20). Paul continues in Colossians 1:21-22 to make it clear that the work of reconciliation involves taking those who 'were enemies and alienated in ... mind by wicked works' and, 'through death', presenting them 'holy, and blameless and irreproachable in [God's] sight'. Cleansing and reconciliation are cause and effect. By his very nature, God is in communion and harmony with all that is perfect, pure and holy. Since the blood of Jesus has cleansed his people *perfectly* (10:14), it has also reconciled them perfectly to God. Indeed, Paul indicates that the whole created order is reconciled along with the primary objects of grace (his elect), so that 'all fulness' should reside in Christ.

Peace through the resurrection (13:20 cont.)

But that does not exhaust the Writer's meaning, for we are told that Christ was **'brought up** [led out] **from the dead'**. Owen explains: 'Christ ... was brought into the state of death by the sentence of the law; and was thence led, recovered and restored, by the God of peace ... to evidence that peace was now perfectly made.'[2] There is an implied parallel between God leading Israel out of Egypt to Sinai, where Moses was the shepherd, and his leading Christ out from the dead to ratify the new covenant—both events were acts of deliverance which made for God 'a glorious name' (Isa. 63:11-14).[3,4]

Thus Paul can declare: '... righteousness ... shall be imputed to us who believe in him who raised up Jesus our Lord from the dead, who was delivered up because of our offences, and was *raised because of our justification*' (Rom. 4:22-25, emphasis added). The resurrection justifies the believing soul because it testifies to the fact that Christ's sacrifice has been accepted by the Father. This is why the Writer says that Jesus was 'brought up from the dead ... *through* the blood...' He means that the shedding of Christ's blood has so perfectly attained its goal that there remains no cause for him to be imprisoned by death. Accordingly, he has been led in triumph from that dark realm as one who has conquered sin, death and hell.

Thus in order to bestow peace on fallen men, the 'God of peace' had also to be the God of power — a power demonstrated *par excellence* by the resurrection of Christ. Paul tells us that 'Jesus Christ our Lord ... was born of the seed of David according to the flesh, and declared to be the Son of God with power, according to the Spirit of holiness, by the resurrection from the dead' (Rom. 1:4). The resurrection, therefore, demonstrates both the reality of justification and the glory and power of the Father.

But it does more. By way of practical application, Paul adds, '... just as Christ was raised from the dead by the glory of the Father, even so we also should walk in newness of life' (Rom. 6:4). The same power and glory that brought Jesus back from the realm of death, works in the believer, both now through the manifestation of new life in Christ, and in the future in the resurrection of the body.

Finally, the resurrection of Christ is proof of two further aspects of the gospel. It demonstrates that Jesus Christ is indeed the eternal Son of God (Acts 2:24-36; Rom. 1:4), and it gives assurance to all men that God has appointed both a Judge and a judgement day (Acts 17:31). Little wonder, then, that the apostles preached 'Jesus *and the resurrection*' (Acts 17:18, emphasis added). So should we!

But why does the Writer remind us of these things so late in the epistle? The physical resurrection of Christ, while implied by such passages as 1:3; 4:14; 6:2; 11:19, is not specifically mentioned anywhere else in Hebrews. There is a straightforward answer to this question, suggested by the appearance of several new elements in this concluding doxology — the God of peace, the resurrection, and Jesus as the Shepherd. As he brings his letter to a close, the Writer is conscious that he has left so much unsaid concerning Christ and the new covenant. The apostle John faced a similar dilemma in writing his Gospel: 'There are also many other things that Jesus did which, if they were written one by one, I suppose that even the world itself could not contain the books that would be written' (John 21:25). Hebrews 'majors' on Christ, the great High Priest who offered himself a 'full, perfect and sufficient' sacrifice for sin. The ramifications are eternal and the personal implications profound, but by concentrating on this theme and all that flows from it, the Writer has necessarily neglected some other great new-covenant truths. He gives notice of this fact by signalling some of them, without elaboration, in his closing prayer.

Peace through the covenant (13:20 cont.)

The Writer describes Christ's sacrifice as **'the blood of the everlasting covenant'** (13:20). He thereby reminds us that the peace established by that offering is in no way fortuitous. Rather it was planned in grace and purposed by God 'before time began' (2 Tim. 1:9). It is the outworking of a covenant put in place long before Sinai, or even Abraham. Yet this 'everlasting' covenant is one and the same with the new covenant in Christ's blood — the 'better covenant' built on 'better promises' (8:6; 1 Cor. 11:25). How can this be? Because the covenant is 'new' only in terms of human history and by contrast with the 'first' or 'old' covenant. In reality it has existed since eternity past and will continue in force for ever. Like the God who ordained it for our blessing, it is truly 'from everlasting to everlasting' (Ps. 90:2; 103:17).

Peace from God — indeed, salvation in all its aspects — is the fruit of this eternal covenant of grace. And that covenant has been ratified by the oath of God and the blood of Christ (6:17; 10:29). The covenant of Sinai failed because it could be broken by man (8:9). But the 'better covenant' cannot fail because it *is* everlasting — ordained by God (8:10-12); sealed with the blood of his Son (1:3; 9:12); and actualised by the inner working of the Holy Spirit (8:10; Gal. 4:6-7). It was *this* covenant that Christ came to establish, inaugurate, mediate and carry to its glorious completion. Richard Lee understood this when he wrote:

> O, how sweet to view the flowing
> Of his soul-redeeming blood!
> With divine assurance, knowing
> That it made my peace with God.
>
> Freely thou wilt bring to heaven
> All thy chosen, ransomed race,
> Who to thee, their head, were given
> In the covenant of grace.

The great Shepherd (13:20-21)

The benediction contains one final jewel — Jesus Christ is now, finally, introduced to us as **'that great Shepherd of the sheep'** (13:20). The Writer has characterised the Lord Jesus Christ in many ways. He is the eternal Son; the creator and upholder of all things; the incarnate Christ made flesh to save his 'brethren' from their sins. He is, above all, the Mediator of the new covenant — our great High Priest who offered his own blood to sanctify his people and make them fit for heaven. He is our forerunner and example; our comforter and King. But, as the epistle draws to its close, the Writer chooses to present this most tranquil portrait of Christ — the Shepherd of the sheep.

The allusion would have needed no explanation, for the Hebrews were familiar with Scriptures such as Psalm 23; 80:1; 100:3; Isaiah 40:11 and others like them. In all these cases, of course, the Shepherd is none other than *Jahweh*, the LORD of hosts. In calling Jesus Christ the 'great Shepherd' the Writer makes a final affirmation of his divine and eternal nature.

Yet the Scriptures cited tell us far more than that, for they emphasise the mighty tenderness of God towards his flock — his chosen people. Christ is not just the Shepherd, he is the Shepherd *of the sheep*. The verbal redundancy is intentional and emphasises the intensely relational nature of the new covenant. 'Christians belong to the fold of the great shepherd', observes Lane, 'because they have been bonded to him by the eternal covenant.'[5] Christ is everything to his sheep, and they mean everything to him. He is their peace in the fullest possible sense. He leads them, feeds them, satisfies them, protects them and endows them with eternal life. He creates them, owns them, rebukes them, saves them, restores them, and carries them in his arms (all this and more can be culled from Psalm 23 alone). In this brief title given to Christ, there is enough content for a whole new epistle!

But the Writer has time only to emphasise one special ministry of the great Shepherd. In doing so, he revisits one of the epistle's major themes — practical fruitfulness in the believer's life. He prays that God would **'make you complete in every good work to do his will'** (13:20-21). This is a most important statement, for it underlines three essential elements

of the new covenant. Firstly, good works are the fruit of salvation, for only God can 'make us complete' (or 'perfect') in
them. Secondly, our works are 'good' only in so far as they
conform to the will of God, but this is possible because his
laws are written on our minds and in our hearts. Thirdly, we
can only perform such works (live such lives) because we are
children of the everlasting covenant, born again and indwelt
by the Spirit of Christ.

It is through the indwelling of the Spirit that God is seen to
be **'working in you what is well-pleasing in his sight,
through Jesus Christ, to whom be glory for ever and ever.
Amen'** (13:21). We were told earlier, in 13:16, that God is
'well pleased' by the 'sacrifice' of good works. What the Writer
adds here is the assurance that even this sacrifice is, in a real
sense, provided by God himself. We are enabled to 'work out
[our] own salvation in fear and trembling' only because 'it is
God who works in [us] both to will and to work on behalf of
his good pleasure' (Phil. 2:13). Again, 'We are his workmanship, created in Christ Jesus for good works' (Eph. 2:10). These
scriptures underline the fact that we can do nothing of ourselves that pleases God. Jesus said, 'I am the vine, you are the
branches. He who abides in me, and I in him, bears much fruit;
for without me you can do nothing' (John 15:5).

But as we abide in him, and bring forth fruit 'through Jesus
Christ', we shall most certainly glorify him. And that is what
the new covenant is all about.

58.
Greeted by brethren

Please read Hebrews 13:22-25

The closing words of Hebrews express the precious reality of fellowship among believers. This is not so much intentional on the Writer's part as intrinsic in the gospel he loves and sets before us in his epistle. That is, he does not mean to launch a belated discussion of the matter, but expresses it naturally — even unconsciously — in his farewell greetings.

He has, throughout the epistle, addressed the Hebrews as a community as well as individuals. He has urged them to 'consider one another in order to stir up love and good works'. He has warned them against 'forsaking the assembling of ourselves together' and counselled them to be diligent in 'exhorting one another' (10:24-25). They are to 'look out' for one another, as their leaders 'watch out' for them (12:14-17; 13:17). They are to 'share' with their brethren (13:16). These and other passages in the epistle emphasise what can easily be forgotten — that Christianity is a shared experience, the expression of a corporate identity. How appropriate it is, therefore, that the epistle should conclude on such a note!

Word of exhortation (13:22)

The Writer makes his final appeal: **'And I appeal to you, brethren, bear with the word of exhortation, for I have**

written to you in few words' (13:22). The 'fellowship dimension' of his words is immediately apparent — he calls them
'brethren', which would also have included the women in the
congregation. He also 'appeals' to them, entreating them as
fellow-believers rather than sternly commanding their obedience. His mode of address breathes the spirit of loving care
that is appropriate (though often neglected) within the family
of God's people.

The key term **'bear with'** has been variously translated.
Delitzsch renders it, 'give a patient willing audience'.[1] while
Andriessen translates the whole clause: 'content yourselves
with this word of encouragement'.[2] The main idea seems to be
that they should receive the epistle as a message of exhortation and encouragement — 'an edifying discourse'[3] — sub-
mitting willingly and patiently to its teaching and its many
injunctions. It is human nature to feel irritated when people
correct us, whether in terms of our understanding or behaviour. The Writer seems to say, 'Do not be offended by the
strength with which I have expressed myself, but rather submit — not to me but to the truth of the Scriptures I have laid
before you.'

The latter point is important. Although the 'word of exhortation' clearly means the epistle itself, the Writer desires his
readers to submit, not to him, but to the Word of God which
he has expounded to them so faithfully, forcefully and cogently.
There can be no greater evidence of true spiritual fellowship
between teacher and taught than such submission to God's
Word. The Scripture is the matrix within which leaders and
led find mutual consolation, edification, respect and joy. Such
submission to Christ is also the cause of peace within the soul
and within the church. It is a characteristic of the new covenant.

But what of the Writer's claim to have written **'in a few
words'**? As New Testament epistles go, Hebrews is among
the longest. However, Kistemaker points out helpfully that 'A

few times in the body of his letter, the author shortened his remarks (5:11; 9:5; 11:32) and stated that he lacked time even though he had much to say.'[4] The term 'few words', therefore, must be considered relative, as Owen explains: '... considering the importance of the cause wherein he was engaged; the necessity that was upon him to unfold the whole design and mystery of the covenant and institutions of the law, with the office of Christ; the great contests that were amongst the Hebrews about these things; and the danger of their eternal ruin through a misapprehension of them; all that he hath written may well be esteemed but a "few words" and such as whereof none could have been spared.'[5]

The Writer had no pastoral charge over the Hebrews, nor was he one of the original apostles. His writing to them must be seen, therefore, not so much as the discharge of a duty as an act of fellowship. His letter expresses a shepherd heart, reflecting the care and concern of the great Shepherd for the welfare of his sheep. He knew these people and their fundamental faithfulness to Christ. But he also knew their weaknesses, trials and temptations, and their constant need of grace from above. He wrote to minister to their needs, and there can be no greater expression of fellowship than that.

Set free (13:23)

The Writer continues, **'Know that our brother Timothy has been set free, with whom I shall see you if he comes shortly'** (13:23). He is happy to be the bearer of good news and anticipates an early opportunity to visit in person the church on which he has lavished so much time and effort by writing his letter.

We know a great deal about Timothy, of course, and two of Paul's letters are addressed to him. Nowhere else in the

New Testament, however, do we read that he had been imprisoned, and this suggests that Hebrews post-dates Paul's last epistle (cf. 2 Tim. 4:6,21). Nevertheless, his acquaintance with Timothy also suggests that the Writer was a member of Paul's circle, and this may well account for the Pauline influence discernible in the epistle.

He expresses the hope that he will visit them shortly, perhaps in company with Timothy. However, he is clearly not prepared to wait too long for a travelling companion, and will come alone if Timothy's arrival is delayed. The implied sense of urgency may well have arisen from a pastoral concern — the need to see how they had responded to the epistle, and to provide further counsel as necessary.

In the light of this verse it is probable that, like Timothy, the Writer was both the pastor of a local congregation and an itinerant preacher, being prepared to travel long distances to visit churches in need of support or counsel. This mixture of roles is illuminating. Such preachers were not necessarily pastoring churches and itinerating at the same time, of course, but the two activities are not incompatible. Either way, it is valuable and encouraging for a church to receive visiting pastors and preachers, and 'preacher mobility' appears to have been practised widely by the New Testament churches.

There is, perhaps, something for us to learn here. Christian fellowship should not be expressed only within the local assembly, or in ministers' fraternals, but between local *churches*. It is good for each church to have a settled pastoral ministry, but this ought not to be to the exclusion of visiting preachers. Nor should such visits be limited to special occasions like anniversaries and Bible rallies (when people's minds may be on other things) but be part and parcel of the ministry enjoyed by the local body of Christ for edification and mutual comfort.

All the leaders, all the saints (13:24)

Greetings can be perfunctory, but they can also convey happy memories, gracious concerns and the warmth of fellowship in Christ. The Writer's greetings here are of the latter kind: **'Greet all those who rule over you, and all the saints. Those from Italy greet you. Grace be with you all. Amen'** (13:24-25). As noted in the introduction, the penultimate sentence suggests that the epistle was written to a church in Italy (probably Rome) and that the Writer was in the company of believers from the Italian fellowship. Other interpretations are possible, of course.

In any case, the important thing at this juncture is that such greetings *were* conveyed. Though far away, the church to which the epistle was addressed was in the hearts and minds of the Writer and his companions. They felt like Paul, who assured the Philippians, 'I thank my God upon every remembrance of you, always ... making request for you all with joy, for your fellowship in the gospel ... because I have you in my heart' (Phil. 1:3-7). Too often today we use the word 'fellowship' when we mean nothing more than socialising. New-covenant fellowship is of the kind described in the verses quoted above — fellowship in the gospel, fellowship in grace, fellowship in suffering, and fellowship in the defence and establishment of the gospel of Jesus Christ. If we can greet our fellow believers and like-minded churches in *these* terms, we shall know what it is to enjoy true Christian fellowship — and thereby anticipate the joys of heaven!

Paul emphasises that his closeness to the Philippians stemmed not from mere acquaintance, but from the fact that they were 'partakers with [him] of grace', both in his imprisonment and his 'defence and confirmation of the gospel' (Phil. 1:7). This is reflected in the Writer's final words: **'Grace be**

with you all.' Grace is, of course, the over-arching premise
of the new covenant. Salvation and glory come to us by grace,
under the covenant of promise fulfilled in Christ. They cannot
be attained by works under the covenant of Sinai. Grace is the
climate of the new Jerusalem, the sunshine of God's love, the
gentle rain of mercy. It is a climate in which Christ is exalted,
the seed of the gospel germinates, and impoverished sinners
are endowed with eternal wealth — the unsearchable riches of
Christ (Eph. 3:8; 2 Cor. 8:9).

Notice, finally, the Writer's emphasis on **'all'** in his personal greeting: 'Greet *all* those who rule over you, and *all* the
saints. Grace be with you *all*. Amen.' Perhaps he was conscious of tensions within the church and wished to underline
the essential unity of the body of Christ.[6] It is more likely,
however, that as he concludes his letter his love for the brethren wells up — stirring a desire to put his arms around them
all in one final protective gesture of affection. It is a perfect
note on which to end.

Bibliography

References for each chapter are given using the name of the author quoted, together with a short title and the relevant volume and page number. This bibliography provides full details of the works in question.

Andrews, E. H. *Free in Christ — The message of Galatians,* Evangelical Press, Darlington (1996).

Andrews, E. H. *The Spirit has Come* (first published as *The Promise of the Spirit*), Evangelical Press, Darlington (1991).

Barnes, Albert. *Notes, Critical, Explanatory and Practical, on the Book of Psalms,* George Routledge & Sons, London (undated) in three volumes.

Berkhof, Louis. *Systematic Theology,* Banner of Truth Trust, London (1959).

Boston, Thomas. *Human Nature in its Fourfold State,* Zondervan (1957). Sovereign Grace Book Club, Evansville, Indiana.

Brown, John. *An Exposition of the Epistle to the Hebrews,* Banner of Truth Trust, Edinburgh (1961).

Brown, Raymond. *The Message of Hebrews* (first published as *Christ above all*), Inter-Varsity Press, Leicester (1982).

Bruce, F. F. *Commentary on the Epistle to the Hebrews,* Marshall, Morgan & Scott, London (1965).

Calvin, John. *The Epistle of Paul the Apostle to the Hebrews and The First and Second Epistles of St Peter,* Oliver and Boyd, Edinburgh (1963).

Carson, D. A., Moo, Douglas J., and Morris, Leon. *An Introduction to the New Testament,* Zondervan, Grand Rapids (1992).

Doddridge, Philip. *A Paraphrase and Notes on the Epistle to the Hebrews, The Family Expositor, vol. 4,* Matthews and Leigh, London (1808).

Delitzsch, Franz. *Commentary on the Epistle to the Hebrews,* T. & T. Clark, Edinburgh (1868) in two volumes.

Eveson, Philip. *The Book of Origins — Genesis simply explained,* Evangelical Press, Darlington (2001).

Gooding, David. *An Unshakeable Kingdom,* Inter-Varsity Press, Leicester (1989).

Guthrie, Donald. *The Letter to the Hebrews,* Inter-Varsity Press, Leicester (1983).

Hagner, Donald A. *Hebrews,* Hendrickson Publishers, Peabody, Mass. (1983).

Hewitt, Thomas. *The Epistle to the Hebrews,* Inter-Varsity Press, Leicester (1960).

Hughes, Philip Edgcumbe. *Commentary on the Epistle to the Hebrews,* Eerdmans, Grand Rapids (1977).

Hughes, Philip Edgcumbe. 'Hebrews 6:4-6 and the Peril of Apostasy,' *Westminster Theological Journal* 35 (1973)

Jones, Hywel R. *Let's Study Hebrews,* Banner of Truth Trust, Edinburgh (2002).

Kistemaker, Simon J. *Exposition of the Epistle to the Hebrews,* Evangelical Press, Welwyn (1984).

Lane, William L. *Hebrews* (in two volumes) Word Biblical Commentaries vols. 47a, 47b, Word Books, Dallas (1991).

Luther, Martin. *Luther's Works, vol. 29, Lectures on Titus, Philemon and Hebrews,* Concordia Publishing House, St. Louis (1968).

McCaul, J. B. *The Epistle to the Hebrews,* London (1871).

Moffatt, J. *The Epistle to the Hebrews,* International Critical Commentaries, Edinburgh (1924).

Newell, William R. *Hebrews Verse by Verse,* Moody Press, Chicago (1947).

Owen, John. *The Works of John Owen,* Johnstone & Hunter (1845-1855), reprinted by Banner of Truth Trust, Edinburgh (1991) in twenty-three volumes. The seven volumes covering the epistle to the Hebrews, and numbered 1-7 in the references in this commentary, correspond to volumes 17-23 of the complete works.

Owen, John. *Temptation and Sin,* The Sovereign Grace Book Club, Evansville, Indiana, (1958). This volume contains three essays, namely, 'Of the mortification of sin in believers', 'Of temptation', and 'Of the remainders of indwelling sin in believers', all of which may be found in the collected works of John Owen.

Pink, Arthur W. *An Exposition of Hebrews,* Baker Book House, Grand Rapids (1954).

Poole, Matthew. *Commentary on the Holy Bible,* Banner of Truth Trust, London (1963) in three volumes.

Robertson, O. Palmer. *The Israel of God — Yesterday, Today and Tomorrow,* P&R Publishing Company, Phillipsburg, NJ (2000).

Trench, Richard C. *Notes on the Parables of our Lord,* 12th edition, Macmillan & Co., London (1874).

Wilson, R. McL. *Hebrews,* Eerdmans, Grand Rapids, and Marshall, Morgan & Scott, Basingstoke (1987).

Notes

Introduction — Understanding Hebrews
1. Owen, *Hebrews,* vol. 6, p.76.
2. Carson, Moo and Morris, *An introduction to the New Testament,* p.398.
3. Carson, Moo, and Morris, *An introduction to the New Testament,* p.397.
4. Bruce, *Hebrews,* p. xxiii *et seq.*

Chapter 1 — Christ the message of God
1. Owen, *Hebrews,* vol. 3, p.12.
2. Lane, *Hebrews,* vol. 1, p.11.

Chapter 2 — Christ the image of God
1. Bruce, *Hebrews,* p.4.
2. Calvin, *Hebrews,* p.7.
3. John Brown, *Hebrews,* p.29.
4. Owen, *Hebrews,* vol. 3, p.99.

Chapter 3 — Christ the Son
1. Lane, *Hebrews,* vol. 1, p.7.
2. Kistemaker, *Hebrews,* p.37.
3. Bruce, *Hebrews,* p.15.
4. Bruce, *Hebrews,* pp.15-16.
5. Guthrie, *Hebrews,* p.74.

Chapter 4 — Christ the King
1. Bruce, *Hebrews,* p.18.
2. Jones, *Hebrews,* p.13.
3. Pink, *Hebrews,* p.58.
4. John Brown, *Hebrews,* p.57.
5. Guthrie, *Hebrews,* p.77.

Chapter 5 — Christ the Creator

1. Eveson, *The Book of Origins,* p.23.
2. Barnes, *Notes on the Psalms,* vol. 3, p.72.
3. John Brown, *Hebrews,* p.63.
4. Owen, *Hebrews,* vol. 3, p.213.
5. Owen, *Hebrews,* vol. 3, pp.231-2.
6. Barnes, *Notes on the Psalms,* vol. 3, p.137.
7. Bruce, *Hebrews,* p.24.

Chapter 6 — Christ the Saviour

1. Owen, *Hebrews,* vol. 3, pp.261-2.
2. Teodorico, cited by Lane, *Hebrews,* vol. 1, p.33.
3. John Brown, *Hebrews,* p.75.
4. Kistemaker, *Hebrews,* p.59.
5. Lane, *Hebrews,* vol. 1, p.40.
6. Andrews, *The Spirit has Come,* pp.169-253.

Chapter 7 — Christ the Man

1. Poole, *Commentary,* vol. 3, p.814.
2. Jones, *Hebrews,* p. 22.
3. John Brown, *Hebrews,* p.89.
4. Lane, *Hebrews,* vol. 1, p.47.
5. Lane, *Hebrews,* vol. 1, p.50.

Chapter 8 — Christ the Deliverer

1. Lane, *Hebrews,* vol. 1, p.57.
2. Philip Doddridge, *A Paraphrase and Notes on ... Hebrews,* p.65.
3. John Brown, *Hebrews,* p.113.
4. Bruce, *Hebrews,* p.44.
5. Poole, *Commentary,* vol. 3, p.816.
6. Lane, *Hebrews,* vol. 1, p.60.
7. Owen, *Hebrews,* vol. 3, pp.448-9.
8. The Greek term translated 'give aid' denotes 'a gracious laying hold in order to redeem' (Delitzsch, *Hebrews,* vol. 1, p.139).

Chapter 9 — Christ the faithful Son

1. Calvin, *Hebrews,* p.34.
2. Lane, *Hebrews,* vol. 1, p.74.
3. Robertson, *The Israel of God,* p.44.
4. Robertson, *The Israel of God,* p.108.
5. Kistemaker, *Hebrews,* p.87.

Chapter 10 — The deceitfulness of sin
1. Bruce, *Hebrews,* p.62.
2. Newell, *Hebrews,* p.96.
3. Calvin, *Hebrews,* p.42.

Chapter 11 — The promise of rest
1. Pink, *Hebrews,* p.204.
2. Calvin, *Hebrews,* p.45.
3. John Brown, *Hebrews,* p.203.
4. Owen, *Hebrews,* vol. 4, p.17.

Chapter 12 — The accountability of man
1. *Strong's Concordance.*
2. Kistemaker, *Hebrews,* p.116.
3. Owen, *Hebrews,* vol. 4, pp.363-4.
4. Guthrie, *Hebrews,* p.119.

Chapter 13 — The throne of grace
1. Calvin, *Hebrews,* p.54.
2. Guthrie, *Hebrews,* p.121.
3. Owen, *Hebrews,* vol. 4, p.396.
4. Kistemaker, *Hebrews,* p.124.
5. Hughes, *Hebrews,* p.171.
6. Owen, *Hebrews,* vol. 4, p.417.
7. Calvin, *Hebrews,* p.57.
8. Berkhof, *Systematic Theology,* p.427.

Chapter 14 — The author of salvation
1. Lane, *Hebrews,* vol. 1, p.119.
2. Luther, *Hebrews,* p.177.
3. Lane, *Hebrews,* vol. 1, p.120.
4. Calvin, *Hebrews,* p.65.
5. John Brown, *Hebrews,* p.250.
6. Bruce, *Hebrews,* p.105.

Chapter 15 — The need to progress
1. Carson, Moo and Morris, *Introduction to the New Testament,* p.400
2. Bruce, *Hebrews,* pp.108-9.
3. Calvin, *Hebrews,* p.68.
4. Lane, *Hebrews,* vol. 1, p.138.

5. Hughes, *Peril of Apostasy*, p.191.
6. Owen, *Hebrews*, vol. 4, p.599.
7. Jones, *Hebrews*, p.55.

Chapter 16 — The danger of apostasy
1. Guthrie, *Hebrews*, p.145.
2. Calvin, *Hebrews*, p.76.
3. Trench, *Notes on the Parables*, p.72.
4. Bruce, *Hebrews*, p.120.
5. *Strong's Concordance*.
6. Owen, *Hebrews*, vol. 5, pp.80, 81.
7. Bruce, *Hebrews*, p.121.

Chapter 17 — The need for diligence
1. Owen, *Hebrews*, vol. 5, p.145.
2. Hewitt, *Hebrews*, p.111.
3. Calvin, *Hebrews*, p.79.
4. Lane, *Hebrews*, vol. 1, p.146.
5. Wilson, *Hebrews*, p.113.

Chapter 18 — The unchanging purpose
1. Lane, *Hebrews*, vol. 1, p.151.
2. John Brown, *Hebrews*, p.315.
3. Hagner, *Hebrews*, p.98.
4. Gooding, *An Unshakeable kingdom*, p.152.

Chapter 19 — An eternal priesthood
1. Bruce, *Hebrews*, p.136.
2. Guthrie, *Hebrews*, p.155.
3. McCaul, *Hebrews*, pp.75, 80.
4. Calvin, *Hebrews*, p. 89.
5. Guthrie, *Hebrews*, p.156.

Chapter 20 — An endless life
1. Jones, *Hebrews*, p.75.
2. Bruce, *Hebrews*, p.146.
3. John Brown, *Hebrews*, p.344.
4. Lane, *Hebrews*, vol. 1, p.185.
5. Lane, *Hebrews*, vol. 1, p.188.

Chapter 21 — A perfect Saviour
1. John Brown, *Hebrews*, p.347.
2. *Strong's Concordance.*
3. Bruce, *Hebrews*, p.151.
4. Pink, *Hebrews*, p.411.
5. Lane, *Hebrews*, vol. 1, p.190.
6. Lane, *Hebrews*, vol. 1, p.192

Chapter 22 — A revealed pattern
1. Jones, *Hebrews*, pp.80-81.
2. Lane, *Hebrews*, vol. 1, p.200.
3. Hewitt, *Hebrews*, p.129.
4. Owen, *Hebrews*, vol. 6, p.6.
5. Bruce, *Hebrews*, p.164.
6. Guthrie, *Hebrews*, p.172.

Chapter 23 — A new covenant (I)
1. Calvin, *Hebrews*, p.109.
2. John Brown, *Hebrews*, p.372.
3. Guthrie, *Hebrews*, p.176.
4. Owen, *Hebrews*, vol. 6, pp.148-50
5. Owen, *Hebrews*, vol. 6, p.149.

Chapter 24 — A new covenant (II)
1. Robertson, *The Israel of God*, p.43.
2. Calvin, *Hebrews*, p.112.
3. Owen, *Hebrews*, vol. 6, p.163.
4. Boston, *Human Nature*, pp.194-5.
5. John Brown, *Hebrews*, p.374.

Chapter 25 — A symbol of Christ (I)
1. Calvin, *Hebrews*, p.116.
2. John Brown, *Hebrews*, p.382.
3. Owen, *Hebrews*, vol. 6, p.122.
4. Owen, *Hebrews*, vol. 6, p.195.
5. Hagner, *Hebrews*, p.128.

Chapter 26 — A symbol of Christ (II)
1. John Brown, *Hebrews*, p.384.
2. Lane, *Hebrews*, vol. 2, p.222.

3. Lane, *Hebrews,* vol. 2, p.226.
4. Pink, *Hebrews,* p.477.
5. Guthrie, *Hebrews,* p.184.

Chapter 27 — An eternal redemption
1. Kistemaker, *Hebrews,* p.248.
2. Owen, *Hebrews,* vol. 6, p.281.
3. Guthrie *Hebrews,* pp.188-9.
4. Pink, *Hebrews,* p.493.
5. John Brown, *Hebrews,* pp.401-2.
6. John Brown, *Hebrews,* p.412.

Chapter 28 — A better sacrifice
1. Kistemaker, *Hebrews,* p.256.
2. Delitzsch, *Hebrews,* vol. 2, p.111.
3. Gooding, *An unshakeable kingdom,* p.190.
4. For a fuller treatment of this subject see Andrews, *Free in Christ,* ch. 17.
5. Delitzsch, *Hebrews,* vol. 2, p.109.
6. Bruce, *Hebrews,* pp.214-15.
7. Owen, *Hebrews,* vol. 6, p.376.

Chapter 29 — A sufficient offering
1. Calvin, *Hebrews,* p.130.
2. John Brown, *Hebrews,* p.431.

Chapter 30 — A body prepared
1. Kistemaker, *Hebrews,* p.272.
2. Delitzsch, *Hebrews,* vol. 2, p.145.
3. Lane, *Hebrews,* vol. 2, p.261.
4. Owen, *Hebrews,* vol. 6, pp.457-60

Chapter 31 — A purpose fulfilled
1. Calvin, *Hebrews,* p.136.
2. Lane, *Hebrews,* vol. 2, p.265.
3. Kistemaker, *Hebrews,* p.277.
4. Delitzsch, *Hebrews,* vol. 2, p.156.
5. Lane, *Hebrews,* vol. 2, p.264.
6. Andrews, *Free in Christ,* pp.52-4.
7. Guthrie, *Hebrews,* pp. 205-6.

Chapter 32 — An eternal perfection
1. Bruce, *Hebrews,* p.239.
2. Lane, *Hebrews,* vol. 2, p.267.
3. Bruce, *Hebrews,* p.241.
4. John Brown, *Hebrews,* p.447.
5. Calvin, *Hebrews,* p.138.

Chapter 33 — An entry into the holiest
1. Lane, *Hebrews,* vol. 2, p.274.
2. Owen, *Hebrews,* vol. 6, p.505.
3. Calvin, *Hebrews,* p.140.
4. John Brown, *Hebrews,* pp.456-7.
5. Lane, *Hebrews,* vol. 2, p.284.
6. Moffatt, *Hebrews,* p.143.
7. Kistemaker, *Hebrews,* p.287.
8. Delitzsch, *Hebrews,* vol. 2, p.172.

Chapter 34 — An approach to God
1. Owen, *Hebrews,* vol. 6, p.509.
2. Lane, *Hebrews,* vol. 2, p.286.
3. Lane, *Hebrews,* vol. 2, p.287.
4. Calvin, *Hebrews,* p.142.
5. Bruce, *Hebrews,* p.252.
6. Jones, *Hebrews,* p.116.
7. Kistemaker, *Hebrews,* p.290.
8. Lane, *Hebrews,* vol. 2, p.290.

Chapter 35 — A fearful thing
1. Kistemaker, *Hebrews,* p.295.
2. Owen, *Hebrews,* vol. 6, p.545.
3. John Brown, *Hebrews,* p.474.
4. Bruce, *Hebrews,* p.263.

Chapter 36 — A need to endure
1. Calvin, *Hebrews,* p.152.
2. Delitzsch, *Hebrews,* vol. 2, p.194.
3. *Strong's Concordance;* see also Lane, *Hebrews,* vol. 2, p.299.
4. John Brown, *Hebrews,* p.484.
5. Lane, *Hebrews,* vol. 2, pp. 303-4
6. Owen, *Hebrews,* vol. 6, p.585.

Chapter 37 — Defining faith
1. Jones, *Hebrews*, p.122.
2. Kistemaker, *Hebrews*, pp.309-11.
3. Bruce, *Hebrews*, p.279.
4. Lane, *Hebrews*, vol. 2, pp.328-9.
5. Owen, *Hebrews*, vol. 7, p.7.
6. Owen, *Hebrews*, vol. 7, p.8.
7. Bruce, *Hebrews*, p.279.
8. Lane, *Hebrews*, vol. 2, p.332.

Chapter 38 — Pleasing God
1. Owen, *Hebrews*, vol. 7, p.24.
2. Owen, *Hebrews*, vol. 7, p.26.
3. Lane, *Hebrews*, vol. 2, p.334.
4. Pink, *Hebrews*, p.665.
5. Eveson, *The Book of Origins*, p.144.
6. Calvin, *Hebrews*, p.165.

Chapter 39 — Waiting for a city
1. Owen, *Hebrews*, vol. 7, p.57.
2. Owen, *Hebrews*, vol. 7, p.59.
3. Pink, *Hebrews*, p.703.
4. Lane, *Hebrews*, vol. 2, p.351.
5. Calvin, *Hebrews*, p.168.
6. Lane, *Hebrews*, vol. 2, p.352.
7. Bruce, *Hebrews*, p.302.

Chapter 40 — Seeking a homeland
1. Delitzsch, *Hebrews*, vol. 2, p.247.
2. Pink, *Hebrews*, p.722.
3. Owen, *Hebrews*, vol. 7, p.88.
4. John Brown, *Hebrews*, p.518.

Chapter 41 — Believing God
1. Lane, *Hebrews*, vol. 2, p.360.
2. Bruce, *Hebrews*, p.312.
3. Owen, *Hebrews*, vol. 7, p.122.
4. Lane, *Hebrews*, vol. 2, p.365.

Chapter 42 — Seeing the invisible

1. Owen, *Hebrews,* vol. 7, p.150.
2. John Brown, *Hebrews,* p.544.
3. Bruce, *Hebrews,* p.319.
4. Lane, *Hebrews,* vol. 2, p.373.
5. John Brown, *Hebrews,* p.545.
6. Owen, *Hebrews,* vol. 7, p.163.

Chapter 43 — Shaming the world

1. John Brown, *Hebrews,* p.584.
2. Owen, *Hebrews,* vol. 7, p.189.
3. Bruce, *Hebrews,* p.334.
4. Lane, *Hebrews,* vol. 2, p.386.
5. Delitzsch, *Hebrews,* vol. 2, p.281.
6. Lane, *Hebrews,* vol. 2, p.389.

Chapter 44 — Looking to Jesus

1. Lane, *Hebrews,* vol. 2, p.409.
2. Bruce, *Hebrews,* p.346.
3. Lane, *Hebrews,* vol. 2, p.408.
4. Lane, *Hebrews,* vol. 2, p.409.
5. Owen, *Hebrews,* vol. 7, p.225.
6. Käsemann, cited by Lane, *Hebrews,* vol. 2, p.409.
7. Owen, *Temptation and Sin,* p.11.
8. Lane, *Hebrews,* vol. 2, p.399.
9. Lane, *Hebrews,* vol. 2, p.411.
10. John Brown, *Hebrews,* pp.611-12.
11. Owen, *Hebrews,* vol. 7, p.239.
12. Lane, *Hebrews,* vol. 2, p.399.

Chapter 45 — Facing hostility

1. Pink, *Hebrews,* p.913.
2. Lane, *Hebrews,* vol. 2, p.418.

Chapter 46 — Enduring chastening

1. Lane, *Hebrews,* vol. 2, p.401.
2. Owen, *Hebrews,* vol. 7, p.263.
3. Delitzsch, *Hebrews,* vol. 2, p.316.
4. Bruce, *Hebrews,* p.360.
5. John Brown, *Hebrews,* p.627.

6. Guthrie, *Hebrews,* p.255.
7. John Brown, *Hebrews,* p.630.

Chapter 47 — Running straight
1. Delitzsch, *Hebrews,* vol. 2, p.325.
2. Owen, *Hebrews,* vol. 7, p.281.
3. Lane, *Hebrews,* vol. 2, p.450.
4. Kistemaker, *Hebrews,* p.384.
5. Lane, *Hebrews,* vol. 2, p.450.
6. Boston, *Human nature,* p.201.

Chapter 48 — Looking carefully
1. John Brown, *Hebrews,* p.639.
2. Lane, *Hebrews,* vol. 2, p.454.
3. Kistemaker, *Hebrews,* p.387.
4. Calvin, *Hebrews,* p.197.

Chapter 49 — Coming to Zion
1. Boston, *Human nature,* p.191.
2. John Brown, *Hebrews,* p.644.
3. Lane, *Hebrews,* vol. 2, p.461.
4. Jones, *Hebrews,* p.144.
5. Delitzsch, *Hebrews,* vol. 2, p.343.
6. Robertson, *The Israel of God,* p.30.
7. Lane, *Hebrews,* vol. 2, p.465.
8. Pink, *Hebrews,* p.1052.

Chapter 50 — Mediating the new covenant
1. Pink, *Hebrews,* p.1051.
2. John Brown, *Hebrews,* p.652.
3. Lane, *Hebrews,* vol. 2, p.467.
4. Owen, *Hebrews,* vol. 7, pp.337-8.
5. Bruce, *Hebrews,* pp.376-7.
6. Lane, *Hebrews,* vol. 2, p.470.

Chapter 51 — Shaking the heavens
1. Owen, *Hebrews,* vol. 7, pp.364-5.
2. Lane, *Hebrews,* vol. 2, p.479.
3. Bruce, *Hebrews,* p.383.
4. John Brown, *Hebrews,* p.662.
5. John Brown, *Hebrews,* pp.662-3.

Chapter 52 — Receiving a kingdom
1. Owen, *Hebrews,* vol. 7, p.369.
2. Owen, *Hebrews,* vol. 7, p.371.
3. Delitzsch, *Hebrews,* vol. 2, p.366.
4. Bruce, *Hebrews,* p.380.
5. Lane, *Hebrews,* vol. 2, p.486.
6. Pink, *Hebrews,* p.1103.

Chapter 53 — Led by love
1. Lane, *Hebrews,* vol. 2, p.495.
2. Lane, *Hebrews,* vol. 2, p.496.
3. Owen, *Hebrews,* vol. 7, pp.386-7.
4. Kistemaker, *Hebrews,* p.408.
5. Guthrie, *Hebrews,* p.268.
6. Bruce, *Hebrews,* p.392.
7. Kistemaker, *Hebrews,* p.409.
8. Bruce, *Hebrews,* p.392.
9. Robertson, *The Israel of God,* p.25.

Chapter 54 — Established by grace
1. Delitzsch, *Hebrews,* vol. 2, p.375.
2. Kistemaker, *Hebrews,* p.415.
3. *Young's Concordance.*
4. Pink, *Hebrews,* p.1157.
5. Raymond Brown, *Hebrews,* p.256.
6. Calvin, *Hebrews,* p.207.
7. Calvin, *Hebrews,* p.208.
8. Delitzsch, *Hebrews,* vol. 2, p.382.
9. Owen, *Hebrews,* vol. 7, p.432.

Chapter 55 — Sanctified by Christ
1. Bruce, *Hebrews,* p.398.
2. Owen, *Hebrews,* vol. 7, p.438.
3. Lane, *Hebrews,* vol. 2, p.538.
4. Calvin, *Hebrews,* p.210.
5. Delitzsch, *Hebrews,* vol. 2, p.389.
6. Raymond Brown, *Hebrews,* p.258.

Chapter 56 — Well-pleasing to God
1. Owen, *Hebrews,* vol. 7, pp.456-7.
2. Calvin, *Hebrews,* p.212.

3. Lane, *Hebrews,* vol. 2, p.526.

4. Lane, *Hebrews,* vol. 2, p.555.

5. Calvin, *Hebrews,* p.213.

Chapter 57 — Loved by the Shepherd

1. Lane, *Hebrews,* vol. 2, p.560.

2. Owen, *Hebrews,* vol. 7, p.475.

3. Lane, *Hebrews,* vol. 2, pp.561-2.

4. Delitzsch, *Hebrews,* vol. 2, p.399.

5. Lane, *Hebrews,* vol. 2, p.563.

Chapter 58 — Greeted by brethren

1. Delitzsch, *Hebrews,* vol. 2, p.403.

2. Andriessen cited by Lane, *Hebrews,* vol.2, p.566.

3. Lane, *Hebrews,* vol. 2, p.568.

4. Kistemaker, *Hebrews,* p.435.

5. Owen, *Hebrews,* vol. 7, pp. 482-3.

6. Raymond Brown, *Hebrews,* p.271.

A wide range of excellent books on spiritual subjects is available from Evangelical Press. Please write to us for your free catalogue or contact us by e-mail.

Evangelical Press
Faverdale North, Darlington, DL3 0PH, England

Evangelical Press USA
P. O. Box 825, Webster, New York 14580, USA

e-mail: sales@evangelicalpress.org

web: http://www.evangelicalpress.org